Edward E. McCullough

HOW THE FIRST WORLD WAR BEGAN

The Triple Entente

and the

Coming of the Great War of 1914—1918

BLACK
ROSE
BOOKS

Montréal/New York
London

Black Rose Books No. BB270
Hardcover ISBN: 1-55164-141-0 (bound)
Paperback ISBN: 1-55164-140-2 (pbk.)
Library of Congress Catalog Card Number: 98-73614

Canadian Cataloguing in Publication Data

McCullough, Edward E. (Edward Eastman), 1917-
How the First World War began : the Triple Entente and
the coming of the great war of 1914-1918

Includes bibliographical references and index.
Hardcover ISBN: 1-55164-141-0(bound)
Paperback ISBN: 1-55164-140-2 (pbk.)

1. Triple Entente, 1907. 2. World War, 1914-1918—
Causes I. Title.

D511.M24 1998   940.2'8   C98-901068-6

Cover Design by Associés libres, Montréal

**BLACK
ROSE
BOOKS**

C.P. 1258	2250 Military Road	99 Wallis Road
Succ. Place du Parc	Tonawanda, New York	London, E9 5LN
Montréal, H2W 2R3	14150	England
Canada	USA	UK

To order books in North America: (phone) 1-800-565-9523 (fax) 1-800-221-9985
In Europe: (phone) 0181-986-4854 (fax) 0181-533-5821

Our Web Site address: http://www.web.net/blackrosebooks

A publication of the Institute of Policy Alternatives of Montréal (IPAM)
Printed in Canada

Le Conseil des Arts | The Canada Council
du Canada | for the arts
depuis 1957 | since 1957

Contents

Acknowledgements

———————————▪———————————

I should like to express my gratitude to my late wife Beryl, without whose encouragement and support this book could not have been written.

I wish to acknowledge the kind permission of the officials of the Public Record Office, London, for the use of the archives in their care. I am indebted to the Interlibrary Loan staff of the Brock University Library for their courtesy and consideration. I should like to thank my computerists, Angela Klassen and Maja Ruscher-Bose, and my editor, Marcia Sweet, for their able assistance.

Dedication

To Beryl

Preface

Seventy years have passed since the publication of Sidney Fay's *Origins of the World War*, and the mass of documentary material of which Fay wrote has become a mountain, yet that epoch-making work still stands as a unique attempt by a great scholar "to tell how it really came about." The years have dealt more kindly, however, with the second volume of Fay's opus than with the first.

Little new evidence has been produced to challenge his story of the last five weeks before the war, although recent years have seen much manipulation of old evidence designed to force a one-sided interpretation of those events. On the other hand, our knowledge of the preceding forty years has been revolutionized, not only by the opening of archives and the release of private papers, but also by the appearance of valuable monographs based on these sources.

Unfortunately, most current general histories dealing with that momentous time remain untouched by the archival revelations and scholarly achievements of the past seventy years and proceed as though we knew little more about the background of the war than we did in 1916. I have attempted to bring the story of the events leading to the Great War into line with present knowledge, and to correct the distortion of the story of the period June 28 to August 1, 1914. This work, based partly on original sources, where possible makes use of archival work done by other scholars.

Introduction

---◼---

One of the central problems of our time is the domination of the world by militarism. Never since the dawn of history has so great a proportion of human and material resources been devoted to preparation for war; never have militarist ideals held so prominent a place in human minds.

The narrow nationalism of the scribblers of twentieth-century history has played a notable part in this development. Ignoring the fact that war is an integral part of the current international political system, and that every sovereign state arrogates to itself the right to make war whenever it sees fit to do so, they have promoted the militarist myth that wars are caused by evil people on the other side of the world who refuse to get along with the kindly and pacific folk on their side. The moral of this myth is of course that the way to avert war is to prepare for it The way to end war is to annihilate, or at least emasculate, those evil people on the other side of the world. In other words, war is best avoided by militarism, that is, by preparation for war and by war itself.

The promulgation of this militarist myth has been achieved by the falsification or distortion of historical fact. This process is best exemplified by the widely accepted mythological history of the events leading to the Great War of 1914-18. The conflict known as World War II brought to an end the rational discussion of the Great War which was under way during the 1930s and ushered in a new period of ultra-nationalist history. The result is that many people believe that the two wars of the twentieth century have their origins in the peculiar mentality characteristic of the Germans. They believe that nearly all the evil tendencies of European society have emanated from Germany or reached their worst form in that country. To move such a mountain of misconception is a task beyond my power. I shall attempt the more modest feat of bringing into some rational order the main events of the international scene related to the coming of the Great War.

Since its aim is to investigate the background of one specific conflict, this study will not concern itself primarily with the general causes which predispose the sovereign state system to recurrent war. An outline of these causes will indicate the general context in which the coming of this particular war will be discussed.

Sovereign states, recognizing no superior authority, exist in relation to other states under conditions of anarchy. They must depend on their own power, or on that of a powerful neighbour, to maintain their rights and interests, and the ultimate arbiter between sovereign states is war. The essential element guaranteeing the existence of a state is power, which is so important that it tends to become an end in itself.

All the other general underlying causes of war flow from the drive for power. The state naturally makes use of nationalist feeling to strengthen the allegiance of its citizens; it strives to expand its wealth and power through the addition of territories and the exploitation of their resources; it builds up its armed forces in competition with those of other Powers; and it allies itself with some Powers in order to obtain by combination greater influence than it could exert alone.

These general causes, all of which operated strongly during the period under discussion, conspired to create a situation especially conducive to war. My concern is to isolate the elements which directed the great European Powers towards the war that eventually took place. The role each played in bringing on the Great War will be apparent as the narrative unfolds.

Since the war that came was between Germany and Austria-Hungary on the one side and the Triple Entente—Great Britain, France and Russia—on the other, this inquiry must concentrate on the formation of these combinations and on how their opposition led them to war. The story opens with a defeated and isolated France facing a triumphant Germany, which is surrounded by friends and dominates Europe; it ends with the outbreak of a war in which France, assisted by two Great Powers, confronts Germany and her one remaining ally. The main theme is the creation of the Triple Entente.

The crucial episode in this development was the making of the Anglo-French entente. To entice a Russia jilted by Germany into the arms of France and divorce Italy from her unnatural bedfellows needed no great diplomatic skill: to bring England into partnership with her two principal rivals required luck of rare occurrence combined with diplomacy of the highest order.

The centre-piece of this work is therefore the creation of the Anglo-French entente. That triumph of French diplomacy is one of the great historical watersheds which determine the course of events for years to come. With dramatic suddenness the equilibrium established by the Franco-Russian alliance was shattered and a new era of turbulence and change involving all the European Powers began. Within a decade it led them into the Great War.

One

———————————————————◼———————————————————

Prologue: The Bismarckian System

The Franco-Prussian war of 1870 marked the end of an era. France's last hope of restoring her long-held predominance in western Europe perished with the battle of Sedan. Since that predominance had depended on German disunity, French opposition to the creation of a German state had been axiomatic. The sequel enforced the conclusion that France alone could not oppose the German Empire. Only in alliance with other Powers could she regain a strong voice in European affairs.

The humiliation of military defeat was reinforced for France by the Treaty of Frankfurt, which by the seizure of Alsace and Lorraine reversed three centuries of French advance into Charlemagne's "Middle Kingdom." This act ensured continued French resistance to any agreement with Germany which implied acceptance of the territorial *status quo* and thus required France "to approve the Treaty of Frankfurt all over again," to use Théophile Delcassé's phrase.[1] Without this depredation Franco-German reconciliation might have been possible, with it no accommodation was attainable in the foreseeable future. The German Empire was thus assured of the permanent hostility of France.

So long as France remained isolated, she was not powerful enough to launch a war of revenge. Otto von Bismarck, the German chancellor, realized that his main task must be to prevent France from acquiring allies, which could best be done by attaching as many powerful countries as possible to Germany. To this end he created a series of alliances which at times included all the Powers except England, which steadily resisted involvement in the European system. Even England, however, usually aligned herself with the German Empire, particularly after the occupation of Egypt in 1882 led her into perpetual friction with France.

The cornerstone of Otto von Bismarck's edifice was a close relationship with the Russian Empire. The friendship of Russia had protected his rear in the war with France, and he never lost sight of the necessity to avoid a war in which Germany would be attacked on two fronts. At the same time he was determined to achieve a closer link with Austria-Hungary.

The first fruit of Bismarck's policy was the establishment in 1873 of a loose association with Russia and Austria known as the League of the Three Emperors. It was not an alliance but rather an agreement for cooperation in case of a crisis which required military or political action. Its significance lay in the fact that it precluded an alliance between Austria or Russia and France.

Italy, too, gravitated towards the German grouping. Her seizure of Rome and the consequent support of the papacy by France had driven a wedge between France and Italy and forced the latter to look elsewhere for support. The Italian advances were welcomed by Bismarck as another link in the chain which encircled France.

The fragility of these friendships was exposed by the war scare of 1875, which showed that while no Power was prepared to ally itself with France, none was willing to see France further crushed and humiliated. British statesmen, in particular, exhibited a remarkable tendency to believe any alarming report from France and to credit Bismarck with the most sinister designs.

A rebellion against Turkish misrule, which broke out in Bosnia and Herzegovina in 1875, touched off a Balkan crisis which would end in a Russo-Turkish war. The Serbs believed they had a divine mission to free all the Slavs from Turkish rule, and in May, 1876, Serbia and Montenegro declared war on Turkey. The war continued for several months, arousing Slav nationalism throughout the area.

Although the Serbs were assisted by thousands of volunteers from Russia, the Turks advanced so rapidly that Belgrade, the Serbian capital, was soon in danger. Russia decided that action must be taken to stop the Turks. Diplomacy and threats stopped the Turkish advance, but the Turks were not amenable to persuasion by the European powers to make reforms which would alleviate the oppression of their Slav subjects.

Bismarck's attempts to work with England, whose aim was to maintain Turkish control of the Straits, were frustrated by British suspicion of his motives, but England nevertheless leaned towards friendship with Germany.

It proved impossible for the Powers to arrive at an arrangement which satisfied all their various views and was acceptable to the Turks, and in the end there was no way of preventing a Russo-Turkish war. Russia declared war on Turkey on April 24, 1877.

The Russian victory was a foregone conclusion, but the Powers refused to allow her to enjoy the fruits of her success. The Congress of Berlin was organized in 1878 to rewrite the terms of the Treaty of San Stefano which ended the war. The Russian defeat by England and Austria at the Congress strained the relations of Germany and Austria with Russia and led to the temporary demise of the League of the Three Emperors. Bismarck found compensation for this in the better relations with England which resulted from their cooperation at Berlin.

To guard against the possibility that Austria might gravitate towards France or Russia Bismarck decided that the time had come to bind Austria with a definite alliance. This Dual Alliance, contracted in October, 1879, provided that if either of the Powers should be attacked by Russia, or by another Power supported by Russia, the other party would come to the assistance of the one attacked. The Berlin treaty, which was the written embodiment of the alliance, was to last five years and to be renewed for another three years if neither Party wished to renegotiate it: it was to be kept secret "to avoid any misinterpretation."[2]

This alliance, together with Germany's intimacy with England, aroused Russian fear of isolation. The Russians therefore approached Bismarck with proposals for an agreement which would secure them against German hostility. The Chancellor insisted on including Austria in any such arrangement and in substance proposed a revival of the Three Emperors' League. This was accomplished in June, 1881, by a treaty of alliance accompanied by a protocol which aimed at solving the knotty problems which might bring Austria and Russia into conflict. Some provisions of the treaty which ended the Congress of Berlin were reaffirmed and possible friction over others was foreseen and guarded against. The three Powers agreed to work out their differences by "friendly explanations." One of the interesting clauses of the protocol reserved to Austria the right to annex Bosnia and Herzegovina whenever she wished to do so.[3]

It is hard to overestimate the significance of this treaty in the Bismarckian system. While it could not eliminate the opposition of Russia and Austria in the Balkans, it did succeed in preventing the outbreak of war and at the same time in providing insurance against a Franco-Russian alliance.

Bismarck's edifice was completed in the following year by the addition of Italy to the alliance with Austria. The approach was made by Italy, whose conflict with France over the occupation of Rome had been embittered by the French seizure of Tunisia in 1881. The Triple Alliance treaty bound Italy and Germany to mutual assistance if either party should be attacked by France, and required all three to fight together in case of an attack by two or more Great Powers. If one of the high contracting parties should be forced by a threat to its security to make war on another Great Power, the others were bound to observe a benevolent neutrality towards their ally. The treaty was to last for five years and was, as usual, to be kept secret. Italy made the very significant reservation that the treaty could not "in any case be regarded as being directed against England."[4] Bismarck had no illusions about the value of Italian military support, which he neither needed nor wanted. His aim was to ensure Italian neutrality in case of war between Austria and Russia.[5]

Although Bismarck now appeared to hold in his hands all the threads which bound the European Powers to Germany and guarded her against a French-inspired coalition, there were serious weaknesses in his system which eventually led to its demise. The most dangerous of these was the collision of Austrian and Russian interests in the Balkans, where the Russian desire for expansion threatened the security of the Austro-Hungarian Empire. Germany's tie with Italy was endangered by Italy's ancient antagonism to Austria which, although temporarily overshadowed by her quarrel with France, could never be erased. These problems loomed larger with every passing year and were to prove in the end insuperable.

The breach between Austria and Russia was not long postponed. The Three Emperors' treaty was renewed in 1884, but the Russians were alarmed by Austria's economic penetration of the Balkans and by her creation of close ties with Serbia and Roumania. The Austro-Russian confrontation during the Bulgarian crisis of 1885-86 completed Russia's disenchantment with the Three Emperors' League. When it came up for renewal in 1887 the tsar refused to continue the agreement.

Bismarck, however, fearing the possibility of a Franco-Russian alliance, was determined to continue the connection with the Russian Empire. This was done by means of a secret "Reinsurance Treaty," in which Germany recognized "the rights historically acquired by Russia in the Balkan peninsula, and in particular the legitimacy of her preponderant and decisive influence in Bulgaria and in Eastern Rumelia." The two Powers agreed on the principle of the closure of the Straits of Bosporus and Dardenelles and expressed their intention to act in common to prevent its violation. The clause which has been cited as an instance of Bismarck's double dealing is the one which bound each Power to maintain a "benevolent neutrality" if the other found itself at war with a third Great Power. This requirement did not apply if one of the signatories was the attacking party. Bismarck had always warned Austria that Germany would not support an aggressive policy and would support Austria only if she were attacked, so the new treaty did not violate the letter of his obligation to Austria. The Reinsurance Treaty was to last three years, and no specific provision was made for its renewal.[6]

At that moment the Bismarckian system appeared to have reached its zenith, but already it was in the process of being weakened by other agreements to whose conclusion Bismarck himself made a notable contribution. In December, 1887, England aligned her Near Eastern policy with that of Italy and Austria in the second Mediterranean agreement, some provisions of which conflicted with those of the Reinsurance Treaty. Although

Germany was not a party to this agreement, its existence greatly increased the difficulty of harmonizing Russian aspirations with the existence of Bismarck's complicated alliance system.[7]

We can never know how long the genius of Bismarck could have managed to maintain an association which included Russia on the one hand and Austria and England on the other. In any event, the matter was taken out of his hands when the new emperor, Kaiser Wilhelm II, accepted the chancellor's resignation in 1890. Although the kaiser's conflict with Bismarck arose mainly over internal matters, his disagreement with what he considered a pro-Russian policy also had a significant influence. Wilhelm, closely associated with the military faction, was alarmed by Russia's warlike preparations and wished to move closer to England and Austria.[8]

The Russians were eager to extend the Reinsurance Treaty, and the emperor was not averse to this course, but the arguments of Baron von Holstein prevailed and it was allowed to lapse.[9] A memorandum by General Georg Leo von Caprivi, the next chancellor, explains the reasoning which led to this decision. It was concluded that the Reinsurance Treaty "could not be well harmonized with the Triple Alliance, with the Treaties between Roumania and ourselves, or with the influence that Germany exercises upon England." If the treaty should become known, the Triple Alliance would be endangered and England alienated.[10]

Although the cogency of the arguments adduced to persuade the kaiser to reject the treaty has often been questioned, the fact that all his ministers were satisfied by them suggests that they were not entirely unconvincing. Most important was the belief, shared even by Bismarck, that Russia was making military preparations for aggressive action. If this expectation became a reality, the Russians would have a strong interest in sowing discord amongst their prospective enemies, and might well do this by disclosing the contradictions in Bismarck's arrangements with the various Powers.

The Russians were much alarmed by Germany's refusal to renew the Reinsurance Treaty, and begged for some written assurance that Germany had not decided to leave them in the lurch entirely and throw in her lot with their enemies. Evidently they would have been satisfied with any scrap of paper which promised the continuity of German policy. The German government, however, while insisting that its policy remained unchanged, declined to put anything in writing, with the predictable result that the Russians believed they were being isolated and were forced to act accordingly.[11]

Whatever the justification for the change, the repudiation of the Reinsurance Treaty was charged with momentous consequences for Germany. The fact that the desire to maintain the friendship of England was one of the major motives for their repudiating the treaty is a striking example of dramatic irony. The Russians, cast adrift by Germany, soon melted into the willing arms of France, bringing to an end the era of German predominance and setting the stage for the creation of the overwhelmingly powerful coalition which brought about the destruction of the German Empire.

Notes

1.Christopher Andrew, *Théophile Delcassé and the Making of the Entente Cordiale*, p. 173.

2.Louis L. Snyder, *Historic Documents of World War I*, pp. 9-12.

3.*Ibid.*, pp. 12-15.

4.*Ibid.*, pp. 16-18.

5.William L. Langer, *European Alliances and Alignments, 1871-1890*, p. 246.

6.Snyder, pp. 18-20.

7.H. Temperley and L. M. Penson, *Foundations of British Foreign Policy, 1792 - 1902*, pp. 455-61.

8.Langer, pp. 494-6.

9.*Ibid.*, pp.500-502.

10.E. T. S. Dugdale, *German Diplomatic Documents*, II, 2-3.

11.William L. Langer, *The Franco-Russian Alliance, 1890-1914*, pp. 65-6.

Two

The Franco-Russian Alliance

Just as German security required the continued isolation of France, so France's desire to restore her past prestige and regain the lost provinces of Alsace and Lorraine dictated the pursuit of powerful allies. It was evident that the Russian Empire was the natural ally, but no move in that direction was made until Léon Gambetta came to power as premier of France in 1881. Although Gambetta hoped that in the course of time both England and Russia could be brought into alliance with France, he realized that neither Power was yet ready for such a departure. His more moderate aim was to improve relations with the two Powers and wait upon events which might draw them together.[1]

Developments in Russia already foretold the day when that Power would no longer remain in harmony with Germany: pan-Slavic nationalists denounced Germany as the ally of the Austrian oppressors of the Slavs. During the fall and winter of 1881-82, nationalist agitation reached a point which caused Bismarck such alarm that he urged Austria to make further concessions to Italy to induce her to join the Austro-German Alliance. The agitation in Russia receded for the moment, but not before the signature of the Triple Alliance treaty on May 20, 1882.[2]

By 1886 the nationalist current was once again on the rise in Russia, and its resurgence coincided with the advent of the Boulangist movement in France. The result was agitation in both countries in favour of a Franco-Russian alliance. French attempts to persuade the Russian government to commit itself to the support of France in case of a Franco-German war were unsuccessful, but the uncertainty of Russian policy induced Bismarck to work for closer relations with Italy and England.[3]

In the summer of 1887 Paul Déroulède, the leader of the *revanche* movement in France, made a second visit to Russia, where he was received with great enthusiasm in military and nationalist circles. The press organs of those groups called for a Franco-Russian alliance and the call was echoed by many figures prominent in Russian officialdom.[4]

The signing of the Reinsurance Treaty in June, 1887, led the Russians to expect more support from Germany in the solution of the Bulgarian problem than Bismarck was prepared to give. His furtherance of the Russian programme fell short of any disposition that Germany should take the lead there, while at the same time he took pains to forward the Mediterranean agreement of 1887, which associated England with Austria and Italy in opposition to the Russian advance against the Turks.[5]

This policy precipitated the formation of a Franco-Russian combination against the British attempt to come to agreement with the sultan of Turkey concerning the British occupation of Egypt. The abortive Wolff Convention of 1887 between England and Turkey, which in effect allowed the British to stay in Egypt indefinitely, was successfully opposed by the combined efforts of France and Russia. This partnership raised in advance the spectre of the coming alliance.[6]

One of the most ominous manifestations of the approaching revolution was the development of strong financial ties between France and Russia. This process was inspired by Bismarck himself when in the fall of 1887 the German government, in response to Russian measures designed to lessen German influence, issued a decree prohibiting the acceptance of Russian securities by the *Reichsbank*. The Russians were able to improve their position by floating loans on more advantageous terms in France. A radical financial change saw German capital withdrawn from Russia and replaced by loans from France.[7]

In November, 1888, a loan of 500 million francs was negotiated successfully. Within a year and a half four enormous Russian loans were arranged in France, prompting the Russian press to rejoice that it was no longer necessary to go to Berlin. Even during the time of Russo-German friendship, Berlin had imposed terms "incompatible with the dignity of a great country."[8]

Bismarck's attempt in 1889 to draw closer to England, coupled with the pro-English proclivities of Wilhelm II, further alarmed the Russians, and it remained only for Germany to repudiate the Reinsurance Treaty to convince them that their sole safeguard lay in seeking closer ties with France. From that moment an eventual Franco-Russian Alliance became no longer a distant menace but a certainty. Already in the summer of 1889 the Russian government offered to support France against England in Egypt, and Nicolas Giers, the Russian foreign minister, suggested that France should profit from the conversion of the Egyptian debt to raise the question of the British evacuation from Egypt.[9]

After Bismarck's fall the new orientation of German policy led to further demonstrations of Germany's desire for closer relations with England. Negotiations aimed at settling colonial disputes in East Africa resulted, in May, 1890, in a treaty which, amongst other provisions, involved the cession of Heligoland to Germany. When this was followed in August by the kaiser's visit to England, widely acclaimed as the seal on a virtual Anglo-German alliance, the last traces of Russian belief in the good will of Germany's new leaders vanished. Russia's only escape from isolation was association with France, the adamant adversary of both England and Germany.[10]

Russian policy since 1870 had been aimed at securing control of the Bosporus and the Dardanelles. This policy brought them into conflict with both England and Austria, the former considering Russian command of the straits a threat to her position in the Mediterranean. The latter believed that Russian tutelage of the Balkans would lead to the unification of the area under Russian leadership and thus to disruption of her empire through its attraction for her subject Slavs.

The second Mediterranean agreement of December, 1887, between England, Italy and Austria-Hungary, guaranteed the *status quo* throughout the Mediterranean basin, thus blocking the advance of both France and Russia in this area. These Powers could free themselves of this obstruction only by destroying the Mediterranean coalition. While the Reinsurance Treaty remained in force cooperation with France had no real attraction for Russia, but the failure to renew the treaty convinced the Russians that Germany had joined their enemies.

Nicolas Giers continued to hope for a Russian reconciliation with Germany, and in August, 1890, during the meeting of tsar Alexander with the kaiser, he attempted to extract from the German government some assurance that Bismarck's support of Russian policy with regard to Constantinople and the straits would be continued. His failure finally convinced him that no agreement with Germany was possible.[11]

At the same time contact was established between the French and Russian military general staffs, and Antoine de Laboulaye, the French ambassador to Russia, exulted that the *rapprochement* which three years ago had seemed an illusion had become real and solid.[12] General le Mouton de Boisdeffre, the French deputy chief of staff who attended the Russian maneuvers, reported that Russia had warned Wilhelm II that he mustn't touch France, whose strong existence was indispensable for the balance of power. At this meeting, Boisdeffre insisted on the absolute necessity of "immediate and simultaneous mobilisation" of the two armies.[13]

The Russian government was initially against any written agreement, but favoured closer relations with France. By March, 1891, the Russian ambassador in Paris was instructed to say that "while the Triple Alliance ruins itself with armaments, the *accord intime* of the two countries is needed to maintain the European balance of power."[14] This idea appeared again and again before 1899, when it became an official aim of the Franco-Russian alliance.

The principal preoccupation of the French government and general staff was the signing of a military convention. The Russians agreed in principle, but hesitated for some time before actually drawing up a convention. Meanwhile, Giers came to the conclusion that England had in effect joined the Triple Alliance, and he proposed that the Franco-Russian entente should be strengthened by an accord between the two governments.[15] The French government in reply pointed out that the maintenance of peace, which was the object of the constant efforts of France and Russia, was closely connected with the maintenance of the balance of power, which was threatened by the Triple Alliance and especially by the adherence of England.[16] The French reply reached Russia just as a French naval squadron arrived at Cronstadt in Russia for a visit. The enthusiasm with which the tsar welcomed the French squadron and his encouragement of popular demonstrations in favour of France were a clear indication of his enthusiasm for a French alliance.[17]

It was decided that the accord should be formalized by an exchange of letters, of which Russia would write the first one. These letters, written in August, 1891, fell short of achieving the French aim of establishing a military convention. In the first clause, the two governments declared that they would act together in all questions which threatened the general peace; in the second they agreed that, if peace was in danger or one of them was threatened by aggression, they would immediately and simultaneously come to an agreement on the measures which this eventuality would require them to take. The French government drew attention to the resulting need for a military convention.[18]

While the Russians appeared willing to discuss military cooperation in general terms, they hesitated for many months before committing themselves to the actual signing of a military convention. When Giers visited Paris in November, 1891, he indicated his satisfaction with the existing state of affairs. The Franco-Russian entente, he said, had changed the situation. The balance of power had been re-established, and there was no longer a question of German hegemony.[19]

In December the tsar, who was much more amenable to the French blandishments than any of his ministers, expressed his willingness to open negotiations for a military convention.[20] General J. de Miribel, chief of the French general staff, was therefore instructed to draw up a draft for submission to the Russians. Miribel's draft aimed at gaining Russian acceptance of the proposition that if one of the two Powers was attacked the other would come to its aid with all of its forces.[21]

General Miribel included an interesting survey of the opposing forces' which presumed a Franco-Russian superiority over the Triple Alliance Powers. According to his figures France and Russia could oppose 3,150,000 men and 7160 artillery pieces to the 2,810,000 men and 6432 artillery pieces of the Triple Alliance. Their superiority over Germany and Austria alone was 700,000 men and 1820 artillery pieces. France, it was declared, would send sixty-five of her seventy-five divisions against Germany, leaving only ten to face Italy's twenty-two divisions. Russia could send thirty-three divisions against Germany.[22]

The French minister of war undertook to send 1,300,000 men and expected Russia to send 700,000 to 800,000 men against Germany. This would give the Franco-Russian forces a superiority of 500,000 men, an advantage of four to three.[23] It was necessary that they should be concentrated with the greatest rapidity and should make contact with the German army as quickly as possible. In May, 1892, the tsar instructed his war minister to prepare a written project of a military convention. He proposed to invite a French general to the Russian military maneuvers in July to discuss the plan.[24] The French were eager to hasten the affair, and in July Alexandre Ribot, deputy minister of foreign affairs, wrote to Count Lannes de Montebello, French ambassador to Russia, that the convention had taken overlong and it was necessary to bring it to a successful conclusion. The need for it had been recognized the preceding August and months had passed with nothing done.[25]

The final draft of the military convention was agreed upon by General Boisdeffre and chief of the Russian general staff, General Nicholas Obruchev, in August and signed by them on August 17. Article I provided that if France was attacked by Germany or by Italy supported by Germany, Russia would attack Germany with all her disposable forces, and that if Russia was attacked by Germany or by Austria supported by Germany, France would use all her available forces against Germany. Article II stipulated that if the Triple Alliance Powers, or any one of them, mobilised, France and Russia, without any previous agreement, would immediately and simultaneously mobilise all their forces and advance them as quickly as possible to their frontiers. Article III pledged France to employ 1,300,000 men against Germany, while Russia would supply 700,000 to 800,000. They were to engage as quickly as possible so Germany would have to fight on the east and on the west at the same time. Article IV required the General Staffs of the two countries to consult together continuously to plan the required measures and to exchange any information about the armaments of the Triple Alliance which might come to their knowledge. The remaining articles provided that France and Russia would not make peace separately, that the convention should last as long as the Triple Alliance and that all should be kept secret.[26] The signature of the convention by the two generals did not end the matter. The agreement could not come into force until it was approved by the tsar, who stalled because he was disgusted by the evidence of corruption in French politics. The Russians postponed the inevitable because they were disturbed by the instability of French ministries. They feared that once the French were assured of Russian support they would not try to maintain the peace.[27]

What followed was a temporary cooling of relations between France and Russia. The French were unwilling to support the Russians in a conflict with England on the Indian frontier and Russia would not join France in protesting British policy in Egypt. At the same time Russia was able to improve her relations with both Germany and Austria, and indeed negotiated with Germany throughout the fall and winter of 1892-93 for the conclusion of a treaty, which it was hoped would result in the re-opening of the German money market to Russian loans. Germany also tended to revert to Bismarck's policy of cooperation with Russia, partly as the result of the advent of a Gladstone government in England.[28] During the course of the year 1893, however, relations between Russia and Germany grew steadily worse. The commercial negotiations failed, largely because of the excessive demands of Germany, and the result was a tariff war, triggered by a substantial increase in the Russian tariff on manufactured goods.[29]

The passing of a new German army bill on July 15, 1893, increased the German army by 1800 officers and 70,000 other ranks. General Miribel at once called for the ratification of the military alliance by the tsar and the increase of the French and Russian forces. France, he said, had already reinforced her trained personnel and would now make every effort to increase her peace effectives.[30] Russia was already engaged in the work of concentrating her military forces on the German and Austrian frontiers, and had made Poland a vast fortified camp with 650,000 men close to the German frontier and almost as many near by. It appears that both France and Russia had anticipated the new German law and had taken steps to forestall it in advance.[31]

These developments were accompanied by a significant increase in Franco-Russian friendliness, culminating in the visit of a Russian naval squadron to Toulon. Russian agreement to this visit followed immediately on the Siamese crisis, which had almost led to war between France and England. French hostility to England during this period greatly overshadowed the question of Alsace-Lorraine, and it appeared to the Russians that the Russo-French entente was at last assuming its proper direction. The Toulon visit was to be followed by the establishment of a Russian squadron in the

Mediterranean, which had been advocated by the French for some time, and which would threaten England's position in the Near East.[32]

By December the tsar was ready to authorize the definite adoption of the military convention with France, which took place in January, 1894. The alliance was now an accomplished fact, but for the moment antagonism to England was the common ground on which the partners met. The Russians made it perfectly clear that they would have nothing to do with the reconquest of Alsace and Lorraine, and the French were equally determined not to support a Russian advance to Constantinople. For the moment at least the alliance was strictly defensive as far as European questions were concerned.[33] More than a decade was to pass before the French could succeed in fashioning the anti-German coalition which would enable them to regain the lost provinces.

The next few years saw little cooperation between the two Powers, and the French complained that Russia was not acting as an ally, but was ignoring France and making up to other Powers. Gabriel Hanotaux, the French foreign minister, complained in May, 1895, that Russia had made no action or gesture favourable to France for six months.[34] By 1898, however, he was satisfied by Russian support of French policy in China, Turkey, Egypt and the Sudan.[35]

In the meantime Count Sergei Witte, the Russian minister of finance, expressed to the French military attaché at Berlin his surprise that France was reducing her military expenditures when other powers were increasing theirs. The attaché replied that France had spent more than others for twenty years and had largely attained her aims of constructing fortresses, perfecting her armaments and acquiring large stores of munitions, so she could now afford to economize.[36]

While making these expenditures on armaments, the French had been able to continue extending credit to Russia on a large scale. In February, 1897, when Russia requested a new loan of two billion francs, the political director noted that loans to Russia already amounted to eight billion francs, nearly half of French funds abroad.[37]

In August, 1898, the French were alarmed by a Russian proposal for a conference to discuss ways of lessening the burden of armaments. Paul Cambon, French ambassador in London, thought that if this proposal had any practical consequences its first effect would be to force France to give up any idea of taking back Alsace-Lorraine by force of arms.[38] France was assured, however, that Russia was not proposing general disarmament but a halt to further increases. When the tsar promised that, in view of the special considerations which applied to France, he would not allow any political questions to be discussed, Théophile Delcassé, French foreign minister, accepted the idea of a conference.[39] In fact, the idea of such a conference originated with the Russian general staff. General Kouropatkin, minister of war, in discussions with Witte concerning the credits needed for new artillery and rifles, had the idea of getting an agreement to freeze the number of peace effectives. This would enable Russia to divert money to the construction of strategic railways and thus to increase her offensive power. Some funds could also be used for the development of industry.[40] The effect of what the Russians were proposing was that the Triple Alliance Powers should agree to the continued preponderance of the Russian army to allow it to increase its mobility and thus to facilitate an attack on Germany. The tsar had no illusions about the practical results of such a conference, but thought it would be useful and would have a "moral effect."[41]

Russian foreign minister Count Michael Mouravieff's circular note proposing the programme for the conference cited as its objects the search for a means of "putting a limit to the progressive increase of military and naval armaments," and discussion of "the possibility of preventing armed conflicts by the pacific means at the disposal of international diplomacy." He suggested as subjects for discussion the "non-augmentation...of the present effective armed land and sea forces, as well as the war budgets pertaining to them;" the prohibition of new firearms and explosives, the prohibition of the use of submarines or diving torpedo boats and acceptance of "the use of good offices, mediation and voluntary arbitration" to prevent armed conflicts. Political questions were to be excluded.[42]

The French continued to fear that the tsar's proposal was for "disarmament," despite Russian assurances that what was proposed was not disarmament but a halt to any increase. They were particularly concerned to prevent a discussion about the use of submarines, in which France had gained an advantage. Nicholas II promised to oppose any discussion of submarines in accordance with French wishes.[43]

Delcassé instructed the French delegates to the conference to take no initiative regarding the limitation of the effectives of the armed forces, but to agree to the maintenance of the *status quo* for five years if the majority so wished. If it was proposed to limit the effectives to a percentage of the population, France would specify that the population of France included her colonial empire. French delegates were told to oppose the limitation of defence budgets or a discussion of the use of submarines. They were to pay particular attention to suggestions concerning mediation, arbitration and good offices.[44]

As was to be expected, no agreement was reached on the limitation of armed forces, armaments or defence expenditures. Conventions were signed concerning the pacific settlement of disputes and the laws and customs of war on land.

Meanwhile the Franco-Russian accords were confirmed and extended by correspondence between Delcassé and Mouravieff. In particular the maintenance of the balance of power now became an official aim of the Allied Powers.[45] This was indicative of the more adventurous policy which followed the accession of Delcassé to the post of minister of foreign affairs. It led gradually to greater and greater French involvement in Russia's plans for an advance on Constantinople and thus contributed to the situation which produced the Great War.

The meeting of the two general staffs in February, 1901, concentrated its attention on the speed with which the Russian troops could reach the German frontier. General Pendezac, chief of the French general staff, told the Russians that their army should cross the German frontier by the fourteenth day after mobilisation in order to divert a large enough portion of the German army to give the French the best possible chance of success in the opening battle. If this battle should, by some accident, not turn out in favour of the French army, the news of the advance of the Russian forces into Germany should reach France on the fourteenth day to compensate "for the effect on public opinion and the morale of the army by good news coming from the Russian front." General Sakharoff, chief of the Russian general staff, could promise to cross the frontier only on the eighteenth day, and said that to cut this to fourteen days would require improvements in the Russian transportation system which would impose great sacrifices on Russian finances. Pendezac replied that the entry of the Russian contingent into action on the fourteenth day was so important to French security that France was ready to provide the financial wherewithal to make possible the construction of the necessary strategic railways with the least possible delay.[46]

This set the stage for the long series of French loans directed to the specific purpose of constructing strategic railways to expedite the concentration of the Russian armies on the eastern frontier. In March the French minister of war was informed that the Russian general staff attached great importance to the construction of a railway joining the St. Petersburg-Vitebsk line then under construction to Bielostok. This would speed up by four days the concentration on the Narev and the Bohr, and in consequence the invasion of East Prussia, by the same time. France authorized a loan of 425 million francs. The tsar decided to use it to build a new line which would connect St. Petersburg and Moscow with the heart of Poland.[47]

By July the Russians were asking for another loan of 500 million francs over three years for railway construction. Strong objections to this further loan were made in the French cabinet, which was concerned about the large demands being made on French resources, but the loan was nevertheless approved when the cabinet was persuaded that it was necessary for political and military reasons.[48]

While the next few years were uneventful for the Franco-Russian

Alliance, the French made great progress in their aim of isolating Germany. With the neutralization of Italy in 1902 and the realization of the Entente with England in 1904, there remained only to reconcile England and Russia to complete the combination which could overawe the Central Powers. The promotion of an Anglo-Russian entente thus became a primary objective of French policy.

There were some misgivings in Russia concerning the Anglo-French *rapprochement*, and Delcassé felt it necessary to assure the Russian government of France's fidelity to the alliance.[49] The French were also uneasy about the improvement in Russia's relations with Germany and Austria. A dispatch from Maurice Bompard, French ambassador in St. Petersburg, in February, 1904, spoke of the collaboration of the Russians and Austrians in the Balkans and the courteous relations between Russia and Germany. He attributed these developments to the fact that Asia had become the principal object of Russian ambitions, and thought this threatened to absorb Russia's military power. He also believed, however, that Russia realized that she needed the French alliance to protect her rear.[50] Georges Bihourd, the French ambassador in Berlin, thought the alliance's military power would be weakened "to the extent that the tsar's troops mire themselves in the Far East." Germany would thus be free to pursue her bellicose projects, in the belief that she could knock out France before Russia could intervene.[51] Germany's failure to make war on France when the Russians were defeated by Japan demonstrates that Germany's bellicose projects were figments of the French imagination.

The completion of the Anglo-French agreements led to much talk in England about a possible Anglo-Russian *rapprochement*. Paul Cambon, then ambassador in London, wrote that Count Lamsdorff, the Russian foreign minister, and Alexander Nelidoff, the Russian ambassador in Paris, favoured this and wanted France to act as intermediary. He thought this would be a bad idea, because Anglo-Russian differences would be hard to reconcile. In a conversation with Edward VII he advised the king to use his influence with the tsar, whose view was very important for Russia.[52]

A dangerous crisis arose during the Russo-Japanese war when Russia's Baltic fleet attacked British fishing vessels. Initial reports stated that two ships had been sunk, one with all hands on board. The Russians had made no attempt to rescue anyone but had simply steamed away. The British government demanded an apology, reparation, and trial and punishment of the responsible persons. The Russians considered the suggestion that British representatives should take part in the investigation humiliating and unacceptable to a Great Power. They also maintained that their admiral had thought the ships were Japanese torpedo-boats in disguise, a view which foreign secretary Lord Lansdowne refused to accept. When the British sent six battleships, four armoured cruisers and several destroyers to the Baltic, it seemed that a violent clash might occur at any moment.[53]

In these circumstances Delcassé used his good offices to bring about a peaceful settlement. On the one hand he insisted at St. Petersburg on the urgency of making concessions to solve the problem, and on the other he instructed Paul Cambon to warn Lansdowne about the danger of acting precipitately without giving the slow-moving Russian government a chance to respond. He believed his efforts were influential in bringing about a pacific outcome of the dispute.[54]

After the Russo-Japanese war the state of Russia's military preparations continued to excite French concern. When the matter of a new Russian loan was under discussion in 1906, General Moulin, the French military attaché at St. Petersburg, suggested that no loan should be authorized until its purpose was fixed. He thought it was necessary to hasten certain military expenditures concerning the railways, armaments and mobilisation arrangements.[55]

The French government was anxious about the bad state of the Russian army, and inquired about the numbers and armament of the soldiers Russia could put on her western frontier and in how many days they could arrive at the German frontier. They wanted to know how soon the general staff thought the Russian forces could be reconstituted.[56] The Russians stated in November that their army was in no condition to fight Germany until at least 1909.[57]

At the meeting of the French and Russian Chiefs of Staff in September, 1908, General Charles Brun, chief of the French general staff, strongly insisted that Russia should devote all the available financial resources to increasing the efficiency of the railway system. A memorandum by the French minister of war spoke of the need to speed up Russian mobilisation, as well as of the need for new artillery and machine-guns.[58]

The Russians were worried by the French agreement with Germany in 1909, and, when Pichon made a speech in which he mentioned the improvement of Franco-German relations, Isvolsky questioned the use of the word "*rapprochement.*" He noted that the question of relations with Germany was always the sensitive point for the two allies and said it should be understood that neither would engage in important conversations with Berlin without the other immediately being advised.[59]

The 1910 meeting of the French and Russian Chiefs of Staff generally confirmed the point of view of the previous conferences, particularly on the point that German mobilisation obliged France and Russia to mobilise at once without previous consultation; if only Austria or Italy mobilised, agreement was required. The new Russian mobilisation plan, effective September 1, 1910, was said to respond to French requirements. It confirmed that the main Russian forces would act against Germany from the outbreak of the war and that Germany would be hindered from denuding her eastern frontier by the Russian plan to undertake a serious offensive against her. The Russian army would cross the frontier on the twentieth day with forces strong enough to win.[60]

Later in the year the French were alarmed by a report that the Russian armed forces had been redistributed so they would have an "essentially defensive objective." General Brun, however, believed that the offensive value of the Russian army had not been lessened by the change. The Russian General Soukhomlinoff informed him that the new plan had shortened mobilisation time and would enable the army to act totally rather than in little segments.[61]

While the Russians gave full support to France's Morocco policy in the summer of 1911, they made it clear that they expected France to support Russian policy regarding the straits in return. In September Neratov, the acting minister for foreign affairs, expressed his hope that France would not oppose Russia's point of view if she decided "to take definite action." He suggested that an agreement regarding the straits might take the form of a letter between the two ministers for foreign affairs.[62] The next few months saw a stream of dispatches on this subject, with Russia eager to persuade the French government to define its attitude to the action which Russia would "sooner or later undertake concerning the Straits and contiguous territory."[63] The French government remained noncommittal and her foreign minister, Justin de Selves, merely repeated the assurances given in 1908 that France "would look favourably on Russia's interest in the Straits and was ready to support resolutions Russia would have to take in regard to them."[64]

In February, 1912, the Russian government sent France a questionnaire about the possible events which might menace peace in the Near East. The Russians wanted to know what action should be taken if: there was an internal crisis in Turkey; Austria took an active step in the Sandjak of Novi-Bazar or Albania; an armed conflict should break out between Turkey and the Balkan states of Montenegro, Greece and Bulgaria. Raymond Poincaré, French premier, replied that the common examination of these eventualities was "fully authorized by the secret accord of August 8, 1899." The two governments had decided then that "always concerned about the maintenance of general peace, they attached no less importance to the equilibrium of the European forces."[65] Although Poincaré stated that the French government would make no decision on the action to be taken in these matters without consulting the London cabinet, this foreshadowed the participation of France in Russia's Balkan projects.[66]

The summer of 1912 saw the establishment of conversations between the allied naval staffs and the signing of a naval convention. The naval convention, arrived at on July 16, provided that the French and Russian naval forces would cooperate in any situation where the alliance provided for combined action of the two armies. The chiefs of staff were required to meet at least once a year to prepare for this cooperation by studying all the probable cases of war and planning their strategy.[67]

The election of Poincaré as president of France in January, 1913, was hailed by Alexandre Isvolsky, Russian ambassador in Paris, as a guarantee that France would continue to support Russia in the Balkans. M. Jonnart, the new French foreign minister, expressed the hope that Russia would continue to act in strict union with France and would take no initiative without previous discussion.[68]

In June, 1913, Stephen Pichon, French foreign minister, was authorized to tell the Russians that France would allow the Russian government to borrow 400 or 500 million francs a year to realize a programme of railway construction throughout the Empire, on two conditions. These conditions were that the strategic lines provided for on the western frontier would be begun immediately, and that the peace-time strength of the Russian army would be increased. Delcassé reported that in March the tsar had approved the construction, improvement or conversion of the strategic rail lines which the general staffs had declared indispensable to effect the concentration of the army on the western frontier. He asserted that since that time he had insisted incessantly on the need to have "as soon as possible the equipment which, enabling the Russian army to take the offensive at the same time as ours, would oblige Germany to divide her forces."[69]

Delcassé's report on the progress of work on the strategic railways stated that the doubling of the Moscow to Warsaw line between Briansk and Gomel was nearly finished and that the quadrupling of the Zabinka to Brest-Litovsk line would soon be finished. He announced that the works that had been finished or were in progress would assure a gain of four days in the concentration of the army.[70] A short time later he reported that Russia would now be able to send thirteen army corps against Germany on the thirteenth day after mobilisation, and that French general Joffre was well satisfied with the measures being taken for increasing the effectives on the western frontier.[71]

The French and Russian general staff conference of 1913 decided that not only mobilisation by Germany but any act of war would require mobilisation by France and Russia. Joffre announced that France would have more than 1,500,000 men, that concentration would be completed on the tenth day and the offensive taken on the eleventh day. General Jilinski said Russia would have at least 800,000 men, who would be concentrated on the fifteenth day and would be ready to take the offensive shortly after.[72]

In December Delcassé reported that the railway works which the general staffs had considered as necessary in 1912 had almost entirely been completed. Measures had also been taken to increase the effectives on the western front. These had received three reinforcements of 25,000 men each, and an increase of 90,000 was projected for 1914. Meanwhile, arrangements had been made for loans of 500 million francs a year for five years, to enable Russia to complete her railway programme.[73]

The tsar's increasing bellicosity was a significant feature of the last six months before the war. In an interview with Maurice Paléologue, the new French ambassador, he expressed his disappointment with England's lukewarm attitude, which he thought prevented the Triple Entente from asserting its power more vigorously. "Think how much force our representations would have, all three together," he said, "from the triple viewpoint, military, naval and financial." The tsar therefore wanted to make the Entente a formal alliance. Paléologue told him the military and naval agreements France had with England were good enough, and that Jonnart would encourage Sir Edward Grey, the British foreign secretary, to make similar arrangements with Russia if he wished it. The tsar did wish it, and the result was the negotiation of an Anglo-Russian naval agreement, which had no real strategic significance but was meant to reassure the tsar of British support.[74] The tsar also informed Paléologue that he had recently increased his army by 75,000 men and would soon add 300,000 more, to which the ambassador replied that France was making an equal effort and that France's three years law would be maintained.[75]

The tsar's desire for an Anglo-Russian Alliance arose from his apprehension of the risk of a war with Germany. He feared the outbreak of war between Greece and Turkey, in which case the Turkish government would want to close the straits. This Russia could not tolerate because it would be damaging to her commerce and her prestige. If it happened, he said that to reopen the straits he "would even employ force." He needed an alliance with England to ensure that Germany would not intervene to support Turkey.[76]

In May Paléologue expatiated at length in a dispatch to Paris on the possibility that war might produce a revolution in Russia. He discussed the two wings of the revolutionary forces, the intellectual proletariat and the working men's proletariat. He dismissed the former as having "a vague programme, full of dreams and Utopianism," but thought the workers had "a formidable power of revolt and subversion." He then surveyed the powers of repression, the police, the Cossacks and the army, and concluded that these forces greatly surpassed those of revolution, and that the government was strong enough to maintain the tsar's absolute rule.[77]

On the same day Paléologue reported that a ukase had just been published fixing the contingent of recruits for 1914 at 585,100 men, an increase of 130,000 over 1913. Considering the measures taken in 1913 and the fact that about one-tenth of the contingent stayed in service four or five years instead of only three, the total increase of effectives in three years would be a half million men.[78]

By July, 1914, great progress had been made in expanding the French and Russian armies and in shortening the time required for their mobilisation and transportation to the German frontier. The Russian army now required only four more days for concentration than the French and German armies, and its numerical advantage over the German army was almost one million men. While the Franco-Russian superiority over the Central Powers was not as overwhelming as it would have been three years later, it seemed great enough to justify their confidence that victory was certain.

Notes

1. William L. Langer, *European Alliances and Alignments, 1871-1890*, pp. 238-9.
2. *Ibid.*, pp. 240-5.
3. *Ibid.*, pp. 371-394.
4. *Ibid.*, p. 426.
5. *Ibid.*, pp. 427-8.
6. *Ibid.*, pp. 428-9.
7. *Ibid.*, pp. 441, 491-2.
8. DDF1, VIII, no. 11.
9. *Ibid.*, no. 399.
10. William L. Langer, *The Franco-Russian Alliance 1890-1914*, pp. 79-81.
11. *Ibid.*, pp. 101-4.
12. DDF1, VIII, no. 160.
13. *Ibid.*, no. 165.
14. *Ibid.*, no. 304.
15. *Ibid.*, no. 430.
16. *Ibid.*, no. 434.
17. William L. Langer, *The Diplomacy of Imperialism*, p. 21.
18. DDF1, VIII, nos. 514, 515, 516, 517.
19. *Ibid.*, IX, no. 76.
20. *Ibid.*, no. 104.
21. *Ibid.*, no. 182.
22. *Ibid.*
23. *Ibid.*, no. 218.
24. *Ibid.*, nos. 296, 300.
25. *Ibid.*, no 318.
26. *Ibid.*, no. 444.
27. Langer, *Diplomacy*, pp. 35, 37.
28. *Ibid.*, pp. 38-41.
29. Langer, *Franco-Russian Alliance*, pp. 304-6.
30. DDF1, X, no. 331.
31. *Ibid.*, no. 362.
32. Langer, *Franco-Russian Alliance*, pp. 335-6.

33.*Ibid.*, pp. 393, 395-7.

34.DDF1, XII, no. 32.

35.*Ibid.*, XIV, nos. 14, 104, 197.

36.*Ibid.*, XII, no. 164.

37.*Ibid.*, XIII, no. 16.

38.*Ibid.*, XIV, no. 314.

39.*Ibid.*, nos. 317, 320.

40.*Ibid.*, no. 335.

41.*Ibid.*, XV, no. 126.

42.J. B. Scott, (ed.), *The Hague Conventions and Declarations of 1899 and 1907*, pp. xvii, xviii.

43.DDF1, XV, no. 153.

44.*Ibid.*, no. 175.

45.*Ibid.*, no. 252.

46.DDF2, I, no. 112.

47.*Ibid.*, nos. 159, 251, 263.

48.*Ibid.*, no. 329.

49.*Ibid.*, III, no. 397.

50.*Ibid.*, IV, no. 317.

51.*Ibid.*, no. 366.

52.*Ibid.*, V, no. 73.

53.BD IV, nos. 12, 13, 15, 16, 19.

54.DDF2, V, nos. 389, 390, 401, 406, 413.

55.*Ibid.*, IX, no. 78.

56.*Ibid.*, no. 192.

57.*Ibid.*, X, no. 310.

58.*Ibid.*, XI, nos. 412, 455.

59.*Ibid.*, XII, no. 364.

60.*Ibid.*, no. 573.

61.*Ibid.*, XIII, nos. 63, 83, 157.

62.René Marchand, (ed.), *Un Livre Noir*, I, 140-1.

63.*Ibid.*, pp. 144-7.

64.DDF3, I, no. 18; LNI, 178-80.

65.DDF3, II, no. 202.

66.*Ibid.*, no. 211.

67.LN, I, 299.

68.LN, II, 11, 13, 15, 19, 21.

69.DDF3, VII, nos. 134, 513.

70.*Ibid.*, no. 521.

71.*Ibid.*, VIII, no. 62.

72.*Ibid.*, no. 79.

73.*Ibid.*, no. 698.

74.*Ibid.*, IX, no. 322.

75.*Ibid.*, IX, no. 322.

76.*Ibid.*, X, no. 123.

77.*Ibid.*, no. 267.

78.*Ibid.*, no. 268.

Three

The Detachment Of Italy

Bismarck's choice of Austria rather than Russia as the centre-piece of his continental system built into it the fatal flaws which eventually destroyed his work. The ancient antipathy of Italy to Austria on the one hand and the Austro-Russian conflict of interests in the Balkans on the other made a continuing connection of the two peripheral Powers with Austria precarious from the outset. Eventually France succeeded in allying herself with Russia and neutralizing Italy.

France first attempted to detach Italy from the Triple Alliance in 1889. Economic difficulties in Italy led the Italian government to hope for a commercial agreement with France. In February, 1891, the Italian finance minister inquired whether a new loan could be raised in France. The reply was that this depended on assurances concerning Italian foreign policy. France wanted a promise that Italy was not engaged, and would not engage herself, to make war on France. Until definite assurance was given that Italy would not join Germany in a Franco-German war, France would not send her money to Italy.[1] As Italy was not yet ready to abandon the Triple Alliance, nothing came of this approach.

Throughout the 1890s Italy continued to press for a commercial agreement with France, but the French reply was always the same. In April, 1894, for example, the French foreign minister told the Italian ambassador in Paris that France would make economic concessions only if these were preceded by a political rapprochement. Although Camille Barrère, the French ambassador in Rome, believed French economic concessions would be followed by a political agreement, French policy remained unchanged until Théophile Delcassé succeeded to the French foreign office in 1898. Delcassé was ready to gamble on the probability that his friend Barrère's judgment was correct.

The definite *rapprochement* of the two countries began in November, 1898, with the conclusion of a commercial accord which ended a tariff war between them.[2] By the autumn of 1900 the time was ripe for a further advance. The assassination of King Humbert in July of that year brought his son to the throne as Victor Emmanuel III. The new king was an irredentist who detested Austria, disliked Wilhelm II and wanted out of the Triple Alliance. The Italian press now exhibited great hostility to Austria-Hungary and looked for an accord with France.[3] In December, 1900, therefore, France succeeded in reaching an agreement with Italy on Morocco and Tripoli. France, on her part, declared that she had no designs on Tripoli and recognized Italy's right to extend her influence there without French consent. Italy, in return, recognized France's right to extend her influence in Morocco, with the reservation that, if France imposed direct sovereignty or a protectorate on Morocco, Italy would have the right to take similar steps in Tripoli.[4]

France obviously anticipated further developments in Franco-Italian relations. The French immediately undertook to facilitate negotiations between Russia and Italy for a treaty of commerce, on the ground that it would be advantageous to France to strengthen the ties between Italy and France's ally.[5]

The next step was taken in connection with the projected renewal of the Triple Alliance. In June, 1901, Italy declared that if the Alliance was renewed it would contain no clause which would menace directly or indirectly the security of France.[6] Next came arrangements for French finance to undertake large-scale operations in Italy, which would enable French interests to gain a preponderant position. As it was believed this would have an important bearing on Franco-Italian relations, the French foreign office undertook to support this development.[7]

In January, 1902, Barrère informed Delcassé that the Italian press was unanimous in the belief that the Triple Alliance was useless and would not be renewed.[8] He himself thought that Italy's military obligations to Germany were already a dead letter.[9] The Marquis Rudini, an influential Italian statesman, thought the Triple Alliance treaty should be redrafted so it could be shown to France and she could satisfy herself that it did not threaten her security. It was his understanding that this would mean that Italy would not join with the Alliance against France.[10]

An exchange of letters between France and Italy on July 10, 1902, defined the relations between the two states from that time forward. A letter to Barrère from the Italian foreign minister, Prinetti, read as follows:

> *In case France is the object of direct or indirect aggression on the part of one or more Powers, Italy will maintain strict neutrality. The same will apply in a case where France, as a result of direct provocation, finds herself obliged to take, in defence of her honour or her security, the initiative of declaring war.*

In this eventuality, the government of the Republic should communicate its intention previously to the Royal Government, in order to establish that it actually amounts to a case of direct provocation.[11]

When Prinetti was asked to define direct provocation, two of the examples he gave were Wilhelm I's refusal to receive Vincent Benedetti, the French ambassador in Berlin and the publication of the Ems telegram by Bismarck. It was evident that France would find it easy to persuade Italy that she had been provoked.[12]

In April, 1904, the welcome given to Émile Loubet, President of France, in Rome showed the enthusiasm of the Italian public for Italy's defection from the Triple Alliance.[13] A short time later Barrère reported that the Italian government proposed to ask for extraordinary military credits, which were to be devoted to preparations for war against Austria. He believed that Italian military circles agreed that the Triple Alliance had been paralysed by the Franco-Italian agreement.[14]

After the Algeciras conference, at which Italy had generally supported France, Barrère wrote to Delcassé that Italy was no longer interested in the Triple Alliance. He thought that to most Italians a war with France seemed impossible, and believed that the Anglo-French entente had strengthened this view. A few Italians, he said, might still be ready to fight France, but not one would want to oppose France and England together.[15] As Italy had originally made the reservation that the Alliance did not apply against England, there can be no doubt that this observation was on the mark.

In the summer of 1905, Lieutenant-Colonel Julliann, the French military attaché at Rome, wrote to the French minister of war that it was no longer believable that Italy would take part in a war against France. In his opinion it was now unnecessary for France to have an army on the Alps frontier.[16] Tommasso Tittoni told Barrère that no government could carry Italy into a war with France, and that in case of a Franco-German war Italy would be neutral.[17]

In 1909 Italy completed her *de facto* break with the Triple Alliance by making a secret agreement with Russia at Racconigi. The two Powers agreed that if it proved impossible to maintain the *status quo* in the Balkans they would support the principle of nationality, to the exclusion of all foreign domination, and that they would take common diplomatic action to ensure this. They also declared that they would consider with benevolence, on the one hand the interests of Russia in the straits question, and on the other Italy's interest in Tripoli and Cyrenaica. Finally it was stipulated that each would make agreements concerning the area only with the participation of the other.[18] Although Italy almost immediately signed an agreement with Austria behind Russia's back, Sir Charles Hardinge in the British foreign office, was undoubtedly correct in his belief that Italy was now closer to the Triple Entente than to the Triple Alliance.[19]

When it seemed possible to the British government that the Agadir crisis might result in war, Sir Arthur Nicolson, then undersecretary for foreign affairs, was confident that Italy would remain neutral.[20] Both the French foreign office and the general staff agreed in 1911 that Italy would not take part in a war. In January, 1912, the French council of national defence decided that the whole active army should be sent to the north-east front, with reserves and territorials left to guard the Alps and the Pyrenees.[21]

In December, 1912, Alexandre Isvolsky, the Russian ambassador in Paris, questioned Raymond Poincaré about the value of the Franco-Italian agreement. Poincaré's reply was that its value lay not in the words used but in the fact that since 1902 Italy had ceased all military preparations on the French frontier and had concentrated on the Austrian frontier. He thought neither side could count on Italian loyalty, but that if war came Italy would wait and join the side to which victory inclined.[22]

French war plans were revised at the end of 1912. Plan XVII, which was completed and inspected by June 1, 1914, assumed that Italy was unlikely to enter the war, certainly not at first, and that France could therefore denude the Alps.[23]

Military writers were of the opinion that Italy was unlikely to fight with the Triple Alliance, but that even if she did her assistance would be of little value to Germany and Austria. Major de Civrieux thought Italy would abandon the Triple Alliance in case of war and might fight against Austria.[24] General Friedrich von Bernhardi, the famous German military writer, considered it doubtful that Italy would take part in a war against England and France, although he was obviously unaware of the Franco-Italian accord of 1902.[25]

Fritz Fischer, the German historian, who in his book, *War of Illusions*, is intent on showing that Italy did not join her allies because they were engaged in an offensive war, tells us that the Triple Alliance was strengthened in 1913, but that Italy regarded it as purely defensive.[26] The renewal of the alliance on December 5, 1912, he says, had once more made Italy a military factor to be counted on.[27] Fischer intimates that Germany seriously expected help from Italy and that the Italians promised to send three corps to the western front. He admits, however, that it was only General Pollio who promised this, and that his promises were "vague and of an academic nature." As far as the Italian government was concerned, he pretends that they applied only in case of a defensive war. Evidently he is unaware of the details of the Franco-Italian agreement, which guaranteed Italian neutrality even if France attacked Germany, provided she had been "provoked."[28] In a discussion of the political situation in the Triple Alliance Fischer details the conflicts between Italy and Austria, and shows that the possibility that Italy would join Austria and Germany in war was extremely remote.[29]

The revival of the Triple Alliance in December, 1912, had no influence whatever on Italian policy. The Marquis de San Guiliano, the Italian foreign minister, told Barrère that the alliance was renewed with no change, that the accords of 1902 remained in full force and that they would operate under the same conditions as in the past. In the debate on the renewal of the alliance in· the Italian Chamber of Deputies many voices were raised against renewal, and one deputy said, without fear of contradiction, that "it would be impossible for an Italian army to find itself on the side of the Austrian army." There was no protest from either side of the Chamber.[30]

There is no reason to believe that the French confidence that Italy would remain neutral when war came was misguided. In fact Italy and Austria were engaged in serious conflict over Albania on the eve of the war, which explains Austria's reluctance to keep Italy informed about her projected coup against Serbia.

Notes

1.DDF1, VIII, nos. 256, 258, 290, 324.
2.DDF2, I, no. 396.
3.DDF1, XVI, nos. 373, 394.
4.DDF2, I, no. 17.
5.*Ibid.*, no. 193.
6.*Ibid.*, no. 376.
7.*Ibid.*, no. 579.
8.*Ibid.*, II, no. 19.
9.*Ibid.*, no. 168.
10.*Ibid.*, no. 76.
11.*Ibid.*, no. 329.
12.*Ibid.*, no 390.
13.Paul M. Kennedy, *The Rise of Anglo-German Antagonism*, p. 269.
14.DDF2, V, no. 438.
15.*Ibid.*, X, no. 4.
16.*Ibid.*, XI, no. 508.
17.*Ibid.*, no. 560.
18.René Marchand, *Un Livre Noir*, I, 358.
19.Sidney B. Fay, *The Origins of the World War*, I, 407-9.
20.BD VII, no. 546.
21.General J. J. C. Joffre, *Personal Memoirs of Joffre*, pp. 42, 48.
22.LN, I 361, 365.
23.Joffre, pp. 83-4.
24.Major de Civrieux, *Le Germanisme Encerclé*, pp. 70, 77-8.
25.Friedrich von Bernhardi, *Germany and the Next War*, p. 152.
26.Fritz Fischer, *War of Illusions*, p. 146.
27.*Ibid.*, p. 169.
28.*Ibid.*, pp. 392-7, 401.
29.*Ibid.*, pp. 404-7.
30.DDF3, V, nos. 34, 83.

Four

![■]

England's Estrangement From Germany

From almost every point of view it seems axiomatic that, as Joseph Chamberlain maintained, the natural ally for England was Germany. France, their common enemy for generations, had allied herself with Russia, and these two expansionist powers were England's leading rivals in the contest for Empire. Germany, after a brief flurry of colonialism in the 1880s, was more interested in trade than in territory. Most English statesmen recognized the two countries' common interests, and cooperation with the German Empire had been the normal English posture for many years.

Behind the facade of shared enmities and interests, however, lay a history of English disdain for German weakness and opposition to the growth of German power.[1] During the German struggle for unification, the British interest in controlling the Baltic reinforced by Viscount Henry Palmerston's belief that a united Germany would threaten British commercial supremacy, led the British government to oppose German nationalism in Schleswig-Holstein.[2]

Palmerston, foreign minister at the time, played the leading role in the expulsion of Prussia from the Duchies in 1849,[3] and his successors continued to follow a pro-Danish policy in the face of frequent violation by Denmark of the 1852 Treaty of London, which had confirmed the rights of the German Confederation in the Duchies of Holstein and Lauenburg.[4] British support of Denmark continued during the crisis of 1863-64, Palmerston, now prime minister, maintaining that Denmark should hold "the keys to the Baltic" and that "Kiel, with its great strategic possibilities, should be ruled from Copenhagen, not from Frankfort or Berlin."[5] British advocacy of the Danish cause stopped short of war because Palmerston, whose policy was violently opposed by the queen, was unable to carry the cabinet with him.[6]

In January, 1870, the French foreign minister induced the British government to propose to Prussia that she should reduce her armaments, an initiative warmly approved by William Gladstone, the British prime minister.[7] The French army, which had recently been expanded, was considerably larger than the Prussian army, and Prussia had to the south and east the still larger armies of Austria and Russia.[8] Bismarck naturally assumed that England aimed at so weakening Prussia that she would be unable to resist French opposition to the unification of Germany.

Foreign minister Lord Clarendon's fatuous statement that France was "a nation resolutely pacific," which guaranteed Prussian safety was equalled only by his audacity in preaching economy to a government that spent far less on armaments than his own.[9] In fact, the British government had good evidence that France intended to oppose German unity by force and that the France of 1870 was anything but pacific. In August, 1867, the French ambassador in Berlin told the British ambassador that France could never "permit the formation of a German Empire."[10] In January, 1870, premier Émile Ollivier, discussing the disarmament proposal with Lord Lyons, the British ambassador in Paris, explained that if France made this proposal herself "a public rebuff by Prussia would be fatal:" it would mean war. It was evident to Lord Lyons that France intended to prevent German unification and that in fact she badly wanted a war with Prussia.[11] Given Napoleon III's energetic pursuit of an alliance with Austria and Italy against Prussia, Bismarck's refusal even to mention the British proposal to his kaiser is easy to understand.[12]

British sentiment during the Franco-Prussian war was generally favourable to Prussia, but the completeness of the German victory induced a shift in opinion towards sympathy with France. When the intention to annex Alsace and Lorraine was announced Gladstone attempted to persuade his cabinet to take action, but his colleagues' more cautious view prevailed.[13] He then wrote an article for the *Edinburgh Review*, under an easily detected pseudonym, in which he publicly stated his objections to the annexation. Characterized by intemperate language, a holier-than-thou attitude and a superficial knowledge of history, this article showed an anti-German bias which distinguished Gladstone throughout his career.[14]

The war scare of 1875 provided the British government with another opportunity for gratuitous interference on behalf of France. The supposed crisis began with a significant increase of the French army, already larger than the German army, and was fomented by the French foreign minister, the Duc de Decazes. The British attempt to unite all the European governments to warn Germany against breaking the peace was quite naturally taken by Germany as evidence of English hostility.[15]

During the Near Eastern crisis of the late seventies England and Germany usually worked together. Bismarck favoured cooperation of Austria and France with England, partly because he thought Anglo-French friendship ruled out a Franco-Russian alliance.[16] He considered an Anglo-French alliance a guarantee of peace and German security.[17] Bismarck also agreed to second the British suggestion that France should take Tunis, and supported British policy in Turkey and Egypt.[18] However, a proposal for an Anglo-German alliance, for which each attributed the initiative to the other, aroused little enthusiasm on either side.[19]

The British occupation of Egypt introduced a new phase in Anglo-German relations. Since this action produced almost continual friction with France, and other Powers received it coolly, German support was essential to the success of British policy. This support was forthcoming: Bismarck backed British policy without reservation.[20] However, his expectation that Germany might, in return, reap some positive advantage from British friendship was disappointed. German policy evoked expressions of gratitude, but no reciprocation.

The first serious friction arose over the establishment of a German colony in South West Africa. That this episode is considered a landmark in the history of Anglo-German relations is shown by the fact that it has attracted an unusually large number of books and articles. These invariably take the view that the problems which arose resulted from Bismarck's bad faith and trickery.

A German merchant named Luderitz purchased territory in the bay of Angra Pequena, where he built a factory and raised the German flag. In February, 1883, Count Georg Munster, the German ambassador in London, inquired whether British protection could be given to a German factory between the Orange and Little Fish rivers. The British answer was that more information concerning the location was needed.[21] In August of that year the Cape government became concerned about the settlement and sent a gunboat to investigate the matter.[22]

On September 10, Baron Ludwig von Plessen, a German chargé d'affaires, left a memo at the foreign office requesting unofficially that the German government be informed whether England claimed suzerainty at Angra Pequena and, if so, on what ground the claim rested. He also wished to know whether the British government had any objection to Luderitz's factory project. The British government replied unofficially that a Mr. de Pass, a British subject, claimed prior right of purchase over this territory, but that Her Majesty's government had no claim on or jurisdiction over the area. The colonial secretary at Cape Town later informed the colonial office that no attempt had been made to have Pass's claim recognized by the British government and that the claim had lain dormant for nearly twenty years.[23]

The German government raised the question officially on November 16, 1883, when Munster called at the foreign office to inquire "concerning the British claim to sovereignty over Angra Pequena and adjacent territory and the basis of such claim, if any." Lord Granville, the British foreign minister, replied on November 21 that England had not proclaimed sovereignty over this territory but that any claim by another Power to any jurisdiction between Portuguese territory and Cape Colony would be considered an infringement of her legitimate rights.[24]

Although the British government had previously refused to annex this territory, it now reversed its policy and made strenuous efforts to establish a claim to Angra Pequena during the last months of 1883.[25] At the same time the prime minister of Cape Colony was in London and was urging the government to adopt a Monroe Doctrine for South Africa, warning all the European Powers to keep out.[26]

On December 31 the German ambassador directed a long letter to the foreign office in which he quoted previous documents to show that England had no jurisdiction over Angra Pequena and requested information concerning the basis of any British claim. As the German government owed protection to German trade, he also wished to learn what institutions England had there which would secure such legal protection for German subjects as would relieve the German government of the necessity to provide such protection itself.[27]

The British government made no reply to this communication for six months. Meanwhile, however, Lord Derby, the colonial secretary, attempted on February 5 to anticipate any German action by inducing the Cape government to take control of Angra Pequena, in order to resist the view of the German government that they could only ensure the protection of German subjects by assuming jurisdiction themselves.[28] This action shows that Derby fully realized the possibility that the Germans might make such a claim and that he believed that they intended to take Angra Pequena. The delay in replying to the German inquiries arose from a desire to forestall this eventuality by establishing an actual British claim.

The German government, after waiting nearly four months for an answer to Munster's note of December 31, proceeded to take Angra Pequena under its own protection. Bismarck telegraphed the German consul at Cape Town on April 24, 1884, instructing him to declare officially that Luderitz's establishments were under the protection of the German empire. On the same day the British government was informed of this action by the German chargé d'affaires in London.[29]

This communication has been the subject of much controversy, as Lord Granville did not understand that Germany now claimed Angra Pequena. Count Munster, in London, was unsympathetic to the acquisition of German colonies and apparently gave the impression that the establishment of German protection was meaningless. At the same time Lord Ampthill, the British ambassador in Berlin, was assuring the foreign office that no decisive

German action had been taken. It is rather curious, however, that on April 25 Ampthill drafted a despatch in which he noted that the British colony at Cape Town had raised a doubt as to whether Luderitz was entitled to German protection and that Bismarck had instructed the German consul on the spot to say that no doubt existed as to this right.[30]

It has been maintained that a German dispatch of February, 1883, which used the term "protection" to mean something less than annexation, confused the British ministers and led them to believe that Bismarck had taken no decisive action. As this dispatch had never been contradicted, they were justified, according to this view, in refusing to believe that Bismarck was actually declaring the area of Angra Pequena a part of the German Empire. In view of Munster's insistence on denying any British claim in his long letter of December 31, and Derby's determined attempts to establish a British claim, it is hard to take this argument seriously.

In any case, the British government continued to insist that, although the area was not claimed by England, they had the right to exclude other Powers because it was so close to British settlements. This policy was restated by Lord Derby in the House of Lords on May 19.[31] This was quite correctly described by Bismarck as "a Monroe Doctrine for Africa" and an insult to Germany.[32]

Finally, after much urging by the colonial office, the Cape government agreed to take control of Angra Pequena, and Germany was informed that German subjects would be given protection under the British flag.[33] Bismarck refused to recognize this British claim, and the German right to colonize Angra Pequena was finally conceded on July 14, 1884.[34]

British historians have performed miracles of double-think in their efforts to turn this episode into an example of Bismarckian trickery and bad faith. The most imaginative and least plausible account is given by historian A. J. P. Taylor. According to Taylor, Bismarck was never interested in colonies and his acquisition of almost the whole German colonial empire was an unwarranted by-product of his desire to quarrel with England. Preparation for this conflict, we are told, was made in a dispatch of May 5, 1884. Bismarck had declared that Angra Pequena was under German protection two weeks earlier, after six months of trying to get a rational answer about its status from the British government, so the assertion that Bismarck began the quarrel on May 5 is hard to understand. A perusal of the dispatch of May 5 makes it even more difficult, as it contains nothing to justify such a conclusion.[35] William Aydelotte correctly points out in his book *Bismarck and British Colonial Policy* that what Bismarck wanted was an understanding by which, in return for his support in Egypt, England would accord fair treatment to German trading and overseas interests.[36]

Taylor maintains that Bismarck's colonial ventures were undertaken in order to facilitate an entente with France, but the timing of the approach to

France effectively refutes this theory. The attempt to get French cooperation was actually made as a result of his colonial policy, and for the moment it failed.[37]

Aydelotte, the most prolific writer on the subject, turns in a gold medal performance in mental gymnastics. He tells us that the British government did not oppose German colonial claims once they understood them, and that the German White Book was unscrupulously edited to depict the British as "colonial monopolists making outrageous objections to Germany's legitimate claims."[38] At the same time he is evidently aware of the British statement of November 21, 1883, which in effect claimed the right to exclude other Powers from areas adjacent to British territories.[39] Aydelotte cites the continued efforts of the colonial office to build up a claim to the coast between the Orange River and the Portuguese colonies, including Derby's attempts to have Cape Colony annex these territories. He points out that Derby could have answered Munster's note of December 31 immediately by stating that England had no claim, but instead tried to get Cape Colony to take control.[40] He also notes that on May 19, 1884, Derby repeated the British claim of the right to exclude other Powers from this coast because of its nearness to British possessions.[41] Since the British government continued its attempts to block German colonial expansion all over the world, spectacles of a special kind are needed to perceive that there was no opposition to German colonial claims once they were understood. When Lord Granville said, in May, 1885, that recent British annexations were not anti-German because these territories were "deemed essential to the safety or welfare of some neighbouring British possession," Bismarck's comment was, "That is the entire world."[42]

Aydelotte also attempts to explain the slowness and stupidity of British policy by asserting that there was a fundamental difference between German and British diplomacy, in that Bismarck had absolute control over foreign affairs while in England an important measure of foreign policy had to secure the approval of about fifteen cabinet members whose ideas differed.[43] He says the leading British ministers, except Derby, didn't oppose German colonization and were ready to meet Bismarck's wishes when they understood them.[44] Lord Granville completely delegated his authority to Derby in the matter of Angra Pequena, and the other members of the cabinet knew nothing about it until June, 1884, so it is obvious that up to that time Derby alone carried out British policy in this affair.[45] It is true that on June 21 the cabinet decided unanimously to accept the German claim to the coast between the Orange River and the Portuguese colonies, largely because their weak diplomatic position left them no alternative. Nevertheless, the continued activity of the colonial office in opposing German aims in the Cameroons, in East Africa and in the Pacific indicates that Derby was allowed to continue his anti-German policy in other areas.[46]

Aydelotte also tells us that Bismarck deliberately deceived the British government, which was completely surprised by the German decision to take control of Angra Pequena.[47] In view of the fact that no member of the cabinet except Derby knew what was happening, it appears that it was he who was responsible for the deception. Bismarck did keep his intention from the British government in June, 1884, but this was because "he feared that the frankness with which he had acted formerly had been abused." England had left his inquiries about her possessions unanswered "in order to use the intervening time in an attempt to increase them."[48]

Aydelotte writes of a "contrived dispute" with the British government. He says that Bismarck went out of his way to foment a quarrel to stimulate national emotion, deluding Germans with "charges against the monopolistic colonial practices of the British government which were quite unjustified by the facts."[49] Unfortunately, the facts cited by Aydelotte himself fully justify such charges.

A great deal has been written about the reasons behind Bismarck's sudden adoption of a "colonial policy." Recent writers have pointed out that Bismarck understood quite well the need for the promotion of foreign trade to support an industrial economy. He introduced a variety of measures to support the export industries, including subsidies for the transportation of goods and the establishment of banks and consular offices overseas. He preferred to have private interests take the lead through the creation of chartered companies, but the wave of imperial expansion in the 1880s led him to fear that the seizure of more and more territory by other powers, particularly England, would leave Germany out in the cold.[50]

It should also be pointed out that this affair highlighted the British government's persistent refusal to accept any idea that German support for British policy should be requited by British goodwill towards Germany. Any suggestion that in return for German assistance in Egypt the British government might reduce its opposition to German colonization somewhere was considered "bullying" and "blackmail." German support was not to be "bought," but must be given freely, with no thought that England might reciprocate. The role of a subordinate power was to follow in the wake of the British ship of state, not to have the temerity to adopt an independent course.

The German chancellor was intensely irritated by the conduct of the British ministers throughout the whole affair. Count Herbert von Bismarck, a German diplomat, spoke to Ampthill of the long delay in answering questions, a delay objectionable in itself but doubly so because Lord Derby had used it to anticipate any action by Germany.[51] The pretense that the delay had been caused by the necessity of consulting an "independent" government at the Cape was treated with the scorn it deserved. The role of the Cape legislature was dictated by the British government's desire to forestall the Germans without incurring the expense of establishing a new colony.

Bismarck's belief that the Gladstone ministry was determined to oppose German colonization and trade in Africa led to an attempt at cooperation with France in order to thwart British intentions. A French ministry headed by the colonial enthusiast Jules Ferry stood ready to join him in ensuring that Africa should be open to the trade of all the Powers. The result was the Berlin Conference of 1884-85, which demarcated spheres of influence and established the doctrine that territory could be claimed only by effective occupation. In unclaimed areas freedom of trade would prevail.

The *rapprochement* between Germany and France could be only temporary, as long as Alsace-Lorraine remained in German hands. Their fragile fraternity was already precarious when the fall of Ferry at the end of March, 1885, sealed its fate. When Lord Salisbury returned to office a few months later, Bismarck undertook to resume his normal policy of friendship with England. Gladstone's restoration to power for a short time, however, soon poisoned relations again. British representatives abroad worked to thwart German colonial ambitions at every turn, and protests from Berlin brought nothing but kind words. An inquiry concerning British claims on the Somali coast produced the same delaying tactics which had been tried in the case of Angra Pequena, evidently with the same purpose of creating a British claim to forestall Germany.[52] When the Gladstone ministry was replaced by another Salisbury cabinet in July, 1886, agreement was eventually reached on the spheres of interest of the two Powers in East Africa. Friction continued for some time over the anti-German activities of the British representatives in Zanzibar, but by the end of 1888 affairs had been smoothed over once again.

Meanwhile the Mediterranean agreements of 1887 had brought England into close cooperation with Italy and Austria, and the cordiality of Anglo-German relations improved accordingly. Encouraged by what seemed a new decisiveness in British policy, Bismarck sounded out Salisbury on the possibility of a short-term alliance against France. The answer was, in accordance with Salisbury's usual reason for inaction, that parliamentary considerations made such an alliance impossible.[53]

Bismarck's dismissal in March, 1890, made little immediate difference in Anglo-German relations, but Salisbury feared that German policy would be more changeable and less reliable than before.[54] The two governments remained in friendly communication during the Balkan crisis which followed, although Germany as usual refused to take any action which might endanger her relations with Russia. The German decision not to renew the Reinsurance Treaty was not intended as a break with Russia, but merely as a simplification of Bismarck's complicated and less than honest policy. One consideration, however, was the fear that its possible disclosure would alienate England.[55]

Meanwhile colonial disputes in East Africa had been disturbing the two governments, and discussions aimed at resolving these problems had begun while Bismarck was still in power. The points at issue concerned the delimitation of spheres of influence in East Africa, rivalry for control of Zanzibar and wrangling between the British and German East African companies. Salisbury proposed arbitration, which was accepted by Germany but proved to be unnecessary. Negotiations were temporarily suspended, to be resumed by Bismarck's successor, General Count Georg von Caprivi. When Salisbury offered to cede the island of Heligoland to Germany the way was opened for territorial concessions by Germany which made a settlement possible. The German government considered that the possession of Heligoland was "by far the most serious matter in the whole negotiation," as "without Heligoland the Kiel Canal is useless to our navy."[56] An agreement was therefore reached on the boundaries of the respective spheres of influence in East Africa, while Germany ceded Witu and other territories and acknowledged England's protectorate over Zanzibar. In return Heligoland was turned over to Germany.[57] With the conclusion of this treaty continued friendly cooperation seemed assured.

During the Arab war in North Nyasaland (1893-95) Germany cooperated with the British in stopping the slave trade and in preventing the importation of guns and ammunition by the Arabs. On at least one occasion a German steamer assisted in the transportation of British troops.[58]

Meanwhile, Germany continued to uphold British policy in Egypt. In 1890, she followed the British lead exactly in the conversion of the Egyptian debt, and the German government made great efforts to support England against France in the question of Turkish suzerainty.[59] In December, 1892, Germany consented at once to the use of the surplus of the Privileged Debt for increasing the Egyptian army. The next few years saw Germany giving "practically unqualified support" of the British control of Egypt.[60]

Throughout the whole period 1890-95 the consistent aim of German policy was to bring England into a closer relationship with the Triple Alliance. Italy was the key to this problem, since the friendship of Italy was important for the British position in the Mediterranean. An attempt by Italy, supported by Austria and Germany, to make a more binding commitment regarding the defence of Italy against France, succeeded in producing reassuring statements by the British government, but no definite obligation. When the Russians threatened Constantinople or the French advanced in Morocco, Germany regularly advised Austria and Italy to act only in conjunction with England and not to allow themselves to be pushed into war without British support. Faced with a possible Russian attack on the Dardanelles the chancellor, Prince zu Hohenlohe-Schillingsfürst, insisted that England must involve herself by treaty or action before Austria and Italy committed themselves.[61] This "anti-British" attitude was shared by all the leading statesmen of the Triple Alliance, who feared that England's refusal to define her attitude meant that they would be left in the lurch if they took action on their own.

Although every British government of this period looked to Germany for support against France and Russia, and the Triple Alliance was generally considered a guarantor of peace, it was never thought possible for England to undertake any explicit obligation. During the Salisbury ministries, the Conservatives' precarious hold on power precluded the possibility of making any definite commitment in the face of public opinion. When Gladstone took office, the anti-German and pro-French tendencies of the Liberals held sway, and friction with Germany was the general rule.

One stratagem the Germans employed, quite erroneously and ineffectively, was to try to frighten the British into a closer relationship with the Triple Alliance by cooperating with France and Russia. This was, at least in part, the explanation of the hard line taken by Germany over the Congo treaty of May 12, 1894. Count Paul Hatzfeld-Wildenburg proposed, on June 1, that Germany should join France in opposing the treaty in order to "exert pressure on England and make her more amenable."[62] Germany had already protested against Article III of this treaty, on the ground that German East Africa would be hemmed in on all sides by British territory, which she had expressly rejected in the Anglo-German agreement of July 1, 1890.[63] Joint action with France had not yet been considered, however, and this approach was made after Hatzfeld-Wildenburg's suggestion. Baron Friedrich von Holstein's later plan of joining with France and Russia for certain *definite* objects had the same aim. In a memorandum of December 30, 1895, he expressed the view that England would not understand the necessity of drawing nearer to the Triple Alliance "until she finds that the Triple Alliance will not follow her lead under *every* circumstance."[64]

Meanwhile, British officialdom was characterized by a growing hostility to Germany. Although the Liberal government was itself attempting to cooperate with France, any German leaning in this direction was considered unacceptable. A German obligation to support British policy under all circumstances was taken for granted, but any suggestion that this should be reciprocated by a friendly attitude towards Germany was considered "blackmail." Baron von Rotenham in the Berlin foreign office wrote in September, 1893, that "all British colonial authorities systematically show ill-will towards our wishes, aspirations and *rights*" where even passive agreement by the British authorities would be helpful. He complained that the British treated the rebels in south west Africa on an equal footing with the German government, and in fact gave assistance to them. The German perception was that "England now shows herself unfriendly to us in every colonial question, however unimportant."[65] This belief was undoubtedly correct, as Lord Rosebery, the leading Liberal imperialist, advocated a British monopoly in the colonial field.

Sir Edward Grey reveals the view which distinguished the Liberal administration in his imaginative account of an incident connected with the Egyptian army increase. British and German firms were applying for railway concessions in Asia Minor when the question of using the surplus of the Privileged Debt to increase the Egyptian army arose. According to Grey, there suddenly came a "sort of ultimatum" from Berlin, requiring the British to stop competing for railway concessions in Turkey for which Germans were applying and threatening to withdraw support for British policy in Egypt unless this was agreed upon. Thereupon, Lord Rosebery "withdrew competition for railway concessions in Turkey."[66]

What actually happened was that, after the German consul-general in Cairo had handed in a note consenting to the army increase, he received a telegram from Berlin stating that the British embassy in Constantinople was "assisting French interests to the injury of Germany" in connection with the Turkish railways, and asking him to hold back his consent if he had not already given it. He acquainted Lord Cromer, consul-general in Egypt, with the contents of the telegram and Cromer informed Lord Rosebery.[67]

In January, 1893, the preoccupation of Sir Francis Clare Ford, the British ambassador in Constantinople, was to prevent the granting of a concession to a German firm for the building of a railway from Eskecheir to Konieb.[68] Acting on instructions from Lord Rosebery, Ford sent a strong *pro memoria* to the Grand Vizier on January 14, insisting that British interests would be injured by this concession and that Turkey should avoid inflicting such injury.[69] The British-owned Smyrna and Cassaba Railway Company had written to both Lord Rosebery and Ford, maintaining that the building of the German line would block further extension of the railway system. The lines projected by the petitioning "British" company were, however, a joint Anglo-French enterprise, and Prince Radolin, the German ambassador, argued that Ford's efforts would actually further French interests without protecting those of the British company.[70] The railway concession was granted to the German firm, in spite of Ford's objections, before Lord Rosebery's intervention to stop British opposition.[71]

No threat was ever made by Germany to withdraw consent already given to the Egyptian army increase, and German support for British policy in Egypt continued uninterrupted. Lord Rosebery repeatedly expressed his gratitude for German assistance in Egypt and Turkey, and his immediate reaction was to move closer to the Triple Alliance.[72] Lord Cromer made no mention of the incident in his book on Egypt, nor can any trace of it be found in his correspondence. In a telegram of January 14, 1893, he informed Rosebery that France had refused to allow the proposed increase of the Egyptian army, while all the other Powers except Russia had consented.[73]

The Germanophobes in England evidently exaggerated this affair to arouse antagonism against Germany, as is shown in Grey's memoirs. Sir Edward Malet, British ambassador in Berlin, opined that Baron Marschall von Bieberstein, the German foreign minister, had resorted to dangerous methods to gain an advantage and that his victory "was a dearly bought one."[74] That these efforts were successful is emphasized by the fact that Harold Nicolson, writing in 1930 in his book *Lord Carnock*, falsely stated that the German government had threatened to withdraw its consent to the army increase.[75]

These official disturbances of Anglo-German cooperation had the additional result of producing newspaper polemics which aroused public hostility on both sides. Germans did not understand that the objective of their government's policy was to convince England that she must join the Triple Alliance. They saw only that Germany was standing up to England and wresting from her the share in colonial spoils their country rightly deserved, but which England's dog-in-the-manger attitude had prevented it from obtaining. Their love-hate sentiment towards England, compounded of admiration, jealousy and resentment at former slights, was turning to unalloyed antipathy.

British public opinion had been schooled in the belief that Germany was a continental power whose real interests could not lie in colonization. Since colonies did not fill a genuine German need, it followed that these persistent German tantrums must hide some sinister design. It appeared that the upstart German Empire, properly a subservient satellite, was deliberately challenging England's position in the world.

At the same time, German competition in trade aroused alarm and resentment in England. As early as the 1870s other European countries had begun to cut into British markets, and by 1885 this was considered so serious that a royal commission was appointed to examine the causes for the depression of trade and industry.[76] Newspapers also began to carry a great deal of news about German commercial progress, and, as R. J. S. Hoffman points out in *Great Britain and the German Trade Rivalry*, this coincided with the colonial dispute of 1884/85. On August 14, 1886, a *Spectator* article maintained that German competition was the cause of the depression of British industry.[77]

Another period of trade depression in 1894-95 produced still greater fear of German competition. *The Times* repeatedly called attention to the advance of German business, and its Berlin dispatch of November 25, 1895, described Germany as "by far the most dangerous of our industrial competitors...all the world over." A few weeks later the *Morning Post* declared that the entire trade of South America was controlled by German merchants.[78]

A rapid increase in the importation of German goods into England also caused concern. Many British specialties were threatened by German competition, including sugar, iron and steel, chemicals, textiles, china and earthenware.[79] There was much anxiety about German competition in the iron trade, and in 1895 a deputation of employers and workmen visited Germany and Belgium to discover the cause of their success.[80]

Increasing German rivalry in the British colonies was a further source of irritation, and although British preponderance was still overwhelming, this issue provided one of the favourite arguments for tariff reform.[81] The most serious aspect of this colonial rivalry was German progress in the Transvaal, where German trade and enterprise grew dramatically between 1889 and 1894. Economic conflict in this area set the stage for a political crisis which would signal a new orientation of British policy.[82]

The injury done to British trade by the advance of Germany was much exaggerated, particularly during periods of depression. In fact, British trade continued to grow, although less rapidly than that of Germany, and the British lead was maintained, except in some continental markets. Nevertheless, trade rivalry must be considered one of the significant causes of growing resentment against Germany.

Although many causes of irritation existed on both sides, Anglo-German antagonism had not yet reached the point of no return. It would still have been possible for either government to reconcile public opinion to a closer relationship, perhaps even to an alliance. Certainly most German statesmen would have welcomed such a development, and this was probably the case in England as well. It was evident, however, that relations had reached a crucial stage, at which some vexatious incident could produce a bitterness which would never be forgiven, particularly in England. This was to happen at the beginning of 1896, when events in South Africa produced the Jameson raid and the Kruger telegram.

The Transvaal had become almost an independent state, but the British government took the view that no other Powers had any standing there, while England's position under the convention of February 27, 1884, with the Transvaal gave her the right to intervene under certain circumstances. The Transvaal rejected the idea of British suzerainty, no mention of which appeared in the convention. British authority to intervene in the Transvaal appeared only in Article IV, which provided that the Transvaal could make treaties or engagements with other countries or with native tribes only with the consent of the British government.[83]

Within the Transvaal conflict arose from the fact that the discovery of gold in 1884 had produced a great influx of foreigners, mainly English, who by 1895 comprised about two-thirds of the population of Johannesburg. According to Cecil Rhodes in an article in *The Graphic,* the *Uitlanders* possessed half the land, owned nine-tenths of the wealth and paid nineteen-twentieths of the taxes, although they were totally without civil rights.[84] Charles Leonard, president of the Transvaal National Union, wrote that the oppression practised by the

Transvaal government was unparalleled in any modern state.[85] The National Union carried on a feverish agitation for the extension of the franchise, which was resisted by the Boers for the very natural reason that they were outnumbered,. and that the granting of the franchise to all newcomers would have meant the loss of independence for the Transvaal.

Rhodes and his associates were interested, not in the grievances of the foreigners in the Transvaal, but in the success of the Cape railway system, which was heavily dependent on the trade with Johannesburg. A new line from Delagoa Bay to Johannesburg menaced the Cape's monopoly of this trade, and Rhodes had tried in vain to come to some agreement with President Paul Kruger which would protect his investment. The new situation also jeopardized his hope of uniting all the South African territories as part of his scheme for a Cape-to-Cairo railroad.[86]

Early in 1895 Rhodes' group decided to join forces with the National Union, which was planning a revolution in Johannesburg. Rhodes and his colleagues provided the foreigners with arms and ammunition and prepared to assist them by invading the Transvaal with a police force of the South African Company.[87] These plans culminated at the end of December in the Jameson raid.

On December 26, 1895, the National Union issued a manifesto to the people of Johannesburg, detailing the reforms the foreigners required and demanding a reply by January 6. The most important demands were those calling for an extension of the franchise, equality of the Dutch and English languages, education for all on an equal basis and free trade in African products.[88]

By the time Dr. Jameson entered the Boer republic on December 30, the movement at Johannesburg had already collapsed and the foreigners there were unable to give him the assistance he expected. The high commissioner for South Africa, Sir Hercules Robinson, sent a messenger to Jameson, informing him that the British government repudiated his action and ordering him to return, but Jameson disregarded this order and the raiders rode on. Met by an overwhelming force of Boer riflemen, the band of about 600 policemen was defeated and forced to surrender.[89]

The German reaction to this seemingly minor incident was destined to have a devastating effect on Anglo-German relations. Germany's interest in the Transvaal had been increasing rapidly, and by 1895, according to a memorandum Count Hatzfeld-Wildenburg delivered to the British foreign office, there were 15,000 Germans living in Johannesburg, and German investments in the Transvaal totalled 500 million Marks.[90] Baron Marschall von Bieberstein insisted that Germany required the maintenance of the *status quo*, and that this attitude was dictated by German commercial and economic interests and by public opinion.[91]

The British government disowned Jameson, and Salisbury informed

Hatzfeld-Wildenburg that Jameson had been ordered to retire and assured him that England had no intention of taking over the Transvaal.[92] Marschall was sceptical about these assurances, but the problem appeared to be solved by the defeat of Jameson's forces. The Germans, however, now made the fatal error of sending a telegram to Kruger congratulating him on his success in safeguarding the independence of his country without calling on the help of friendly powers.[93]

Although this gaucherie was taken calmly by the Salisbury government, it produced a perfect furor of anti-German rage in the press and amongst the public. The reference to the help of friendly powers was naturally interpreted as an intimation that Germany would have given such help if it had been requested. This was considered an intolerable insult, and even such a serious journal as the *Economist* wrote of resisting such an affront by war if necessary.[94]

The response of the English people to the Kruger telegram was as extreme as the German action in sending it. The British government itself brought Jameson and the other ringleaders of the expedition to England, where six of them were convicted of violation of the Foreign Enlistment Act and sentenced to terms in prison.[95] United States President Grover Cleveland's message concerning the Venezuela boundary dispute was a much more offensive document, but it aroused little public indignation. Why, then, did the Kruger telegram produce such a storm of rage?

The answer must be found in the mood of the English public and in the prevailing view of Germany. Undoubtedly the irritation aroused by the American insult was diverted to the Germans, who felt the full force of the explosion of wrath. There was great interest in the Transvaal, where large amounts of speculative capital had been invested, and the German threat to these investments was exaggerated and feared. At the same time, the English were shaken out of the comfortable belief that Germany, for her own preservation, must side with England in any conflict with France and Russia, and that therefore the German army formed a part of her defence.[96]

There was, it is true, no immediate official change in Anglo-German relations. Nevertheless, the Kruger telegram marks a crucial turning-point in British policy. Discussion of the dangers of splendid isolation was already underway, and many English people believed a decision to join one or other of the continental groups was fast becoming a necessity. Before 1896 the most favoured partner was the German Empire; after the Kruger telegram Russia replaced Germany as the preferred ally in the minds of the British public.[97] Thus, while a British government could still cooperate on occasion with Germany, and even toy with the idea of establishing a closer relationship, public opinion decried such cooperation and would almost certainly have repudiated any attempt to create a formal alliance.

The German government, unaware that its policy was now doomed to failure, still cherished the illusion that in the end England would be forced to join the Triple Alliance. German opinion was still hostile, but no doubt this attitude could have been changed by a friendly policy on England's part. In England, however, suspicion and distrust of Germany had gone so far that this was no longer possible.

The year 1898 saw the opening of the new phase in the history of British foreign policy foreshadowed by the Kruger telegram. The conviction that England could no longer depend on German friendship raised the spectre of a continental coalition against the British Empire and inspired some British statesmen with the belief that the policy of isolation should be abandoned and that England should join one of the continental alliance systems. There was as yet no general agreement either on the necessity of this move or on the direction in which it should be made, but the signs of change were unmistakable.

The first approach was made to England's most troublesome enemy. In January, 1898, Salisbury indicated his desire for a *rapprochement* with the Russian Empire by proposing that the two Powers should work together in China.[98] When it became evident that the Russian appetite was insatiable, the negotiations were broken off, and Sir Nicholas O'Conor, the British ambassador at Constantinople, suggested that Russian designs might be blocked by a combination of powers.[99]

The collapse of the negotiations with Russia was followed immediately by colonial secretary Joseph Chamberlain's first unofficial attempt to arrive at a basis for agreement with Germany. It should be noted that, while each side was under the impression that the initiative had been taken by the other, no *official* action was taken by either government.

The first important conversation took place on March 29, 1898, when Chamberlain informed Hatzfeld-Wildenburg that England could no longer continue her policy of isolation and wished to come to an understanding with Germany. Hatzfeld-Wildenburg's account represents Chamberlain as expressing "the desire for a binding agreement between England and the Triple Alliance" while Chamberlain's memorandum says he suggested a defensive alliance between England and Germany.[100] Since it was agreed by both that the talk was unofficial, each "speaking in his private and personal capacity," it is quite clear that no official offer of an alliance was made.[101]

The German government found Chamberlain's ideas unsatisfactory and discouraged continuation of the discussions. When Prince Bernhard von Bülow, German foreign minister, asked what support England would give if Germany was attacked by the Dual Alliance there was no decisive answer.[102] Bülow thought a treaty entered into by one British government might be repudiated when the government changed, and that Germany might be left in the lurch in case of a Franco-Russian attack.[103] It is interesting that this view coincides almost exactly with that expressed by Lord Salisbury in his famous memorandum of May 29, 1901, although Salisbury thought a German pledge would be almost equally unreliable.[104]

Although Chamberlain believed that any alliance agreement should be laid before Parliament, there was considerable doubt that any such treaty would be acceptable to that body. Arthur James Balfour did not agree that a treaty should be laid before Parliament, and admitted to Hatzfeld-Wildenburg that Germany would be undertaking a risk in concluding a treaty which would result in a Franco-Russian attack if Parliament rejected it.[105]

When Chamberlain saw that his proposals were unacceptable, he fell back on his real purpose, which was to involve Germany in protecting British interests in China against Russian encroachment. He therefore proposed a division of China into spheres of influence, with a German sphere between the British and Russian ones. The Germans were understandably unwilling to take on the task of containing the Russian advance in China.

A certain air of unreality pervades these conversations on both sides. On the British side, Chamberlain was unable to give any opinion as to the views of his colleagues in the cabinet, and it was evident that Salisbury, who was informed only later of the conversations, would oppose anything more than what he called a "closer relationship" with Germany.[106] The Germans clearly had no intention of laying themselves open to the risk of a war with Russia and France unless they had an absolute guarantee of British support. They were also justifiably sceptical about the possibility of a British agreement with Russia, which was made possible only by Japan's unforeseen victory in the Russo-Japanese war. At the same time, it seemed unlikely that the public in either country would welcome an Anglo-German alliance. Balfour and Hatzfeld-Wildenburg were agreed that public opinion should be prepared for a *rapprochement* by an accommodating attitude by both governments in small questions.[107]

The first "small question" to be taken up concerned the disposition of the Portuguese colonies. In June, 1898, Luiz de Soveral was sent to London to raise a loan on the security of the revenues of Angola, Mozambique and Timor, with the possibility that Portugal's sovereignty over its African possessions would be included in the mortgage. The German government believed that if England and Portugal came to an agreement on this basis it would "cause a complete revolution to the disadvantage of the Powers with interests in Africa, or whose nationals are creditors of Portugal."[108] Germany therefore intervened with a request that she should join England in the loan to Portugal, that other Powers should be excluded and that the two Powers should agree on a partition of Portugal's colonies if she should be forced to relinquish them. The German government evidently believed that England was dependent on Germany for support in Africa, particularly in Egypt, and that England should be prepared to cooperate with Germany in the disposition of African territories.[109] The Germans also thought Lord Salisbury was eager to acquire the Portuguese colonies for England, although it appears that this was not actually the case. In fact, Salisbury informed Count Hatzfeld-Wildenburg at once that England was bound by old treaties to guarantee Portugal in her possessions.[110]

During the course of the negotiations Wilhelm II told the British ambassador that colonial expansion was now a necessity for Germany. According to the ambassador, he said he would "prefer to obtain what he wanted by friendly arrangement with England, but if this were not possible he would have to seek assistance elsewhere." This had been the case with regard to securing coaling stations in China, where he had been opposed consistently by England and had been forced to turn to Russia.[111]

An agreement was finally reached under which the two Powers were to notify each other of loans made to Portugal on the security of her colonial revenues. One of them would take over the administration of the customs houses in assigned places in case of default by Portugal. A secret convention provided that, if the integrity of Portugal could not be maintained, England and Germany would oppose intervention by any other Power and that neither would advance any claim in the territories assigned to the other Power.[112]

Whatever may have been Salisbury's original intention he obviously preferred Portugal to Germany as a neighbour in South Africa. He therefore did everything in his power to ensure that the Portuguese agreement would not take effect.[113] The next year Salisbury negotiated an agreement with Portugal under which Portugal would join England in the prospective war with the Transvaal and England would reaffirm her obligation to defend "all conquests or colonies belonging to the Crown of Portugal."[114] When Hatzfeld-Wildenburg asked him about this Anglo-Portuguese treaty, however, he "blatantly denied its existence."[115]

The agreement on the Portuguese colonies marked another widening of the gulf between England and Germany. The Germans believed that Salisbury had shown bad faith by abandoning the idea of acquiring the colonies rather than to risk sharing them with Germany, while the British believed that Germany's "enormous...colonial demands" stamped Germany as a "pushing and greedy power."[116] It is worth noting that during the 1890s this pushing and greedy power added 1000 square miles to its territory, while the satisfied, generous British Empire acquired nearly 2 million square miles in Africa alone.

The assertion frequently made that Germany arrived at the colonial feast too late, after all the desirable areas had already been gobbled up by other Powers, is nonsense. Between 1890 and 1914, the supposed period of aggressive German expansionism, the British Empire added more than 2 million square miles to its possessions, while the Germans obtained 102,000 square miles, all of it by negotiation. At the same time, the French conquest of Morocco was carried through with the support of an England ready to fight to exclude Germany.

The next event to disturb Anglo-German relations was a dispute over the administration of Samoa. The Samoan trade had been developed largely by German companies, following the improvement of methods of drying coconut and handling coconut oil by a German company. Trade and politics were dominated by Germans during the 1870s and 1880s, and land for coconut plantations was acquired.[117] By 1880 traders from the United States and England had become interested in Samoa also, with consequent rivalry amongst the three groups. None of the three governments, however, was interested in annexing the islands, although all three signed treaties of friendship with the native authorities in 1878 and 1879, which gave them most-favoured-nation privileges.[118]

In 1889 a conference at Berlin established a tripartite supervision of the islands by England, Germany and the United States.[119] Tripartite rule of Samoa failed to end the rivalry amongst the three Powers for control. Germany made several proposals for a division of the various Pacific territories, but England and the United States both opposed any agreement which would give Germany control of Samoa. The Liberal administration of 1892-95 followed the usual anti-German policy and colonial quarrels multiplied.[120] Salisbury's return to power, however, was not followed by any significant change in British policy. German attempts to get British agreement to a partition of Samoa met with no success.[121]

When the King of Samoa died in August, 1898, trouble arose over the appointment of a successor. The immediate German reaction was to propose a partition of the islands. The British government rejected this, on the ground that Australia would object to any alteration.[122] Leaders of two Samoan factions contended for the kingship, with the Germans supporting one group and the British and Americans the other. The issue was decided temporarily by a six-week war between the German-supported faction and British and American naval forces.[123]

Chamberlain's desire for cooperation with Germany prompted him to advance various proposals for an exchange of colonial territories, including an advantageous deal for Germany which would have given her valuable colonies for relinquishing her claims in Samoa.[124] Although Bülow agreed with the German colonial office that the territories offered were worth more than Samoa, the sentimental views of the kaiser and public opinion prevailed, and Germany insisted on remaining in Samoa. The final agreement gave Savaii and Upolu to Germany and Tonga and the German Solomons to England.[125]

The long-drawn-out bickering over Samoa produced a great deal of bad feeling, which affected public opinion in both countries. It also affected the attitude of both governments by increasing suspicion concerning the motives and methods which governed their policies.

The outbreak of the Boer War once again brought to light the difficulties which attended any attempt to realize a German partnership with England. Despite the fact that the German government maintained a friendly attitude, Bülow was unable to prevent the expression of antagonism to England by some sections of the German press.

As Caroline Playne remarks, "the passion of indignation which rang through Europe" concerning British policy and the barbaric treatment of Boer women and children, who were shut up in concentration camps where thousands died, was never understood in England.[126] This indignation was expressed in France more widely than in Germany, and was supported by the French government. On November 16, 1900, the British ambassador in Paris wrote that "nine-tenths of the papers circulating both in Paris and the Provinces are maliciously set against us." He also reported that the municipal council of Paris had decided unanimously to go to the railway terminus to receive President Kruger.[127]

At the same time the anti-German faction in England seized the opportunity to arouse distrust of Germany and to magnify every sign of hostility to England which appeared. In particular, the German government deplored the activities of *The Times* correspondent in Berlin who, it was said, collected criticisms of England from the anti-government German press and sent them to London, where they were described as coming from "authoritative sources."[128] The British press also fostered distrust of Germany by spreading rumours that German soldiers were being sent to assist the Boers, and even that German officers were leading the Boer army. At the official level, Joseph Chamberlain received information which led him to believe that a group of German officers and noncommissioned officers (N.C.O.s) had proceeded to Pretoria to take part in the war. If there was any truth in such allegations these men were acting in direct violation of strict orders given to them by the kaiser.[129]

That the distrust of Germany was shared by many Britons in responsible positions is shown by the action of the British admiralty in stopping and searching German steamers on suspicion that they were carrying contraband to the Transvaal. On December 29, 1899, the German mail steamer *Bundesrath* was captured and taken to Durban for examination before a prize-court.[130] Although the German government declared that the ship was not carrying contraband, and a search carried out on January 6 showed that this was correct, the *Bundesrath* was detained for three weeks.[131]

Meanwhile two other German steamers were stopped and searched, one at Aden and the other at Durban. The senior naval officer at Durban reported on January 4 that he was carrying out a search of the German ship, the *General*, which he had detained on "strong suspicion."[132] Although instructions were sent that the *General* should be released as soon as possible, the search, which disclosed no contraband, took five days, and the ship did not leave Aden until January 10.[133] Another German ship, the *Herzog*, was brought into Durban as a prize but was soon released.

The action against the *General* produced from the German government a request that commanders of British ships should be instructed to respect the rules of international law.[134] Salisbury was insulted at receiving a communication containing such language from a friendly Power. One wonders why the Germans should believe that England considered Germany a friendly Power, in view of the detention of German ships, which Salisbury later agreed was unjustified. Furthermore, in disregarding the German government's assurances that its mail ships were not carrying contraband, Salisbury had clearly indicated his belief that the Germans were lying. Apparently unfriendly actions on the part of the British government did not merit unfriendly words from Germany.

These incidents naturally unleashed a storm of invective in the German press. As J. L. Garvin tells us in his book *The Life of Joseph Chamberlain*, this was "officially stimulated by propaganda in the interests of the new fleet."[135] While it is true that Bülow instructed the press bureau to use the detention of German ships to support the fleet measure, there is no reason to suppose that official stimulation was really necessary.[136] In fact, Bülow postponed discussion of the matter in the Reichstag as long as possible, and did not speak about it until January 19.[137] By that time he was able to inform the Reichstag that the British government had agreed not to arrest mail steamers on suspicion only, not to molest any ships as far from South Africa as Aden and to pay compensation for the detention of the *Bundesrath*.[138]

Since Bülow felt it necessary to appease German opinion by emphasizing that the British had given in on all points, his speech was received with indignation in England and the British government replied by publishing the objectionable notes in the Blue Book on the subject. The conclusion of the affair did not, therefore, pacify public opinion in either country, nor did it allay suspicion of Germany in England.

Meanwhile, Wilhelm II had shown his sympathy for England by visiting that country on November 20, 1899, despite the fact that this action was very unpopular in Germany. Chamberlain took advantage of this opportunity to reopen the discussion of an alliance with Bülow and the kaiser. Chamberlain still believed that Germany was England's natural ally, since "the immediate threat to British interests arose from the expansionist policies of France and Russia."[139]

Bülow has given a full account of his talks with Chamberlain and

Balfour, with comments on Chamberlain's conversation with the kaiser. He did not see Salisbury, who was attending his wife's deathbed, but received a letter from him explaining that he would be seeing Chamberlain instead. It was emphasized, however, that Chamberlain spoke "only for himself, not for the Cabinet."[140]

Chamberlain told Wilhelm II he wanted a general understanding between Germany, England and America, to which, according to Bülow, the kaiser answered that "it was not in the British tradition to conclude formal alliances," and that Germany's relations with Russia made a general *rapprochement* undesirable. He suggested that the method of special agreements should be followed instead.[141]

When Chamberlain declared that a *rapprochement* with America was one of the cardinal points of his policy, Bülow told him that if he wanted an Anglo-German-American grouping he should use his political and personal influence with the Americans to persuade them to conciliate Germany in politics and business.[142] This remark seems to be the basis for Chamberlain's advocacy of an alliance of England, Germany and the United States in a speech at Leicester.[143] If Bülow's version is correct Chamberlain took a casual statement as an invitation to make a public speech on the subject. Bülow felt compelled by the resulting violent attacks on his policy in the Reichstag to deny any closer relationship with England than "to live with her in peace and harmony."[144] Although Bülow did not mention Chamberlain's Leicester speech, Chamberlain considered that he himself had been insulted. In fact, both parties must be considered guilty of bumbling diplomacy, which could only harm Anglo-German relations.

In his conversations with Balfour and Lansdowne, Bülow gained the impression that both these statesmen were much less interested in a comprehensive Anglo-German alliance than was Chamberlain.[145] Balfour said that all parties wanted a *rapprochement* with Germany, and declared, as Chamberlain had also done, that he would not object to German construction of the Anatolian railway. It was clear, however, that his view of an Anglo-German *rapprochement* was quite limited, since he spoke of the probable disintegration of the Austro-Hungarian Empire as an event of little interest to England. Balfour had obviously no intention of advocating a British association with the Triple Alliance, which was probably not considered seriously even by Chamberlain.[146] Thus, if Germany had been prepared to discuss an alliance on the basis contemplated by the British, she would have been forced to abandon Austria, since if she had been required to go to war over an Austro-Russian quarrel, a not improbable event, England would have been under no obligation to come to her support. It is hardly surprising that the German government was unenthusiastic about a tentative proposal which would have left her alone in the centre of Europe to face the greatly superior armies of France and Russia with the possible assistance only of the British navy.

The winter of 1900 saw the Russians propose joint action by Russia, France and Germany to put pressure on England to end the Boer war. Although the German government, in accordance with the pro-British policy it maintained throughout the war, rejected any idea of such action, a myth grew up in England that the move had been inspired by Germany. Despite officially expressed appreciation for continued German friendship, this myth acquired such vitality that it appeared in Sir Eyre Crowe's famous anti-German memorandum of 1907. The only evidence to support Crowe's view is a statement to the British ambassador by Delcassé, who privately blamed Germany for the failure of the Russian overture.[147]

During the Boxer rebellion, which began in May, England and Germany cooperated in a friendly way but the sequel was another ill-fated agreement. The Germans wished to forestall British monopolization of the Yang-tsze valley, and in August, 1900, the kaiser proposed that England and Germany should agree on a policy of maintaining the Open Door in that area, and that France, the United States and Japan should be invited to join in the agreement.[148] The British, whose principal aim was to involve the Germans in blocking the Russian advance in China, saw this as an opportunity to accomplish their purpose, and agreed to an accord with Germany, which was signed on October 15, 1900.

The first clause of this agreement pledged the two governments to uphold the principle that Chinese ports should be kept open to trade and commerce in "all Chinese territory as far as they can exercise influence," while in the second they promised to maintain the "territorial condition" of China. England and Germany were to consult on the steps to be taken if another Power tried to gain territorial advantages, and the other Powers were to be asked to accept the principle of the Open Door.[149]

Since the Germans made it clear from the outset that they had no intention of opposing Russia in Manchuria, there is no substance to the charge made in the Eyre Crowe memorandum that there was bad faith on their side. In fact, Salisbury told Sir Frank Lascelles, the British ambassador in Berlin, in his despatch of October 15 that Hatzfeld-Wildenburg had objected to any agreement requiring German opposition to Russia in Manchuria, and that the phrase "as far as they can exercise influence" covered this.[150] On March 17, 1901, Lascelles informed Lansdowne, who had now taken over the foreign office, that he was convinced that the German interpretation that the agreement excluded Manchuria was correct.[151]

The British cabinet, with the important exception of Salisbury, was more and more in favour of a German alliance. In September, 1900, Chamberlain, cabinet members George Goschen, Balfour, Lansdowne and

Hamilton all opposed Salisbury.[152] Shortly after Lansdowne's accession to the foreign office discussions concerning a possible Anglo-German alliance were resumed for the last time. As usual, each side thought the initiative had been taken by the other, and both sometimes waited in vain for further advances which were never made. Since Lansdowne was lukewarm about the matter and Salisbury was definitely opposed to any agreement with Germany, these discussions were doomed from the start.[153]

Lansdowne informed Lascelles on March 18, 1901, that he had spoken to Baron von Eckardstein, secretary of the German embassy in London, about cooperation against Russia and that Eckardstein had suggested a defensive alliance. Lansdowne threw cold water on this idea, and told Lascelles there were "obvious difficulties." Two weeks later he wrote that it would be hard to make anything of the German proposal, "but knowing the quarter in which it probably originated I wished to treat it with all possible deference."[154] On May 24 Lansdowne wrote a memorandum to Salisbury explaining the supposed German overture as a proposal that England should join the Triple Alliance. He himself objected even to an alliance with Germany, on the ground that the country "might find itself dragged into a quarrel in which we had no concern" and which might have been provoked by Germany.[155] Nevertheless, on his instructions, two possible drafts were produced by Sir Thomas Sanderson, permanent under-secretary at the foreign office, who discouraged the idea. Sanderson thought the problem of qualifying the treaty to prevent either side from being drawn into a quarrel which its public would not support was insoluble. He also believed Germany had more to gain from an alliance than England had. His drafts were never shown to the Germans.[156]

Salisbury's reply to Lansdowne was his long memorandum of May 29, 1901, in which he repudiated the idea that England's isolation placed her in danger and maintained that to join the Triple Alliance would bring no advantage. He also argued that neither the British nor the German government was competent to make promises to go to war for any purpose of which their public opinion did not approve.[157]

The notion of a possible alliance between England and Germany finally died in December, 1901, when Lansdowne, in another memorandum to Salisbury, proposed a treaty in which the two Powers would agree as follows: to maintain peace, to maintain the *status quo* on the shores of the Mediterranean, Adriatic, Aegean and Black Seas; to support freedom of navigation in the Persian Gulf and prevention of territorial acquisitions there by other Powers; to cooperate in furthering this policy; and to consult when events threatened these interests. Such an agreement, he believed, "would amount to little more than a declaration of common policy and of a desire to maintain close diplomatic relations." He thought it would be advantageous to

England, but expressed no view on its advantages to Germany.[158] Salisbury was opposed even to this innocuous agreement, which indicates the illusory character of the whole proceeding. When Lansdowne discussed the question with Count Paul von Metternich, the German ambassador in London, the latter told him that for Germany it was "all or none" and that his government was not interested in special agreements.[159]

When the British finally realized the futility of expecting Germany to pull British chestnuts out of the Russian fire, their first reaction was to negotiate an alliance with Japan, which was concluded in January, 1902. This alliance provided for mutual assistance in case either Power went to war with more than one Power, thus ensuring that if Japan and Russia should come to blows England would prevent France from intervening. Although this did not signify an immediate intention of coming to terms with France, it did mark a definite end to any idea of an alliance with Germany. The Japanese, in fact, proposed on several occasions that Germany should be invited to join the alliance, but Lansdowne refused to entertain any such idea.[160]

Many English writers have poured scorn on the stupidity of the German leaders in not perceiving their desperate need of an alliance with England, to save them from the fate they were destined to suffer. They do not seem to realize that the parting of the ways which led Germany to defeat led also to the destruction of the British Empire and the reduction of England to the rank of a second-rate power.

The truth is that there was miscalculation on both sides, and that this stemmed in part from the same cause, namely an overestimation of the power of the Russian Empire. The German fear of Russia precluded her from accepting anything less than an absolute guarantee that she would have British assistance in case association with England led to war with the Dual Alliance. The British fear of Russia convinced the government that some solution to continued confrontation with that Power was necessary, and that they must either secure German assistance or come to some agreement with France and Russia. A further error on the British side was miscalculation of the strength of Germany, which resulted in a failure to appreciate either the value of German support or the disadvantage of German enmity. Sir Francis Bertie even doubted that Germany was strong enough to be a worthwhile ally, while Sir Frank Lascelles thought that "if England were to cease to exist as a great Power, they [Germany] would be at the mercy of Russia and France" because these two Powers would be able to defeat Germany.[161] It is also evident that they did not fully consider the consequences of abandoning their long-standing relationship with the Powers whose interests lay in maintaining the *status quo* and associating themselves with the expansionist policies of France and Russia.

Paul Kennedy, in an article in the *Journal of Modern History*, adheres strictly to the modern line that German policy was governed by the need for "a manipulated social imperialism" to capture the support of the masses. He tells us that this factor determined Germany's naval policy and her colonial ambitions, and that these policies played a decisive negative role in the alliance talks. We are told that Bülow said at his first meeting with the kaiser and Admiral Alfred von Tirpitz that naval expansion was incompatible with an English alliance.[162] Nevertheless, according to Bülow's despatches, he was ready to negotiate an alliance in 1901 provided that England would associate herself with the Triple Alliance and that the Alliance would be ratified by Parliament.

H. W. Koch, on the other hand, maintains that the German foreign office was genuinely interested in an alliance with England in 1901. By this time the second German navy bill had been passed, and German naval policy, which was never mentioned, had no effect on the negotiations. Koch confirms that no serious offer of an alliance was made by either Chamberlain or Lansdowne, and points out that what the British wanted was the support of the Triple Alliance without the conclusion of a formal treaty. The British had no interest in supporting Austria, but hoped they could get German support without making any commitments themselves.[163]

Since no actual offer of an alliance was ever made by the British, it is difficult to estimate the probability that any agreement could have been reached. What is certain is that there was no possibility that England would join the Triple Alliance: it is also very unlikely that an open Anglo-German alliance treaty ratified by Parliament could have been achieved, and even a secret treaty would have been strongly opposed by Salisbury.

There can be little doubt that Germany was justified in refusing to abandon Austria while exposing herself to a Franco-Russian attack. Without German support Austria would have been forced either into agreement with Russia or disintegration with a consequent augmentation of Russian power. It would have been foolhardy to exchange the Austro-Hungarian Empire for the possibility that a British expeditionary force might arrive soon enough to save Germany from defeat by the Dual Alliance.

In any case, it is probable that Germany could have achieved no more than friendly agreements for cooperation, which under certain conditions might have led to something similar to the Anglo-French entente. Germany, however, had had twenty-five years of experience during which grudging cooperation by English Conservative governments had been followed by the advent of Liberal administrations hostile to Germany and friendly to France. When a Conservative government made an agreement with France, a Liberal successor could be counted on to carry it on with even more enthusiasm. It is almost impossible to imagine Sir Edward Grey as a friendly collaborator with Germany.

Finally, there remains the lack of foresight shown by the Germans in their refusal to believe in the possibility of a British agreement with France and Russia. The history of British attempts to arrive at some accommodation with Russia shows clearly that any such result would have been extremely difficult to achieve if Russia had been able to continue her advance in the Far East and to maintain the prestige of her armed forces. The Russian defeat by Japan was a dramatic revelation of the actual weakness of the Russian Empire and the death-blow to Russia's hopes of further expansion in the Far East. This defeat, as unforeseen by British statesmen as by the Germans, turned Russia back on Europe and made her amenable to British advances.

Notes

1. Raymond J. Sontag, *Germany and England*, pp. 31-9.

2. K. A. P. Sandiford, *Great Britain and the Schleswig-Holstein Question, 1848-1864*, pp. 20, 24.

3.*Ibid.*, p. 26.

4.Sir Augustus Oakes and R. B. Mowat, *The Great European Treaties of the Nineteenth Century*, p. 199.

5.H. C. F. Bell, *Lord Palmerston*, II, 367.

6.*Ibid.*, pp. 373-8.

7.John Morley, *The Life of William Ewart Gladstone*, II, 321-2.

8.Lord Newton, *Lord Lyons*, I, 263.

9.*Ibid.*, pp. 268-9, 278.

10.Morley, p. 219.

11.Newton, pp. 249, 277, 296-7.

12.H. Oncken, *Napoleon III and the Rhine*, pp. 90, 142.

13.H. W. V. Temperley and L. M. Penson, *Foundations of British Foreign Policy, 1792-1902*, pp. 323-4.

14.*Edinburgh Review*, October, 1870, "Germany, France and England," pp. 582-3.

15.W. L. Langer, *European Alliances and Alignments*, pp. 45-53; E. T. S. Dugdale, *German Diplomatic Documents*, I, 8-12.

16.W. N. Medlicott, *The Congress of Berlin and After*, p. 205.

17.*Ibid.*, p. 227.

18.*Ibid.*, pp. 113, 315.

19.Medlicott, pp. 385-9; Dugdale, I, 144-51.

20.Dugdale, I, 161-8.

21.FO64/1101.

22.Accounts and Papers, 1884, LVI, C4190, p. 449.

23.FO64/1101.

24.C4190, p. 460; F064/1101.

25.W. O. Aydelotte, *Bismarck and British Colonial Policy*, pp. 44-5.

26.*Ibid.*, pp. 35-6.

27.FO64/1101.

28.C4190, p. 478.

29.Aydelotte, p. 55.

30.FO64/1102.

31.Deb. Lords, 3rd ser., CCLXXXIII, col. 646.

32.Dugdale, I, 174, 176.

33.C4190, p. 482.

34.*Ibid.*, p. 497.

35.A. J. P. Taylor, *Germany's First Bid for Colonies, 1884-1885*, p. 33; Dugdale, I, 170-1.

36.Aydelotte, p. 62.

37.Taylor, p. 35; P. Gifford and W. R. Louis, *Britain and Germany in Africa*, pp. 77-80.

38.Aydelotte, pp. xvii, 187.

39.*Ibid.*, p. 36.

40.*Ibid.*, pp. 45-50.

41.*Ibid.*, p. 65.

42.Paul M. Kennedy, *The Rise of Anglo-German Antagonism*, p. 175; Gifford and Louis, pp. 76-7.

43.Aydelotte, p. 3.

44.*Ibid.*, p. 127.

45.*Ibid.*, pp. 43, 99-100, 163.

46.*Ibid.*, p. 99; Kennedy, p. 175; Gifford and Louis, pp. 76-7.

47.Aydelotte, p. 76.

48.*Ibid.*, p. 97.

49.*Ibid.*, pp. 191, 193.

50.James J. Sheehan (ed.), *Imperial Germany*, pp. 192-5.

51.FO64/1102.

52.Dugdale, I, 218-9.

53.*Ibid.*, pp. 369-74.

54.Temperley and Penson, pp. 462-7.

55.Dugdale, II, 2.

56.*Ibid.*, p. 37.

57.*Ibid.*, p. 25.

58.Sir Harry Johnston, "The Arab War in North Nyasaland," *The Graphic*, April 18, 1896, pp. 470-1.

59.Dugdale, II, 67, 70-93.

60.*Ibid.*, p. 295, Ed. note.

61.*Ibid.*, p. 356.

62.*Ibid.*, p. 294.

63.*Ibid.*, pp. 312-3; Hansard, 3, Vol. 346, col 1268.

64.Dugdale, II, 373-4.

65.*Ibid.*, pp. 281-2.

66.Grey of Falloden, *Twenty-five Years*, I, 9-11.

67.Dugdale, II, 180.

68.FO78/4477.

69.FO78/4477, 4500.

70.FO78/4477.

71.FO64/1293; H. Nicolson, *Lord Carnock*, p. 96.

72.Dugdale, II, 182-3; FO64/1293.

73.FO78/4513.

74.FO64/1293.

75.Nicolson, p. 96.

76.R. J. S. Hoffman, *Great Britain and the German Trade Rivalry*, p. 28.

77.*Ibid.*, pp. 73-4.

78.*Ibid.*, pp. 230-3.

79.*Ibid.*, p. 108.

80.*Ibid.*, pp. 239-43.

81.*Ibid.*, pp. 199-201.

82.*Ibid.*, pp. 206-7.

83.British and Foreign State Papers, 1883-1884, Vol. LXXV, pp. 5-13.

84.*The Graphic*, Feb. 20, 1897, p. 219.

85.*Ibid.*, March 20, 1896, p. 366.

86.W. L. Langer, *The Diplomacy of Imperialism*, pp. 218-222.

87.*Ibid.*, p. 224.

88.J. C. Ridpath, *et al.*, *The Story of South Africa*, p. 189.

89.*Ibid.*, pp. 190-7.

90.Dugdale, II, 387.

91.*Ibid.*, pp. 370-1.

92.*Ibid.*, pp. 380-1.

93.*Ibid.*, p. 387.

94.Langer, *Diplomacy*, p. 241.

95.Ridpath, p. 387.

96.Langer, *Diplomacy*, p. 241.

97.Helmuth Hoffmann, *The English Periodical Press and the End of British Isolation, 1894-1904*, p. 19-21.

98.BD, I, no. 5.

99.*Ibid.*, no. 23.

100.Dugdale, III, 21-3; J. L. Garvin, *The Life of Joseph Chamberlain*, III, 259-60.

101.*Ibid.*, p. 260.

102.*Ibid.*, p. 290.

103.Dugdale, III, 23-4.

104.BD, II, no. 86.

105.Dugdale, III, 24-5.

106.Garvin, pp. 266, 272, 279.

107.Dugdale, III, 24-5.

108.*Ibid.*, pp. 30-1.

109.*Ibid.*, pp. 32-4.

110.*Ibid.*, p. 29.

111.BD, I, no. 87.

112.*Ibid.*, nos. 90, 91.

113.Paul M. Kennedy, *The Samoan Tangle*, p. 131.

114.Temperley and Penson, pp. 515-6.

115.Kennedy, *Tangle*, p. 295.

116.*Ibid.*, pp. 128, 295.

117.*Ibid.*, p. 6.

118.*Ibid.*, pp. 12-20.

119.*Ibid.*, pp. 69, 74, 94.

120.*Ibid.*, pp. 108-114.

121.*Ibid.*, pp. 155-9.

122.Dugdale, III, 42-3, 45.

123.Kennedy, *Tangle*, pp. 146-54.

124.*Ibid.*, pp. 205-6, 215-16.

125.*Ibid.*, p. 238.

126.Caroline E. Playne, *The Pre-War Mind in Britain*, p. 197.

127.FO800/125.

128.Dugdale, III, 107.

129.*Ibid.*, p. 116.

130.Accounts and Papers, 1900, LVI, Cd. 33, Africa No. 1, no. 4, p. 88.

131.Cd. 33, no. 55, p. 108.

132.*Ibid.*, no. 15., p. 92.

133.*Ibid.*, no. 22, p. 94, no. 46., p. 103.

134.*Ibid.*, no. 21, p. 94.

135.Garvin, III, 514.

136.Kennedy, *Tangle*, p. 301.

137.Langer, *Diplomacy*, p. 661.

138.Cd. 33, p. 111.

139.Julian Amery, *The Life of Joseph Chamberlain*, IV, 135.

140.Prince von Bülow, *Memoirs*, I, 312.

141.Dugdale, III, 108.

141.*Ibid.*, p. 111.

143.Bülow, I, 313.

144.J. M. Goudswaard, *Some Aspects of the end of Britain's "splendid isolation,"* p. 46.

145.Bülow I, 315.

146.Dugdale III, 109-10.

147.Christopher Andrew, *Théophilé Delcassé and the Making of the Entente Cordiale*, pp. 164.

148.Dugdale, III, 132.

149.BD, II, no. 17.

150.*Ibid.*

151.*Ibid.*, no. 135.

152.George Monger, *The End of Isolation*, p. 18.

153.Lord Newton, *Lord Lansdowne*, pp. 199-200.

154.FO800/128.

155.BD, II, no. 82.

156.*Ibid.*, no. 84.

157.*Ibid.*, no. 86.

158.*Ibid.*, no. 93.

159.*Ibid.*, no. 94.

160.*Ibid.*, no. 126.

161.FO800/128, 129.

162.Paul M. Kennedy, "German World Policy and the Alliance Negotiations with England, 1897-1900," *Journal of Modern History*, December 1973, pp. 606-7, 610.

163.H. W. Koch, "The Anglo-German Alliance Negotiations: Missed Opportunity or Myth," *History*, Vol. 54, 1969, pp. 388-90.

Five

────────────■────────────

The Creation Of The Triple Entente

The events of 1902 and early 1903 finally convinced the British government that public opinion would not tolerate cooperation with Germany. From 1901 on the conservative press, led by *The Times*, conducted a campaign for a reorientation of British policy away from Germany and towards an understanding with France and Russia. *The Times* was followed by the *Morning Post*, the *Spectator*, *Fortnightly Review*, the *Observer* and the *Daily Mail*. The *National Review* under Leo Maxse was a strong voice leading in the same direction.[1]

The first incident to evoke public wrath was the attempt to cooperate with Germany to collect the Venezuelan debts. The British role in this fiasco was so unsavoury that Eyre Crowe "forgot" to mention the matter in his anti-German memorandum.

Germany would have preferred a "pacific blockade" of Venezuela, but Lord Lansdowne thought this would be useless and proposed the seizure of Venezuelan gunboats.[2] After discussion at some length, the German government accepted the idea of seizing the gunboats, and a short time later also every British suggestion concerning procedure.[3] On December 2 Lansdowne informed Count Paul Metternich by memorandum that it was necessary to decide what to do if the seizure of the gunboats produced no results. The British government favoured a blockade, but the measures suggested by Germany would be acts of war.[4] The Germans accepted this point of view and the two governments proceeded to take action. The Germans cooperated fully in the endeavour.

The future course of events was foreshadowed when Sir Michael Herbert, the British ambassador in Washington, reported that there was irritation over the bombardment and sinking of Venezuelan ships, and suspicion of the intentions of Germany, who was suspected of "using" England.[5] How far this was from the truth is shown by Lansdowne's dispatch to Sir Frank Lascelles two days later, in which he said that the German government was "prepared to accept at every point the suggestions which we have made to them."[6] A week later Herbert reported that Lord Cranbourne's statement that British ships had not taken part in the sinking of the Venezuelan ships, and the outcry against cooperation with Germany in the English press, had "produced a revulsion of feeling in favour of Great Britain" and a great outburst against Germany. Herbert regarded this with a feeling of "complacency, if not of satisfaction."[7]

According to the German report of these affairs, a British ship did take part in the action against the Venezuelan ships and the fort at Puerto Cabello.[8] In fact, the bombardment of Puerto Cabello on December 13 was undertaken on the initiative of Commodore Montgomery, captain of H.M.S. *Charybdis*. Montgomery had arrived at Puerto Cabello to find that the captain and crew of the British ship *Topaze* had been imprisoned and mistreated, and that the captain had been compelled to haul down his colours. Montgomery demanded an apology for this insult to the British flag and an assurance that such incidents would not be repeated. When these were not forthcoming, he shelled the forts Libertador and Vigia, then landed and destroyed their guns. His report included the statement, "The German Commodore backed me up most loyally."[9]

The British government soon decided, however, that good relations with the United States and the appeasement of British opinion were more important than keeping faith with Germany. When, on January 17, the fort of San Carlos at Maracaibo fired on a German ship and the commander bombarded and destroyed the fort, the British commander-in-chief refused to support him. Lansdowne agreed, and hoped that he would "be careful to avoid associating himself with any such severe measures," and the admiralty wired to him that it was "of the utmost importance" that British ships should not take part in "any indiscreet or violent action."[10] Thus the British, who had insisted on a war blockade and had themselves bombarded one fort with German assistance, now pretended to be innocent lambs and threw Germany to the wolves. The storm of abuse which arose in the British press must have been music to the ears of the Germanophobes in the foreign office.

It is interesting to note that, when joint Anglo-German action against Venezuela was first proposed, the kaiser agreed, but only "if we can be assured that the Britons will not use the opportunity to make the Americans suspicious of us and so weaken the effect of my brother's visit." Prince Henry of Prussia was scheduled to visit the United States shortly on a goodwill tour. When the Venezuelan government tried to separate Germany from England by offering to satisfy the German claims in return for the abandonment of cooperation with England, the German government refused to entertain this proposal.[11]

At the same time the kaiser's visit to the king at Sandringham provided an opportunity for the press to vent its spleen against Germany. The announcement that he would visit the king in November "stung the Germanophobe agitators into a fury." The daily and weekly press attributed all sorts of projects to him.[12] The *Spectator* thought the kaiser must want something, and speculated that this was to involve England in the Baghdad railway in order to turn Russian hostility towards England. The German aim was to keep England from coming to an agreement with Russia and France, for if this took place "it would hardly be too much to say that the position of Germany would be a desperate one." The kaiser should be told that the history of the last three years had shown that the less the British have to do with Germany the better. Friendship with Germany would produce French and Russian hostility, which would be "infinitely more inconvenient and dangerous to us" than the ill-feeling of Germany.[13] The *National Review* wrote that it was unthinkable that any patriotic British statesman would so far forget his duties as to think of a *rapprochement* with Germany. It was to be hoped that the leading newspapers would protest against any such policy.[14] A Liberal imperialist proposed that the kaiser should be told that Germany had no need for a navy and asked what purpose the German fleet had if not for use against England.[15]

Hard on the heels of the Venezuela affair came the attempt to associate British capitalists with the building of the Baghdad railway. Lansdowne and most of his associates agreed that the bargain reached with Germany would be advantageous to England, and Lansdowne himself thought it would be a "national misfortune" if the railway was built without British participation.[16] The German navy bill, the conduct of the German press during the Boer War and the joint intervention in Venezuela had caused so much anger, however, that there was an open revolt of the right-wing press against any cooperation with Germany. Violent anti-German agitation caused the government to drop the project.[17]

While these events were taking place, negotiations were already under way for the *rapprochement* with France which had been so often threatened. Théophile Delcassé, the French foreign minister, had long cherished the idea of a settlement with England, and as early as September 1, 1898, he had told Sir Edmund Monson, the British ambassador in Paris, that he had always thought an understanding between England, France and Russia would be desirable.[18] At that time, however, he was not yet ready to give up the hope of driving the British out of Egypt.

The Fashoda crisis convinced an important group of colonial enthusiasts, led by Eugene Étienne, to advocate giving up the policy of opposing England in Egypt and working for compensation in Morocco instead. Étienne's group pressed this policy on Delcassé for several years, and in 1903 they succeeded in converting him to their point of view.[19]

Delcassé was also enthusiastic about the conquest of Morocco, and envisioned a greater France built around the shores of the Mediterranean, but for a time he hoped to acquire it without agreement with England.[20] His first step was to conclude an accord with Italy which recognized the "right" of France and Italy to extend their influence in Morocco and Tripoli respectively without opposition by the other Power. It provided that, if France imposed direct sovereignty or a protectorate on Morocco, Italy should be allowed to do the same in Tripoli.[21]

The conclusion of this bargain with Italy was followed by an attempt to agree with Spain on a future partition of Morocco. Fear of England had led Spain to make overtures for a *rapprochement* with France, and this encouraged Delcassé to hope that Spain would be amenable to an arrangement concerning Morocco. A change of government in Spain interrupted these negotiations, and although they were resumed in the summer of 1902, they were again inconclusive.[22]

The first approach to England was taken by Paul Cambon in March 1901, apparently on his own initiative. Cambon proposed an agreement giving France freedom in the Moroccan interior while England would control the coast. Lansdowne described this to Joseph Chamberlain as a proposal that "we should be complaisant at the intended plundering of Morocco by the French." The country, he said "did not belong to us," and he could not see how France and England could announce to the world that they had come to terms "on so questionable a basis."[23] Chamberlain replied, "If we are to discuss such a large question as Morocco please bear in mind that the Germans will have something to say—and both they and we will want compensation."[24]

Approaches to England in the summer of 1902 met with a discouraging response. On August 9 Cambon reported on a discussion with Lansdowne about the possibility of an agreement on Morocco and Siam. About Siam he proposed that the two Powers should cooperate to keep Germany out. On Morocco he offered the neutralization of Tangier and freedom of trade for a fixed time. He also mentioned the interests of Spain and suggested that she should have a zone of expansion if Morocco was liquidated.[25] Lansdowne responded by saying he "regarded with the greatest apprehension the idea of provoking an international controversy" over Morocco. He pointed out that Italy, Spain and Germany also had interests in Morocco, and expressed the idea that a premature "liquidation" of Morocco would be "sure to lead to serious complications."[26]

No doubt this conversation confirmed in Delcassé's mind the necessity of pretending that France wanted to maintain the *status quo* in Morocco. At the time of the Morocco-Tripoli agreement with Italy he had told Camille Barrère, the French ambassador to Italy, that the agreement should not be made public for reasons "which do not permit us to raise the veil on the possibility of a future action of France in Morocco."[27] Lansdowne's reaction to the mention of liquidation warned him that these reasons still applied, and in particular in discussions with England.

Lansdowne's reluctance to allow the French to take Morocco continued through the fall of 1902. In October he informed Sir Harry Maclean, the British officer commanding the sultan's army, that there was "not the slightest chance of any one Power being given a free hand in that country," and that England would not agree to any attempt at such a development.[28] The director of military intelligence thought that if Morocco disintegrated it would be to England's advantage for Germany to have a share.[29] Increasing disturbances in Morocco in December led the British government to believe that the country was about to fall apart and they would soon be unable to prevent a French takeover. Lansdowne therefore decided that something should be salvaged from the wreckage before it was too late. When Cambon opened the subject again at the end of December, Lansdowne was ready to embark on serious discussions.[30]

On December 31, 1902, Paul Cambon, acting for the first time on definite instructions from Delcassé, initiated a conversation which charted the course of future negotiations on Morocco. He began by asserting that France wanted to maintain the *status quo* and to avoid interference in Morocco's internal affairs. Lansdowne agreed on the maintenance of the *status quo* and on the importance of avoiding isolated action by any one Power if intervention became necessary. Cambon then proceeded to reveal Delcassé's intention of excluding Germany from the question by proposing that the supervision of Moroccan affairs should be kept in the hands of the three "interested" Powers, France, England and Spain, and stating definitely that the French government wished to exclude Germany. Lansdowne agreed that this was desirable, but wondered how it could be accomplished. He pointed out that this emphasized the need to maintain the *status quo*, since if Morocco were partitioned it would be hard to keep the German kaiser from getting his share. Cambon replied that the only way to prevent German interference was for England, France and Spain to take concerted action if danger arose and "face Germany with an established agreement and with accomplished facts." Although Lansdowne expressed general agreement with these views, he thought it necessary to give the matter more thought before making a definite commitment.[31]

This conversation contains all the seeds from which were to spring many years of conflict over Morocco. Public acceptance of Delcassé's profession of adherence to the *status quo* obliged the British government to continue pretending, in the face of all the evidence, that the French were really trying to maintain it. Acquiescence in the exclusion of Germany from Morocco embroiled them in supporting Delcassé's challenge to the German government, which in turn involved pretending to believe that Germany had no interests in Morocco.

The British government had been aware of the French designs on Morocco for many years. In 1892 Lord Salisbury had made an effort to persuade the sultan to institute reforms which would protect him from aggression by the European Powers by regularizing trade and improving his own position. The British mission, whose aims were welcomed by Germany, Italy and Austria, failed entirely due to the intrigues of France. The French were opposed to any measures which might strengthen the sultan and enable him to defend his country against French domination.[32]

By 1900 the French were ready to begin the military conquest of Morocco. Early in that year they occupied Tuat, a "vast oasis complex in the north-central Sahara," which was recognized as being part of Morocco.[33] From here they continued to occupy other points, taking control of a long stretch of Moroccan territory.[34] The sultan tried to negotiate a precise boundary line between Algeria and Morocco, but the French refused this, because it would have limited their freedom of action on the frontier. In July, 1901, the two agreed on joint control of the frontier zone, which left the way open for French expansion: the sultan was too weak to take effective military action. The French advance could therefore continue as part of a supposed joint programme of pacification.[35]

Between 1900 and 1903 the French occupied large areas of southeast Morocco, and by the fall of 1903 Moroccan resistance there was in a state of collapse. The French advance to military control of new territory continued while Delcassé was assuring Lansdowne that France wanted to preserve the *status quo*. By the time the Anglo-French agreement was signed General Louis Lyautey, the French commander in the area from 1903 to 1906, was aiming at extending control of the southern frontier area to the Atlantic.[36]

It seems probable that Lansdowne's impression that anarchy was increasing in Morocco in December, 1902, was a result of French propaganda. The so-called disorders were the popular answer to the French advance, and what the French called "banditry" consisted of attacks on French outposts and convoys. It was widely understood that the destabilization of Morocco was a result of French military activity.[37]

The French pretense of adhering to the *status quo* was so transparent that it could have deceived no one. Lansdowne was warned of the real situation in February, 1903, when Sir Mortimer Durand, British ambassador in Madrid, reported that the Spanish foreign minister had told him of a French proposal to divide Morocco between France and Spain.[38] Delcassé made his conception of the matter quite plain in a conversation with Lansdowne during President Émile Loubet's visit to London in July, 1903. He told the British foreign minister that he did not want to get rid of the sultan or annex Morocco, because rule through the sultan would be "much more convenient than French administration pure and simple." He added that he "had often wished that they still had a Dey at Algiers." Thus the sultan would remain as a French puppet, perhaps partly to maintain the facade of adherence to the *status quo*.[39] This was underlined by a despatch from Delcassé on October 26, 1903, in which he said, "As soon as its financial preponderance is established in Morocco, by means of an effective control, the government of the Republic will be ready to renounce its part in the financial control of Egypt." He thought a similar agreement could be arrived at concerning the administration of the Egyptian railways when France "has established its control over the public works of Morocco." Paul Cambon elucidated the matter by saying, "In a word, we give you Egypt in exchange for Morocco."[40]

During Loubet's visit to London, Eugene Étienne had a long conversation with Lansdowne, in the course of which he said that the sultan's government seemed to be about to fall to pieces and it would be "prudent to provide for the event of its complete collapse."[41] Lansdowne replied that such governments sometimes survive a long time, but when he reported this to British consul-general Lord Cromer in Egypt, Cromer's answer was that once the French were assured they could get Morocco, its "agony would not be of long duration" and it would soon become a French province.[42]

That Lansdowne was well aware of French intentions is shown by foreign office inquiries in July, 1903, to both the war office and the director of naval intelligence on their views on Morocco. One of the questions posed was the amount and location of territory England could agree to Spain receiving as her part of the bargain. Both replies discussed the problem on the premise that France would establish a protectorate in Morocco. The war office believed the French colonial party aimed at establishing a protectorate over the whole of north-west Africa, while the main concern of the navy was whether or not France would be able to use the Moroccan coast in time of war.[43] In this connection, there were several discussions between Cambon and Lansdowne on the question of fortifications on the Moroccan coast.

In January, 1904, Lansdowne told Monson that Delcassé had assured Spain that any Anglo-French arrangement would be based on the assumption that the *status quo* would be maintained "as far as the form of government was concerned."[44] Again, this obviously meant that the sultan would remain as the nominal ruler of a French protectorate.

Just before the signing of the Anglo-French agreement, Cambon called attention to the fact that England had signed a treaty with the sultan obliging him not to alienate any territory to another Power without British consent. The French government wanted "formal assurance by letter" that the British would not take advantage of the treaty to make difficulties for France in any agreement she might make with Spain for disposing of Moroccan territory.[45]

When the question of recording the arrangements for the liquidation of Morocco arose, Lansdowne suggested that these should be included in "a separate and secret document" which would not be laid before Parliament.[46] The first French draft of this secret document openly mentioned annexation of the French and Spanish zones, but Lansdowne objected to such frankness even in secret and it was therefore necessary to find a more innocuous wording. The final treaty merely provided for the possibility that either government might find it necessary to modify its policy with respect to Egypt or Morocco. If this happened in Morocco, certain specified territories were to be allotted to Spain.[47] When Lansdowne wanted to publish this secret article, Cambon "informed him of the reasons which must prevent us from appearing to dispose of the future of Morocco."[48]

In an interesting despatch to Cromer, Lansdowne expressed the opinion that an "open announcement" that England had gone over to the side of international law-breakers would be a "fatal blow" to her reputation.[49] It was therefore necessary to pretend that no such interpretation could be put on the Anglo-French agreement. His expressions of belief in French sincerity may be taken as evidence of his determination to turn a blind eye to reality and put the best possible face on the deal he was making with France.

Sir Edward Grey, soon to become foreign secretary, was also under no illusion about the fate of Morocco. In the parliamentary debate on the ratification of the agreement he noted that a declaration by two Powers of devotion to the independence of a small country was usually a prelude to its absorption. Grey evidently did not expect that the *status quo* would be maintained.[50] In the same debate, M. P. Gibson Bowles drew attention to the fact that the denial of the sultan's right to erect fortifications in parts of his domain deprived him of sovereignty. He called the whole agreement a "compact of plunder" made at the expense of other countries.[51]

Balfour denied that anything had been done to prejudice the interests of any other Power, and presented the agreement as a step towards the "peace and amity of the world." He declared that the Moroccan agreement removed a danger to European peace and spoke of the elimination of other such dangers as well. The irony may have been unintentional, but Balfour knew quite well that the exclusion of Germany promised trouble.[52]

It is unnecessary to examine in detail the German interest in Morocco, which dated from the early days of European penetration of that country and was well known to everyone. It should be noted, however, that, as a signatory of the Treaty of Madrid of 1880, Germany had the same legal position in Morocco as any other Power. That treaty gave all the Powers most-favoured-nation treatment and the right to own property in Morocco.[53] In Germany's case this was reinforced by a trade treaty negotiated in 1890.[54]

Although Lansdowne's initial reaction to the French proposal to exclude Germany was cautious, he agreed to it when it became apparent that France would negotiate only on this condition. His repeated references to Germany in his conversations with Cambon show that he was well aware of the consequences of this decision. On November 17, 1903, he told Cromer that both he and Cambon had expected from the beginning that Germany would have to be taken into account. He thought the Germans might ask for Rabat and Cromer agreed that they were certain to ask for something, either

Rabat or a coaling station on the Red Sea.[55] Balfour revealed a similar opinion when he reported to the king that Germany, "when she hears that Morocco is the subject of negotiations, will doubtless do her best to make things difficult for us all."[56] In March, 1904, Lansdowne thought it would be "interesting to see how Germany takes our transaction with regard to Morocco," since she was always supposed to be casting her eyes in that direction.[57] Both Lansdowne and Balfour evidently accepted probable conflict with Germany as part of the price to be paid for French friendship.

It is not hard to see the reasons for these expectations. It was not long since Chamberlain had proposed a settlement of the Moroccan question with Germany, and when Chamberlain first heard of the French suggestion he had warned Lansdowne that Germany would have something to say and would want compensation.[58] A memorandum by the British military intelligence division, dated September 9, 1902, had expressed the view that if Morocco should disintegrate or be absorbed by France, England and Germany would have to stake out their claims and suggested that Germany should get the coast south of Casablanca.[59]

Lansdowne was also well informed about German trading interests in Morocco. Statistics provided to the cabinet showed Germany in third place behind England and France, but consular reports detailed many lines in which German goods were replacing those produced in England. In shipping entering Moroccan ports Germany led all countries in 1896 and 1897, but was second to England in later years.[60]

The French government was actually alarmed at the rapid advance of Germany in Morocco, and in May, 1903, Delcassé told a friend that "the Moroccan question must be solved within three years" or France would be forestalled by Germany.[61] Delcassé's apprehension stemmed from frequent dispatches from French representatives concerning German progress in Morocco. In July, 1901, a long report from the French vice-consul at Rabat had described the rapid advance of German commerce and shipping, the increasing German activity in administrative matters and the study of the country by German scholars and explorers.[62] Saint-René Taillandier, the French minister at Tangier, was also concerned about the advance of German political influence and Delcassé advised him that France must not be left behind.[63]

Anxiety about German activity in Morocco continued in 1902 although the French were also busy blocking British moves at that time. A foreign office note on the Moroccan question stated that the promise of commercial liberty and the freedom of the Strait of Gibraltar near Tangier would not be enough to placate Germany but that she would also want compensation elsewhere in Africa to consent to French acquisition of Morocco.[64] The projected Franco-Spanish agreement of November, 1902, also recognized Germany's interests in Morocco, and suggested offering Germany the lease of a port on the Atlantic as a *quid pro quo*.[65]

Delcassé was thus well aware that Germany had large and growing interests in Morocco. Nevertheless, in January, 1903, he told Georges Bihourd in Berlin that he did not want to discuss Morocco with the German government, since it "might see this as an encouragement to its pretensions which in our view nothing could justify." If Bihourd was questioned on the matter he was to maintain "the greatest reserve."[66] Since reports from both Morocco and Berlin were at this same time detailing the growth of German interests in Morocco, where the largest foreign colony was now German, the intention to affront Germany is obvious.[67]

The attitude which Germany would take to the Moroccan question was already evident early in 1903. Bihourd noted that, while Germany was declaring that she had only insignificant political interests in Morocco, there was insistence on the importance of her commercial interests there. He wrote that German commerce had passed that of France and menaced that of England.[68] Prince Radolin, the German ambassador in Paris, told Saint-René Taillandier that "as for us, it will always suffice to have in Morocco the freedom necessary to develop our commerce."[69] An "eminent German diplomat" was quoted as saying that "if France holds to the basis of the open door in Morocco, her civilizing efforts will meet only with sympathy."[70]

These statements forecast the policy to which Germany would adhere for the next eight years. Bülow's speech after the signing of the Morocco agreement warned that Germany could and would protect her economic interests in Morocco. When it became evident that France was bent on monopolizing economic activity in Morocco, German opposition to this policy produced the conflict which was to be expected. Delcassé's deliberate decision to ignore Germany's claims, while coming to terms with Italy, Spain and England, arose from his belief that no agreement with Germany was possible unless France was prepared to renounce Alsace-Lorraine, and was predicated on the assumption that Germany was powerless to oppose his plans if he could enlist British support.

In fact the exclusion of Germany must be construed as an attempt to fashion an anti-German coalition, about which Delcassé now believed the British leaders were as enthusiastic as himself. Both he and Cambon saw the British willingness to deal with France as the result of the rise of anti-German sentiment in England. Early in 1903 Cambon wrote of the British public's hostility to Germany, which he thought stemmed from profound causes and hoped would last. In his view France was benefitting from the irritation against Germany produced by the Venezuelan incident.[71] Delcassé's determination to ignore Germany was therefore reinforced by his belief that if complications ensued, British support would be forthcoming.

Lansdowne himself had no particular dislike of Germany and no wish to become embroiled with her. He had, however, no apprehension that Germany posed any threat to the British empire, and cared little if she was a friend or an enemy. He merely accepted the certainty of antagonizing Germany as part of the price to be paid for French friendship.

The apprehension that the entente might lead to complications which would be unpalatable to some sections of the British public required another elaborate game of make-believe. It was necessary to pretend that the entente was merely a settling of differences between England and France, aimed at ending Anglo-French antagonism but having no political significance. It was even publicly suggested that it might be a prelude to a similar agreement with Germany, if only points of disagreement could be found on which to agree.

The acceptance of this myth by some historians rests partly on the belief that the colonial agreements of April, 1904, constitute the entente. In fact, these agreements were made possible by the Entente Cordiale, which came into existence slowly and was established in the summer of 1903 by Edward VII's visit to Paris in May and President Loubet's visit to London in July. On March 13, 1903, the British ambassador in Paris reported to Lansdowne that Loubet had said to him that the king's visit "would be the seal of the rapidly strengthening cordiality, and would be universally recognized as such."[72] When Eugene Étienne visited London in July he told Lansdowne he believed that "the most serious menace to the peace of Europe lay in Germany" and that an Anglo-French understanding "was the only means of holding German designs in check." France would also be able to influence Russia and relieve England of many of her troubles with that country.[73] Lord Cromer expressed to Lansdowne the opinion that one of the main attractions of the *rapprochement* for France was the hope that it would lead to an Anglo-Russian arrangement and thus isolate Germany.[74]

Many English newspapers showed a good understanding of the events of May and July, 1903. *The Times's* Paris correspondent declared that the ending of Anglo-French tension, which had become "a useful factor for the diplomacy of certain Great Powers," would produce "some interesting modifications in European politics."[75] *Le Figaro*, he wrote, thought the new Anglo-French relations would open to French diplomacy "a field of action of which it would not fail to take advantage."[76] The editor of the *Daily Telegraph* said on the day President Loubet landed in England, "So long as the English and French fleets are ranged together in the concord symbolized by the meeting of the squadrons under the white cliffs of Dover today, there is no Power or influence in existence which can menace the vast colonial dominion of either country."[77] On the same day the *Standard* thought Delcassé had "brought France and England as close together politically as is perhaps possible without a formal alliance."[78]

In March, 1904, *The Times* correspondent wrote that Anglo-French relations "promise to assume a substantial character which could scarcely be fortified by a treaty of alliance."[79] The editor of *The Times* thought the entente possessed "an importance in our foreign policy that can hardly be overrated."[80]

The Paris correspondent quoted the *Petit Parisien* as saying that "Germany, who for 30 years has had an exaggerated weight in the world, has no longer the preponderance which she in vain seeks to assert." His own view was that "the Triple Alliance only appears as the ghost of its former self."[81]

There can be little doubt that *The Times'* perception of the matter was correct. Lansdowne was simply carrying out the policy which aimed at ending British isolation. Having given up the possibility of attaining a closer relationship with Germany, he had turned to France and Russia, as Chamberlain had warned the Germans would be the case. It has been argued that Lansdowne's offhand acceptance of the French proposal that each should give the other diplomatic support in carrying out the agreement shows that he did not understand what he was doing.[82] Since it was Lansdowne himself who requested French support for British policy in Egypt, it is equally logical, and much more plausible, to assume that this clause of the agreement was in accordance with Lansdowne's conception of the entente, and that he was quite ready to commit it to writing.

Lord Percy, under-secretary of state for foreign affairs, confirmed this view in the debate on ratification of the Anglo-French convention. He told the House of Commons that the proposals being presented were to be "explained or defended in the light of the larger issues of policy embodied in the general agreement" and said he expected the debate would be mainly concerned with these larger issues rather than with the details of the settlement. He declared that the distinctive feature of the agreement was that the parties promised "to do all in their power to further one another's interests" and "to give one another, as friends, advantages which are ordinarily given only to allies."[83]

This broad interpretation is confirmed by subsequent events. When Delcassé's determination to ignore Germany led to complications, he looked for British military support, and the British response convinced him that they were eager to supply it.[84] And when, despite the most determined British efforts to support Delcassé's policy, he was forced to resign, Lansdowne wrote to Bertie that "the entente is quoted at a much lower price than it was a fortnight ago." To another friend he wrote that Delcassé's fall had "sent the entente down any number of points in the market."[85] A cabinet report to the king said that Delcassé's dismissal under pressure "displays a weakness on the part of France which indicates that she could not at present be counted on as an effective force in international politics."[86] If the entente was nothing more than an ending of differences with France it is hard to see how either French weakness or a French agreement with Germany would lessen its value.

The suggestion made by Lord Percy, under-secretary of state for foreign affairs, that the Anglo-French agreement would "provide a working model" for the adjustment of differences between England and other nations was obviously another attempt to confuse the public concerning the meaning of the entente.[87] Actually, Lansdowne had already rejected German proposals for an all-round settlement of differences.

Among those who appear to have taken British statements about the nature of the entente at their face value was Wilhelm II, who told Lascelles on May 18, 1904, that his "Government were preparing proposals for an arrangement similar to that recently concluded between England and France for the settlement of all questions pending between the two Governments."[88] Bülow had been working for some time on proposals for a general agreement with England, and believed that Egypt was "the best nail to hang all the rest on."[89]

Lansdowne described the German request for an agreement similar to that made with France as "a great piece of effrontery."[90] His reasons for refusing to entertain the German proposals were detailed in a memorandum for the cabinet dated June 13, 1904. He admitted that the German government's position was not unreasonable and that the bargain they proposed would not be a bad one, and explained that his objection to such a transaction was mainly political. "We do not desire," he wrote, "that it should be within the power of Germany to parade an Anglo-German agreement of any considerable dimensions at this juncture, and such an agreement might be looked at askance by our friends in France."[91] The cabinet agreed on "the avoidance of anything in the nature of a treaty with Germany which could be compared with the recent Anglo-French agreement."[92] This disposes of the myth that the reason there was no similar agreement with Germany was because there were no differences to be settled.

There still remained the completion of the planned evolution of British policy by the negotiation of a settlement with Russia. The failure of Salisbury's initial approach to Russia in 1898 gave some indication of the difficulties involved in harmonizing the expansionist aims of the Russian Empire with British interests. Already there was agreement that the objective was to achieve a close understanding between the two countries which would put their political relations on "a friendly and durable basis."[93] The idea that between them the two countries could hold Germany in check was also mentioned.[94] The negotiations were broken off when it became apparent that only a one-sided bargain would satisfy Russian greed.

Discussions with Russia were begun in November, 1903. They showed that Russia wished to monopolize Persia and was unready to agree to a British sphere of influence there. In January, 1904, a draft of a possible agreement was drawn up by the foreign office. According to this plan Russia was to recognize Afghanistan and Tibet as being in the British sphere of influence, while Persia was to be divided, with predominance for Russia in the north and for England in the south.[95]

The Russo-Japanese war intervened the next month, and England's position as an ally of Japan put a damper on the negotiations for the time being. The completion of the Anglo-French agreement, however, produced a flurry of interest in the addition of Russia to the entente. The French press was inclined "to regard the agreement as a possible precursor to a similar understanding with Russia."[96] An editorial in the *Pall Mall Gazette* advocated an invitation to Russia to join England and France in a new Triple Alliance, "with a view to the realization of the ideal of universal peace." The editor thought there was room in the world for "the three great expansive, centrifugal Powers," which were England, France and Russia.[97] The Russian press and diplomatic circles both expressed a desire for an Anglo-Russian agreement, which would give Russia an ally in her economic struggle with Germany, and would remove the latter Power "still further from the friendly concert of the Powers."[98] In May Count Ai Benckendorff, the Russian ambassador in London, told Lansdowne the Russian government would be willing to reach an understanding on all questions as soon as the end of the war made negotiations possible.[99]

On October 21, 1904, the Russian Baltic fleet attacked British fishing vessels off the Dogger Bank, sinking two and damaging two others, with the loss of all on board one ship. The British government demanded an apology, reparations, trial and punishment of those responsible for the outrage and required that British representatives should oversee the proceedings.[100] The Russians considered the British demands humiliating and unacceptable to a Great Power, and put forward the Russian admiral's claim that the boats were Japanese torpedo boats.[101] The British government reacted by sending six battleships, four armoured cruisers and several destroyers to the Baltic to contain the Russian fleet.[102]

The matter was referred to an international commission of inquiry, before which moderate British claims were put forward. An amicable settlement was arrived at, compensation was made and the tsar apologized for the error of his admiral.[103]

Clearly the British government, while it had felt it necessary to react strongly in the face of an outraged British public, was not eager to break with Russia if this could be avoided. In fact the British press eventually blamed Germany for the Dogger Bank incident. Arnold White and the lead writers of *Vanity Fair* and the *Army and Navy Gazette* called for the German navy to be "Copenhagened."[104] [On May 2, 1801, Nelson had made a surprise attack on the Danish fleet at Copenhagen and destroyed it. Denmark was not at war with England.] Some British authorities even accepted with approval the idea that Germany had been responsible for the Russo-Japanese War. When Count Sergei Witte told Sir Cecil Spring-Rice at the British embassy in St. Petersburg that Germany's whole policy for years had been to create hostility between Russia and

Japan, and that Germany had encouraged both Russia and Japan to fight, King Edward commented that his remarks were "very much to the point."[105]

In October, 1905, Lansdowne asked the Russian ambassador about the possibility of an "amicable arrangement," but Count Benckendorff thought this should wait until the effect of the Anglo-Japanese treaty had worn off. He also specified that any arrangement arrived at should not be directed against Germany.[106]

While the effect of the Anglo-Japanese treaty on Russian public opinion might be lessened in time, neither its real effects nor those of the Russian defeat could be changed for many years. The Russian drive to the Far East had come to an end, and Russian ambitions inevitably turned back to Europe and the Near East. More important still for the success of an Anglo-Russian entente, the clay feet of the Russian colossus had been revealed for all to see: Russia's bargaining power had been drastically reduced, and her new-found moderation made an agreement with England possible on terms which the British government could consider reasonable.

A significant shift in British policy came with the accession of Sir Edward Grey to the position of foreign minister. The primary purpose of the approach to Russia remained what it had been for Lansdowne, to secure England against "further Russian advances in the direction of the Indian frontier,"[107] and thus to free British policy from the constraints imposed by perpetual conflict with Russia. For Grey, however, an additional object was the creation of an anti-German coalition. This is evident from the fact that the pursuit of an entente with Russia continued with even greater energy after the Russian defeat by Japan. With the Russian navy destroyed, the Russian army defeated and demoralized, and the Russian autocracy mired in domestic problems, there was now no longer any immediate need to protect the British Empire against Russian aggression. What remained was the need to check the growing industrial and commercial power of Germany.

In January, 1906, the Russians made proposals for an understanding which would settle all differences between the two countries, but this was to follow an immediate loan to the Russian government.[108] Although Liberal opinion in both England and Russia opposed the granting of a loan before the meeting of the Duma, the British money market was opened to the Russians for the first time in many years, and a joint Anglo-French loan was approved in April. This assistance in the maintenance of Russian autocracy earned the gratitude of the tsar and smoothed the way to an agreement.[109]

By September, 1906, the British and the Russians were acting in common to shut out German financial influence in Persia.[110] When Alexandre Isvolsky visited Berlin the next month British suspicions were aroused and Grey wanted to know what was said there. He was assured that Isvolsky had made no embarrassing engagements. A Russian proposal that the two Powers should promise to prevent third Powers from obtaining concessions in Persia was opposed by Grey. He told Sir Arthur Nicolson that the same objective could be obtained by getting Persia to agree not to make concessions to other Powers. This would give other countries no pretext for saying the settlement had infringed the Open Door principle.[111] It would thus be possible to close the door while maintaining the pretense that it was being kept open. A short time later the French minister at Teheran reported that Isvolsky and Nicolson had agreed on the desirability of excluding Germany from Persian affairs.[112] The Russians believed that the main purpose of the Anglo-Russian convention was to shut Germany out of Persia.[113] When the Germans complained that England and Russia were trying to do just that, they were told there was no idea of excluding German commerce.[114] It is interesting that the British later protested against Russian attempts to exclude their trade from the northern zone.[115] At the same time Grey considered that any attempt by Germany to do business in Persia was aimed at breaking the entente.[116] A Hardinge minute of October, 1907, explained the foreign office point of view. "I hope," it read, "that the developments of Russian foreign policy in the near future may show themselves in the Near East, where it will not be easy for Russia and Germany to work together."[117]

An agreement on Persia, Afghanistan and Tibet was signed on August 31, 1907. The most important section of this agreement was the division of Persia into three parts, with a Russian sphere of influence in the north, a British sphere of influence in the south, and a neutral sphere separating them. The preamble paid the usual lip-service to the integrity and independence of Persia, which was already practically non-existent.[118]

This agreement caused Grey a great deal of trouble with his opposition in the Liberal party, because the Russians paid no attention to the idea of the independence of Persia. They quite naturally assumed that the British government had no more interest in the integrity and independence of Persia than in the integrity and independence of Morocco, which was also supposed to be maintained. The difference, of course, was that England had surrendered Morocco wholly to French control, while in Persia they were interested in maintaining equal opportunities with Russia in the neutral zone.

As Grey's overriding concern was to preserve the unity of the entente and the common front against Germany, he had no alternative but to allow the Russians to get away with whatever they wished to do. This included the intervention of the Russian army in the war between the shah and his constitutionalist opponents. The Russians, with the connivance of the British government, procured the defeat of the elements in Persia which opposed the absolutism of the shah.

In December, 1911, Russian troops entered Tabriz, where they established a reign of terror featured by atrocities of the most horrible kind.[119]

The reaction of Sir George Buchanan, British ambassador in St. Petersburg, to these events was to express his fear that Russian actions in Persia would be detrimental to Anglo-Russian relations, because British public opinion was concerned about the independence of Persia. Sergei Sazonov, the Russian foreign minister, assured him that Russia would not violate the integrity and independence of Persia. Buchanan must have exercised great restraint to avoid laughing when he heard this statement.[120]

Grey wanted the Russians to agree to the installation of a Persian government corresponding to the Anglo-Russian agreement, whatever that may mean. He also wished for agreement on a financial adviser to the Persian government, and hoped that the military occupation would end when the Russian demands, including payment of an indemnity, were met and order was restored.[121] There is no record of these British wishes being met.

A few weeks later Buchanan reported that Russia wished to broaden the Anglo-Russian understanding. Grey replied that this was not the moment for such a move, as British public opinion thought Russia was pushing Persia too hard. The strengthening of England's ties with Russia was thus postponed until a more propitious time. This time did not arrive until shortly before the war, as British public opinion continued its vocal opposition to Russian policy in Persia.[122]

In February, 1914, Buchanan reported that Sazonov was dissatisfied "with the influence which the Triple Entente at present exercises in international questions." Sazonov thought the entente would be more effective if it could be converted into an alliance. Buchanan agreed that if Germany knew beforehand that France and Russia would have British support she would not risk war. Although Grey was still unhappy about Russian action in the neutral sphere in Persia, he was eventually persuaded to undertake negotiations for an Anglo-Russian naval convention.[123]

In April, 1914, George V visited Paris and Grey accompanied him. Sazonov had suggested that Gaston Doumergue, the French premier, should let them know that the Russians believed a closer relationship between England and Russia would be very desirable. Doumergue promised to do this, and on the last morning of King George's visit he asked Grey to visit the Quai d'Orsay, where he took up this intermediary task.[124]

From the Russian point of view the need for assurance of British support in war was urgent. The tsar feared that war between Greece and Turkey might be renewed and that Turkey would react by closing the straits. In that case Russia would use force to reopen them and wanted British support to prevent Germany from supporting Turkey.[125]

What the French proposed was naval conversations between the British and Russian naval staffs. Neither they nor Grey believed such conversations would have any strategic value: it was simply a matter of assuring the Russians that they were being treated on equal terms with France, and that

the British had not closed their minds "against participation in a war."[126]
Grey agreed to make an agreement with Russia similar to those between
England and France, although some members of his party and even some in
the cabinet were against closer relations with Russia. He also approved the
Franco-Russian aim of maintaining the balance of power as well as peace, a
balance which was heavily against the Central Powers. By May 20 Sazonov
was able to inform the tsar that the British government had agreed to staff
conversations to elaborate the conditions of cooperation of the British, French
and Russian fleets.[127]

As Grey's opposition in Parliament was naturally opposed to the forging
of closer ties with the world's most brutal autocracy, questions were raised
about the reported negotiations. He was asked in Parliament if any naval
agreement had been entered into with Russia, or if any negotiations for such
an agreement had taken place or were pending.[128] Grey, who prided himself
on his ability to deceive people without directly lying to them, replied that
Prime Minister H. H. Asquith's answer to a similar question had been that
"there were no unpublished agreements which would restrict or hamper the
freedom of the government, or of Parliament, to decide whether or not Great
Britain should participate in a war." He said this statement was still true, and
that no negotiations were in progress, or were contemplated, which would
make it less true. In his memoirs he claims that this statement was absolutely
true, so it must be supposed that he himself believed it. He admits that it does
not answer the question and excuses this on the ground that Parliament
"cannot be told of military and naval measures to meet possible
contingencies."[129] As he has himself stated that the agreement with Russia
had no strategic significance, his excuse is irrelevant. As usual, he did not
want to allow Parliament to understand his policy for fear it would repudiate
it. He was also, of course, well aware that Parliament would have nothing to
say about a declaration of war in any case, and that therefore it made little
difference whether or not that body knew what the government was doing.

Grey had discussed the proposed evasive answer to Parliament with
Benckendorff, who thought it was excellent. To the German ambassador he
stated that London and St. Petersburg had not discussed the straits question
for five years, which was true but completely irrelevant. Although the
Germans actually knew for certain that the Anglo-Russian conversations were
taking place, such ingenious irrelevancies did not prevent Prince Karl
Lichnowsky from continuing to take anything Grey told him seriously.
Benckendorff thought it was difficult for Grey to deny that he was carrying on
negotiations and to carry them on at the same time.[130]

Grey's willingness to undertake this gesture of entente solidarity, in
defiance of a hostile public opinion and despite his own misgivings about
Russian policy in Persia, must have convinced France and Russia that they

were assured of British cooperation when war came. The fear that Grey might consider peace as important as the cohesion of the entente could be banished from their minds.

Notes

1.O. J. Hale, *Publicity and Diplomacy*, pp. 263-4; Paul M. Kennedy, *The Rise of Anglo-German Antagonism*, p. 56.
2.BD, II, nos. 171, 172.
3.*Ibid.*, nos. 174, 176.
4.*Ibid.*, no. 177.
5.*Ibid.*, no. 180.
6.*Ibid.*, no. 181.
7.*Ibid.*, no. 184.
8.E. T. S. Dugdale, *German Diplomatic Documents*, III, 163.
9.Accounts and Papers, 1903, Venezuela, no. 1, LXXVII, Cd. 1399.
10.BD, II, nos. 186, 187.
11.Dugdale, III, 161-2.
12.*The Graphic*, January 3, 1903, p. 12.
13.*The Spectator*, November 8, 1902, p. 688.
14.Caroline E. Playne, *The Pre-War Mind in Britain*, p. 117.
15.*Ibid.*, p. 139.
16.BD, II, no. 216.
17.Kennedy, p. 367; R. J. S. Hoffman, *Great Britain and the German Trade Rivalry*, pp. 143-5.
18.BD, I, no. 262.
19.Christopher Andrew, *Théophile Delcassé and the Making of the Entente Cordiale*, pp. 197-9.
20.*Ibid.*, p. 86.
21.DDF2, I, no. 17.
22.Andrew, pp. 147-51, 191-2.
23.Lansdowne to Chamberlain, March 16, 1901, Chamberlain MSS, Box J. C. 11/4, quoted in George W. Monger, *The End of Isolation*, p. 39.
24.Julian Amery, *The Life of Joseph Chamberlain*, IV, 163.
25.DDF2, II, no. 369.
26.BD, II, no. 322.
27.DDF2, I, no. 508.
28.BD, II, no. 328.
29.DMI Memoranda, October 24 and November 22, 1902, F099/400.
30.Andrew, pp. 194-5.
31.BD, II, no 330; DDF2, II, no. 552.
32.E. D. Morel, *Ten Years of Secret Diplomacy*, pp. 8-11.
33.Ross E. Dunn, *Resistance in the Desert*, p. 23.
34.*Ibid.*, pp. 176-7.
35.*Ibid.*, pp. 178-9.
36.*Ibid.*, p. 208.
37.*Ibid.*, p. 209.
38.BD, II, no. 336.
39.*Ibid.*, no. 357.

40.DDF2, IV, nos. 40, 46.
41.BD, II, no. 356.
42.*Ibid.*, no. 359.
43.FO800/126.
44.BD, II, no. 388.
45.*Ibid.*, no. 414.
46.*Ibid.*, no. 398.
47.*Ibid.*, no. 416.
48.DDF2, IV, no. 370.
49.BD, II, no. 402.
50.HCD, Vol. 135, cols. 518-9.
51.*Ibid.*, cols. 524-33.
52.*Ibid.*, cols. 572-5.
53.British and Foreign State Papers, Vol. 71, pp. 639 ff.
54.*Ibid.*, Vol. 82, p. 969.
55.Lord Newton, *Lord Lansdowne*, pp. 285-6.
56.CAB 41/28/14.
57.FO800/129.
58.Amery, IV, 163-4.
59.FO99/400.
60.CAB 37/65/63.
61.Andrew, p. 211.
62.DDF2, II, no. 324.
63.*Ibid.*, no. 448.
64.*Ibid.*, no. 333.
65.BD, III, 70, Ed. note.
66.DDF2, III, no. 26.
67.*Ibid.*, no. 44.
68.*Ibid.*, no. 51.
69.*Ibid.*, no. 131.
70.*Ibid.*, no. 432.
71.*Ibid.*, nos. 37, 192.
72.FO800/125.
73.BD, II, no. 356.
74.Lansdowne, MSS, vol. viii, quoted in Monger, p. 145.
75.*The Times*, July 6, 1903.
76.*Ibid.*, July 11, 1903.
77.*Daily Telegraph*, July 6, 1903.
78.The *Standard*, July 6, 1903.
79.*The Times*, March 18, 1904.
80.*Ibid.*, March 26, 1904.
81.*Ibid.*, April 14, 1904.
82.Monger, pp. 158-9.
83.HCD, Vol. 135, Cols. 499, 515.
84.See Chapter VI.
85.Newton, p. 341.

86.CAB 41/30/21.

87.HCD, Col. 516.

88.BD, III, no. 1.

89.Dugdale, III, 192.

90.Newton, p. 329.

91.CAB 37/71/78.

92.CAB 41/29/19.

93.BD, I, nos. 6, 12.

94.*Ibid.*, no. 8.

95.CAB 37/68/1.

96.BD, II, no. 418.

97.*Pall Mall Gazette*, March 22, 1904, p. 1.

98.*Sunday Times*, April 17, 1904, p. 7.

99.BD, IV, no. 184.

100.*Ibid.*, no. 12.

101.*Ibid.*, nos. 13, 15, 16.

102.*Ibid.*, no. 19.

103.*Ibid.*, no. 25.

104.Kennedy, pp. 271-2.

105.BD, IV, no. 69.

106.*Ibid.*, no. 196.

107.Grey of Falloden, *Twenty-five Years*, I, 154.

108.FO800/72.

109.Bertrand Russell, *Justice in War Time*, pp. 167-70.

110.BD, IV, nos. 344, 345.

111.FO800/72.

112.DDF2, X, no. 401.

113.B. de Siebert, *Entente Diplomacy and the World*, p. 557.

114.FO800/62.

115.FO800/74.

116.FO800/93.

117.BD, IV, no. 544.

118.Grey, I, 159-161.

119.Russell, pp. 172-91.

120.FO800/74.

121.LN, I, 171-3.

122.*Ibid.*

123.FO800/74.

124.Grey, p. 273; LN, II, 255-7.

125.LN, II, 258.

126.Grey, I, 274.

127.LN, II, 260-1, 266-7.

128.Grey, I, 278.

129.*Ibid.*, p. 279.

130.LN, II, 326-8.

Six

———————————————◼︎———————————————

The First Morocco Crisis

The first Morocco crisis was the inevitable result of the determination of Théophile Delcassé, the French foreign minister, to demonstrate to Germany that she was powerless in the face of Anglo-French solidarity. The policy of ignoring Germany while disposing of Morocco was Delcassé's personal policy, and was opposed by the diplomatic corps, the Colonial party, the Chamber of Deputies and eventually all his cabinet colleagues.[1] Many French publications insisted on the necessity of negotiating with Germany. The *Questions diplomatique et coloniale*, for example, warned Delcassé not to forget that a solution in Morocco required agreement with three Powers: England, Germany and Spain. Suggestions of compensation for Germany came from many sources.[2]

Delcassé's refusal to discuss Morocco with Germany continued throughout the negotiations with England, and was emphatically affirmed by his failure to give the German government official notification of the agreement of April 8, 1904. Germany was thus given no opportunity to discuss the possible effects of the agreement on German interests in Morocco.

Georges Bihourd, the French ambassador in Berlin, was greatly concerned by Delcassé's policy and during April, 1904, he repeatedly warned of possible action by Germany aimed at belying her impotence, "which," he said, "our press proclaims a little too loudly."[3] When he asked permission to discuss the Anglo-French agreement with Baron Oswald von Richthoven, Delcassé did not allow him to do so. He authorized him merely to repeat a declaration he himself had made to Prince Radolin, the German ambassador in Paris, on March 27 to the effect that France intended to maintain the *status quo* in Morocco and that freedom of trade would be respected.[4] A few days later Bihourd mentioned Chancellor Bülow's Reichstag statement that he intended to protect Germany's commercial interests in Morocco and predicted that Wilhelm II would take some action to show that Germany was "neither isolated nor disarmed." "I find it hard to believe," he wrote, "that Wilhelm II will tolerate, not the isolation, but the obliteration of Germany without trying some demonstration, cautious or vociferous."[5]

The British foreign office was ready to give the French flouting of Germany unconditional support, but at least one official took a more moderate view. Sir Thomas Sanderson's comments on the Crowe memorandum show that he thought Bülow's statement in the Reichstag was an invitation to England and France to discuss the bearing of the Anglo-French agreement on German interests. He also remarked that Delcassé was pursuing a series of maneuvers to isolate Germany, which was, of course, obvious to any disinterested observer.

The German foreign office considered that Germany had been affronted by the settlement of Morocco without consultation with her, and that this had been a blow to the prestige of the Empire.[6] They were also convinced that France would exclude German trade and industry from Morocco, as she had done in all French colonies.[7] The elimination of foreign trade in French colonies, in contrast with the freedom of trade in German colonies, was well known in England and was drawn to the attention of the British government by British businessmen during the negotiations with France.[8]

The published portion of the Anglo-French agreement made it clear that German economic interests were threatened, and with regard to trade this was confirmed by Lansdowne's statement to Count Metternich on June 6 that "the commercial arrangement with France was strictly bilateral" affecting only British commerce in Morocco and French commerce in Egypt.[9] Article IV of the agreement also provided that "concessions for roads, railways, ports, etc." would be controlled by the government concerned, that is by France in Morocco and by England in Egypt.

Delcassé had told Radolin that France wanted to maintain the *status quo* and protect trade "in the common interest."[10] Pierre Guillen in his book *L'Allemagne et le Maroc, 1870-1905*, considers Delcassé's statement to Radolin "a vague assurance," which "could not be considered an official notification." The Quai d'Orsay, he says, "contented itself with verbal promises of a vague character without diplomatic value."[11] The French intention to exclude Germany from Moroccan trade is further shown in Bihourd's dispatch from Berlin on April 21, in which he expressed the expectation that Wilhelm II would "try to creep into the settlement of the Moroccan question," perhaps by "demanding for German commerce the same treatment given to that of England." He remarked that the guarantees Germany could claim were contained in Article IV of the Anglo-French agreement, which, as we have seen, applied only to British commerce.[12]

In the months following April 8, 1904, German policy was uncertain. The German leaders thought a great deal about what action they should take, but were unable to come to a decision, mainly because of differences of opinion between the foreign office and Wilhelm II.[13]

Holstein thought Germany should retreat before the hostility of all the interested Powers, but Bülow insisted on action. Bülow and Richthoven wanted to seize a territorial pledge on the Atlantic coast of Morocco, where a naval base and a coaling station could be established, and Bülow made this suggestion soon after the signing of the Anglo-French agreement. The kaiser, however, rejected the idea, as he had previously declared that he wanted no Moroccan territory, but only advantages for German commerce.[14] The naval office also objected to this plan, believing no place on the Moroccan coast was suitable for a naval base and that in any case the navy would be too weak to protect it against either the British or the French navy.[15]

As an alternative, Radolin, in a dispatch from Paris dated July 27, proposed a policy of forcing France to open negotiations by proceeding step by step with her in Morocco. If France sent a squadron to Tangier, Germany would send one; if France obtained a concession, Germany would claim a similar one; French pacific penetration of Morocco would be matched by Germany. This plan was also vetoed by the kaiser, who did not want to oppose France openly at this time.[16]

The German foreign office then suggested that Germany should make a naval demonstration, which would show that she did not recognize French predominance. Once again Wilhelm II refused to give his consent, even when the French and British governments made a naval demonstration. He thought this would create an Anglo-French front against Germany, apparently not realizing that such a front already existed.[17]

The German government then sounded out other countries, including England, about support for the Open Door policy. The foreign office refused to believe that England would actually give France a free hand in Morocco, and some British actions, such as the sending of ships when there were troubles at Tangier, seemed to support this view. When Germany asked what action England would take if she acted to protect her interests, Lansdowne replied that England would not prevent a third Power from protecting its rights based on previous treaties.[18] Lansdowne also stated mendaciously that England and France had "made no attempt to dispose of the rights of other Powers," and Count Metternich received the correct impression that, if France and Germany clashed over Morocco, England would support France. The Germans therefore dropped the idea of a declaration of the Powers on the maintenance of the Open Door. Count Metternich nevertheless informed Lansdowne clearly that "Germany intended to uphold any rights which she was entitled to claim under existing treaties."[19]

Unable to devise a plan for action, the German government finally decided to await events, meanwhile refusing to recognize French predominance and showing by its attitude that the Anglo-French convention had no relevance to Germany. This policy of reservation was forced on the foreign office by the refusal of the kaiser to countenance the strong line advocated by Bülow and Richthoven.[20]

Meanwhile, Bülow continued for some time to think that Delcassé still intended to negotiate with Germany, as he had done with all the other interested Powers.[21] When he declared before the Reichstag in 1904 that he had no objection to the Anglo-French treaty, provided that German interests were preserved, he "was addressing a cautious appeal to Delcassé." Similar hints were given in Paris, Madrid and Tangier, and the German press announced as a trial balloon that talks were about to begin. To all this Delcassé paid no attention.[22]

By October it had become apparent that the hope for negotiations was illusory and that there was no possibility of reaching agreement with France. At this point the conclusion of the Franco-Spanish agreement of October 3 forced the German government to find some way of protecting Germany's economic interests in Morocco and set the stage for the next phase of the Moroccan question.

The public declaration by France and Spain was communicated to all the Powers, but as it merely stated that Spain adhered to the Anglo-French declaration and that both Powers were "firmly attached to the integrity of the Moroccan Empire under the sovereignty of the Sultan," it had little relation to the real agreement, which was secret.[23] The secret agreement provided for the division of Morocco into spheres of influence and its partition when, for "any cause established by common agreement," the maintenance of the *status quo* should become impossible. Meanwhile, public works, including railways, roads and canals, were to be carried out by companies made up of Frenchmen and Spaniards. The exploitation of mines and quarries and economic enterprises generally were also reserved for the nationals of these two countries.[24] British endorsement of the agreement in effect pledged England to support a Franco-Spanish partition of Morocco, to take place at a time to be determined by France and Spain. Meanwhile, France and Spain would monopolize the economic exploitation of Morocco. By early November these secret clauses were known to the German government through the Spanish minister at Tangier.[25]

Although the French had been moving slowly in Morocco while the negotiations with Spain were in progress, there had already been indications of the direction their policy was to follow. Even before the conclusion of the Anglo-French agreement the *Journal des Debats* had published articles forecasting later developments. On April 5, 1904, one of these said:

The nation that aids Morocco to civilize herself will evidently monopolize the public works; why should not the nation that builds the ports and railroads be our own? And if the country possesses rich mineral deposits, as they say, why should they not be exploited by our compatriots?[26]

On May 23 Saint-René Taillandier had suggested immediately placing the Moroccan police under French control, before other Powers could act to protect their nationals themselves.[27] When Delcassé authorized him to make proposals to the sultan in this regard, Taillandier had set forth a programme in which Algerian police and gunners were to play an important part.[28] By June the entire Moroccan debt had been refunded and brought into French hands. A French syndicate got an option on future loans, the coinage of money and the trade in silver and gold.[29] In July a state bank was created to take control of Morocco's finances, and this had been supplemented by French control of the customs. The placing of French officers in charge of the Tangier police force was a further sign of French determination to move quickly to establish their authority.[30]

French official statements to Germany after the signing of the accord with Spain were such as could only confirm the German government's view of French policy. When Bihourd reported that Richthoven had asked him about the bearing of the agreement with Spain on Germany's commercial interests, Delcassé described that agreement as one which had obtained "the adhesion of the Spanish Government to the principle of commercial liberty inscribed in the declaration of April 8," and instructed Bihourd to declare that this had "further increased the guarantees which international commerce will enjoy in Morocco."[31] Richthoven was naturally suspicious, and the revelation of the real meaning of the accord with Spain fully confirmed his suspicions.

Shortly after the conclusion of the Franco-Spanish agreement Delcassé prepared to send Saint-René Taillandier on a mission to Fez which would initiate the establishment of the French protectorate. The belief that German industry and capital would be shut out of the Moroccan market was meanwhile supported by two actions of the French government. When English and German companies tried to organize a port service, the French insisted that such an action required their consent and the British foreign office supported them. The second incident occurred when Sir Mohamed Tazi, brother of the Moroccan minister of finance, was preparing to visit Germany to discuss with German industrialists the purchase of war *matériel*. French protests forced him to go first to Paris, and to give most of the business to French industry.[32]

Delcassé set forth the details of the proposed mission to Fez in a dispatch to Taillandier on December 15, 1904. First on the list came the establishment of order in Morocco by the creation of a military force under French officers, the basis of which should be Algerian gunners and "Muhammadans" from the Algerian police. Next came the proposal that a

French financial adviser should be appointed to the *Maghzen*, the officials around the sultan. Then followed a series of measures designed to compensate the French government "for the sacrifices it is ready to impose on itself to improve the welfare of the Sherifian Empire" by acquiring for France the right to monopolize Moroccan commerce and industry. These measures involved the construction of railways which would join Fez to the Algerian system, a motor road between Marnia and Oudjda, requested by the governor of Algeria, and a telegraph network also linked with that of Algeria. A consortium had been established to undertake these public works and the industrial enterprises of Morocco, as well as a programme of port construction for which Taillandier was to get the sultan's authorization. French mining companies were also prepared to exploit the mineral wealth of Morocco, and some had already applied for concessions. The dispatch concluded by instructing Taillandier to convey to the Moroccan government the minatory intimation that France had both the power and the will to carry out this programme with or without its consent.[33]

When the German consul at Fez got the details of the French programme the German government decided that some action was necessary to force Delcassé to take German interests into consideration. The United States was also alarmed, and the American consul proposed that American trade should be secured by a commercial treaty with the sultan. He thought that if Morocco came under French political and economic control trade would be monopolized by France, as in Algeria and Tunis.[34]

Richard von Kühlmann, the German chargé d'affaires at Tangier, took a leading part in trying to block the French plans. He warned Taillandier in November, 1904, that Germany expected France to come to an agreement with her.[35] His idea, that if Germany let it be known that she was ready to intervene energetically France would negotiate, was adopted, and in December he began throwing out hints about a pending German initiative.[36]

The German campaign was stepped up early in January, assisted by the kaiser's realization that his hope of a continental alliance including France was illusory. On January 2, Bülow instructed Kühlmann to tell the sultan that Germany had not agreed to the arrangements of France, England and Spain concerning Morocco. The sultan was informed that Germany opposed any change in the *status quo* and was assured of Germany's moral support. Bülow was careful, however, not to make any definite promise of German aid, which might provoke a crisis with France.[37]

When Taillandier arrived at Fez on January 25, 1905, the sultan undertook a reform programme of his own by summoning two men from every town and district to form an assembly which would consider the French proposals. On February 11, Bülow urged the sultan to reorganize his country and restore order himself with the aid of the assembly. At the same time

Kühlmann informed the French chargé d'affaires at Tangier that Germany did not recognize the French agreements concerning Morocco and was not bound by them.[38]

The French represented these actions as a complete reversal of German policy, a view which was taken up in England in support of the myth that German action had nothing to do with Morocco but was merely an attempt to smash the Anglo-French entente. Sir Arthur Nicolson told Jules Cambon, however, that in his view Germany simply wanted to show that because they had not been officially informed of the Anglo-French agreement they were free to ignore its existence. He thought the German action was "perfectly legitimate" and was an indication they wanted France to discuss the Morocco question with them.[39]

Searching for a method of intervention which would reassure the sultan without provoking a rupture with France, the German foreign office came up with the idea of Wilhelm II's visit to Tangier. This would encourage the Moroccans to oppose the French plans and show that Germany was not to be ignored. At the same time such a pacific demonstration would not have the appearance of a menace designed to inflame France.[40]

The speeches attributed to Wilhelm II at Tangier were more provocative than had been intended by the foreign office, largely because of their tone and phraseology. In substance, the kaiser did no more than recognize the sultan as the sovereign of an independent country, which was the same view openly proclaimed, although secretly repudiated, by France and England.

It should be emphasized that the kaiser's visit to Tangier represented no change in German policy. The frequently repeated statements of that policy never varied from the line laid down by Bülow in April, 1904, that, while Germany had no territorial ambitions in Morocco, she intended to maintain her economic interests there. These statements were made many months before the defeat of Russia by Japan was anticipated, and German documents show that the decision to take action in Morocco was made long before the battle of Mukden.[41] There is no evidence to indicate that German policy was influenced by the Russian disasters of 1905. The decisive German action began early in January when the French intention to proceed rapidly with the "Tunisification" of Morocco—bringing it under French control—became apparent, and when the kaiser dropped his objections to opposing France.

The French government received the news of the Tangier visit quite calmly. Maurice Rouvier, the premier, thought it had little political significance and was not menacing; Paul Cambon and Bihourd both thought it was not directed against France. Even the French colony in Morocco was not hostile. Its main organ, Le Journal de Maroc, attacked not Germany but Delcassé and his shortsighted policy.[42]

The immediate reaction in England was quite different. Ignorant of the Franco-Spanish agreement for the partition of Morocco and the monopolization of its economy, British public opinion assumed that Germany was challenging the published portion of the Anglo-French declaration, which proclaimed Morocco's independence and integrity. The British public therefore leaped to the conclusion that Germany was in fact challenging the Anglo-French entente. This belief, for which there is no evidence whatsoever, rested on a whole series of falsehoods, all of which were deliberately fostered by the British foreign office. It was believed that Germany had negligible interests in Morocco, and that these were not threatened by French action, since France was bent on maintaining the *status quo*. Further, Germany was supposed to have taken no interest in the matter until France was weakened by the Russian defeats in the Far East, when it was suddenly decided that the kaiser should visit Tangier.

The French foreign office was naturally encouraged by the anti-German furore in England, and Jules Cambon reinforced the British view by quoting Delcassé's vague and misleading statements to Germany about the maintenance of the *status quo* and commercial freedom. He pretended that Germany had been fully informed about the agreements concerning Morocco and professed to think the German government's conduct "incomprehensible." Delcassé told Bertie Germany had given him no idea what she wanted and that "he could not understand what objects the German Emperor had in view."[43]

The pretense of believing that Germany had no legitimate complaint concerning Morocco led to the idea that the German government must have some other reason for its action. This in turn supported the myth that Germany was actually trying to "smash" the Anglo-French entente, although the British had taken pains to publicize the entente as merely an agreement to end differences with France.

Although the Germans were concerned about the *rapprochement* between England and France, it is evident that they underestimated the significance of the Anglo-French entente. Their attempt to come to a similar agreement with England themselves indicates that they had failed to realize that England and France had reached what amounted to a virtual alliance. In June, 1904, Lansdowne told Metternich that England had agreed to disinterest herself in Morocco but had not "engaged herself to take France's part in the relations of third parties towards Morocco."[44] Bülow and Holstein thus failed to realize the extent to which the British cabinet had committed itself to the support of France and refused to believe that England would lend countenance to a policy aimed at the humiliation of Germany. No doubt they should have known better than to take seriously British assurances about the character of the Anglo-French agreement, but one cannot ignore the possibility that they believed what they were told.

At the same time they were sceptical about a British commitment to give France a completely free hand in Morocco. They had no way of knowing that the British government was pledged to support the establishment of a

French protectorate and the partition of Morocco between France and Spain. There were indications that many people in England, as well as the British colony in Morocco, were opposed to handing over Morocco to France. Sections of the English press opposed the French action, and the reports of *The Times's* correspondent in Tangier were hostile.[45] Holstein's assumption that British backing of France would remain platonic can hardly be considered unreasonable.[46]

Even after the kaiser's visit to Tangier Delcassé refused to make an open approach to Germany to initiate discussions. He tried instead to persuade the German government to ask for negotiations by hints to the press and to the foreign ambassadors in Paris. On April 9, when Bülow was to dine at the French embassy next day, Delcassé authorized Bihourd to indicate that he was ready to clear up any misunderstanding if the Morocco question should arise in conversation. Bülow, however, did not mention Morocco, and nothing came of this suggestion.[47]

Finally, pressure from Maurice Rouvier, the premier, from his advisers and from other members of the cabinet forced Delcassé to open the subject himself. On April 14, he instructed Bihourd to inform the German government that he was ready to dispel any misunderstandings. The Germans replied by proposing an international conference on Morocco.[48] When Delcassé was attacked in the chamber on April 19 by deputies of all shades of opinion, Rouvier gave him lukewarm support and he offered his resignation the following day. Although this resignation was withdrawn when the cabinet agreed to support him, Rouvier now took a hand in foreign policy himself.[49]

An international conference was naturally anathema to Delcassé since a conference could hardly be expected to hand Morocco over to France. He therefore at last decided, under pressure again from his advisers and his cabinet colleagues, to try for direct talks with Germany.[50] The German government, however, believing that nothing could be obtained from Delcassé, was no longer interested in bilateral negotiations. That their judgment was accurate is shown by a draft prepared for them by Delcassé which merely repeated the meaningless formula that France had bound herself to uphold freedom of commerce in Morocco by her agreements with England and Spain.[51] The German government now understood the real meaning of these agreements, and their acceptance of such a formula was out of the question.

When it became apparent that the Germans would accept nothing but an international conference, Delcassé decided to defy them, confident in the belief that they would not risk a war in which he was sure England would side with France. This assumption was certainly correct, since the German government had no intention of going to war over Morocco. His equal certainty that the German conference proposal would never be adopted was misplaced.[52]

Delcassé's conviction that England would fight alongside France if war came was undoubtedly correct. On April 22, Lord Lansdowne informed Sir Francis Bertie that, if the German government asked for a port on the coast of Morocco, England would join France in "strong opposition." He also thought the behaviour of Germany was "most unreasonable having regard to M. Delcassé's attitude" and expressed the British government's wish to give him all possible support.[53] In reporting this communication to Delcassé, Bertie changed the order of Lansdowne's instructions, putting the British desire to give France all the support in their power at the beginning. This "changed the emphasis from that of helping France to oppose the German acquisition of a port to that of helping her to oppose Germany in the whole Moroccan question."[54] The belief that Lansdowne had no such intention, however, goes too far, since Lansdowne's dispatch is certainly open to this interpretation. He was aware of the plans which were being made for military cooperation with France and also knew, as did every observer at the time, that the British public would enthusiastically favour a decision to go to war with Germany.[55]

Delcassé's belief in the British determination to side with France depended not only on Bertie's communiqué but also on "indiscretions" by British service chiefs and by Bertie himself as well as on other official actions by the British government. The evidence that Sir John Fisher, First Sea Lord, disclosed his plan to the French for attacking Kiel and landing 100,000 men in Schleswig-Holstein is "almost conclusive."[56] It is also highly probable that in March, 1905, British General Sir James Grierson discussed war plans with the French and encouraged them to count on British support in a war with Germany.[57] Both Fisher and Grierson were spoiling for a fight with Germany, and Delcassé assumed that they were speaking for the British government.

Sir Francis Bertie was a confirmed Germanophobe and an enthusiast for a military alliance with France. Bertie called on Delcassé on April 22. Although there is no record of what he said, Delcassé told Maurice Paléologue on the evening of that same day that "France was assured of English support in the event of war."[58]

At the same time, the British government gave other unmistakable signs of its desire to show solidarity with France. Shortly after the announcement of the kaiser's proposed visit to Tangier, the British suggested an exchange of visits between the British and French fleets. This was understood everywhere as a sign of British determination to support France.[59]

In April, Edward VII embarked on a Mediterranean cruise which "seemed designed by England as a sustained exhibition of Anglo-French solidarity."[60] He called only at French ports and while at Algiers he appealed to Delcassé by telegram not to resign. The king also visited Paris, where he had two meetings with Delcassé, emphasizing still further the British resolve to uphold his policy. It must have appeared to Delcassé that King Edward's assurances were made in the certainty that he was expressing the policy of his ministers.

These official actions were accompanied by a press campaign of unexampled malevolence, undoubtedly encouraged by the diplomatic machine. The animosity of the English press towards Germany had been evident for some time before the kaiser's landing at Tangier, but that event unleashed an even greater outburst of vituperation, which continued throughout the summer and fall of 1905.[61] Thus the British actions described above "took place against the background of a British public more Germanophobe than at any time in living memory."[62]

It is with these antecedents in view that we must approach Lansdowne's assurances to the French government on May 17 and 25, 1905. When his belated attempts to open talks with Germany failed, Delcassé instructed Paul Cambon to ask Lansdowne for an official pledge of British support. Already certain that he would receive a favourable reply, Delcassé interpreted Lansdowne's response in the light of his preconceived ideas.[63]

Lansdowne's account of the first interview records that he told Cambon:

our two Governments should continue to treat one another with the most absolute confidence, should keep one another fully informed of everything which came to their knowledge, and should...discuss in advance any contingencies by which they might...find themselves confronted.[64]

Cambon's account reports that he asked whether, if "we had serious cause to believe in an unjustified aggression" the British government would "concert with the French government on the measures to be taken?" Lansdowne replied in the affirmative.[65]

Lansdowne's attempt on May 25 to lessen the force of his previous declaration only succeeded in convincing the French that he had strengthened it. In his explanation to Cambon he stated that he had wanted discussion with the French government, not as a result of "unprovoked aggression," but in anticipation of "complications to be apprehended." Cambon thought he had broadened his previous offer from a desire for consultation in case of aggression to a wish to examine the general situation. He believed this meant "a general agreement which would in reality constitute an alliance."[66]

Delcassé's belief in a defensive and offensive alliance rests, therefore, not merely on these conversations with Lansdowne, but on a whole series of actions by British officials. These actions culminated in avowals by Lansdowne which he understood as confirmation of a British intention previously made clear but now validated by the official sanction of the secretary of state for foreign affairs.

In fact, Delcassé's perception of the matter was quite correct. No one in a position to understand the situation doubted that if war came over Morocco England would side with France. Many Frenchmen, including Rouvier, believed that England was trying to push France into war with Germany.[67] Rouvier agreed with Delcassé that the British navy could destroy the German fleet and wipe out German commerce, but he thought it would be unable to prevent a German invasion of France.[68]

The English press paid no attention to the legitimate grounds of the German protest against French policy and declared that this was a pretext to cover an attack on the Anglo-French entente. English editors, with a few exceptions, showed themselves more French than the French and loudly proclaimed the solidarity of the entente. This campaign helped to convince French statesmen that "the English wished to embroil them with their neighbors across the Vosges." Far from helping Delcassé, it contributed to his downfall.[69]

German statesmen have been ridiculed for their belief in the reality of a defensive and offensive alliance between France and England, but although wrong in letter, they were right in fact. British readiness to go to war to promote the French conquest of Morocco indicates that they were prepared not only to defend France but were willing to support an aggressive French policy.

Lansdowne's belief that the French were proceeding too rapidly in Morocco did not deter him from this course of action. On December 26, 1904, he had written to Sir Edmund Monson that although he did not think the French had intended to "force the pace in Morocco," he now thought events might be too strong for them. He had therefore begged that he might "be given ample notice of any vigorous measures which they find themselves obliged to take, for it is evident that Europeans may have a very dangerous time ahead of them."[70] In August, 1905, he thought the French had been imprudent and that they had "played their cards badly in Morocco" and were suffering for it.[71] His continued strong support of the French action reveals the extent of his commitment to put them in possession of Morocco at all costs.

Delcassé's colleagues shared his belief in the certainty of British support, but they were not prepared to carry his vendetta against Germany to the point of war, since they did not subscribe to his opinion that fear of the British navy would deter Germany from taking drastic action. Although the Germans had not yet made any threat of war, French premier Rouvier was frightened by the possibility that they might do so, and the cabinet as a whole accepted his judgement.[72] They therefore decided to refuse the supposed British offer of a formal alliance and to repudiate Delcassé's policy.

When Rouvier dined with Prince Radolin, the German ambassador, on April 26 he told him he was anxious to satisfy Germany and live on the best terms with her. Bülow's comment was that France should then stop trying to break up the Triple Alliance and inciting England against Germany.[73] On the same day Rouvier made an indirect offer to discard Delcassé, whose conduct of the Moroccan affair was deplored by all his colleagues, by the majority of the chamber and by French public opinion.[74]

The French press had been attacking Delcassé's policy with remarkable unanimity for some time, and his conduct of Moroccan affairs was almost universally condemned. Many journalists believed his failure to agree with Germany was a grave mistake, and some accused him of wanting to provoke a war with Germany.[75] The English press, on the other hand, was loud in its praise of Delcassé and critical of those who attacked his policy in the chamber.[76]

Rouvier changed his mind early in May, when it seemed possible that Delcassé might succeed in arranging peace between Russia and Japan. The German government was seriously alarmed by this possibility, which would not only consolidate Delcassé's position with the cabinet but might lead to the formation of a quadruple alliance of England, France, Russia and Japan.[77] The danger of the situation increased at the end of May, when the destruction of the Russian fleet by the Japanese at Tsushima made the beginning of peace talks seem near at hand. Bülow, therefore, deciding that the time had come to apply pressure to force Delcassé's dismissal, instructed Radolin to demand an immediate agreement, failing which there would be "an open breach."[78] As it was obvious that no agreement was possible with Delcassé at the helm, this was equivalent to demanding his dismissal.

It appears that, as Delcassé insisted, Bülow was bluffing, but if the threat was meant seriously it was a misfortune for Germany that Delcassé was overthrown. Both France and England were less well prepared for a land war than at any later time, and German inability to cope with the British navy was a constant factor which would never change. Russia was in disarray and was unlikely to play a significant part. Unluckily for Germany, Rouvier, the premier, and his colleagues saw this quite clearly and they were unanimous in their determination to sacrifice Delcassé rather than take the risk of war over Morocco.

Delcassé's dismissal on June 6 was by no means solely, or even mainly, the result of German pressure. Almost no one in France approved of his determination to exclude Germany from discussion of the Moroccan question, and Rouvier's earlier spontaneous offers to remove him had been a recognition of that fact. The morning papers on June 6 demanded that Delcassé should resign, and "satisfaction at the news of his resignation was expressed by organs of all parties." Thirteen of the fifteen leading newspapers published on June 7 condemned his policy.[79]

The press, in general, estimated that the minister had pursued a personal policy without regard to the principle of collective ministerial responsibility; he had attempted to treat Germany as a Power isolated by his astute diplomacy; his Moroccan policy had been badly conceived and grave

*mistakes had been made in carrying it out; and, blinded by his own egotism
and desire for a personal triumph, he had pursued a bellicose policy that
endangered the security of France. Beneath the press comment ran a strong
current of opinion favorable to Germany, and opposed to a closer
understanding with England.*[80]

Even Bertie, strongly inclined to blame Germany and support any French
policy, admitted that Delcassé's fall came about because he did not disclose
his policy to his colleagues and did not carry out cabinet decisions. On June
15, writing to Lansdowne about Delcassé's removal, he said, "It has the
appearance of being a sacrifice to a German menace, but it is not entirely
so."[81]

Apparently Rouvier believed that with the fall of Delcassé the German
government would drop the idea of a conference and come to an agreement
directly with France. Although Rouvier indicated a willingness to negotiate he
failed to make any definite proposals when asked by Germany to do so. In
pressing for an international conference Germany stood on solid legal
ground. If she abandoned that position to engage in discussions which might
well be fruitless, she would forfeit her opportunity to influence the course of
events in Morocco, as Kiderlen-Wächter, the German foreign minister,
pointed out in his speech to the Reichstag on November 17, 1911.[82]
Furthermore, Bülow had insisted repeatedly that Germany had only
economic interests in Morocco and Wilhelm II had stated publicly on March
16, 1904, that Germany had no intention of acquiring Moroccan territory.[83]
Having committed herself to the proposition that the Moroccan question
should be settled by an international conference, Germany had no viable
alternative to maintaining that stand.

It should be added that anyone who approaches the matter with an
open mind must admit that a European conference was the proper, civilized
way to arrive at an arrangement which would take into account the rights of
all the Powers who had interests in Morocco. Germany had suggested, in
September, 1903, that the affairs of Morocco should be regulated by an
international conference, but the idea had received no support.[84] The plain
fact is that German policy was open, correct and perfectly justified: the secret,
dishonest and aggressive policy was that pursued by England and France.

Immediately after Delcassé's resignation, Germany circularized all the
Powers which had signed the convention of Madrid in 1880, asking them to
support the holding of a new conference. All the powers except England and
France adopted a noncommittal attitude, while these two strongly opposed
the German proposal.[85]

Lansdowne's comment on the German note is particularly interesting:
he thought the conference "would be expected to deal not only with the
introduction of reforms, but with the maintenance of the independence and

integrity of Morocco, and the preservation of the open door." On being assured that this was indeed the case, he pretended to believe that French action did not jeopardize either Moroccan independence or the Open Door, although he knew very well that this was not so.[86]

Rouvier, feeling that acceptance of a conference would be humiliating to France, tried to avoid it by coming to some arrangement directly with Germany. When this failed he insisted that, if the conference were to be held, agreement on its programme should be reached beforehand. Despite strong pressure by England to prevent acceptance, Rouvier finally consented to the convoking of the conference, provided that an accord on its agenda satisfactory to France could be reached. At the same time, he informed the British government that once the conference was over "it would be possible to see that Germany did not get too much in Morocco."[87] This clearly foreshadowed the determination of France to pay no attention to such decisions of the conference as did not harmonize with the plan to make Morocco a French protectorate.

On July 8, 1905, an agreement was concluded by which Germany consented to recognize the special interests of France resulting from the common border between Morocco and Algeria as well as French rights derived from existing treaties. Radolin specifically declared that this included the Anglo-French and Franco-Spanish treaties on Morocco.[88] The conference decisions were to be compatible with the sovereignty and independence of the sultan, the integrity of his empire and equality of economic freedom. The German government admitted the necessity of military and financial reforms, to be regulated for a short time by an international agreement.[89]

This seeming harmony hid a wide divergence of viewpoint. In accepting France's treaties with England and Spain the Germans no doubt thought they were consenting to the published portions of those agreements, while the French assumed that they were agreeing to the partition of Morocco and the elimination of German business interests there as provided in the treaty between France and Spain. Rouvier therefore proceeded to reassure the Spanish government definitely that commercial and industrial enterprises would be carried out by Franco-Spanish groups. He also promised that Spain would share in the policing of Morocco and that she should have a larger share in the state bank than any country except France.[90]

The French and German governments now began conversations to determine a programme for the conference. At first their views seemed irreconcilable, but the signing of the abortive Bjorko treaty on July 24 led the Germans to believe that if they were to conciliate France in the Morocco question she could be brought into alliance with Germany.[91] It is almost impossible to understand how the German leaders could have believed that they were about to achieve an alliance of France and Russia with Germany. In persuading themselves that the French renunciation of Delcassé's policy meant that France was now reconciled to the loss of Alsace-Lorraine they displayed density of an exceptional degree. At the moment when France had succeeded in detaching Italy from the Triple Alliance and in bringing England into virtual alliance with herself, it was folly to imagine that she would abandon the cherished hopes of thirty-five years in order to ally herself with her foremost enemy.

At the same time, the usual divisions within the German government led to a confusion of policy which antagonized both the government and public opinion in France. While Bülow was attempting to smooth the way towards agreement with France, Count Tattenbach, the German minister at Tangier, proceeded with arrangements for a loan to the sultan by a group of German banks and also persuaded the Moroccan government to give a German firm a contract to build a mole in Tangier harbour.[92] Bülow felt himself obliged to support these concessions once they had been agreed upon, and after much wrangling France consented to overlook these transgressions in return for German agreement concerning the site of the conference and the exclusion of the policing of the frontier region from its agenda.[93]

An agreement was finally signed on September 28, 1905, which set forth the programme for the conference which France and Germany would propose to the sultan. The police outside the frontier region were to be organized by an international accord, while the contraband arms trade on the frontier would be controlled exclusively by France and Morocco. Financial reforms were to be undertaken by a state bank, which would reorganize Moroccan finances and direct revenues to the pay and equipment of the police forces and the provision of urgent public works. The organization and control of this state bank were left to the conference, which would also study tax collection and the creation of new sources of revenue. Contracts for public works were to be awarded to all nationalities without preference. On the same day the two Powers agreed that a consortium of French banks should share the loan arranged by Tattenbach with the German group and that the German company should build the mole in Tangier harbour unless the French company involved could claim an equal right to build it.[94]

In August, 1905, the commercial division of the German foreign office had drawn up a memorandum defining the points Germany should be firm about at the conference. In order to preserve existing German interests they should maintain the most-favoured-nation clause, freedom of the coastal trade and liberty to fish in Moroccan waters. For the development of her interests in the future Germany required freedom of exports, the lowering of customs duties and the opening of all ports. In addition, the Moroccan government should have complete independence in granting concessions and Germans should be able to participate in government orders, port development works and railway and mineral concessions on an equal basis with other foreigners. Germany should also have equal participation in a state bank.[95] The only other important part in the German programme was to prevent France from acquiring a police mandate for the whole of Morocco.[96]

French aims were somewhat modified since the time when they had hoped to have a completely free hand in Morocco. In July, 1904, Delcassé had refused Spanish participation in the police forces "absolutely," holding that Spain should be satisfied with sharing in the customs and in economic enterprises.[97] After accepting the idea of a conference, the French had abandoned their intention of monopolizing the police control and had agreed to share it with Spain. This would be more acceptable to the conference Powers, while still leaving France in a dominant position. Their original plan to staff the police with Muslims from the Algerian police and Algerian gunners, while not specifically abandoned, was probably considered impractical of realization.[98] France still hoped to obtain the largest share in the state bank, with Spain in second place. Their acquiescence in the awarding of public works contracts to all nationalities was more apparent than real, since they expected to obtain a position which would enable them to direct most contracts to French and Spanish companies, as provided in their agreements with Spain. Their devotion to the sovereignty and independence of the sultan was as insincere as ever.

The British aims were quite simple: they were determined to maintain their close relationship with France and to put her in control of Morocco in accordance with their agreement. The foreign office instructed Sir Arthur Nicolson, the British delegate to the conference, that British policy would be "to give fullest support to the French delegate." French success would be a success for the entente, while failure would lower its prestige and diminish its vitality. "Our main object therefore must be to help France carry her point at the Conference."[99]

The French government was determined to make no further concessions to Germany, and Bertie reported that the French military authorities were quietly making preparations for war and were buying large quantities of stores and guns.[100] Paul Cambon told Sir Edward Grey, the new Liberal foreign minister, that if Germany attempted at the conference "to take a hand in the military, financial and police administration" it would mean war.[101] Cambon therefore asked Grey whether, if the conference ended in a rupture between France and Germany, France could count on British "armed assistance." Grey made no definite promise, but expressed the opinion that if Germany attacked France over the Anglo-French agreement, public opinion "would be strongly moved in favour of France." When Cambon then suggested military and naval conversations, Grey agreed that these were advisable.[102]

Grey told the Germans that England had conceded a special position to France in the Anglo-French agreement and that England could not "suggest to France any departure from the attitude prescribed by the terms" of this agreement. To Nicolson he wrote that the four Powers directly interested in the Mediterranean had made arrangements with each other which were satisfactory to themselves and "it was most undesirable that they should allow these arrangements to be disturbed."[103] In other words, he insisted on the right of England and France to dispose of Morocco, regardless of any German interest. In fact, Grey was already prepared to adopt the whole French programme, and was ready to support France even in an invasion of Morocco. He thus indicated his willingness to go to all extremes to put France in possession of the country.[104]

Grey therefore accepted without question the premise implicit in the agreements of England, France and Spain concerning Morocco, that Germany had no rights or interests in that country. Any attempt to protect German interests there constituted an aggressive policy, to be righteously resisted by the countries pledged to the conquest and partition of Morocco.[105] Grey thus embraced from the outset the policy of humiliating Germany which had been instituted by Delcassé.

When Sir Francis Bertie urged that a positive promise of British support should be given, Grey replied that, although he could make no absolute commitment, England could not stand aside if war came. Regarding advance precautions, he pointed out that Sir John Fisher had "long ago" prepared naval plans with the French naval attaché. Although England could send only 80,000 men to the continent she could, of course, protect herself, since she was more powerful at sea than she had ever been.[106]

Grey authorized military conversations after consulting only three members of the cabinet, Sir Henry Campbell-Bannerman, Asquith and Lord Haldane. He told Bertie in Paris that to give France a definite promise of military aid would mean an alliance, which would have to be disclosed to Parliament. The existing situation, with the secret military and naval conversations assuring British readiness if war came, was more satisfactory.[107]

According to Cambon's account, Grey told him on January 10, 1905, that the military and naval conversations already in progress should continue.[108] Major Victor Huguet, the French military attaché in London, had reported on December 20 and 21 conversations with General Grierson, director of military operations at the war office, in which Grierson had told him that England could send a minimum of 100,000 men to the continent, which would be raised to 120,000 if possible. Grierson stated that the war office had just completed a study of the intervention of a British army in a war between France and Germany. Arrangements were being made with the admiralty for the transport of these troops to the continent. General Grierson had pointed out that this did not prejudge the decision of his government on going to war, but had expressed the belief that public opinion in favour of cooperating with France was so strong that no British government could withstand it. He thought the German kaiser must be aware of this and must know he would be foolish to undertake a war with France in which England would certainly take part with all her forces.[109]

Grey was thus simply carrying on a policy begun by his predecessor, Lansdowne, and doing so with great enthusiasm. This naturally involved continuing the various deceptions practised by Lansdowne, particularly the pretense that the Anglo-French agreement on Morocco was not aimed at putting France in control of that country. While assuring the French that the British public was ready to fight if a quarrel arose over that agreement, he asserted that they would not do so to put France in possession of Morocco.[110] Since the British had promised France support for the establishment of French jurisdiction there, this was precisely what they would have been fighting for if war had come.

The Germans entered the Algeciras Conference confident in the belief that they could prevent France from obtaining her objectives, but they were only partially successful. England gave France unconditional support throughout while Spain, Russia and Italy leaned heavily in the French direction. Clever French diplomacy succeeded in isolating Germany on some issues, even in the end hoodwinking President Theodore Roosevelt into believing that it was Germany who threatened Moroccan independence while France was trying to maintain it.[111] Nevertheless, in the final clash over the police mandate, when France insisted that not even one port should be under international control, only England supported her, while at the same time advising her to give way. When England and France stood firm, Germany conceded the point in preference to breaking up the conference.[112]

The Act of Algeciras began with the recognition of three principles, namely the sovereignty and independence of the sultan, the integrity of his state, and economic freedom without inequality. Although France's agreements with England and Spain had paid lip-service to these principles, their inclusion in a treaty signed by all the European Powers might have been thought to make French adherence to them somewhat less dubious.

Since the right to supply instructors for the Moroccan police played so prominent a part in the conference and was endowed with such exaggerated influence on the later history of Morocco, it is worthwhile to detail exactly what authority the Act of Algeciras gave to France and Spain. The first chapter of the act, which dealt with the organization of the police forces, provided that these were to be under the sovereign authority of the sultan, recruited from amongst Moroccan Muslims, commanded by Moroccan chiefs and distributed in the eight ports open to commerce. To organize the police

French and Spanish officers and noncommissioned officers (N.C.O.s) agreeable to the sultan would be put at his disposal by their respective governments as instructors. These officers and N.C.O.s would, for a period of five years, supervise instruction, discipline, administration and payment of the police and give technical assistance to the Moroccan commanders. The rules for assuring the recruitment, discipline, instruction and administration of the police forces were to be agreed upon by the sultan's minister of war, the Swiss inspector and the two French and Spanish superior officers and submitted to the diplomatic corps at Tangier for approval. The police were to number from 2,000 to 2,500 men, distributed at the ports in groups of 150 to 600. The number of French and Spanish officers would be sixteen to twenty and that of N.C.O.s thirty to forty. A superior officer of the Swiss army, appointed by the sultan as inspector general, would submit copies of his reports to the diplomatic corps at Tangier in order to insure that the police duties were carried out in accordance with the decisions of the conference. The instructors were to be Spanish at Tetouan and Larache, mixed at Tangier and Casablanca and French at the four remaining ports.

It should be noted that these rules were far from conforming to the original French plans and that they had no relation to the military operations later undertaken by France and Spain. Sir Arthur Nicolson thought control of the state bank would be more important than the police duties and that whoever held the purse strings would have more influence than someone "cooped up with a few police at a coastal town."[113] As France did not conquer Morocco by instructing the police, it is impossible to prove him wrong.

The most important provision regarding the state bank, established under Chapter III, was the requirement that the Powers should have equal shares in the bank, which was placed under international control. Although the bank was to operate under French law, France received neither the largest share nor a monopoly on loans to the Moroccan government, both privileges she had coveted.

Under the heading of "Regulations concerning a better tax yield and the creation of new revenues," import duties were set and provision made for the reduction of export duties on some products. Foreigners were to have the right to own property, with certain specified limitations, and the coastal trade was to be open to all nations. Foreign supervision of all these matters was to be carried out by the diplomatic corps at Tangier.

Chapter IV covered public services and public works, including the granting of concessions. Public works and concessions were to be under the complete control of the Moroccan government, which was to submit plans for public works projects to the diplomatic corps so that all Powers would be able to compete in submitting tenders. All nations would have an equal chance to tender, and the Moroccan government would accept the most advantageous tender. These same provisions were to apply to concessions to exploit the cork-oak forests. A Moroccan decree would lay down the conditions for concessions to exploit mines and quarries.

The final article provided that all existing treaties, conventions and arrangements between the Powers and Morocco should remain in force, but that if any of these conflicted with the Act of Algeciras, the latter should prevail. This meant that any agreement with France which infringed the sovereignty or integrity of Morocco was no longer valid. It did not, however, touch the agreements which France had made with Spain and England, although many of the provisions of these agreements were also invalidated by the act.[114]

The Algeciras conference is usually described as a defeat for Germany, although the Germans attained most of their objectives there. Señor Ojeda, the acting foreign minister of Spain, thought Germany had "secured a good share of the objects she was contending for." He believed she would likely try "to tempt France into compliance with German schemes elsewhere by offering to leave her alone in Morocco."[115] It has been said that while Germany won in principle, France won in practical results. This was no doubt true, simply because France was under no necessity to abide by the decisions of the conference.

The Act of Algeciras of 1906, if adhered to, would have involved a dramatic curtailment of France's Morocco programme. The provisions for economic equality of all nations, in particular, would have prevented the French and Spanish monopolization of the economy envisioned in the Franco-Spanish agreement. Actual recognition of the sovereignty and independence of the sultan would have postponed the French military campaign for at least five years. The proceedings of the conference had shown, however, that no power except Germany was interested in preventing a French absorption of Morocco. France, now assured of British military support, realized that she had been given a green light to undertake the subjugation of the country.

The limitation of the Algeciras provisions to five years set the deadline: the operation must be completed by 1911 to avoid possible intervention by the Powers. France therefore abandoned the pretense of pacific penetration and proceeded with the military conquest of Morocco. This conquest was pushed forward in defiance of the frequently expressed wishes of the French Chamber, which between 1906 and 1911 passed resolution after resolution in favour of maintaining the Act of Algeciras and the independence of Morocco.[116] The French government paid little attention to these resolutions, and the army in Morocco ignored any direction from the government which might have held back its progress. The continuing destruction of the authority of the sultan and the steady advance of the French army culminated in the spring of 1911 in the march to Fez, which brought the sultan under the complete control of France. This produced a final attempt by Germany to come to some agreement with France which would either ensure her economic interests in Morocco or award her the compensation for relinquishing them to which she had as much right as England, Spain and Italy. This in turn resulted in another "crisis" over Morocco, which entente propaganda has christened the Agadir crisis.

Notes

1.Christopher Andrew, *Théophile Delcassé and the Making of the Entente Cordiale*, pp. 270-72, 276, 298.

2.Pierre Guillen, *L'Allemagne et le Maroc, 1870-1905*, pp. 660-62.

3.DDF2, V, no. 28.

4.*Ibid.*, no. 29.

5.*Ibid.*, no. 44.

6.Guillen, p. 757.

7.E. T. S. Dugdale, *German Diplomatic Documents*, III, 220.

8.CAB 37/65/53.

9.BD, III, no. 18.

10.GPXX, pt. 1, 5, no. 6368.

11.Guillen, p. 788.

12.DDF2, V, no. 44.

13.Guillen, p. 764.

14.*Ibid.*, pp. 695, 764-6.

15.*Ibid.*, pp. 766-7.

16.*Ibid.*, p. 768.

17.*Ibid.*, pp. 770-2.

18.*Ibid.*, pp. 773-4.

19.BD, II, no. 62; Guillen, p. 774.

20.Guillen, pp. 775-6.

21.Dugdale, III, 221.

22.Guillen, p. 787.

23.DDF2, V, no. 361.

24.*Ibid.*, no. 358.

25.Guillen, p. 782.

26.O. J. Hale, *Germany and the Diplomatic Revolution*, p. 84.

27.DDF2, V, no. 167.

28.*Ibid.*, p. 268, fn.

29.Hale, p. 86.

30.Guillen, pp. 762-4.

31.DDF2, V, no. 371.

32.Guillen, pp. 813-15.

33.DDF2, V, no. 479.

34.Hale, pp. 95-6.

35.*Ibid.*, p. 96.

36.Guillen, pp. 815-18.
37.*Ibid.*, pp. 825-827, 832.
38.Hale, pp. 97-8.
39.BD, III, no. 66.
40.Guillen, pp. 832, 838.
41.Hale, p. 117.
42.Guillen, pp. 844-6.
43.BD, III, nos. 84, 86.
44.Dugdale, III, 19 ff.
45.Guillen, pp. 845, 878-80; Hale, p. 100.
46.Dugdale, III, 221.
47.Andrew, pp. 274-5.
48.*Ibid.*, p. 275.
49.*Ibid.*, pp. 276-7.
50.*Ibid.*, p. 277.
51.*Ibid.*, p. 274.
52.*Ibid.*, p. 278.
53.BD, III, no. 90.
54.E. N. Anderson, *The First Moroccan Crisis*, p. 211.
55.Andrew, pp. 280, 282 fn.
56.*Ibid.*, p. 283.
57.*Ibid.*, p. 284.
58.*Ibid.*, p. 279, 286.
59.*Ibid.*, p. 280.
60.*Ibid.*
61.E. D. Morel, *Ten Years of Secret Diplomacy*, pp. 76-80.
62.Andrew, p. 281.
63.*Ibid.*, pp. 287-8.
64.BD, III, no. 94.
65.DDF2, VI, No. 443, quoted in Andrew, p. 287.
66.*Ibid.*, no. 465, quoted in Andrew, p. 288.
67.Andrew, p. 287, Dugdale, III, 229.
68.Andrew, p. 289.
69.Hale, pp. 105-6.
70.FO800/126.
71.FO800/130.
72.Andrew, pp. 288-9.
73.Anderson, p. 213, fn.
74.Andrew, p. 290; Dugdale, III, 229, no. 625.
75.Hale, pp. 107-115.
76.*Ibid.*, pp. 115-16.
77.Andrew, pp. 290-3.
78.*Ibid.*, pp. 296-7.
79.Hale, pp. 131-2.
80.*Ibid.*, p. 132.
81.FO800/127.

82.Cd. 5992, 1911.
83.Anderson, p. 151.
84.Guillen, p. 689.
85.Anderson, pp. 234-7.
86.BD, III, no. 117.
87.*Ibid.*, no. 134.
88.DDF2, VII, no. 199.
89.*Ibid.*, no. 209.
90.BD, III, no. 181.
91.Anderson, pp. 263-4.
92.*Ibid.*, p. 264.
93.*Ibid.*, p. 270.
94.DDF2, VII, no. 467.
95.Guillen, p. 861.
96.Anderson, pp. 311 ff.
97.DDF2, V, no. 252.
98.*Ibid.*, no. 583.
99.BD, III, nos. 199, 200.
100.FO800/49.
101.BD, III, no. 224.
102.*Ibid.*, no. 210.
103.*Ibid.*, nos. 230, 234.
104.*Ibid.*, no. 243.
105.BD, III, no. 230, 234; FO800/61.
106.*Ibid.*, no. 216.
107.*Ibid.*, no. 219.
108.DDF2, VIII, no. 285.
109.*Ibid.*, no. 256.
110.BD, III, nos. 216, 219.
111.Anderson, p. 388.
112.BD, II, nos. 338, 344.
113.FO800/337.
114.DDF2, IX^2, 223-53.
115.BD, III, no. 397.
116.Morel, p. 102.

Seven

The Anglo-German Naval Race

The view that British antagonism to Germany arose from the German decision to build a larger navy is probably the most widely-believed myth of the pre-1914 period. This belief is supported by descriptions of a supposed Anglo-German naval race, which presumably began with the German Navy Bill of 1898.

The unprecedented expansion of the British navy which took place at this time was actually begun and continued by the British themselves and was largely unrelated to the strength of other navies. The British admiralty needed periodic naval scares to frighten Parliament into providing the money for this programme and some foreign navy was used to provide the necessary bogeyman.

The first naval "scare" came in 1884 when unemployment in the shipbuilding industry encouraged the journalist W. T. Stead to launch a campaign for an increase in naval strength in the *Pall Mall Gazette*.[1] Stead was supported by various admirals and vice-admirals, by speeches and by letters in the press. The main thrust of Stead's article was a comparison of the French and British navies by classes of ships, in which he professed to show that the French navy was almost as strong as that of England.[2]

An article in the *Manchester Guardian* disputed Stead's conclusions and argued that he had classified some French ships incorrectly. A close examination of Stead's article appears to confirm this judgement.[3] A few weeks later, however the *Guardian* reported a speech by Sir E. J. Reed, formerly chief constructor of the navy, who said that it was doubtful that in three or four years the navy would be equal to that of a single European Power. The result of this campaign was a five-year programme during which British naval expenditure rose from £11 million to £17 million while French expenditure rose from £7,653,000 to £8,126,000.[4]

The naval scare of 1888 was begun by the *Standard* in January with an account of "extraordinary naval preparations at Toulon," which turned out to be a tempest in a teapot.[5]

Nevertheless, according to A.J. Marder, in his book *The Anatomy of British Sea Power*, the panic of 1888 was inevitable, due to a remarkable increase in French spending on new construction. According to his figures, for which he quotes no source, France spent £7,960,000 in the four years 1885-88 compared with £12,500,000 for England.[6] However, on April 1, 1888, England had forty-two battleships built and seven building while France and Russia had twenty-four with fifteen building. Germany had thirteen battleships but was building none. The British navy had six armoured cruisers built and six more building, compared with ten built and one building for France, Russia and Germany.[7]

Although the naval estimates did not increase between 1889 and 1893, a new building programme was adopted which called for the addition of 113 ships to the navy between April 1, 1889, and April 1, 1894. These included eight first-class battleships and nine first-class protected cruisers. Five first-class battleships and two first-class protected cruisers were already in progress at the time.[8] On December 31, 1893, England had fifteen first-class, twelve second-class and eleven third-class battleships and seven first-class ships being built. The corresponding figures for France, Russia and Germany combined were thirteen first-class, twenty second-class and twelve third-class battleships with fifteen first-class ships, six second-class and five third-class in progress. In cruisers, England had overwhelming superiority over the other three navies together.[9]

The naval scare of 1893 was the most successful effort up to that time. It was touched off by the visit of the Russian navy to Toulon on October 13. A series of articles in *The Times* aroused the country with sensational descriptions of the menace posed by the combination of the French and Russian fleets.[10] Although everyone agreed that the navy was stronger than those of France and Russia combined, the result was the beginning of the greatest decade of expansion in the history of the British navy, before or since.

During the ten years 1894/95 to 1903/04 naval expenditure grew from £17,366,100 to £38,970,560, and in the latter year expenditure on new construction amounted to over £12 million, a more than £9 million increase since 1893-94. In addition Asquith stated in the House of Commons on March 2, 1908, that under the Conservative government a great deal of money had been spent which did not appear in the estimates and that for several years the loan expenditure had been nearly £3,500,000 a year.[11] This decade saw the launching of thirty-six battleships and the addition of 53,700 men to the roster.[12]

In the same period the combined expenditures of France and Russia on new construction increased from £4,600,000 to just under £9 million.[13] The British navy added more tonnage than the navies of France, Russia and Germany combined. Between 1900 and 1904 her navy estimates increased from £27,522,000 to £36,889,000, although there was "no corresponding increase on the part of the other naval powers."[14]

Meanwhile Germany had begun to expand her navy, the last of the Great Powers to do so. Germany had the second largest merchant marine but only the fifth largest navy. It was generally believed that a navy was needed to protect trade and the fact that Germany was now dependent on food supplies from overseas added a still further argument for naval expansion.

Much has been made of the fact that Admiral Alfred von Tirpitz, secretary of state to the admiralty, argued that in choosing the type of ships to be built the basis to be used should be the most difficult situation into which the fleet could come. Since the most dangerous naval enemy was obviously England, the fleet should be built with a view to a possible war with that power. British authorities had concluded by 1902 that war with Germany had become a possibility, and Tirpitz evidently agreed with them. His reasoning was exactly the same as that used by the British in the expansion of their navy, and the German navy was built against England in the same sense that the British navy was built against France and Russia in the early stages and against Germany later.

Tirpitz also pointed out that the German shortage of bases prevented the German fleet from acting at a distance from its home ports, and that therefore it should be able to "unfold its greatest potential between Heligoland and the Thames." This required a coal capacity great enough to permit a radius of action as far as Brest or Cherbourg. He thought such a navy also corresponded with German requirements against France and Russia.[15] This limitation on German action was recognized by the British admiralty, which thought that protection of commerce would be easier in a war with Germany than with France.[16]

Paul Kennedy tells us that if the Germans had wanted to protect their commerce they would have built overseas cruisers instead of battleships.[17] There is no explanation of the fact that all the other European Powers, as well as the United States, also built battleships, and all entered the battleship race before Germany. As the British view was that the Germans had no right to establish bases or coaling stations, it is unlikely that they would have conceded Germany's right to build a fleet of overseas cruisers. The plain fact is that, according to the British propaganda machine, Germany had no right to have a navy at all.

A further cause of British concern was Tirpitz's idea of building a navy strong enough that the greatest naval power, which was England, would be taking a risk in attacking Germany. Why this should have been considered a threat to England is hard to understand. It can only be assumed that the British wanted to be able to attack Germany without risk and thought Germany's unsuccessful attempt to deprive them of this advantage was unfair. V. R. Berghahn, an extreme critic of German policy, admits in his book *Germany and the Approach to War in 1914*, that Tirpitz had no idea of attacking England but wanted to make it difficult for England to attack Germany.[18] He does, however, fully endorse the British attitude throughout this whole period, which held that Germany alone among the Great Powers had no right and no reason to build a navy.[19] Another modern writer tells us that Tirpitz's risk theory was neither a striving for hegemony in Europe or a determination to "wrestle with the British Empire for naval supremacy." German naval policy, H. W. Koch says in an article in *History*, was at the outset defensive, taking into account the French and Russian navies.[20]

The most noteworthy circumstance about the "risk navy" is that Germany never came close to achieving such an aim. In 1904 the German navy was smaller and weaker in relation to the British navy than it had been ten years earlier, and when the Anglo-French entente ranged the two largest navies in the world together, the idea of the risk navy became nothing but a pipe-dream. British writers agree that the entente made the risk navy policy obsolete, but none explain why the British government continued to pretend that the German navy was a threat to England.[21]

Germany had the same argument for building a navy that England had, namely that she depended on overseas sources for food and raw materials. This was recognized by British politicians on some occasions, as when Asquith said in Parliament that Germany was a country with "a rapidly growing population becoming more and more dependent both for food and raw materials on overseas sources of supply and with an expanding maritime commerce which she is bound to protect."[22] A much more common view was that expressed by Churchill when he described the German fleet as an unnecessary luxury. Modern writers continue to quote these ideas with approval, after a war which saw the starvation death of over 600,000 Germans by the illegal food blockade of the British navy.[23]

Although Germany had the same argument for building a navy that England had, protection of commerce was not the real purpose of either navy. This is shown for the British navy by the report in March, 1907, of a committee considering a proposal to abolish the right of capture of private property at sea. The proposal presumably would have protected the commerce of belligerents: the committee unanimously agreed that England should oppose the idea. The proposal was seen as unfair because it required a greater sacrifice from England than from the other Powers. The committee thought England's naval supremacy assured her ability to protect her own commerce, which made the proposal unnecessary from the British point of view. On the other hand, since England's "striking arm" in European warfare was naval, the proposal demanded "a reduction of the effectiveness of our one weapon of offence." The following statement indicates their line of thought:

We are assured, and we feel bound to accept the assurance, that our navy is now, and for some years may be expected to be equal to the task of capturing or confining to port very shortly after the outbreak of any war within reasonable contemplation, the greater part of the marine, both belligerent and mercantile, of our enemy.

In other words, the main purpose of the British navy was not to protect British commerce but to destroy the commerce of other Powers.

V. R. Berghahn devotes considerable space to the building of the German fleet as an instrument to wring concessions from England.[24] A. J. Marder also remarks in a similar vein that "the new fleet would be used as an instrument of coercion."[25] Evidently England was to be "coerced" by ensuring that she would be taking a risk in attacking Germany.

The British navy, intended as an instrument of offence in war, was also useful in the same way in time of peace. As Winston Churchill explained to Parliament on March 26, 1913, England could not allow another naval power to come close enough "to deflect or restrict her political action." Restricting England's political action would mean England couldn't freely intervene in European affairs and would lead to war.[26] There is no reason to believe that the fighting navies of other Powers had a different purpose.

Kennedy pointed out that German business interests were strongly in favour of naval expansion, because it would assist the shipbuilding and related industries.[27] In this connection it should be noted that the British naval scares of 1884 and 1909 were both preceded by depression in the shipbuilding industry, and the rumours of German acceleration in 1908 were started by the head of a company which expected to profit from naval expansion.

Berghahn's conclusion is that Tirpitz hoped to force the British to give Germany "fair play," and thought that "perhaps even a partnership based on equality would be possible." Berghahn calls this aim of achieving equality with the other Great Powers "a very dangerous strategy," presumably on the ground that Germany should properly have been satisfied with an inferior position.[28]

As far as British public opinion was concerned, the basis for alarm about the German navy was already laid by the time of the first German navy bill. In January, 1896, before Tirpitz took office, British naval writers like H. W. Wilson and Arnold White took alarm at Germany's naval ambitions.[29] According to A.J. Marder, the psychological background can be found in the Kruger telegram, commercial rivalry and the anti-English tone of the German press. When the German government prepared estimates for 1897/98 which called for a large increase in expenditure and the building of one battleship and four cruisers, the *Saturday Review* called this an "astounding naval programme" which had no relation to defence. H.W. Wilson thought it showed Germany's intention to measure herself with England. The fact that the Reichstag refused to pass nearly half the proposed increase did not seem to impress these observers.[30]

Archibald Hurd and Henry Castle remark that "In the light of the vast development of Germany's colonial and commercial interest the navy Act of 1898 was of an unambitious character."[31] Germany had a smaller fleet than any Great Power except Austria-Hungary, and it is obvious that the infant German navy could not have been considered a real threat by any stretch of the imagination. There can be little doubt that the real reason for this unjustified alarm was, as Marder concludes, commercial and colonial rivalry.[32]

The German navy bill of 1900 was greeted by a section of the press as evidence that Germany "was bent on displacing Great Britain as the Mistress of the seas" and would soon attempt to crush her.[33] No doubt the furore in Germany over the detention of mail steamers by the British navy facilitated the passing of this bill. The British admiralty, however, was still concentrating its attention on France and Russia and did not take the growth of the German navy very seriously. Lord Selborne's memorandum of January, 1901, said: "I propose therefore to consider our position almost exclusively from its relative strength to that of France and Russia combined."[34]

In the fall of 1902, a memorandum by Lord Selborne developed the idea that the German navy was being built simply to fight England. It was based on his argument that the German fleet appeared to be designed to operate only in the North Sea.[35] All the efforts of British diplomacy were being used to prevent Germany from acquiring a port or a coaling station anywhere in the world, so the German shortage of bases dictated this German strategy. Both Tirpitz and the British admiralty recognized this. Selborne was thus using a symptom of German inferiority as proof that Germany intended to attack England.[36]

Although Selborne still considered France and Russia England's most important rivals, Marder states that by 1902 public opinion, the government and the admiralty all saw the German fleet as a greater potential menace than those of the Dual Alliance.[37] Since the French and Russian navies were both stronger than that of Germany and were still increasing faster, this potentiality was clearly something to cause concern in the distant future. The real cause of concern was the growing British antagonism to Germany, which had nothing to do with the building of the German navy. British officialdom and the general public were becoming more and more hostile to Germany, and this antagonism produced doubt at the admiralty about the wisdom of continuing to concentrate attention only on France and Russia.[38] Sir Frank Lascelles, the then British ambassador to Germany, was asked his opinion on the policy and aims of Germany in April, 1902, and he replied that the German navy was "aimed at that of the greatest naval Power."[39]

On April 8, 1904, the entente with France eliminated the French navy as England's foremost competitor. In the next year the Russian navy was almost destroyed by Japan and the Russian threat also disappeared. It was impossible to pretend that England's naval supremacy was threatened and expenditure on new construction decreased steadily for the four years, 1905-08.[40] This followed on the report of a special committee which met in November, 1904, and concluded that the battleship situation was so favourable that a reduction in the programme was in order.[41]

Under these circumstances the admiralty desperately needed a new adversary, and Germany was chosen for the role. The weakness of the German fleet, however, posed a difficult problem, which meant that it took some time to devise a workable strategy. The navy therefore had to live with declining appropriations for new construction until 1909.

Sir John Fisher's repeated statements about the superiority of the British navy and the need for economy show that the reductions were fully supported by the admiralty. On September 26, 1906, he wrote that "our curtailed shipbuilding policy is so enormously in advance of our requirements that it's simply stupid to talk of the loss of our naval supremacy." He thought the navy's margin of superiority over Germany was so great that this talk was absurd even if England stopped building altogether.[42] In January, 1907, he thought the navy was "incomparably stronger and more ready for fighting than it was two years ago," although the estimates had been reduced by five million and would, he said, be reduced still more.[43]

Popular myth holds that these British reductions encouraged Tirpitz to believe that he was on the verge of catching up to the British navy and were thus responsible for a speeding up of the German programme. In fact, the German programme, far from being speeded up, lagged behind the provisions of the navy law for some time. Fisher pointed out in 1907 that in March of that year it had been eighteen months since Germany had begun to build a battleship or large cruiser. The Germans had been paralysed by the launching by the British in 1906 of the H.M.S. *Dreadnought*, which convinced them that their existing fleet was useless.[44]

When the Germans did begin building again they not only had to make up for lost time but faced greatly increased costs for the new ships. The greater size and power of the Dreadnought battleships and battle-cruisers approximately doubled the cost of each new ship.[45] The first four German Dreadnoughts, about equal to the Lord Nelson in size, speed and fire-power, each cost £338,000 more. The first ten British Dreadnoughts cost less than twenty percent more than the previous ten British battleships. The German cost of building a ship mounting 12" guns was £600,000 more than the British cost. These facts account for the large increase in the German expenditure on new construction between 1907 and 1909.[46]

Again it is pretended by pro-entente historians that a policy forced on Germany by the British initiative in building the Dreadnought signified sinister intentions on the part of Germany. Modern Germanophobe writers do not, of course, accept the view that Germany was forced to build Dreadnoughts. Germany had no right to build a navy in the first place, so according to them, she had no right to build Dreadnoughts either. Holger Herwig, who considers the German navy bill of 1900 "a unilateral challenge to Great Britain's dominant sea power," tells us that the German decision to build Dreadnoughts "made it clear to British leaders that Berlin intended to compete with the Royal navy."[47] Apparently similar decisions by the United States and France had no such significance.

Marder lends support to the supposed fear of the German navy by the statement that between 1900 and 1905 Germany launched fourteen battleships, only two fewer than the British. The fact that this ignores the two ships bought by the British from Chile in 1903 is a minor omission; much more important is the failure to note that in the previous five years, 1895-99, the British had launched twenty battleships and the Germans four. By 1903 England was "equal to a combination of any three powers in completed first-class battleships."[48] At the end of 1905 the British navy had thirty-seven battleships completed in the preceding ten years while the German navy had fourteen. A mere recital of numbers, however, greatly understates the British superiority. The British ships outweighed the German ones by an average of 2,648 tons and the total projectile weight of their broadsides in guns with a calibre of 9.2" and above was nearly six times that of the German battleships. The British ships carried four 13.5," one hundred thiry-six 12," eight 10" and twenty 9.2" guns; the German ships carried sixteen 11" and forty 9.4" guns.[49]

It is quite clear that no one in a position to know the facts had any reason to be alarmed about a threat to British naval supremacy. In April, 1905, Lord Lansdowne agreed with the British ambassador to Washington, Sir Michael Herbert, that Germany was much too weak at sea to think of attacking England.[50] Sir Edward Grey expressed a similar opinion in January, 1906, when he stated that England was more supreme at sea than she had ever been.[51] In a memorandum a short time later he asserted that in case of war England could shut up the German fleet in Kiel and keep it there without losing a ship or a man or firing a shot.[52] Lord Esher, chairman of the committee of imperial defense, thought British power was "six times that of Germany at the given point of battle."[53]

The following year Sir John Fisher, First Sea Lord, agreed with Tirpitz that the British navy was four times stronger than the German navy. In a letter to Edward VII he wrote that England had seven Dreadnoughts and three Dreadnought battle-cruisers built and building while Germany had not begun a single Dreadnought. Fisher thought half the German battle fleet was about equal to the British armoured cruisers. An admiralty memorandum of August 22 said that England had one hundred and twenty-three destroyers and forty submarines, while Germany had forty-eight destroyers and one submarine.[54]

At the same time Fisher drew attention to the admiralty's problem when he noted that one hundred fifty members of Parliament had just prepared one of the best papers he had ever read showing that the navy was so strong that no new ships were needed at all. Fisher thought it was unwise to parade the fact of England's great superiority, as this might cause parliamentary trouble.[55]

In 1908 Fisher suggested to King Edward that it would be a good idea to "Copenhagen" the German fleet—that is, to attack it without warning. This has usually been dismissed as a joke, but Fisher himself insists that he was quite serious. He thought it would be wise "to seize the German Fleet when it was so very easy of accomplishment."[56] This was not because Fisher feared the German fleet, but because it was necessary to eliminate Germany as a commercial competitor.[57] One can imagine how a similar proposal made by Tirpitz to the kaiser would be treated by modern historians.

In March, 1908, Germany had no Dreadnoughts in service, and at that time Herbert Asquith, chancellor of the exchequer, stated in Parliament that the British naval position was "one of unassailable supremacy." The debate in Parliament produced much controversy concerning the German fleet, and the question whether or not by the end of 1911 Germany would have thirteen Dreadnoughts against England's twelve was raised. The fact that the Germans were still eighteen months from completing their first Dreadnought gives some indication of the extremes to which some were prepared to go to support continued expansion of the British navy and arouse antagonism against Germany.[58]

A short time after Asquith's statement in Parliament, on May 5, 1908, Reginald McKenna, the civilian first lord of the admiralty, "formally agreed to 4 Dreadnoughts and if necessary 6 Dreadnoughts" for 1909-10.[59] This promise, given before any alarm about the acceleration of German building had been raised, set the stage for the naval scare of March 1909.

The naval scare of 1909 required the acceptance of three propositions, all of which were false, and two at least of which were known to be false by the British admiralty. These were, first, that the Dreadnought was so great an advance on all earlier ships that this type should be the measure of naval strength; second, that Germany was accelerating the building of battleships beyond those authorized by the naval law; and third, that Germany could now build battleships as quickly as the British could.

McKenna began his speech on March 16, 1909, by stating that the increase in the naval estimates over the previous year amounted to £2,803,000, most of which was for new construction. The estimates provided for the building of only four battleships, but he gave notice that four more might be ordered during the year. He named Germany as the country whose naval strength was increasing most rapidly and therefore as the standard by which British requirements should be measured.[60]

Although McKenna stated that the Dreadnought had not rendered the earlier ships obsolete but had merely shortened their life, he proceeded to compare British and German strength in Dreadnoughts. Germany still had no Dreadnoughts in service so this exercise required a projection of German building into the future, and here he gave full rein to his imagination. In November, 1908, a rumour had been circulated that Germany was accelerating the construction of battleships, and on this basis McKenna created an imaginary fleet of German Dreadnoughts which by the fall of 1910 would number nine against England's ten, and in 1911 would reach thirteen against England's sixteen. By April, 1912, Germany would have seventeen Dreadnoughts to England's sixteen unless the British navy could add four additional ships to bring its total to twenty. He also declared that there had been "extraordinary growth" in the German capacity to construct big ships and that England would have difficulty keeping pace.[61]

Arthur J. Balfour, the leader of the opposition, managed to outbid McKenna by a considerable margin. He was sure Germany would have thirteen Dreadnoughts to England's ten by December, 1910, and he achieved even wilder flights of fancy for succeeding years. He strongly emphasized that only Dreadnoughts should be counted and was quite certain Germany could now build battleships as quickly as the British could.[62]

Asquith disputed some of Balfour's figures, but asserted that the Germans were certain to have thirteen by November, 1911. He also supported the statements concerning acceleration and speed of building.[63] These tactics were so successful that all eight ships were included in the estimates at once, by public demand.

These parliamentary statements were so widely at variance with the facts that it is hardly possible to believe the government took them seriously. In the first place, the Dreadnought was not a radically new type of ship, its only claim to distinction being the fact that the intermediate armament of earlier ships was replaced by six additional 12" guns. The fine line separating the Dreadnought from the Lord Nelson class which immediately preceded it can be seen by examining Winston Churchill's list of British and German Dreadnoughts at the outbreak of the war. The two ships at the top of the

British list are the *Lord Nelson* and the *Agamemnon*. That this classification is justified is shown by the fact that the weight of broadside of the primary guns is almost the same as that of the first four German Dreadnoughts and the speed is only a half-knot slower.[64] Marder, who usually endorses all the opinions of the most extreme naval writers, ends his discussion of the subject with the statement that it was the development of long-range shooting and not the Dreadnought herself "which made all existing ships obsolete."[65] The fact that the guns mounted on the Dreadnought were the same 12" guns used on the *Lord Nelson* and that their range was little different from that of those mounted on British battleships since 1898, disposes of the myth of the obsolescence of the pre-Dreadnoughts. Twenty-six of these ships composed the four battle squadrons of the Channel fleet when the war began. The eight King Edwards made up the third battle squadron of the Grand fleet.[66] The guns on all these ships were equal to those of any German ship afloat on August 1, 1914.

The only evidence of German acceleration was that advance orders had been placed for some equipment to forestall a rise in prices. As Germany had not laid down a single battleship from the summer of 1905 until July, 1907, it is clear that Fisher's statement that she had been paralysed by the Dreadnought was correct and that her earlier programme was therefore in arrears.[67] Furthermore, it should be pointed out that the German navy law of 1900 provided for the laying down of two battleships for the replacement of older ships in each of the four years 1906, 1907, 1908 and 1909 and that a total of ten was actually laid down in those years, two more than were needed to replace the ones being retired. The amended law of 1908 increased the number of replacements to three for 1908, 1909 and 1910, with the number falling to two in 1911 and one for each year thereafter.[68] This added three battleships to the total Germany was to build by 1917.

In any case, the projections of German building given to Parliament were wildly incorrect. The first two German Dreadnoughts were completed in October, 1909, and the next two in March 1910. At the end of 1910 Germany had completed four Dreadnoughts and one battle-cruiser, while the British had completed seven Dreadnoughts and three battle-cruisers. In 1911 the score was even, and the year ended with the British ahead by fourteen to nine. For succeeding years the figures were twenty-one to thirteen in 1912 and twenty-six to seventeen in 1913. Before the war began the British had completed four more Dreadnoughts and one battle-cruiser while the Germans had completed one battle-cruiser, leaving the final tally at thirty-one to eighteen in favour of England, not counting the two Lord Nelsons.[69]

It should be added that even with regard to Dreadnoughts, the numbers understate British superiority. Sixteen of these British ships were equipped with 13.5" guns and the remainder with 12" guns; ten German ships had 12" batteries, the other eight only 11" ones. The British advantage in fire-power was thus much greater than the numbers indicate.[70]

Although the Germans were not, in fact, accelerating the building of battleships, it is at least possible that the British admiralty may have believed this particular story. Fisher's statement that lack of information should be acted on as if they were accelerating indicates that the admiralty had no actual evidence on the matter.[71] The German government provided McKenna with the correct information and assured him that there was no acceleration, but he chose to disbelieve them.   /

The statements about German speed of building were simply nonsense. Marder says we know today that Germany could build a Dreadnought in twenty-seven to thirty-three months, based on statements by the German admiralty.[72] It is true that Germany did build the first four small Dreadnoughts in twenty-seven to thirty-two months. The average building time for those completed before the war, however, was thirty-four and a half months. The normal British time was twenty-four months and the average was twenty-four and a half months, ten months less than the German time.[73] The *Navy League Annual* for 1910 stated that the speed of Dreadnought construction was twenty-six months in England and thirty-four months in Germany.[74] The admiralty must have been well aware of these facts, but may have taken advantage of the German admiralty's optimistic statements to confuse the issue.[75]

This particular sham originated in May, 1906, when a businessman named Mulliner, head of a British company which manufactured guns and gun mountings, sent a letter to the British war office stating that Krupp had developed a new method for making 12" guns which saved one-third of the required time. Some opposition members of Parliament were evidently in touch with Mulliner in March, 1909, and they cited his warnings in the debate on the estimates. Samuel Roberts, M.P., a former director of Mulliner's firm, stated that Germany could make the complete armament for ten battleships in one year.[76]

The *Navy League Annual* for 1909/10, on the other hand, stated that it was impossible to accept the idea that Germany would mass many years of naval programmes into a single year. The editor described the German navy bill as "immutable" and added that "so far it has been much delayed."[77] The Germans, far from accelerating, were actually behind schedule at the end of 1909, and, when the critical date of April, 1912, arrived, had completed nine Dreadnoughts, instead of the seventeen which had been declared certain.[78]

By March 22, Asquith realized that the scare had been overdone, and made a speech in which he tried to calm the storm which had been raised. He called the stories about the country's naval unpreparedness "absurd and mischievous legends," and gave the correct Dreadnought figures for 1909. He then drew attention to the British pre-Dreadnought battleships, stating that England had forty first-class battleships of that type compared with twenty for Germany. He pointed out that the British ships had one hundred fifty-two 12" guns against forty 11" guns on the German ships. After detailing an even greater British superiority in armoured cruisers he concluded with the assertion that it was "absurd to attempt to suggest that we are in a condition which ought to excite alarm and disquietude."[79] He did not mention that this absurdity had just been committed by a member of his own cabinet, who, in introducing the increased naval estimates, had intimated that he was acting out of concern for the safety of the Empire.

Stephen McKenna, in his biography of his father, devotes a whole chapter to the naval scare of 1909. He maintains that McKenna's statements in Parliament were made in accordance with information supplied by the admiralty.[80] No doubt this is so, but that he did not know the information was false is unlikely. The fact that he had promised an increased programme before any knowledge of the supposed German acceleration came to light is surely an indication that he was privy to the deception practised on Parliament and the public. When it is remembered that England was now acting in concert with France and Russia, whose combined navies were almost equal to those of Germany and Austria, it is hard to believe that any British government had the effrontery to suggest that England was threatened by the German navy.

The real balance of naval power is shown in a letter from Fisher to Lord Esher, written on March 21, 1909, while the debate on the estimates was in progress. Fisher imagines a speech he could make to squash his opponents, in which he would say that England has now "two Fleets in Home Waters, each of which is incomparably superior to the whole German Fleet mobilized for war...This can't alter for years, even were we supinely passive in our building..." Of course he did not make this speech, because it would have been "an effectual cold douche to the 8 Dreadnoughts a year."[81]

Marder, who as usual sides with the extreme naval historians, takes this performance seriously, and appears to think the alarm about the German navy was genuine. He thinks it was "curious" that the service organs took no part in the hysteria.[82] Presumably the editors of the service publications were well enough informed to recognize a hoax when they saw one. One footnote was supplied by the editor of the *Navy League Annual*, who described the scare of 1909 as "one of the most portentous pieces of Parliamentary humbug ever practised upon the electorate."[83]

Sir John Fisher wrote on January 19, 1910, "We shall be 2 keels to 1 in March 1912 and 2 keels to 1 at the end of the German navy law...we shall have 22 Dreadnoughts in March 1912 and the Germans will only have 11! This is all absolute fact! But as I've often told you, 'the truth is that we don't want anyone to know the truth.' "[84] On October 15 he wrote that a friend had informed him that "retardation not acceleration is the present aspect of German shipbuilding."[85]

Sir John Fisher played the most important part in creating the panic of 1909 by stimulating a press campaign and supplying McKenna with false information. Peter Padfield, in his book, *The Great Naval Race*, describes him as the centre of an "alarmist web" and says he kept busy "firing off red-hot letters to the select band of editors and naval correspondents whom he trusted." Fisher lent support to the counting of Dreadnoughts only in a memorandum in which he said: "we are fighting for our lives, and for a one-Power standard now, when the pre-Dreadnoughts shortly go the way of all flesh and die out."[86] He told McKenna the only issue was the number of Dreadnoughts, and supported this by a reference to the Canopus class of battleships, which he said could be "gobbled up" by the Dreadnoughts.[87] The Canopus class, launched in 1897/98 were the last British battleships to be armed with 35 calibre (AAA) 12" guns. But even these guns had a range almost the same as that of the guns on the first four German Dreadnoughts and the first battle-cruiser. The British navy had twenty-three pre-Dreadnought battleships built after the Canopus class which mounted guns with a range as great as those on any ship completed by Germany before the war.[88] In January, 1909, Fisher wrote to McKenna that building only six ships in 1909/10 would jeopardize England's national existence. As his letter to Lord Esher in March shows, he knew quite well that this was false.[89]

This pretence of a German naval threat set the stage for the farcical discussions with Germany aimed at persuading the Germans to stop building a navy. Asquith told Parliament during the 1909 debate that England had more than once raised the question of a mutual reduction of naval expenditures. This was not strictly accurate, because there was never any British offer to limit British naval building, only statements that a German slowdown would result in similar action by England. The same tactics were to be repeated in succeeding years, as the British government continued to act as if British naval expansion depended on that of Germany. Interestingly, Sir Eyre Crowe pointed out on April 13, 1909, that a naval agreement with Germany would be dangerous if a third Power, such as Austria, should take up the race. The danger posed to Germany by the French and Russian navies does not seem to have occurred to him.[90]

Discussions of this nature were a new departure in British policy. No such step was taken during the long period when France and Russia were supposed to be the antagonists against which the British navy was being built. During the debate on the estimates of 1905/06 the secretary of the admiralty had stated that for the country "to discuss directly with Foreign Powers its Navy Estimates was an impossibility" and that "direct negotiations on questions of the Navy and the construction programme were impossible."[91] This was exactly the view taken by the kaiser when British envoys approached him on the matter.

Grey and David Lloyd George, the chancellor of the exchequer, raised the naval question with the German ambassador in the summer of 1908. Both ministers insisted that British naval expenditure had risen because of the German programme and the increased speed of construction in Germany, and that Anglo-German relations centred on the fleet problem. The kaiser's minutes on Metternich's dispatch reporting this conversation show that, unlike most German statesmen of the time, he was shrewd enough to see through this charade. He remarked, correctly, that there had been no increase in the German speed of construction and that the British navy was already three times as strong as Germany's. He understood quite well that naval construction was not a basic cause of British enmity and applauded Metternich's view that a slackening of tension between the two countries was the primary need. He was opposed to any discussion of the size of the German navy and thought "France and Russia might equally well demand a reduction of our land armaments." Any British statesman would have taken the same view if the positions had been reversed.[92]

Two weeks later Lloyd George told Metternich he understood that Germany needed a larger navy, and suggested that the ratio between the two navies should be fixed at 3:2. Since the German navy had little hope of approaching British strength so closely, an agreement on this basis would have cost the Germans nothing. In fact, when the British government later proposed a ratio of 16:10 Tirpitz was quite ready to accept it.[93]

When King Edward visited Germany in August, Sir Charles Hardinge discussed the naval question with Wilhelm II. Armed with false information from the admiralty, he told the kaiser that by 1912 Germany would be equal or superior to England in Dreadnought strength. The kaiser naturally informed him that his figures were incorrect, but Hardinge was unimpressed and concluded with the words "You must stop or build slower," to which Wilhelm II replied "Then we shall fight, for it is a question of national honour and dignity."[94]

In December, 1908, Grey told Metternich that England must increase her naval spending or Germany would soon be superior. He said the pace depended on Germany, as other countries were either not building Dreadnoughts or doing so slowly. The French had six battleships under construction at the time, and although *Jane's Fighting Ships* calls these "semi-Dreadnoughts," they were in fact slightly superior to the Lord Nelson in weight, speed and fire-power and were approximately equal in these respects to the first four German Dreadnoughts.[95]

Reviewing Metternich's report of his conversation with Grey, Bülow suggested to Tirpitz that a slowing down of German building might be advisable. He correctly predicted that the German navy could not act against the superior British forces, but would be shut up in harbour by a British blockade. He thought the best course might be to concentrate on coast defence, increasing the stock of sea mines and creating a strong fleet of submarines. While Bülow did not maintain that such a policy would remove British hostility, it might postpone a conflict until Germany was stronger.[96] Tirpitz disputed Bülow's belief that a slowing down of construction would have a mitigating effect on British antagonism and insisted that on the contrary it would be taken as a sign of weakness and would result in further attempts to humiliate Germany.[97]

In the spring of 1909 Sir William Goschen, British ambassador in Berlin, expressed the view that the four extra ships should be laid down as soon as possible, because as soon as the Germans were convinced that they could not compete they would cut back their programme.[98] Similarly, when the new chancellor, Bethmann-Hollweg, proposed negotiations for a naval arrangement, William Tyrrell thought it was a result of the British decision to build the eight Dreadnoughts in 1909 and 1910.[99] Actually it is clear that there is little relation between the two naval programmes. German building was governed throughout by the navy law while the British programme depended on the success of the admiralty in deceiving Parliament into believing that more ships were necessary. Grey stated on one occasion that if Germany would arrest her increase in naval expansion England would do the same:[100] what actually happened was that between 1910 and 1914 German expenditure on new construction remained constant while that of England increased by £4 million.[101]

On August 21, 1909, Goschen reported to Grey that Bethmann-Hollweg was ready to make proposals for a naval agreement, but that this would have to be part of a general understanding. Goschen replied that the conclusion of a formal understanding would be difficult in view of the existing friendships and alliances. To this Grey answered that nothing in the British agreements with France and Russia was directed against Germany and that these were no bar to a friendly arrangement with Germany.[102]

When Bethmann asked what England would do in return for a modification of the German navy law, Goschen told him that England could make no promise about her rate of naval construction, because the navy was her first line of defence and she had to regulate it in relation to those of her neighbours. Apparently the Germans were expected to believe that the French and Russian navies were a possible threat to England but not to Germany.[103] Grey also insisted that the navy was a matter of life and death to England in a way which could not possibly apply to Germany. Evidently he believed that the British ability to destroy German commerce was no threat to a Germany which depended for existence on imported food and raw materials.[104]

Negotiations continued for four years, although Grey believed nothing could come of them. He maintained throughout that the cause of Anglo-German tension was the German navy, but was unable to come to any agreement because it was necessary to maintain the alliance with France and Russia.[105] When Count Metternich told him that the word "neutrality" must be part of any formula, Grey suggested the promise that England would "neither make nor join in any unprovoked attack" on Germany. This formula of the unprovoked attack shows the unreal character of this supposed attempt to come to an agreement with Germany. The British government wished Germany to bind herself to halt the expansion of her navy. Meanwhile England would continue to increase her own naval power and retain the right to oppose German interests throughout the world. However naive he thought Bethmann-Hollweg to be, Grey can hardly have imagined that he would be taken in by such transparent phraseology. The Germans were already aware that Grey would consider any attempt to protect their interests against French encroachment a provocation, and they knew quite well the emptiness of his protestations that British policy was not inspired by any animosity to Germany and that her engagements with France and Russia were not inimical to Germany.

As the naval authorities in France and England had made arrangements for cooperation in time of war, the two navies would act together against Germany. It remained only for England to sign a naval agreement with Russia to establish common action by the three entente navies in case of war. Signing was projected on the eve of the war. Thus when the war began in August, 1914, Germany and Austria were faced by a combination of naval power more than three times as great as their own. Against such overwhelming superiority they had little chance of saving their people from the rigours of a ruthless starvation blockade.

The last act in the naval negotiation farce was the so-called Haldane mission. Grey had no expectation that he could persuade the Germans to stop building a navy unless there was some prospect that they could improve their relations with England by doing so. He had no intention of renouncing his resolve that when the war came he would take England into it on the side of France and Russia. Thus he could offer the Germans nothing to induce them to undertake a unilateral reduction of their naval expenditure. War secretary Lord Haldane was sent to Germany with no power to do anything but engage in friendly conversation. Grey explains the two purposes of the visit in his memoirs. The first was to avoid openly offending the Germans by refusing to respond to the German kaiser's intimation that he would welcome a visit from a British minister. The second was to convince the opponents of his policy in the cabinet and the Liberal party that he was trying to be friendly with Germany.[106] Haldane was given no authority to make any definite proposals on behalf of the British government, but there was some discussion of the naval question and some talk of assisting Germany to acquire African colonies. Metternich told Haldane that if the British government offered a suitable formula the navy law could be changed. Grey drafted a reply which repeated the same empty phrases denying an "aggressive policy" and promising not to make an "unprovoked attack" on Germany. The Germans' recent experience at the time of the Agadir crisis had shown how easy it would be for them to provoke an attack, and they were understandably as unreceptive as before. Wilhelm II concluded that the British hoped to persuade Germany to give up the navy law "in return for an African empire made up of other people's territories."[107] Baron Greindl, the Belgian ambassador in Berlin, wondered whether Belgium was the intended victim.[108] The "failure" of the Haldane mission marked the end of the naval negotiations comedy, which no longer served a useful purpose. The inevitability of an early war was now widely accepted, and increasing naval appropriations became a matter of routine. At the same time German expenditures were stabilized at the level required for building the new larger, more expensive ships.

The modern expansion of the British navy, which began in 1884, bore little relation to the strength of other navies. The existence of these navies, however, provided the admiralty with ammunition to pressure Parliament into voting increasing naval estimates. The French navy had played the role until it was joined by the Russian fleet, and the two furnished the needed stimulus until 1904. When the French entente and the destruction of the Russian fleet by Japan removed those threats, it was necessary to find a new bogeyman, and Germany was chosen for the part. Since the real German navy was too weak to endanger British naval supremacy an imaginary one had to be created. Continuing increases in the naval budget could be maintained by periodically deluding the public into believing that the growing expenditures were caused by Germany.

The plain fact, evident in retrospect to anyone who takes the trouble to follow the course of events, is that throughout the whole period the lead was taken by the British navy. When the opponents were France and Russia, British naval expansion proceeded faster than that of France, Russia and Germany combined. During the time of the so-called naval race with Germany the British set the pace, initiated the construction of the *Dreadnought*, introduced the turbine and the use of oil and led the way in increasing the size and speed of ships and the calibre of guns. Fisher's nucleus crew system, which ensured that the whole British fleet was "instantly ready for war," anticipated by six years the reorganization of the German navy decreed by the Navy Bill of 1912.[109] The slow-down of 1905 to 1908 was forced on the admiralty by an overwhelming superiority which no deception could disguise.

The building of the German navy was neither a basic cause of British hostility to Germany nor a significant factor in the British decision to join France and Russia in a war with Germany. Given the industrial and commercial development of Germany, which threatened England's economic domination of the world, a clash between the two Powers was probably inevitable. The growing rift between them was responsible for their failure to become allied, and this in turn convinced the British government to adopt the alternative policy of coming to terms with England's two foremost imperial rivals. The German navy had nothing to do with either the failure of the alliance negotiations or the making of the Anglo-French entente. A division of the spoils of imperialism was preferable to the surrender of commercial supremacy.

A subsidiary role of the German navy, in addition to supporting increased British naval estimates, was to provide British Germanophobes with a lever they could use to increase anti-German feeling, and this may have eased the task of uniting the public behind the war when it came. It is probable that some other stimulus would have been found to arouse antipathy to Germany if she had failed to follow the lead of all the other Powers in expanding her navy. The fact that British leaders believed already in 1905 that public opinion would support the government in going to war with Germany shows that the agitation about the navy was not needed to produce this result.

Periodic alarms about the German navy bills nevertheless featured the period from 1898 on. One example is the fuss about the German *Flottennovelle* of 1908, which provided for the replacement of battleships after twenty years instead of twenty-five years. The British admiralty had already adopted a similar policy, and Germany merely followed suit, in the same way as she followed other British innovations.

Bülow was undoubtedly right in his opinion that the German navy could never hope to challenge British supremacy and that it would have been better to build submarines. It was England's good fortune that Tirpitz's view prevailed and that Germany persisted in building a fleet of battleships which could never be used against the overwhelming British superiority.

It is also true that a change of German naval policy would have done nothing to lessen British hostility to Germany, and it is unlikely that it would have made any difference to the timing of the war. The Germans would have been better advised to spend their money on training a larger proportion of their young men as soldiers. An additional million trained men would have enabled them properly to carry out the Schlieffen plan and might well have enabled them to accomplish the really vital task of knocking the French out of the war in six weeks. While this would not have made it possible for Germany to defeat the British Empire, it would have changed the whole course of the war to her advantage.

The German navy law of 1900 provided for the creation of a fleet of thirty-eight battleships and fourteen large cruisers by 1917, and the only important change in this objective before the outbreak of the war was the addition of six large cruisers by the supplementary law of 1906.[110] German building of battleships proceeded on the basis laid down in 1900, so that in the normal course of events Germany would have had thirty-eight battleships of twenty years vintage or less in 1917. Germany actually had thirty-three such ships when the war began, with seven more due for completion by 1917. Two older ships would require replacement by that time, and the total of thirty-eight would be obtained. It seems unlikely that the six large cruisers provided for by the 1906 addition would have been afloat by that time, because only the original fourteen of 1900 were scheduled for completion by the end of 1916.[111] At no time was German building in advance of the navy law, and in March, 1909, at the time of the naval scare, it was behind schedule. Holger Herwig says that in 1914 the German building programme was eight battleships and thirteen battle- cruisers in arrears, but this seems to be an exaggeration based on a faulty interpretation of the supplementary laws passed since 1900.[112]

It thus appears that German building of both battleships and cruisers took place within the limits of the navy Law of 1900, with the exception that two battleships required for earlier replacement would have been built by 1917. Slowed momentarily by the introduction of the *Dreadnought*, German construction soon resumed its normal course, uninfluenced by external pressures and undeterred by external criticism.

Churchill has explained in full the situation at the outbreak of World War I. British superiority in home waters, he says, "was smaller than at any subsequent moment in the war...If the German navy was ever to fight a battle, now at the beginning was its best chance." The British navy would have welcomed a battle at that moment, particularly since the fleet was ready as a result of the test mobilization, while only the active German fleet was mobilised. But, says Churchill, "The German staff felt that even if this was the best chance for a trial of strength, it was a chance so hazardous and even so forlorn that it was not worth taking..." Churchill professes to believe that "there was not much margin for mischance," but his figures lend little support to this view. The British Dreadnoughts had almost twice the fire-power of their German counterparts, and the superiority of the British pre-Dreadnoughts was much greater still. The British navy was more than twice as large as the German navy, and ship for ship it was superior in every respect.[113]

The Anglo-German naval race existed only in the British imagination. The Anglo race was under way long before the passage of the first German navy law, and the British raced harder before 1905 than after. The only relation between the two navies was that Germany followed British innovations, usually at some distance, as did all the other naval Powers. The British presumed that Germany had no right to build a navy, and that she should have refused to make any advances in size and speed of ships or in fire-power after 1898. It was Germany's failure to conform to the pattern proper to an inferior upstart Power which made possible the campaign against the German navy. This in turn has provided us with the fairy-tale known to British propaganda as "the Anglo-German naval race."

Notes

1. F. W. Hirst, *The Six Panics and Other Essays*, pp. 41-9.

2. *Pall Mall Gazette*, September 18, 1884.

3. *Manchester Guardian*, September 20, 1884, p. 9.

4. Hirst, pp. 48-9; Parliamentary Paper no. 129, Accounts and Papers, LIII, 1904, pp. 83 ff.

5. A. J. Marder, *The Anatomy of British Sea Power*, pp. 126-8.

6. *Ibid.*, p. 123.

7. Parliamentary Paper no. 218, 1888, LXVIII, p. 683.

8. Accounts and Papers, L, Cmd. 5648b, p. 341.

9. Parliamentary Paper no. 465, 1893-4, LIV, p. 185.

10. Marder, pp. 179-80.

11. Accounts and Papers, 1894, Cmd. 7295, LIV, 475; 1904, no. 129, LIII, 83; 1908, no. 281, LXV, 771; HCD, 4th ser. XVII, col. 659, CLXXXV, col. 371.

12. *Jane's Fighting Ships*, 1905-06, pp. 40-46; Accounts and Papers, 1894, LIV3, 1903, XXXIX, 309.

13. Accounts and Papers, 1904, no. 281; HCD, XVII Col. 659.

14. A. J. Marder, *From the Dreadnought to Scapa Flow*, I, 23.

15. Jonathan Steinberg, *Yesterday's Deterrent*, p. 209.

16. Marder, *Anatomy*, p. 481.

17. Paul M. Kennedy, "German World Policy and the Alliance Negotiations with England," *Journal of Modern History*, Vol. 45, December, 1973, p. 608.

18. V. R. Berghahn, *Germany and the Approach of War in 1914*, pp. 38-9.

19. *Ibid.*, pp. 50 ff.

20. H. W. Koch, "The Anglo-German Alliance Negotiations," *History*, Vol. 54, 1969, p. 379.

21. E. L. Woodward, *Great Britain and the German Navy*, pp. 32-3, 37, 62; Peter Padfield, *The Great Naval Race*, p. 137.

22. HCD, CLXXXV, col. 376.

23. Woodward, p. 15.

24. Berghahn, pp. 34-40.

25. Marder, *Anatomy*, p. 457.

26. Padfield, p. 293.

27.Berghahn, pp. 26-28.

28.*Ibid.*, pp. 38-9.

29.Paul M. Kennedy, *The Rise of Anglo-German Antagonism, 1860-1914*, p. 248.

30.Marder, *Anatomy*, pp. 288-90.

31.Archibald Hurd and Henry Castle, *German Sea Power*, p. 115.

32. Marder, *Anatomy*, p. 300.

33.*Ibid.*, p. 458.

34.*Ibid.*, p. 463; G. W. Monger, *The End of Isolation*, p. 11.

35.Marder, *Anatomy*, p. 465.

36.FO800/100.

37.Marder, *Anatomy*, pp. 464-5.

38.Monger, p. 68.

39.Lansdowne, MSS, Vol. XIII, quoted in Monger, p. 69.

40.Accounts and Papers, 1908, LXV, 771, no. 281.

41.Marder, *Anatomy*, p. 510.

42.Marder, *Fear God and Dread Nought*, p. 91.

43.*Ibid.*, p. 112.

44.Lord John Fisher, *Memories and Records*, I, 31.

45.Padfield, p. 163.

46.*Jane's Fighting Ships*, 1914, pp. 36-41, 46, 118, 120.

47.Holger H. Herwig, *"Luxury" Fleet*, pp. 47, 58.

48.Marder, *Anatomy*, pp. 417, 460.

49.*Jane's Fighting Ships*, 1905-6, pp. 34, 40-46, 177, 181-3.

50.BD, III, nos. 82, 83.

51.*Ibid.*, no. 216.

52.FO800/92.

53.Maurice V. Brett, *Journals and Letters of Reginald Viscount Esher*, II, 210.

54.Fisher, I, 31-2.

55.*Ibid.*, pp. 32-3.

56.*Ibid.*, pp. 134-5.

57.*Ibid.*, p. 22; II, 108.

58.HCD, 4th ser., CLXXXV, col. 1335.

59.Fisher, I, 186.

60.HCD, 5th ser., II, cols. 930 ff.

61.*Ibid.*, cols. 933-6.

62.*Ibid.*, cols. 946-52.

63.*Ibid.*, cols. 960-62.

64.W. S. Churchill, *The World Crisis*, I, 698-9.

65.Marder, *Dreadnought to Scapa Flow*, I, 57.

66.Churchill, p. 701.

67.Hurd and Castle, p. 139.

68.*Ibid.*, pp. 335-6; *Jane's Fighting Ships*, 1914, pp. 118-120.

69.*Jane's Fighting Ships*, 1914, pp. 34-41, 118-124.

70.*Ibid.*

71.Fisher, I, 190.

72.Marder, *Road*, I, 153.

73.*Jane's Fighting Ships*, 1914, pp. 34-41, 118-120.

74.Hirst, p. 97.

75.A. J. Marder, *Fear God*, II, 379.

76.*Daily News and Leader*, May 23, 24, 1913.

77.*Navy League Annual*, 1909-10, pp. 64-5.

78.Marder, *Fear God*, II, 208.

79.HCD, *Ibid.*, col. 1507.

80.Stephen McKenna, *Reginald McKenna*, 1863-1943, pp. 70-83.

81.Fisher, I, 189.

82.Marder, *Road*, p. 168.

83.E. D. Morel, *Truth and the War*, p. 157.

84.Marder, *Fear God*, III, 290.

85.*Ibid.*, p. 31.

86.Padfield, p. 206.

87.Marder, *Fear God*, II, 221.

88.*Jane's Fighting Ships*, 1914, pp. 46-53, 118-124.

89.Marder, *Fear God*, II, 222.

90.FO371,673/13621, quoted in C. J. Lowe and M. L. Dockrill, *The Mirage of Power*, III, 430.

91.HCD, 4th ser., CXLII, col. 465.

92.E. T. S. Dugdale, *German Diplomatic Documents*, III, 284.

93.*Ibid.*, pp. 289-91.

94.*Ibid.*, pp. 291-5.

95.*Jane's Fighting Ships*, 1914. pp. 118, 258.

96.Dugdale, III, 331-3.

97.*Ibid.*, pp. 335-40.

98.FO800/61.

99.FO800/93.

100.FO800/92.

101.Accounts and Papers, 1914, LIV, no. 137.

102.FO800/61.

103.FO800/62.

104.FO800/93.

105.FO800/62.

106.Grey of Falloden, *Twenty-five years*, I, 241-3.

107.Woodward, pp. 329-55.

108.BDD, pp. 133-4.

109.Marder, *Fear God*, II, 22-3.

110.Dagobert Broh, *Hardinge, the Tirpitz Plan and Anglo-German Relations, 1906-1910*, pp.4, 73, 75.

111.*Jane's Fighting Ships*, 1914, pp. 116-132.

112.Herwig, p. 92.

113.Churchill, I, 197-199, 698-701.

Eight

The Agadir Crisis

The Agadir crisis of 1911 can be understood only in the light of events which
followed the Algeciras conference. That conference had ostensibly provided
conditions under which all countries had equal opportunity to carry on
business in Morocco and participate in competition for public works contracts
and concessions. The extent to which these provisions would enable Germans
to continue economic activity in Morocco would depend on the ability of
France to use her special position to control the Moroccan government.

The French were as eager as ever to get on with the task of taking over
Morocco. They expected that their many years of experience at stirring up
trouble there would enable them to find frequent opportunities for
intervention to preserve order.[1] The financial position of the sultan had by
this time become very precarious. His authority and his ability to collect taxes
had been undermined by abuses of the extraterritorial power exerted by
foreign nations.[2] With sixty percent of the customs duties earmarked for
repayment of the French loan of 1904, and with the customs offices in French
hands, he had no way of raising the money to pay an army to keep order in
his dominions. France was therefore in a strong position to exert pressure on
him to further increase French power.

The murder of a French citizen in Tangier on May 27, 1906, provided
the first occasion for French action. The French government blamed the
incident on anarchy in the Tangier region and quickly sent two cruisers to
Tangier to join the one already there. In accordance with the Franco-Spanish
agreement, Spain was notified of the intention to take this step and invited to
join in the demonstration if she wished to do so.[3] Apparently no landing was
necessary to clear up the anarchy.

A dispatch from August de Saint-Aulaire, the French chargé d'affaires at
Tangier, shows the view of French policy taken by other foreigners in

Morocco. He described the hostility of the Spanish newspapers in Tangier, which he said was shared by the organ of the English colony, *Mogreb el-Axa*. These papers repeated endlessly that France treated with the pretender to the sultan's throne, encouraged contraband arms and used *agents provocateurs* to stir up an anti-dynastic movement which would give France "a favourable opportunity to encroach cunningly on Moroccan territory." The French agreements with England and Spain were considered a menace to all non-French interests, and it was thought that whatever France gained would be lost to Europe.[4]

The next opportunity for French action came in November, 1906, when a brigand protected by the local governor, Raissouli, took control of the town of Arzila with twenty men. The band pillaged, raped and took Europeans hostage, according to the French account. The sultan called on the governor to curb these activities, which resulted in Raissouli's taking control of Arzila and then of nearby Tangier. The French note reported the multiplying of scenes of savagery at Tangier, with brawls, rifle-fire, beatings and sometimes killings. These events, together with the molestation of Europeans, were said to require the sending of a naval force to Tangier, in which project France and Spain would cooperate. The French representative in Morocco called the attention of the government to the possibility that an event which seriously threatened the safety of Europeans might oblige the warships to land a force to protect their nationals. This intimation that nothing had yet threatened the safety of Europeans gives an indication of the way events were exaggerated to justify strong French action.[5]

The British government, inspired by the French reports of disorder at Tangier, urged France and Spain to act more energetically to keep order. When Grey was told that France was considering a landing of forces at Tangier, he expressed himself as strongly favouring this move.[6] On November 15 Paul Cambon informed his chief of a report that England intended to send warships to demonstrate off the coast of Morocco. He warned that if France and Spain did not take action other powers would do so.[7]

The French operation was delayed, however, by the reluctance of Spain to take part in the naval demonstration. The French view was that the Spanish representatives in Morocco had been instructed to act as if there was no need for energetic intervention. The problem was that France needed Spanish cooperation if she wanted her action "to maintain the character of a demonstration performed in the spirit of the Act of Algeciras."[8]

Spain was finally induced to collaborate with France, and the Spanish ship *Princes de Asturias* left for Tangier on December 1. By December 4, France and Spain had prepared a note to send to the signatory Powers of the Act of Algeciras concerning a landing at Tangier. This note informed the

Powers that recent events at Tangier were "of a nature to make foreigners fear that their security is not adequately guaranteed." It continued,

> *If the situation should worsen to the point where more serious disorders would result, the organization of the police, provided for in the Act of Algeciras, would appear to be urgently required, and France and Spain would have to take measures to expedite the organization under the conditions accepted by the Powers which took part in the Conference.*[9]

This reveals, again, that nothing had yet happened which seriously menaced foreigners, and also that the purpose of the operation was to intimidate the sultan, and in particular to force him to organize the police forces which France and Spain were to instruct.

The French and Spanish naval forces arrived at Tangier on December 8 and 12 respectively.[10] Unfortunately, their arrival coincided with the decision of the sultan to send a military force to keep order at Tangier, which was reported on December 10.[11] *The Times* carried a series of reports throughout December, usually headlined "The Anarchy in Morocco," although few of them actually described the "anarchy." As the sultan's troops approached Tangier, *The Times's* reports took the view that his troops would be unable to control the situation, and that they seemed to be afraid to take on the local governor.[12] By December 26 the sultan's army had improved greatly, and on the following day the sultan deposed Raissouli without a battle.[13]

The Times's report from Paris supplied a footnote to the operation when it mentioned a widespread belief in Tangier that the sultan had acted "to prove the futility of a police force organized by foreigners." The dispatch concluded, "The Franco-Spanish police force must be organized before the Franco-Spanish ships can withdraw."[14]

Anti-French feeling grew rapidly as the French pushed to extend their control, and another incident soon opened the way for a further French advance. The establishment of dispensaries staffed by French doctors, begun by Delcassé, aroused great hostility, because the doctors were suspected of poisoning local inhabitants. When a Dr. Mauchamp at Marrakech erected a pole and some cables on the roof of his house, the people thought it was a telegraph system for communication with the French on the coast. Although Mauchamp offered to remove the pole, he was attacked by a mob and murdered.[15]

This was the signal for which French general Louis Lyautey had been waiting. On March 29, 1907, French forces occupied Oudjda, an old and important city on the Moroccan side of the internationally recognized frontier, where they remained until the completion of the conquest of Morocco, despite frequent promises to leave. This was the first beach-head for French expansion into the northern zone of the frontier, which now went forward continuously.[16]

The French government notified Spain of its intention to occupy Oudjda and to remain until the sultan fulfilled all his engagements to France, particularly until he put into force the agreements about organizing the police in the frontier region. Spain was assured that this was not a step on the road to Fez and that in any case it did not affect Spain as Oudjda was not in her zone.[17]

The French blamed the khalifa of Marrakech for inciting the population against France and demanded his arrest and trial. They also pointed once again to the anarchy into which Morocco had fallen and insisted on the organization of the frontier police without further delay.[18] The sultan's advisors, the *Maghzen*, agreed to all the French demands for satisfaction in regard to Dr. Mauchamp's murder, but still failed to enter into negotiations for the organization of the police.[19]

The crucial events which sealed the fate of Morocco and led directly to its incorporation in the French empire took place at Casablanca at the end of July, 1907. A French company had obtained a concession to construct harbour works at Casablanca, and to provide stone to the harbour they ran a railway to a nearby quarry. The Moors in the neighbourhood, already alarmed by the progress of French influence, feared that this railroad further threatened their independence. In addition, the line skirted a Moorish cemetery near the town, where the blowing of the train's whistle was considered an insult to the dead.[20]

On July 28, representatives of the eleven tribes of the surrounding district, the Chaouia, called on the district governor, Ben Bouzid, and demanded the stopping of the harbour works and the dismissal of the French customs officials. The governor, a weakling, neither acceded to the demands of the tribesmen nor excluded them from the town, with fatal results to both the railway workmen and the independence of Morocco.[21] Two days later a group of tribesmen attacked the workmen on the railway and murdered those who were unable to hide or escape. The official French report put the number of those killed at eight, of whom five were French, two Italian and one Spanish.[22]

The French had long been hoping for an excuse to land troops on the Atlantic coast of Morocco. Since naval demonstrations and incursions from Algeria had failed to bring the sultan to heel, it was obvious that stronger measures were needed to induce him to accept French overlordship.[23] Without waiting for instructions from Paris, the chargé d'affaires at Tangier, Saint-Aulaire, immediately ordered the cruiser *Galilée* to proceed to Casablanca to safeguard the lives of Frenchmen and other foreigners. He informed the French government of this move and urged that France should act quickly by sending an expeditionary force to protect the Europeans before another power could intervene.[24] At the same time he took steps to preclude a

German protest by spreading rumours that German agents had fomented the trouble at Casablanca.[25]

The French cabinet decided to send a naval force and a battalion and a half of troops to occupy Casablanca, organize the police force and repress the tribes in the neighbourhood. Spain was to be asked to take part in this action.[26] Pichon informed the German ambassador that French and Spanish troops would disembark to protect foreigners and maintain order, but without any intention "to invade the Sherifian Empire to any extent."[27]

Meanwhile, an uncle of the sultan, Moulay el-Amin, who was camped nearby with 700 men, took charge of the town, expelled the tribesmen and established peace and quiet. He arrested thirty of those involved in the murder of the railway workers and expressed his willingness to hand them over for trial and punishment. From August 1 to August 4 the town was completely quiet.[28]

The French still intended, however, to land an army to take control of the town and pacify the countryside. They had no intention of allowing the restoration of order by Moorish authorities to foil them once again. Spain refused at first to take part in the French action, on the ground that both the occupation of the city and the organization of a police force composed of Frenchmen and Spaniards were contrary to the Act of Algeciras. By August 8, 1907, Spain had agreed to cooperate by sending troops to Casablanca, but only a small detachment of 400 men, sufficient to police the town, was actually sent.[29]

Meanwhile, before the French could arrive in sufficient force to establish complete control, the French cruiser *Galilée* arrived off Casablanca, with officers and crew thirsting to avenge the murder of their compatriots. Commander Ollivier agreed, on the advice of the foreign consuls, not to attempt a landing with the inadequate forces at his disposal, because it would likely result in the massacre of the Europeans. Angry and mutinous, his crew waited impatiently for the signal which would allow them to bombard the town.[30]

On August 4, the officers on the *Galilée*, believing that the main French force would arrive the next morning, sent word to the French vice-consul that they would land at 5:00 A.M. on the 5th. When the defenders of the consulate saw three boatloads of sailors leaving the *Galilée*, they assumed that this was an advance party sent to clear the way for the main force. As the French squadron had not in fact arrived, the landing of the party from the *Galilée* produced exactly the result the consuls had feared. The Moorish soldiers at the city gate, who had not been informed of Ollivier's intention, attempted to close the gate when the sailors appeared. When the sailors forced the gate fighting broke out, with the result that the French party killed not only the

Moorish soldiers in their way but everyone in the street between the gate and the consulate including about sixty men, women and children.[31]

On the arrival of the landing party at the French consulate, the signal was given for the *Galilée* to bombard the town. The bombardment continued for three hours, sparing only the area of the foreign consulates. On the first shot the tribesmen invaded the town and began an orgy of pillage and slaughter directed mainly against Europeans and Jews. During the forenoon the French cruiser *Du Chyala* and the Spanish cruiser *Alvarada de Bazan* arrived with reinforcements of about ninety men, who assisted in the defence of the consulates. The nights of August 5 and 6 saw determined attacks on the consulates by such large numbers as to place them in serious danger, which was relieved only by the arrival of the French squadron on the afternoon of the 7th. The French troops brought the town under control within a few hours, and the marauding Arabs disappeared, not to return until August 18.[32]

"The real slaughter, however, had only begun."[33] The French force, composed of Senegalese tirailleurs and foreign legionnaires, proceeded to complete the blood bath and looting the Arabs had begun. The legionnaires ran amok, killing everyone who remained alive and looting everything that was left to steal. Strong measures were necessary to bring them under control.

On August 6, a French dispatch to all the European capitals announced the landing at Casablanca and the bombardment of the previous day. As usual, it stressed the urgency of organizing the police force in the ports for the protection of Europeans. The message also declared that France would scrupulously respect the integrity of Morocco and the sovereignty of the sultan and that order, security and commercial freedom would be guaranteed.[34] Germany immediately agreed both to the correctness of the French action and on the necessity of organizing the police.[35]

General Drude, in command of the French expedition, was instructed to maintain the role of protecting the Europeans assigned to France by the Act of Algeciras.[36] Once a French army had established itself in western Morocco, however, the enthusiasts on the spot were inspired to take the bit in their teeth. The French government, curbed by a Chamber of Deputies whose majority consistently opposed an aggressive policy, wished to preserve at least a semblance of compliance with the act. Their agents in Morocco, accustomed to acting in the absence of, or even in defiance of, instructions from Paris, wanted to push forward towards the conquest of Morocco.

Arab attacks on the French army at Casablanca began on August 18. Within ten days General Drude realized that it was useless to remain passive in the face of such elusive foes and decided that he must take the offensive. Unfortunately, just as the Arabs were unable to adapt to the French method of warfare, the French army was incapable of changing its tactics to counter the Arab style. Only their crushing superiority in fire-power enabled the French eventually to gain the upper hand. Drude undertook several adroitly devised forays, but succeeded only in producing casualties on both sides without ever coming to grips with the enemy.[37] The failure of his third sortie brought orders from Paris to remain at Casablanca, where the French army stayed for three months.[38]

Meanwhile, great events were taking place in the south, where the acquisition of European weapons had made it possible for one of the local chiefs, Madani el-Glaoui, to establish a position of predominant power. Realizing that the failure of Abd el-Aziz to control the country or resist French encroachments had made him so unpopular that he could not remain as sultan, Madani decided to create a sultan of his own. He fixed on Moulay Hafid, pasha of Marrakech and half-brother of Abd el-Aziz. On August 16, 1907, Moulay Hafid was proclaimed sultan at Marrakech.[39]

Moulay Hafid's cause soon triumphed throughout southern Morocco and his army began to move into the Chaouia. As the rebels advanced, Abd el-Aziz took refuge at Rabat where he expected to be protected by the French. By December, 1907, a Hafidist army was encamped at Settat, fifteen miles from Casablanca.[40] On January 7, 1908, Moulay Hafid was proclaimed sultan of Fez, uniting the Moroccans in declaring a holy war against the infidel.[41]

The French government now decided it was necessary to occupy the Chaouia and a new commander, General Albert d'Amade, was chosen for the task. General Amade, however, with 14,000 men under his command, was no more successful than Drude had been in pinning down the elusive Arabs. Five failed expeditions in five weeks convinced premier Clemenceau that another change of leadership was called for, and he summoned General Lyautey from Algeria. Lyautey refused to replace Amade, but agreed to inquire into his conduct of the war. Amade finally learned his lesson and adopted a scorched earth policy which brought the fighting in the Chaouia to an end. He had captured Settat on two previous occasions, but orders from Paris had prevented him from holding it: in mid-March he occupied it for the third time and remained.[42]

Moulay Hafid now turned his attention to the final overthrow of Abd el-Aziz, who retained control only of the area where he was protected by the French army. Abd el-Aziz insisted that, since his troubles were caused by the reforms imposed on him by France, the French should support him by military intervention. The French government, however, concerned that interference in a civil war would invite international complications, instructed Amade to avoid supporting Abd el-Aziz.[43]

By the end of March, 1908, Spain, believing quite correctly that the military conquest of Morocco had begun and determined not to be left behind, sent an army to occupy part of the zone allotted to her by the partition agreement. Eugenio Regnault, French representative at Tangier, thought

Spain should have secured French assent to its action in accordance with their agreement, and advised that she should be warned about the diplomatic difficulties she was courting.[44] Spain, however, refused to be misled by French protestations of innocence and continued to push forward until by the fall of 1909 more than 30,000 Spanish troops were engaged.[45]

On May 19, instructions to General Amade, repeated to all European capitals, directed him to occupy the Chaouia until indigenous forces could take over. The German reply to this was to insist on the evacuation of Morocco by French troops as soon as possible. The kaiser's perceptive comment was, "The French do not dream of that." When Baron W. von Schoen, the German secretary of state for foreign affairs, inquired about evacuation, Stephen Pichon, minister of foreign affairs, told him it might be more or less than a year, but it would take place as soon as possible.[46]

It was now apparent to everyone that Abd el-Aziz was almost at the end of his rope. The French colonialists in Morocco, however, believing that his downfall would be a defeat for France, continued to support him. General Lyautey protested against both the evacuation of the Chaouia and the recognition of Moulay Hafid: France must keep the Chaouia for security and maintain Abd el-Aziz as a competitor to Hafid. General Amade, with the connivance of others on the spot, aided the sultan with his forces, in defiance of specific orders to the contrary from Paris.[47]

As Moulay Hafid took control of more and more of Morocco, German businessmen began to complain that French policy was destroying their trade. Although France expressed her willingness to recognize Moulay Hafid as early as May 28, 1908, French procrastination, together with Amade's use of French troops to assist Abd el-Aziz, led the Germans to suspect that France was delaying recognition in order to extort special conditions which would extend her control.[48] For some time Baron Schoen acquiesced in French policy, agreeing early in July that all the Powers should act together on the question of recognition.[49] By the end of August, however, German patience came to an end and the German government authorized the sending of a consul to Fez to deal with Moulay Hafid. Schoen advised the French of this move and declared that it had no political purpose. His note specifically stated that Germany considered that the Powers should now proceed to recognize Moulay Hafid, thus indicating that the German step did not constitute recognition. Nevertheless, France suspected that it was Germany who now sought a special position with Moulay Hafid.[50]

By September 11, after more than two months of discussion, France and Spain produced a proposal setting forth the terms on which the Powers should recognize Moulay Hafid. These were that he should declare adherence to the Act of Algeciras, accept all treaties and arrangements made with the Powers by the previous government, assume responsibility for the damage caused at Casablanca, and stop the holy war.[51] Germany agreed to these terms with the qualifications that the representations should be made by the diplomatic corps at Tangier and that the new sultan should be required to accept only those previous treaties and arrangements which conformed to the Act of Algeciras. Although the act had specifically stated that prior treaties contrary to its provisions should be invalid, France objected to both these qualifications, but particularly the second. The French feared that Germany hoped to persuade Moulay Hafid to ask for a delimitation of the frontier between Morocco and Algeria, which would prevent them from sending troops into Morocco at will. In the end, Germany agreed to the Franco-Spanish programme, evidently realizing that there was no prospect of persuading France to observe this, or indeed any other, clause of the Act of Algeciras.[52] This agreement cleared the way for the recognition of Moulay Hafid, which finally took place on December 16, 1908.

Moulay Hafid's agreement to end the *jihad*, accept the Act of Algeciras, and yield to the other French demands was forced on him by France's increasing military and financial control of the country. The French advance on the eastern frontier had continued in the summer of 1908, until it had assumed a significance comparable to that of the invasion of the Chaoiua. A great battle involving fifteen or twenty thousand Moroccans had been fought at Boudenib, "a major event in France's conquest of Morocco." Paris agreed that the occupation of Boudenib would be only temporary, but her army paid no attention to this, and turned it into a strategic centre whose protection required further advances west and north.[53]

While these stirring events were taking place, Germany had been trying to arrange for Franco-German economic cooperation in Morocco. On June 20, 1907, August de Saint-Aulaire, the French chargé d'affaires at Tangier, reported that the German representative at Tangier had proposed an agreement for joint enterprises. These would be submitted for tender where required, but Germany would agree not to enter into competition with France. The proposal that these joint enterprises were to be undertaken on a basis of equality was unacceptable to France.[54] Stephen Pichon stated to Jules Cambon that France would not object in principle to eventual economic association with Germany in Morocco, but that she could only treat with Germany in affairs in which England and Spain refused to take part. France must be careful, however, not to increase German interests to a point which would justify political intervention.[55]

Another dispatch from Saint-Aulaire on July 23 told of renewed German proposals for an agreement. Although the German representative offered a pledge that Germany had no political aims, and would reduce her representation in Morocco from an embassy to a chargé d'affaires, Saint-Aulaire was very suspicious. He thought the Germans must be trying to find an excuse for political interference. When, in January, 1909, Moulay Hafid asked Germany for a loan of military instructors, Germany refused the request and informed the French government. Nevertheless, the French could not be persuaded, despite repeated German insistence for more than three years, that all Germany wanted was to protect her business interests in Morocco.[56]

The negotiations for an agreement on economic cooperation dragged on until February 9, when an accord was finally signed. Meanwhile the Moroccan civil war almost destroyed commerce and delayed public works projects.

In the light of the events of 1907 and 1908, the accord of 1909 appears as something of a joke. It stated that France was firmly attached to the integrity and independence of the Sherifian Empire, large parts of which were occupied by French and Spanish troops. It also declared that France was resolved to safeguard economic equality, not to hinder German commercial and industrial interests and that the nationals of the two countries would join in the operation of concessions. Germany, again declaring that she pursued only economic interests in Morocco, recognized the special political interests of France and their importance in maintaining peace and order, and promised not to interfere in these interests.[57]

This Franco-German agreement was destined to have few practical results. No joint venture was ever undertaken, and the economic clauses remained a dead letter. The Moroccan government was unable to finance any public works because its revenues were almost completely in the hands of France. France also attempted to exclude railways from the operation of the accord on the ground that those proposed were military lines. The exploitation of mining resources was blocked by disputes over the claims of the German Mannesmann brothers to some mineral deposits.[58] Frequent changes of government in France prevented the development of a consistent policy.[59]

When the German government tried to open negotiations on the economic application of the accord, Pichon agreed with Paul Cambon that there was no reason for government involvement and that the accord meant only that the two governments would not hinder Franco-German joint enterprise. Instructions to this effect were sent to the French embassy in Berlin, and Sir Edward Grey was informed at the same time that nothing would be done to interfere with France's previous agreements.[60]

Conversations on Morocco nevertheless took place in Berlin, and on June 2, 1909, the German embassy in Paris delivered an *aide-mémoire* on the subject. The first two sections dealt with the Moroccan debt and the proposed loan: Germany agreed substantially with French proposals, but expressed the view that the loan should include a sum of twelve million francs for the execution of public works. In this regard, the German note pointed out that works in progress at Larache had been promised to German entrepreneurs before the Algeciras conference and that these did not come under the act. It suggested that the cost of 6,300,000 francs should be a first charge on the proposed loan of twelve million, and promised to ensure that the German entrepreneurs would offer French capitalists participation in these works. Works at Casablanca would be under French control, but Franco-German cooperation was suggested at Tangier.[61]

Three months later France submitted a reply which agreed with the German proposals almost entirely, but the Moroccan loan made no provision for expenditures on public works so nothing could be done. By October the German press was insisting that the accord was an illusion, and on January 22, 1910, no understanding had yet been reached between French and German industrialists.[62]

Thus, at the time of the French decision to occupy Fez, Germany had made no headway in her efforts to achieve some measure of Franco-German cooperation either in Morocco or elsewhere in Africa. The disinclination of France to collaborate in any way with Germany is evident in the French documents throughout the period. Although Germany undertook no political initiatives in Morocco, her repeated assurances that her interests there were purely economic failed to alleviate French suspicion that her professions concealed political and territorial aims.

Meanwhile, France had been bringing Morocco more and more completely under her control. By 1910 French authority had been extended to almost all of Morocco east of the Moulaya River, which was about half-way between the Algerian border and Fez.[63] Civil war had made the collection of taxes more difficult, and Moulay Hafid could not raise the money to carry on his government, to say nothing of paying the huge indemnity demanded by France for her military expenses and the damage done at Casablanca. All the Powers concerned agreed that a new loan was needed to enable Morocco to meet the obligations Moulay Hafid had accepted.

France insisted, however, that certain conditions must be fulfilled before the granting of a loan. The principal matters of dispute concerned the French occupation of the eastern and Chaouia areas, where the sultan wanted an early withdrawal of French troops, while France insisted that her forces would leave only when they were replaced by native troops under French officers. It took several months to induce the sultan, by threats and persuasion, to consent to the French demands, but finally on March 1, 1910, the French government was able to announce that he had agreed to all the French terms.[64]

The accord signed by the sultan provided that France would evacuate the Chaouia when her army had been replaced by a Moroccan force of 1500 men and the military expenses of her occupation had been paid. On the Algerian frontier, French troops would evacuate some points when the sultan's cabinet, the *Maghzen*, had stationed 2000 troops there and France believed they could maintain order.[65]

The sultan's principal liabilities were 80 million francs owed to various creditors and 70 million francs due to France for the military expenses involved in occupying Moroccan territory. To meet these obligations and all other engagements of the *Maghzen*, a loan of 90 million francs was arranged. The loan bore interest at 5 percent and was to be paid by instalments over seventy-five years. It was guaranteed by the customs, the rent from the tobacco and sulphur monopoly, taxes on income and markets, revenues from the royal domain in the ports and part of the urban taxes.[66]

The sultan could not touch the proceeds of the loan as it was earmarked to pay off Morocco's previous debts. His only means of raising revenue to carry on his government was the exaction of tribute from the tribes by violence, which naturally produced resistance and soon another revolution. Having thus ensured that the sultan was so completely without resources that he had not the slightest chance of raising forces to police either the Chaouia or the Algerian frontier area, France was in no danger of having to break her promises regarding withdrawal, but could remain in these areas, as the colonialists had always intended she should do, without violating any agreement, except, of course, the Act of Algeciras. That act had now been reduced to a scrap of paper and Moulay Hafid was a helpless puppet in the hands of France.[67]

The curtain was about to rise on the last act of Delcassé's drama, "The Conquest of Morocco." By June, 1910, the new sultan was reported to be as unpopular as his predecessor. It was evident that he was unable to control the country or subdue the rebellious tribes and that French reorganization of his army was necessary if he was to be maintained. This was undertaken by Lieutenant-Colonel Émile Mangin, who attempted to impose French army discipline on the sultan's forces.[68]

The first task of the new army was to tame the rebellious Cherarda tribe and at the end of February, 1911, an expedition was undertaken for this purpose. As an operation to control the Cherarda, the campaign was a complete failure, but it succeeded in its more important object of drawing the sultan's army away from Fez in order to allow other tribes to besiege the capital, and thus give France a pretext for sending an expedition to save the city.[69] If this succeeded the French protectorate would be established.

In March, 1911, the French government sent reinforcements to Casablanca to defend the ports and assure security of commerce in the Chaouia region.[70] The Spanish government now assumed that France was about to take final control of Morocco, and protested against the French tendency to exclude Spain from Moroccan affairs and to obstruct her even in the Spanish zone. As Spain by then had 40,000 troops in Morocco, it was evident that she was determined not to be left behind.[71]

Early in April alarming reports began to come from the French representatives in Morocco, along with suggestions that a military expedition should be sent to Fez.[72] On April 4, Paul Cambon told Sir Arthur Nicolson that France might have to take military measures to protect Europeans at Fez. Nicolson gathered that one purpose might be to maintain the sultan on his throne. He said that if French troops were sent for that purpose "it was clear that they would never be able to leave the country."[73] The Spanish ambassador told Nicolson that "if France occupied Fez it was clear that she would remain there," that the sultan would be completely under French influence and that his independence would have vanished. In this case, Spain would occupy her own zone of Morocco.[74]

The most difficult task was to obtain the consent of the French cabinet for the occupation of Fez. It necessitated a press campaign to convince Paris and Europe that a critical situation in Fez endangered the lives of Europeans and that the fate of civilization in North Africa was at stake. Political manipulation was also needed to manoeuvre the French government into approving the colonialist programme, since neither the Chamber of Deputies nor French public opinion favoured the establishment of a protectorate. Alexandre Ribot, a deputy, generally a supporter of the government, opposed sending an expedition to Fez, arguing in the Chamber that the Algeciras act obliged France to preserve order on the coasts. He thought extending French police activity to the whole country would be equivalent to the conquest of Morocco.[75] The Russian ambassador, Alexandre Isvolsky, thought an expedition to Fez would be an event of European importance of which it would be impossible to foresee the consequences.[76]

The Paris press responded nobly with confused and contradictory reports of the situation at Fez, which nevertheless presented a frightful picture of the probable fate of the European colony. The press campaign depended not on the Act of Algeciras but on the right of the French government to come to the relief of French officers and foreigners in Fez.[77]

These French representations were supported only by England and even the British minister at Tangier, Lister, wavered in his adherence to the French view.[78] The German reports uniformly played down the danger to Europeans at Fez. On April 7, Alfred von Kiderlen-Wächter, the German foreign minister, told Jules Cambon that German news indicated that there was no imminent danger; on April 25, Chancellor Bethmann-Hollweg stated that according to his informants Europeans were not in danger, the price of food stuffs had not risen and the situation did not justify the emotional tone of the French dispatches.[79] Reports from Belgian representatives agreed with the German view. The Belgian consul reported that the life and interests of foreigners at Fez were not threatened and that no one was anxious about his fate. He thought the march of relief columns might put them in danger.[80] A dispatch from Tangier on April 25 informed Sir Edward Grey that British consul Macleod had reported that Fez was quiet on the 20th, and tension had been relieved by the arrival of grain and cattle.[81]

The furore in the French press, however, persuaded the government that France's duty was to save Fez at all costs. On April 23, 1911, the French cabinet, which had as yet authorized only the advance of Moroccan troops led by French officers, decided to send French troops to Fez. General Moinier, in command of these troops, was instructed to announce that France would not occupy new territory but was sending troops to support the sultan and rescue the endangered European colonies. The same dispatch called attention to the importance of getting the sultan to request the cooperation of French troops, while giving him the "most formal assurances" that France did not intend to extend her action beyond the task of relieving the foreign colonies and restoring order and the *Maghzen's* authority.[82] By the time Moulay Hafid was persuaded to request French troops, it was necessary to have him pre-date his letter to make it appear that France had sent troops because he had asked for them.[83]

A footnote to the comedy was supplied by a French publicist who described at length the false and contradictory press reports. He quoted one of the correspondents involved as writing that:

In truth, there had been some exaggeration, that in point of fact, at no moment had the safety of Fez and its inhabitants been seriously menaced; that the idea of a regular siege and of a sudden capture had been alike chimerical and that, moreover, so far as the provisioning of the place was concerned, he could reassure the most timorous that there was sufficient corn in the city to feed the whole population, plus the expeditionary column, for more than a year.[84]

Everyone in Europe understood that, once installed in Fez, the French would never leave and that the French protectorate was in the process of being established. Kiderlen-Wächter's reaction to the French circular was to inform Jules Cambon in Berlin that, if the French remained there and the sultan's power was maintained by French bayonets, Germany would consider that the Act of Algeciras was being violated. She would claim her freedom to act in accordance with her treaty rights.[85]

The Spanish government, which understandably believed that the real French programme was embodied in the Franco-Spanish agreement of October, 1904, assumed from the outset that France was undertaking the completion of the conquest of Morocco. On April 29, the Spanish minister of state handed the French ambassador a letter which quoted the 1904 accord as saying that Spain could exercise freedom of action in her zone "if the weakness of the Government and its persistent inability to keep order" made the maintenance of the *status quo* impossible. The letter asserted that this condition now existed and that therefore Spain would assume liberty of action in her zone.[86]

The French, in accordance with their usual policy of attempting to sow discord between England and Germany, pretended to think that the Spanish reaction was being instigated by Germany. The British ambassador in Madrid saw no reason to believe that this was the case, and in fact the German reaction to the French march to Fez was much more moderate than that of Spain.[87]

Sir Edward Grey was, of course, happy to see the French taking control in Morocco in accordance with the Anglo-French agreement. Publicly, however, he felt it necessary to pretend that the French were acting in accordance with the Act of Algeciras. On May 2, 1911, he told parliament that the French were going to Fez "at the urgent request of the sultan" and that their action was "not intended to alter the political status of Morocco."[88] Later in May he stated that the French "had no choice but to relieve Fez with the least possible delay" and that they were there "to safeguard the lives of the Europeans at Fez" and "to uphold the sovereignty of the sultan."[89] He thought the French would retire when order was restored.

General Moinier arrived in Fez with French troops on May 21 and after settling there requested reinforcements.[90] He met no resistance on his arrival and found the European colonies completely safe and sound.[91] The French government continued to issue a stream of assurances that the occupation would be temporary and that France's purpose was simply to restore the sultan's prestige and establish order. Sir Francis Bertie, who was ready to believe anything the French told him, was alone in taking these effusions at their face value.[92]

By June 1, Grey thought that the French had "enormously strengthened their position in Morocco" and that Spain would have to be given something substantial to keep her quiet. Nine days later he wrote to Bertie:

I am afraid the French have got too deeply in to get out and they will have to go through with a partition of Morocco, in which there will be some difficult and rough water to navigate and some price to be paid.[93]

He was right. On June 22, Jules Cambon reported an important conversation with Kiderlen-Wächter, who said that the sultan was becoming a French puppet and that France was in the process of establishing a protectorate. Cambon replied that if Kiderlen-Wächter, who had expressed interest in Mogador, a port on the west coast of Morocco, wanted part of Morocco, negotiations were useless and added: "One can look elsewhere."[94]

Kiderlen-Wächter said: "You want us to get out of Morocco. Well! if we consent to disinterest ourselves politically from Morocco you must give us something in return. A rectification of frontier in equatorial Africa, or a slice of your Congo, or something of that description."[95] "You must tell us what you want," he added. Cambon had no instructions, but offered to discuss the matter with his government when he went to Paris and suggested that meanwhile Kiderlen-Wächter should think about what Germany wanted. Kiderlen-Wächter's last words were, "Bring us back something from Paris," to which Cambon responded, "I will try."[96]

Cambon arrived in Paris on June 23, 1911, and reported to the foreign ministry the next morning, only to find another change of cabinet which made Justin de Selves the new foreign minister. Before Selves had taken any action on Cambon's report he was faced with the news, presented to him by the German ambassador on July 1, that Germany had sent a warship to Agadir. The stated reason for this action was that some German firms in the vicinity, alarmed by unrest among the tribes, had applied to the German government for protection for their lives and property. The German note declared that when quiet was restored in Morocco the ship would leave Agadir.[97]

Germany's decision to send the *Panther* to Agadir was not a hasty action intended to complicate the negotiations with France. Kiderlen-Wächter had designed this policy early in May when it was already apparent that France was about to take control of Morocco. He reasoned that the French would establish themselves permanently in Fez, that this would mark the final collapse of the Act of Algeciras and that freedom to pursue their own interests would be restored to the signatory Powers. Germany would gain nothing by protesting and should therefore look for an objective which would induce the French to compensate her. If the French remained at Fez, Germany would also have the right to protect her compatriots and could send ships to Mogador and Agadir, where there were large German firms. In possession of this pledge Germany could wait to see if France would offer compensation in her colonial possessions, in return for which Germany would abandon the two ports.[98]

It has been argued that, because negotiations were already in progress, the sending of the *Panther* to Agadir was a brutal act essentially unrelated to the negotiations but designed to intimidate France. If one ignores the whole previous history of the Moroccan affair this criticism is justified, but no one acquainted with French policy over the preceding seven years could suppose that France had any serious intention of conceding substantial compensation to Germany if it could be avoided. The Germans naturally believed that if possible France would prolong the negotiations until she could present Germany with a *fait accompli* which would relieve her of the necessity of making any concessions whatever. No one familiar with the history of French delay, equivocation and obstruction during the three years 1908-11 could doubt the accuracy of this opinion. K.H. Jarausch, in his book *The Enigmatic Chancellor* tells us that the German foreign office "correctly assumed" that Germany would get nothing from France without seizing a trump.[99] Kiderlen-Wächter had already decided that pressure must be exerted to bring about a settlement before it was too late.[100]

It should be noted that already on May 3, Kiderlen-Wächter had been ready to abandon Morocco in return for compensation elsewhere. If he at one time mentioned acquiring Mogador as compensation for being shut out of Morocco this was without the authority of his government, which had always expressly repudiated the desire to obtain Moroccan territory. He could never have secured Wilhelm II's consent for such a project.

The man best acquainted with the Franco-German negotiations of the preceding three years was Jules Cambon, the French ambassador in Berlin. On July 6, in a dispatch to Joseph Caillaux, the French finance minister, he mentioned German complaints that they had been unable to bring the talks they had with France to a conclusion. "The obstacles we have opposed to them," he continued, "have persuaded them that there is no use making economic agreements with us on Morocco and that, in consequence, equal treatment of their economic interests will be menaced if our domination is established. They no longer believe in our good faith."[101]

On July 10, Jules Cambon reported Kiderlen-Wächter's complaints about France's failure to respect her engagements on economic matters contained in the agreement of February, 1909. Kiderlen-Wächter said France had seized every advantage but had not given Germany even the limited guarantees she had asked for her industry. Cambon's comment was, "This observation corresponds with the fears I had expressed before on this subject to your Excellency's predecessor."[102] In a covering letter he said: "I attribute the Agadir action to several causes. The first is the undeniable deception which has led to the failure of M. de Kiderlen's proposals on the subject of the Moroccan railways." He pointed out that he had sent many letters warning against a renewed offensive by Germany and against the negligence with which the French government treated economic questions.[103] To his brother Paul, the French ambassador in London, Cambon wrote that he had "foreseen the Agadir affair for six months."[104]

Once again, as with the kaiser's landing at Tangier, the French were not alarmed by the "*Panther's* spring." They understood that Germany desired an agreement with France which would clear up the Morocco question.[105] Selves received the news of the dispatch of the ship calmly, evidently not yet realizing that the German action had created a crisis. On July 3, 1911, George Grahame, in a letter to Sir William Tyrrell, Grey's private secretary, wrote that Selves's visit to Holland on that day indicated that the French did not take the matter too seriously. He thought the French felt that they had no strong argument against the German move, as they had themselves "played fast and loose with the spirit of the Act of Algeciras." French policy in Morocco, he said, had been "a tissue of sophisms and hypocricies."[106] On July 5, Raymond Poincaré gave a speech calling for a frank, straightforward policy founded on treaties with other nations, which he said would soon cause the clouds to disappear.[107]

Historian K. H. Jarausch maintains that the sending of a ship to Morocco was a "dangerous plan" because the British were disturbed by the possibility of a German port on the Atlantic coast, and that European opinion was shocked and outraged.[108] Grey's later pronouncements show that the British were not particularly concerned about the possible establishment of Germany in Morocco.

It might be worthwhile to ask the critics of German policy what Germany should or could have done, short of acquiescing in the French destruction of the Act of Algeciras. Germany would have been within her legal rights to demand a return to the *status quo*, but "France could no more have evacuated Morocco without national humiliation than Germany could have accepted defeat and retired beaten from the diplomatic field without humiliation."[109] If Germany had wanted war, she would either have demanded a return to the Algeciras act and thus the withdrawal of French and Spanish troops from Morocco, or she would have sent a squadron of warships, landed troops, and done at Agadir what France and Spain had done elsewhere, with as much justification as they had.[110] What made the sending of the *Panther* a "dangerous policy" was simply the determination of the British foreign office to pick a quarrel with Germany if she attempted to protect her rights. The shock and outrage were largely confined to the British foreign office and *The Times*. A *Westminster Gazette* editorial on July 3 was headed "The Expected." The *Gazette* thought the "incident" was "intrinsically unimportant" and meant only that Germany was putting in a claim to be considered, which she had every right to do.[111] Arthur Ponsonby, a Liberal M.P., pointed out in Parliament that England had seen Russian troops pour into Persia, Italy seize Tripoli, French troops go to Fez and had made no protest. "But immediately a German man-of-war goes to Agadir we are told that we are on the eve of a very great crisis."[112] The response of the foreign office to the *Panther's* arrival was simply its usual reflex reaction to any attempt by Germany to protect her rights or to further her trading interests anywhere.

Only when it became apparent that the British foreign office was eager to confront Germany did the French decide that they could take advantage of this to force the Germans to accept a smaller compensation. As early as May 18 French foreign minister J.M. Cruppi had spoken to Bertie about a "supposed German changed attitude if the French troops should remain more than a brief period at Fez," although the German government had already informed him what their attitude would be in that case.[113] The French now saw that some judicious misinformation would enable them to use the British to their own profit.

Grey was much more excited about the German communication than were the French. He called a meeting of the cabinet, which was told that the German case was that France and Spain had by their action created a new situation which made it necessary for Germany, France and Spain to rearrange matters à trois. The cabinet agreed that France and Spain had given Germany a plausible excuse for regarding the Algeciras arrangement as at an end. It was decided, however, that in view of England's commercial interests and treaty obligations, Grey should tell the German ambassador that England could not allow the future of Morocco to be settled behind her back and that any negotiations must be à quatre rather than à trois. Grey was also authorized to tell the French ambassador that England would be loyal to her treaty obligations, but wanted to know what suggestions the French government wished to put forward. They must recognize that their action had made a return to the status quo difficult if not impossible and that it might be necessary "to give a more definite recognition than before to German interests in Morocco." The cabinet also cited the British interests which must be safeguarded as follows: no German fort on the Mediterranean shore; no new fortified port anywhere on the Morocco coast; the Open Door for British trade.[114]

Why should the British government have supposed that any of these interests was threatened? The German communication had stated that the Panther would leave Agadir as soon as the situation returned to normal.

It should be noted that the German government made no mention of negotiations with Spain, that no such negotiations were under way and that France and Germany had no intention of including Spain in their discussions.[115] All the suggestions that Spain should take part in the Franco-German conversations came from Spanish representatives, who were obviously eager to have a hand in the matter.[116] Count Paul von Metternich, the German ambassador in London, had been instructed by his government to draw attention to the changed conditions in Morocco resulting from French and Spanish actions and to assert that these actions made the possibility of a return to the status quo ante doubtful. Germany therefore would be prepared to seek a final understanding with France on the Moroccan question, which should be possible in view of the good relations existing between Germany and France. Metternich had spoken to Nicolson who in his minute to Grey evidently transposed the mention of Spain as one of the Powers engaged in military operations into the part of Metternich's remarks which dealt with the Franco-German negotiations.[117] Paul Cambon had an opportunity on July 4 to disabuse Grey of the idea that Spain was to be included in the negotiations, but he failed to do so.[118]

When Grey saw Metternich on July 4, he told him that the British government was "of the opinion that a new situation had been created by the dispatch of a German ship to Agadir." This was a misrepresentation of the cabinet's position, as its report to the king shows that it clearly understood that the new situation had been created by France and Spain.

Count Metternich disputed Grey's contention, but evidently did not realize its full significance. Grey dictated his interpretation of the cabinet's decision to him, but observed that "he must take this as a conversation, not as a written communication."[119] To Grey's statement that England was an interested party and could not recognize any arrangement which was come to without her participation, Metternich merely replied that the German government would understand that it was natural for England to take an interest. Metternich had been instructed that in case England decided to take active measures, he should say that events in Morocco had made it necessary to safeguard German interests and Germany would understand if England decided to do likewise. In his conversation with Grey Metternich thought the British government had not decided on active intervention and therefore did not carry out these instructions.[120]

Sir Edward Grey's attitude should have warned Metternich, and through him the German government, that he intended to seize the opportunity for a confrontation with Germany and that it was necessary to take every precaution to thwart this intention. Although the German government no doubt believed that their original dispatch had explained the situation, it would have been wiser if they had followed it with more specific assurances. Whether anything they could have done would have quieted British foreign office suspicions is questionable, but they might at least have deprived Grey of the argument that they had ignored him.

The foreign office reaction was the result of two causes, in both of which the sinister influence of Eyre Crowe in that office is readily apparent. There was first the rooted antipathy to Germany, which made rational understanding almost impossible. Little in the way of balanced judgment could be expected from a foreign office which viewed with equanimity the spectacle of nearly 100,000 French and Spanish troops engaged in the conquest of Morocco but decried the "ruthless aggression" which sent a 1000-ton gunboat with a complement of 125 men to anchor off the Moroccan coast. No doubt the danger to Germans in the Agadir hinterland was as unreal as the peril to Europeans which had taken the French to Fez: the German action was, however, an insignificant gesture in comparison with the extensive military operations being carried on by France. In his speech to

Parliament on July 6 Herbert Asquith, the prime minister, took the line the cabinet had authorized and merely stated that a new situation had arisen, not that Germany had created it.[121]

The second irritant for the British foreign office was distrust of France and suspicion of her loyalty to the Triple Entente. On March 15, 1911, Crowe appended a minute to a note from Jules Cambon in which he discussed Franco-German negotiations for a syndicate to build railways in Morocco. Crowe described this as a violation of the Act of Algeciras, which required public tenders for such works. He considered these negotiations "a more flagrant example of the vicious policy which the French government are pursuing," in the course of which they were prepared "to make important political bargains with Germany at our expense." He thought France should be warned that this would lead to an estrangement between France and England. This was, of course, the usual reaction of any member of the entente when one of the others indicated a desire to live at peace with Germany.[122] This view is reflected in Grey's statement to Parliament in November that British intervention was necessary to prevent "the other nations of Europe from being brought into the orbit of a single diplomacy."[123]

When the sending of the *Panther* to Agadir was announced Crowe at once assumed that Germany must have decided to go to war with France and England "before embarking on a policy of aggression." He thought the danger of war depended on Germany feeling she could succeed, and suggested that the British government should refrain "from giving to Germany any clear indication of their real view or of the attitude they may have to adopt." Grey and Nicolson agreed.[124] Crowe's reaction is puzzling, as it seems evident that if the Germans had wanted war they would have demanded a return to the *status quo* of the Algeciras act, which would have been quite within their rights but which the French could not have accepted without suffering a disastrous diplomatic defeat.

By July 17, 1911, Crowe confessed to being "altogether nonplussed" by German policy, and could not understand what Germany was driving at. He thought the original German purpose had been frustrated by England's attitude, that Germany had to adopt a new course and that she now couldn't explain either to France or to herself what she wanted. Again Nicolson and Grey agreed.[125] In fact, it is as clear as crystal that Germany's aim was exactly what it had been for seven years—to persuade France to recognize her legal claim to equality in Morocco in accordance with her treaty rights, or to grant her the compensation which England, Spain and Italy had already received. Anti-German prejudice had so blinded the British foreign office to reality that they had become the captives of their own deceptions.

The foreign office finally determined that the real purpose of the German action was to disrupt the Anglo-French entente. This idea was put forward by Crowe as early as July 4, when he remarked that the German government intended to make use of the good Anglo-German relations they supposed existed to detach England from France.[126] Nicolson had the same idea.[127] Selves encouraged this English view, although he knew very well that it was nonsense. On July 9, Bertie reported that Selves was "quite aware that the German coup at Agadir is for the purpose of testing the solidity of the Entente between England and France."[128] Crowe thought on July 15 that Germany was making "a determined bid for a Franco-German coalition against England."[129]

A memorandum penned by Crowe on January 14, 1912, pretended to clear away all doubts about the aims of German policy. The German objective, which was to destroy the Anglo-French entente, was shared by Joseph Caillaux, who wanted France to join the Triple Alliance. Caillaux, according to this account, had already promised Germany the whole Congo, and the *Panther* was sent to Agadir to strengthen his hand. When public opinion prevented him from keeping his word, Caillaux pretended that British opposition had made it impossible to give Germany the Congo, thus turning German wrath against England.[130] Caillaux's crime was that he preferred conciliation of Germany to war. There were many in both France and England who agreed with him, but unfortunately they were unable to make their view prevail.

As the British foreign office considered that any attempt by Germany to assert a claim to compensation for the surrender of her rights in Morocco aimed at smashing the entente, it was inevitable that they should adopt this view. We need look no farther for the British reaction, which took the form of supporting French resistance to any significant concession to Germany. The French just as naturally encouraged this British policy.

There is not the slightest evidence which suggests that Kiderlen-Wächter imagined he was following a policy which might induce France to sever her ties with England and ally herself with Germany. He knew quite well that England would stand on the side of France and that there was no hope of changing this.[131] In his resignation petition he stated that he had hoped that by finally solving the Moroccan problem "he could free Germany from the continual annoyance of British opposition in all parts of the world and might even win for her British friendship."

The view that Joseph Caillaux, the premier, had similar aims is equally unsupported by evidence, but rests on statements made by his political enemies to discredit him. His account of his conduct of French policy from July 1 onward coincides exactly with the documentary evidence, and shows very clearly that his suspicions of Germany were as profound as those of any other Frenchman.[132]

On July 4, when Grey asked Paul Cambon if France wanted to restore the *status quo* in Morocco, Cambon told him there was no disturbance to the *status quo* as France had already withdrawn from Fez.[133] This was technically correct, as French troops had been removed from Fez for propaganda purposes.[134]

The effect of Cambon's statement was seen the next day, when Grey told the Spanish ambassador German action was not straightforward. The Germans had said they would not complain about the French going to Fez if they withdrew quickly, and now the French had withdrawn.[135] Grey knew the French withdrawal was a trick, because he wrote to Bertie on July 20 that France had turned Morocco into a French protectorate.[136]

From July 5 on, the French repeatedly insisted that France had no intention of allowing Germany a foothold in Morocco, which should have quieted Grey's apprehensions about a partition of the country amongst France, Spain and Germany. Nevertheless, Grey still clung to the idea that Germany was trying to get part of Morocco, and in fact intimated that England had no objection to this, although he thought there would be a "great fuss" from the public.[137]

By July 12, Bertie had informed Grey that Germany's foreign minister Kiderlen-Wächter had agreed to renounce all political interest in Morocco in return for compensation elsewhere. It was at this point that the French began to mislead the foreign office about German intentions. They frequently pretended that they were perplexed about what Germany wanted, an old hoax which Delcassé had employed in 1905. This ploy was calculated to foster British suspicions of German double dealing and ensure continued foreign office support.

When Kiderlen-Wächter's conversation with Jules Cambon concerning the Congo was reported to England, the German suggestions were represented as "demands," playing on the British misunderstanding of the French verb *demander*. Kiderlen-Wächter's offer of the northern part of the Cameroons was described as "frontier rectification" and his mention of Togo was omitted altogether.[138] Jules Cambon's report to Paris paints an entirely different picture. When Cambon asked him what he wanted Kiderlen-Wächter said he had only general ideas, but took a map and showed him the Congo from the ocean to the Sangha River. Cambon then continued, "My feeling is that M. de Kiderlen wants to sound us out. He asks for all; perhaps he wants only part. I believe the German government wants a port on the Atlantic. Failing Agadir, it wants Libreville."[139] The region from the Sangha to the sea was far from the whole French Congo, but it did form a considerable part of it. The idea that France might cede the French Congo in exchange for Togoland had been mooted in Paris as early as May 7th.[140]

Sir Francis Bertie wrote on July 17 that Germany must know that her requirements in the Congo were impossible for France to accept and that they were designed to reconcile the French to the establishment of Germany on the Moroccan coast. He avoided mentioning the Cameroons or Togo, implying that only the cession of the Congo was being discussed. He also stated that Paul Cambon had told him that Germany would claim the right of pre-emption of the Congo Free State when it came up for disposal. As Kiderlen-Wächter had specifically denied this aim, this was obviously an attempt to alarm the British government by false information.[141]

Crowe's minute to this dispatch maintained that if the German demands were met it would "mean definitely the subjection of France." He thought this was a trial of strength and that the "dominant question" was "whether England is prepared to fight by the side of France if necessary." Nicolson wrote to Sir William Goschen, British ambassador in Berlin, in the same vein.[142] As the French were also thinking in terms of taking military measures, it is evident that all three Powers considered the possibility of war if the talks broke down, and that England and France were at least as ready for that eventuality as Germany.[143]

On July 20, 1911, it appeared that Grey was deviating from the belligerent views of the foreign office die-hards and was inclined towards compromise. He was willing to allow Germany to acquire additional territory in Africa and remarked that it was reasonable for Germany to want a larger share, in view of British and French acquisitions. He was even ready to concede to Germany a share in the pre-emption rights to the Belgian Congo. At the same time he asserted that England could not go to war to put France in possession of Morocco.[144]

Nevertheless, the next day he authorized David Lloyd George, the chancellor of the exchequer, to make a bellicose speech at the Mansion House that evening. Lloyd George asked him whether the German government had given any answer to the communication he had made on behalf of the cabinet on July 4. When Grey told him they had not, he asked whether this was not unusual and Grey said it was. Lloyd George evidently believed a letter had been sent to Germany and not answered, and Grey made no effort to correct his misconception.[145] Grey then agreed to Lloyd George's proposed statement on foreign policy.[146] According to Lord Riddell, Lloyd George arrived late at the Mansion House and told him that "the delay was due to a conference with Asquith and Grey as to the precise terms of the speech."[147]

It will be recalled that Grey had told Metternich that he must take his statement of July 4, 1911, informing Metternich of the cabinet's decision as a conversation and not a written communication. Metternich obviously thought, mistakenly it would appear, that Grey was satisfied with his reply and that nothing further was necessary at the moment. Grey saw Metternich on the same day he spoke to Lloyd George and the ambassador immediately communicated Grey's concerns to his government. The German government replied at once, before hearing of Lloyd George's speech. When they did hear of it they told Metternich to refuse to allow the German reply to be used in Parliament "after the speech of the chancellor of the exchequer."[148]

The most important part of Lloyd George's speech was his statement that:

If a situation were to be forced upon us in which peace could only be preserved by the surrender of the great and beneficent position Britain has won by centuries of heroism and achievement, by allowing Britain to be treated, where her interests were vitally affected, as if she were of no account in the Cabinet of nations, then I say emphatically that peace at that price would be a humiliation intolerable for a great country like ours to endure.[149]

Grey maintains in his memoirs that Lloyd George's Mansion House speech "had much to do with preserving the peace in 1911" and that it made "German Chauvinists there doubt whether it would be wise to fire the guns." He also says it "certainly had the effect of making the German government keep in touch with their ambassador in London and send him instructions."[150]

All these statements are completely untrue. The first serious threat to peace was the Mansion House speech; no person in a responsible position in Germany had any intention of firing the guns; and the German government answered Metternich's dispatch reporting Grey's *démarche* of July 21 immediately. Lloyd George's speech was everywhere interpreted as a threat of war directed at Germany, and in fact it was Lloyd George's intention to warn Germany that if war came England would fight along with France.[151] If Wilhelm II had aimed such a belligerent speech at England, the resulting storm would have darkened the English sky for a month, and the incident would still be cited today as an example of the megalomania engendered by a withered arm. Goschen reported from Germany that Jules Cambon was "rather aghast" at the effect of the speech on the French colonial chauvinists.[152] Historian S.R. Williamson maintains in his book, *The Politics of Grand Strategy*, that Lloyd George's speech was "a political move by Asquith and Grey to curtail radical control of British policy," and that it "effectively muted the cabinet's direction of foreign policy, alarmed the Germans, and assured the French."[153]

As the Anglo-French agreement on Morocco, and all the French actions which flowed from it, had been based on the premise that Germany was of no account in the family of nations, a sharp reaction was predictable. The effect in Germany of the Mansion House speech was to produce a riposte so sharp in tone that Grey feared an attack on the British fleet.[154] Sir Henry Wilson, the director of military operations, says the possibility of England being involved in a continental war caused grave anxiety in the cabinet for several weeks.[155]

Discussions on this subject continued until late in September, and both France and England anticipated an outbreak of war. Early in August, Grey instructed Goschen to get any information he could about any increase in German imports of wheat and other foods, which would indicate preparations for war.[156] Goschen does not seem to have reported any such preparations. A special meeting of the Committee of Imperial Defense (C.I.D.) was held on August 23 to consider what action England should take in case of a Franco-German war.[157] British preparations for war were very far advanced and everything was ready for action both at sea and on land. Sir Arthur Nicolson wrote on September 14 that he had talked with Haldane, Lloyd George and Churchill and that he was glad to find that all three were "perfectly ready—I might almost say eager to face all possible eventualities."[158]

Preparations for war were also going on in France. In late August commander in chief Joseph Joffre told a British military attaché that he and his staff were hard at work settling the details of their plan of campaign, which would be ready in a few days.[159] Evidently French public opinion was enthusiastically in favour of a strong stand against Germany. *The Times* reported on September 26 that French opinion was stiffer than for thirty or thirty-five years against anything savouring of an "ignominious peace." There was "nowhere in France the slightest fear of Germany, nor would there be any reluctance to put a vital issue to the test of an encounter." Louis Barthou, a former minister of justice, asserted that France, assured of her right and her strength, "will never be willing to sacrifice honour to peace."[160] Nicolson thought the French army had "never been in a better state of equipment, organisation and armament, or been inspired by so strong a feeling of perfect confidence and unity." They believed they were able to meet Germany on "very nearly equal terms" and that the issue would not necessarily be unfavourable to them.[161] It appears that both England and France were more eager to fight than Germany, and that France thought the issue might be favourable even without Russian help. As Russia had given "formal assurance" of both diplomatic and military support, there could be no doubt of the outcome if war came.[162] All these military preparations followed from Lloyd George's speech, and the war crisis should therefore be known as the Mansion House crisis.

It should be pointed out that no British interests were at any time involved in the Franco-German discussions. If the British government could not be certain of a lack of British involvement in the beginning it knew that fact long before Lloyd George made his speech. From July 5 on, the French had insisted repeatedly and forcefully that under no circumstances would they allow the Germans to set foot in Morocco. This vehemence ensured that there would be no German port on the Mediterranean coast or anywhere else in Morocco, and that the French would remain responsible for maintaining the Open Door. This took care of all three of the British interests enumerated by the cabinet on July 4. The fear of the British foreign office was that France and Germany might end their long feud over Morocco and decide to live at peace with each other, a calamity which must be averted at all costs. As *The Times* had pointed out on July 20, any *rapprochement* between France and Germany would hurt British interests. The *Westminster Gazette* thought the claim that the government was acting to protect British interests enabled them to support France.[163] The Mansion House speech was therefore a threat of war if Germany did not reduce the asked for compensation for giving France a free hand in Morocco. As such it was at least as extreme an example of swashbuckling diplomacy as the sending of the *Panther* to Agadir.

The Franco-German negotiations on Morocco continued without British participation, because the British government now recognized that it had no real reason to take part. Relations between France and Germany had already reached the stage at which both feared the possibility of war if the discussions were broken off. On July 19, Jules Cambon thought this might happen and wrote from Berlin to Selves: "It seems to me necessary to examine immediately what measures, if necessary military, should be taken and what diplomatic situation is to be envisaged in case the discussions are definitely broken off." With regard to military measures, Selves replied that he was in frequent touch with the British government and that the Russian government was being kept informed. He assured Cambon that they would both support France.[164]

Alfred von Kiderlen-Wächter, the German foreign minister, told Jules Cambon the next day that if France wanted to make the conversations impossible, Germany would insist on "complete and entire application of the Act of Algeciras, and if necessary we will go all the way." Cambon assured him that France would go equally far.[165] Neither side, however, wished to break off the negotiations if this could be avoided. German chancellor Bethmann-Hollweg wrote to the kaiser that same day that if France remained obdurate Germany must insist on maintaining the Act of Algeciras. He thought Germany "must seek to avoid this alternative with all the means in our power" as it would "risk a more serious conflict."[166]

Lloyd George's Mansion House speech and the French and British press campaigns it inspired added to the difficulty of the Franco-German discussions. Kiderlen-Wächter told Goschen he could not now modify his position because there would be an outcry in Germany that the government had yielded to threats from England and France.[167] He had already given France complete satisfaction with regard to Morocco, but thought France was offering too little in exchange for this conciliatory attitude and his proposed cession of German territory in the Cameroons and Togo.[168]

Jules Cambon agreed that the French government was being too niggardly and tried to persuade them to be more forthcoming. On July 24, he wrote to Selves, "If we want the negotiations to have results we must show more generosity. Between ourselves, what we are offering is too little and almost ridiculous." He also thought, however, that the menace of English intervention would lead Germany to make concessions and that France would need to make less.[169] This did not happen, and Cambon reported that Kiderlen-Wächter remained adamant, whereupon Joseph Caillaux ordered "the Generals and Admirals concerned in mobilisation to have everything ready."[170]

By September, with the negotiations for compensation to Germany for its lost interests in Morocco still dragging on, Cambon wanted Goschen to ask Grey to advise the French government to be generous and to make "a really acceptable offer." Grey thought that if Germany was prepared to give France a clear bargain in Morocco, it was "sheer unreason to make the difference between peace and war depend upon the Wesso-Alima triangle." The extent of British support if there was trouble depended on its being clear that France had no reasonable way of avoiding it. Selves's reaction to this was to tell Bertie he thought Germany's excessive demands were intended to humiliate France by forcing her to give in. Bertie thought many people in France believed war was inevitable and it was better to have it now when France was well prepared and England's assistance was certain because her interests were involved.[171]

The prolongation of the negotiations led in September to a partial retraction of Kiderlen-Wächter's promise of complete freedom for France in Morocco. He now attempted to establish a privileged position for Germany in southern Morocco. When his proposals made no headway, he was forced to renounce this project and satisfy himself with guarantees for German economic activity and freedom of trade. The centre of attention then shifted to the Congo compensation, and agreement on all issues was finally reached after a month more of discussion.[172]

By the agreement of November 4, 1911, a strip of the French Congo was added to the Cameroons. This included a narrow corridor giving Germany access to the sea as well as to the river Congo. The treaty was denounced by nationalists in both France and Germany, but German dissatisfaction had a much more solid basis. France had achieved her expansionist aims in Morocco at the cost of a relatively worthless piece of territory in Central Africa.

The assumption that Germany would have made a better bargain if the *Panther* had not gone to Agadir cannot be proved or disproved. Kiderlen-Wächter's mistake was his failure to take measures to avert British suspicion of his motives. The foreign office belief that he was aiming at the destruction of the Anglo-French entente brought England into the lists against him and gave France the confidence to limit German gains to as little as possible.

Grey's speech to Parliament on November 27 was calculated to increase suspicion of Germany in England. He stated that the report that France had invaded Fez even though the Germans had objected was incorrect. He made no mention of the actual German reaction. This left the impression that the sending of the *Panther* to Agadir was unconnected to France's march to Fez.[173] His statement that the German government regarded a return to the *status quo* doubtful if not impossible suggested that they were lying and he repeated his contention that the new situation had been created by the dispatch of the *Panther* to Agadir. He also repeated the erroneous view that the German government had wanted to solve the Moroccan question by dividing her between Germany, France and Spain. He pretended to be mystified as to what Germany had wanted.[174] The unacceptable German "demands" were also reaffirmed and the suspicion that the Germans were trying to ensure a French refusal so they could stay in Morocco was maintained. By his statements he gave further credence to the rumours that the Germans had landed, acquired concessions and raised the German flag at Agadir. In this connection, he described Germany as being in occupation of a closed port and acquiring a monopoly of commercial opportunities. He gave no indication that this scenario was false.[175] To deflect parliamentary suspicion of his policy he remarked that people were talking as though war was near in the summer, and dismissed the idea without definitely denying it.

When Selves, the French foreign minister, spoke in the Chamber on December 14, 1911, he gave a true account of the Franco-German negotiations. He pointed out that the negotiations had been proceeding for some time before his appointment as foreign minister. He stated at the start that any German compensation would be outside of Morocco, as France would not allow Germany to have any Moroccan territory. The Germans had agreed at once to France's plan. The first words the German foreign minister had said were, "Morocco you shall have it. Establish therein your protectorate, draw up yourselves the arrangement which shall specify the details." All he asked was that Germany should be compensated for abandoning her treaty rights in Morocco. Such compensation had already been arranged with England, Spain and Italy. Thus, in the end Selves took steps to inform French public opinion of the true nature of the discussions with Germany, while Grey further inflamed English opinion with misrepresentations.[176]

The Agadir crisis was a significant milestone on the road to World War I. Violent press campaigns in all three countries excited public opinion and aroused resentment and hostility. England's one-sided attitude and her eagerness to intervene on behalf of France strongly confirmed the French belief that they could be sure of British support in any conflict with Germany. It also convinced Wilhelm II that the Triple Entente was determined to force Germany to accept whatever limitation it imposed on her or fight.

Notes

1.E. D. Morel, *Ten Years of Secret Diplomacy*, p. 48; Douglas Porch, *The Conquest of Morocco*, pp. 97, 133 ff.

2.I. C. Barlow, *The Agadir Crisis*, pp. 19-21.

3.DDF2, X, no. 88.

4.*Ibid.*, no. 237.

5.*Ibid.*, no. 258.

6.*Ibid.*, no. 265.

7.*Ibid.*, no. 279.

8.*Ibid.*, no. 282.

9.*Ibid.*, no. 337.

10.Ibid no. 366.

11.*The Times*, Dec. 10, 1906.

12.*Ibid.*, Dec. 24, 1906.

13.*Ibid.*, Dec. 27, 28, 1906.

14.*Ibid.*, Dec. 29, 1906.

15.Porch, pp. 147-8.

16.Ross E. Dunn, *Resistance in the Desert*, p. 231.

17.DDF2, X, no. 449.

18.*Ibid.*, no. 448.

19.*Ibid.*, no. 483.

20.Porch, p. 150.

21.E. Ashmead-Bartlett, *The Passing of the Shereefian Empire*, p. 26.

22.DDF2, XI, no. 99.

23.Porch, p. 150.

24.DDF2, XI, no. 99.

25.Porch, p. 153.

26.DDF2, XI, no. 110.

27.*Ibid.*, fn., p. 189.

28.Ashmead-Bartlett, pp. 32-4.

29.DDF2, XI, nos. 118, 122; Ashmead-Bartlett, p. 57.

30.Ashmead-Bartlett, pp. 34-8.

31.*Ibid.*, pp. 41-5.

32.*Ibid.*, pp. 42-53.

33.Porch, p. 157.

34.DDF2, XI, no. 119.

35.*Ibid.*, no. 120.

36.Ashmead-Bartlett, p. 55.

37.*Ibid.*, pp. 54-111.

38.Porch, p. 167.

39.*Ibid.*, pp. 161-5.

40.*Ibid.*, pp. 165, 168.

41.DDF2, XI, no. 239.

42.Porch, pp. 168-80.

43.DDF2, XI, nos. 247, 252.

44.*Ibid.*, no. 318.
45.Ashmead-Bartlett, pp. 529-32.
46.DDF2, XI, no. 376.
47.*Ibid.*, nos. 373, 398.
48.Barlow, pp. 56-7.
49.DDF2, XI, no. 399.
50.Barlow, pp. 57-9.
51.DDF2, XI, no. 446.
52.*Ibid.*, nos. 453, 463, 523.
53.Dunn, pp. 236-7.
54.DDF2, XI, no. 41.
55.*Ibid.*, no. 85.
56.*Ibid.*, no. 89; Morel, p. 116.
57.DDF2, XI, 1065-7.
58.Barlow, pp. 84-152.
59.Morel, pp. 117-8.
60.DDF2, XII, nos. 112, 116.
61.*Ibid.*, no. 207.
62.*Ibid.*, no. 317, 332, 398.
63.Dunn, p. 237.
64.Barlow, pp. 88-95; DDF2, XII, no. 444.
65.Barlow, pp. 95-6; DDF2, XII, no. 293.
66.Barlow, pp. 96-7.
67.Barlow, p. 46; Morel, p. 41; Harold Nicolson, *Lord Carnock*, p. 342.
68.Porch, pp. 212-17.
69.*Ibid.*, pp. 217-8.
70.LN, I, 54.
71.*Ibid.*, pp. 63-4.
72.DDF2, XIII, no. 210.
73.BD, VII, no. 202.
74.*Ibid.*, no. 221.
75.LN, I, 74.
76.*Ibid.*, p. 81.
77.*Ibid.*
78.Barlow, p. 193.
79.DDF2, XIII, nos. 222, 254.
80.E. D. Morel, *Diplomacy Revealed*, p. 215.
81.BD, VII, no. 217.
82.DDF2, XIII, nos. 249, 252.
83.*Ibid.*, no. 295.
84.Morel, *Ten Years of Secret Diplomacy*, pp. 107-8.
85.DDF2, XIII, no 267; E. T. S. Dugdale, *German Diplomatic Documents 1891-1914*, IV, 1.
86.DDF2, XIII, nos. 75, 276.
87.BD, VII, nos. 230, 258.
88.HCD, 5th series, XXV, cols. 184, 574.
89.*Ibid.*, XXVI, cols. 125, 878.

90.DDF2, XIII, nos.313, 328.
91.LN, I, 105-6.
92.Barlow, p. 192.
93.FO800/52.
94.DDF2, XIII, no. 364.
95.FO800/62.
96.DDF2, XIII, no. 364.
97.Dugdale, IV, 6-7.
98.*Ibid.*, pp. 2-4.
99.K. H. Jarausch, *The Enigmatic Chancellor*, pp. 120-1.
100.G. P., Vol. XXIX, no. 10572, p. 142, quoted in Barlow, p. 230.
101.DDF2, XIV, no. 37.
102.*Ibid.*, no. 51.
103.*Ibid.*, no. 54.
104.*Ibid.*, no. 73.
105.Barlow, p. 233.
106.FO800/52.
107.Morel, *Ten Years*, p. 127.
108.Jarausch, pp. 121-2.
109.Morel, *Ten Years*, p. 114.
110.*Ibid.*
111.*Westminster Gazette*, July 3, 1911, p. 1.
112.HCD, XXXI, cols. 2615-6.
113.FO800/52.
114.CAB 41/33/20
115.DDF2, XIV, no. 60.
116.BD, VII, nos. 343, 344, 351, 352, 358.
117.Grey of Falloden, *Twenty-five Years*, I, 213-4; Dugdale, IV, 6-7.
118.DDF2, XIV, no. 19.
119.BD, VII, no. 356.
120.Dugdale, IV, 7-8.
121.HCD, XXVII, col. 1341.
122.BD,VII, min. to no. 192.
123.HCD, XXXII, col. 59.
124.BD, VII, mins. to no. 343.
125.*Ibid.*, min. to no. 373.
126.*Ibid.*, min. to no. 352.
127.*Ibid.*, no. 354.
128.FO800/100.
129.BD, VII, min. to no. 383.
130.*Ibid.*, pp. 821-4, App. III.
131.Barlow, p. 304.
132.Joseph Caillaux, *Agadir: Ma Politique Extérieure*, pp. 107 ff.
133.BD, VII, no. 355.
134.DDF2, XIV, no. 362.
135.BD, VII, no. 358.

136.FO800/52.

137.*Ibid.*

138.BD, VII, no. 392.

139.DDF2, XIV, no. 71.

140.Dugdale, IV, 4.

141.FO800/52.

142.BD, VII, min. to no. 392; no. 395.

143.DDF2, XIV, no. 86.

144.FO800/52.

145.David Lloyd George, *War Memoirs*, I, 25.

146.Grey, I, p. 215.

147.Lord Riddell, *More Pages from My Diary, 1908-1914*, p. 21.

148.Grey, I, p. 220.

149.Lloyd George, p. 26.

150.Grey, I, p. 217.

151.Lloyd George, p. 25.

152.BD, VII, no. 431.

153.S. R. Williamson, *The Politics of Grand Strategy: England and France Prepare for War*, p. 154; see also F0800/100.

154.Winston Churchill, *The World Crisis*, I, 32-3.

155.Major General Sir C. E. Callwell, *Field Marshal Sir Henry Wilson, His Life and Diaries*, I, 97-8.

156.FO800/62.

157.Callwell, p. 99.

158.Nicolson, p. 347.

159.FO800/100.

160.*The Times*, September 26, 1911.

161.Nicolson, pp. 347-8.

162.DDF2, XIV, no. 86; BDVII, no. 496.

163.*The Times*, July 20, 1911, p. 8; *Westminster Gazette*, July 28, 1911, p. 11.

164.DDF2, XIV, nos. 79, 83.

165.*Ibid.*, no. 90.

166.Dugdale, IV, 13.

167.BD, VII, no. 424.

168.DDF2, XIV, no. 97.

169.*Ibid.*, nos. 98, 99.

170.FO800/52.

171.*Ibid.*

172.Barlow, pp. 364-9.

173.HCD, XXXII, col. 45.

174.*Ibid.*, col. 46.

175.*Ibid.*, cols. 48-9.

176.Morel, *Ten Years*, p. 153.

Nine

Russia, France and England Prepare for War with
Germany

One of the most persistent myths of the pre-war era is the idea that the arms
race of that time was begun, led and perpetuated by Germany. The usual
method of omitting essential material is not sufficient to sustain this fiction,
so some historians have had to resort to extensive falsification. Fritz Fischer
presents every increase in the French and Russian armies as a result of
German initiative, and makes the unfounded statement that Germany
launched a preventive war against the "unprepared Entente."[1]

V.R. Berghahn provides a map which purports to show the number of
soldiers available on mobilisation for the various Powers in January, 1914. His
figures are very far from reality.[2] The French supposed strength of 1,250,000
men, for example, compares with the agreement of the French general staff in
the summer of 1913 that France would send more than 1,500,000 men against
Germany, while his Russian total of 1,200,000 is considerably smaller than the
number of soldiers in the Russian standing army at the time. Germany and
Austria are represented as being able to mobilise a half-million more men
than France and Russia, although they were actually outnumbered by more
than one million.

The militarist thesis, of course, requires the maintenance of the belief
that German and Austrian military preparations exceeded those of the
Entente powers. Otherwise the myth, that preparation for war by the "good"
nations would guarantee peace, falls to the ground. The truth about this
matter therefore strikes at the very basis of militarism.

The Franco-Russian Alliance set the stage for a coordinated effort by the
two Powers to establish military domination of the continent. As early as
1888, the successful floating of a French loan of 500 million francs to Russia
prompted the French ambassador at St. Petersburg to write to his minister of

foreign affairs that the loan opened unknown horizons, because the union of Russian men with French money would make a force capable of defeating Germany.[3] In 1890 a French armaments firm signed a contract to make 500,000 rifles for the Russian army, with the possibility that this might be increased to 1,000,000.[4]

On July 23, 1891, France proposed an agreement which would oblige the two Powers to mobilise immediately if a Triple Alliance power mobilised, and this was formalized by an exchange of letters. The French believed France and Russia had enough power to balance the Triple Alliance.[5] Alexandre Ribot, the French minister for foreign affairs, thought that the Franco-Russian entente had re-established the balance of power and that there was no longer a question of German hegemony.[6]

The succeeding five years saw France and Russia acting together in Abyssinia, at Constantinople and in China. At the same time a flood of French money flowed into Russian coffers. The long-continued French drive to speed up the Russian offensive against Germany by the construction of strategic railroads began in 1901. The Russian general staff attached great importance to the building of a line joining the Petersburg-Vitebsk railroad to Bielostok, which would speed up the invasion of East Prussia by four days. A French loan of 425 million francs was issued in May, and in the discussion on the use of the loan the tsar insisted that the strategic lines which were considered urgent should be begun immediately.[7] Later in the year another loan was requested by Russia for the same purpose. The French cabinet objected on the ground that the demands on the French market were excessive, but Théophile Delcassé "set forth the political and military reasons which required a favourable reception" and the cabinet adopted his conclusions.[8]

It was generally believed at this time that the Dual Alliance could defeat the Triple Alliance and that Germany was in a dangerous situation. Sir Francis Bertie, for example, wrote on November 9, 1901, that it was essential for Germany to get the armed support of England

...for the contingency of an attack on Germany by France and Russia combined, for if England be not bound to Germany and H.M.G. [Her Majesty's government] come to a general understanding with France and Russia, or with either of them, the position of Germany in Europe will become critical.[9]

Bertie believed that England held the balance of power between the two alliances, and that Germany would have to fight to prevent England's destruction whether or not the two countries were allied.[10]

In 1902, the *Spectator* thought Germany's position was growing weaker and that France was stronger in relation to Germany than she had been for thirty years. The French army, the writer said, was "strong, vigorous and well-equipped," and "it would be a very rash soldier who would predict that Germany could roll back a French invasion."[11]

The idea that England must side with France and Russia in the interests of the "balance of power" could not have been taken seriously by any informed person at the time. After the defection of Italy in 1902, France and Russia had a superiority of 700,000 men over Germany and Austria. The defeat of Russia by Japan changed the situation for a few years but the advantage of the Dual Alliance was soon restored.

The visit of French president Émile Loubet to London in July, 1903, produced a laudatory editorial in the *Morning Post*, which declared that the French army had been made "identical with the manhood of the nation" and that it had been "brought to a high level of excellence in organization, training and equipment." France had also created a great navy "remarkable for the excellence of its personnel and *matériel*."[12] Citing the approval of the Anglo-French *rapprochement* in the American press, the paper thought England, France and the United States could "impose their will upon the civilized world."[13] The *Westminister Gazette* thought the Entente Cordiale might relieve the competition in naval armaments between "the two countries which led the world in naval power."[14]

The signing of the Anglo-French agreement in April, 1904, brought a flow of press articles extolling the power of France and the weakness of Germany. In anticipation, the *Daily Telegraph* exulted that France's colonial dominion was now "invulnerable by any enemy" and that on the continent France was "released from any danger of an attack in the rear."[15] The London *Standard* said France "had materially strengthened her international position" and the Paris correspondent quoted a French paper as saying that Wilhelm II had been checkmated, because England had thrown her weight on the side of the Dual Alliance, "making war impossible for a long period."[16] Ironically, the general opinion was that the peace of Europe had now been assured for a long time.

At the same time, however, war with Germany was anticipated. In the summer of 1904 "talk of the inevitability of an Anglo-German war was in the air," and specific war plans against Germany were made for the first time.[17] Bertie wrote that Germany was the "real enemy, commercially and politically."[18] Lord Esher thought Germany would consider it vital to absorb Holland, and that the day might not be far off when France and England would have to fight her to prevent this.[19] It was also in 1904 that Sir John Fisher first suggested that England should pre-empt an attack by the German fleet. Although this was never seriously considered by the British government, Fisher insisted that he was serious and later bemoaned the fact that it had not been done.[20] The *Army and Navy Gazette* declared that the German fleet was "the one and only menace to the preservation of peace in Europe" and thought England should ask that it not be increased. *Vanity Fair* said the German fleet should be destroyed.[21]

England's preparation for war, both naval and military, was proceeding apace. The British naval estimates had trebled between 1889 and 1904, and now amounted to £41,400,000. Army expenditure was £36,300,000, a larger sum than was spent on the German army that year, a year during which British defence expenditure was 75 percent greater than that of Germany.[22] England, France and Russia had eighty-five first class battleships to fourteen for Germany.[23] Each was spending more on new construction than Germany.[24]

France, confident that her new closeness to England would allow her to play a more aggressive role in European affairs, began to use her financial power to strengthen her position in the Balkans. Serbia, which had just thrown off Austrian tutelage to come under the influence of Russia, received a loan of sixty million francs, with the understanding that armaments would be ordered from French firms.[25] A loan of forty million francs, half for munitions and half for railways, was floated in 1904. The munitions were to be bought entirely in France, and a French company was to build the railways.[26] A loan to Bulgaria for the purchase of French artillery followed, the loan contract and a deal with the French armaments firm Creusot for eighty-one batteries at a price of 26 million francs being signed at the same time.[27] These loans were indicative of the French decision to become more involved in Russia's activities in the Balkans.

In 1905 France's haste to establish her protectorate in Morocco and the German opposition to it produced the possibility of war. The question of British assistance to France if war came naturally arose, and there could be only one answer. Both assumed that British diplomatic support of France meant nothing unless it involved military support if necessary.

The prospect of assisting France in a war with Germany meant participation in a continental war, which had not previously been considered. Strategic war games were held in April and May, 1905, to evaluate the problems of continental warfare.[28] The editor of *Le Matin*, a close friend of Théophile Delcassé, the French foreign minister, wrote that the British had verbally promised to mobilise the British fleet, seize the Kiel Canal and land 100,000 men in Schleswig-Holstein.[29]

While it is true that formal military discussions did not take place until December, 1905, there had been "a series of unilateral declarations of support made to the French by the English service chiefs." The conversations which were initiated between the French and British general staffs in December, 1905, continued until the outbreak of the war.[30]

Sir John Fisher, First Sea Lord, was one of the greatest enthusiasts for war with Germany. In a letter to Lansdowne in April he wrote that this was "a golden opportunity for fighting Germany in alliance with the French," and that he hoped Lansdowne could bring this about.[31] His principal aim was to wipe out German commerce, and he thought the British navy could easily destroy the whole German merchant navy.[32]

The anti-German sections of the press were eager for a war with Germany. *The Times* said war was so certain that the country should be alerted to the danger it faced.[33] There were articles urging that the German fleet should be destroyed.[34]

Delcassé was also keen for war, or at least for the threat of war to force Germany to back down on matters in conflict with France's interests. He was certain England would support France in a Franco-German war, and that the British navy would annihilate Germany's trade and her merchant marine. He declared that the coalition of the French and British navies was "such a formidable machine of naval war" that no Power "would dare to face such an overwhelming force at sea."[35]

Delcassé's colleagues did not realize, as he did, that Germany had no intention of going to war, and they recoiled in panic from the thought of war without Russian assistance. This mood did not last long after Delcassé's fall; by June 19 Maurice Paléologue noted that there had been a change of feeling. He wrote that there was "no more fear, no more cowardice, no more bending to the German will; the idea of war is accepted." The Belgian minister in Paris wrote in October that nationalist chauvinism had reawakened and that people were ready to make sacrifices for a stronger army and navy.[36] In December, a big increase in armaments was passed by the Chamber by a large majority.[37]

With the accession of the Liberals to power in England at the end of the year, the whole-hearted Germanophobe, Sir Edward Grey, replaced the lukewarm Lansdowne as British foreign minister. This ensured that the foreign office would support the French enthusiastically if there was war. On December 30, 1905, Grey wrote that "he had no hesitation in affirming anything Lansdowne had said in support of the French,"[38] but he soon went beyond anything Lansdowne had said to France.

Lieutenant-Colonel Charles Repington, the military correspondent of *The Times*, was the intermediary who carried on the military conversations with Major Victor Huguet, the French military attaché. He gave Huguet a list of questions for the French government concerning cooperation in war. It was agreed that each service should be under one direction, the French to command on land and the British at sea. The French opposed the idea of landing 100,000 men in Schleswig-Holstein, calling this a "delicate operation." They promised not to violate Belgian neutrality unless the Germans did so, but thought Belgium would not fight. Repington asked if France could capture Togoland and the Cameroons if England took East and

West Africa and the German possessions in the Pacific, and the French replied that they could and would.[39]

On January 22, General Sir James Grierson, director of military operations, informed the French general staff that a British army consisting of 105,000 men, 43,000 horses and 5,000 cars would disembark at Calais, Boulogne and Cherbourg on the 8th to 16th days of English mobilisation. Two other divisions would eventually be available.[40]

Repington also saw Sir John Fisher, who was in the process of creating a new fleet by withdrawing ships from various areas. Fisher told him Admiral Sir Arthur Wilson's channel fleet "was alone strong enough to smash the whole German fleet."[41] Naval conversations with the French were held on an ongoing basis.

Huguet told Repington at the end of December, 1905, that the French navy had already taken certain precautions and was prepared for a German attack. The French army was ready and "reservists were already coming to barracks to ask for orders."[42] It was clear that the French were prepared to go to war to shut Germany out of Morocco, in accordance with their agreements with England and Spain.

When Lord Haldane became war minister in the Liberal cabinet in 1905 he had immediately undertaken a dramatic reform of the army. He planned an expeditionary force of 158,000 men, to be supplemented by special reserves of 80,000. His original goal of a total of 300,000 was nearly reached in 1910, although it declined thereafter.[43] By 1911 the strength of the British army had been approximately doubled, while expenditure had declined.[44]

The army was reorganized in 1908, especially by the building of a general staff to deal with strategy and training. A reserve of officers was created by converting the volunteer corps at the universities into Officers' Training Corps. Universities and schools which did not have volunteer corps were encouraged to form them.[45] The result of these efforts was that, according to the official history, "the British Expeditionary Force of 1914 was incomparably the best trained, best organized, and best equipped British Army that ever went forth to war."[46]

An interesting aspect of the period leading up to the Algeciras conference is the fact that, contrary to the often-expressed opinion, no one in England or France gave the slightest sign that there was any fear of Germany. Confidence that the power of England and France was superior and that they could overawe Germany reigned supreme. At the end of December a memorandum by Sir Charles Dilke, a former cabinet minister and an expert on foreign affairs, indicated his belief that the French army was superior to that of Germany.[47] Charles Repington wrote an article for The Times in which he stated that France and Germany would be able to mobilise an equal number of men, and that the French artillery was certainly better than that of Germany. He thought the French and German fleets were practically equal.[48] On January 15, Paul Cambon, French ambassador in London, told Grey he was sure there would be no trouble with Germany if she knew England and France would act together.[49] A note by Sir Charles Hardinge asserted that if England supported France Germany would avoid a conflict in which she would "lose her entire mercantile marine and almost her whole foreign trade."[50] Lord Tweedmouth thought Germany would not risk a war with England and France for some years.[51] There is no reason to believe that Germany contemplated going to war at the time.

Later in the same year, after the conclusion of the Algeciras conference, war with Germany was still expected. Lord Esher thought a war with Germany was certain in the not too distant future, because Germany was determined to have commercial pre-eminence. He feared it would come before England adopted compulsory service, which would take at least five years.[52] One wonders why he considered conscription necessary, since he believed British naval power was "six times that of Germany at the given point of battle."[53]

Some of those in France who were eager for war in the spring of 1906 believed it would be an antidote to social revolution. In March and April L'Echo de Paris published a daily series of articles on the coming revolution. Le Gaulois also predicted a social revolution, and some novels of the day reflected the same ideas. Paul Doumer, an ardent expansionist and former governor-general of Indo-China, is quoted as saying: "I consider France in a desperate state. We must get out of it at any price by a violent crisis." He favoured an early war as the only way to unite the French people "in the right feeling."[54]

Both France and England took steps to strengthen Russia and support her Balkan policy. Russian bonds were admitted to the London market for the first time since the Crimean war, and the British government recognized the regicide regime in Serbia, which it had refused to do since 1903.[55] France was engaged in arming Serbia, which Russia had chosen to play a leading role in Russia's Balkan offensive.[56]

Although the year 1907 was relatively quiet, the possibility of war with Germany continued to occupy attention. In April and May Fisher was busy with plans for such a war. Admiral Lord Charles Beresford was working on a plan of campaign, and Fisher thought his suggestion about the Atlantic fleet making a surprise attack on Germany was "well worth consideration."[57] The French thought Germany might take up a threatening attitude in connection with the Anglo-French agreement with Spain to guarantee the *status quo* in the Mediterranean. They asked for assurance of British support if this happened, and Cambon asked Grey whether, "if Germany picks a quarrel we can count on you." Grey simply answered "yes." As Germany had given no sign of being disturbed over the agreement, no action was necessary.[58] Conversations between the two general staffs included particular reference to the conveyance of British troops from the landing places to the points of concentration.[59]

Fisher believed that England would eventually have to fight Germany, because Germany could not expand commercially otherwise.[60] German commerce was indeed expanding rapidly, and the reality was that England could not stop this expansion without fighting Germany. In fact, Fisher could not "conceive such German madness as to make war against England," because it would mean the collapse of the German Empire.[61] The Germans were therefore unlikely to attack England, so she must make the attack herself by a surprise attack on the German fleet. Germany was in such a "time of stress and uneasiness" over the building of the *Dreadnought* that it was "peculiarly timely." But "Alas! We had no Pitt, no Bismarck, no Gambetta!" so the opportunity was missed.[62]

The kaiser's letter to Lord Tweedmouth, First Lord of the Admiralty, in March, 1908, in which he explained that he was England's best friend in Germany, excited the press about German intentions. It drew attention to the strong anti-British sentiment in Germany. Lord Esher thought British naval and military forces should be put in good order, because Germany intended to crush England and nothing could "prevent a struggle for life except the certainty that the attack would fail." The extent of his credulity appears in his account of a secret treaty between Germany and Sweden for the partition of Denmark, which would enable Germany to control the Belts [the straits joining the Baltic Sea and the Kattegat] and the Baltic.[63]

An early war was expected in both England and France. There were constant warnings in the press that Germany was preparing to make war on England.[64] Evelyn Baring, Lord Cromer, voiced his apprehension in the House of Lords in July, and his alarm was repeated in the House of Commons by Austen Chamberlain.[65]

The French also predicted that war would come soon. Georges Clemenceau thought war with Germany was "both certain and near."[66] Delcassé thought France was taking too humble a line with Germany, who did not want war any more than did France. The French army was just as good as that of Germany, and there was no need for France to try to conciliate the Germans.[67]

In October Asquith appointed a subcommittee of the Committee of Imperial Defence (C. I. D.) to study the military needs for a continental war.[68] Lord Esher thought the army had been even now so improved in readiness for war that a force of 200,000 men could be ready to fight on the line of the Meuse in eighteen to twenty-one days.[69]

On October 7, Austria proclaimed the annexation of Bosnia-Herzegovina, to which Alexandre Isvolsky, the Russian foreign minister, had agreed at a meeting with the Austrian foreign minister, Baron Ai von Aehrenthal, on September 16. In return Aehrenthal had agreed to support the opening of the straits to Russian warships. Isvolsky was unable to persuade England to agree to the opening of the straits, so he felt he had been cheated. He denied that he had made any bargain and fomented a crisis by encouraging the Serbs to oppose the annexation by force. The British government supported his policy, ostensibly on the moral ground that international treaties were inviolate. Although the Russians believed this question must eventually be decided by war, they had to postpone war because it would be two or three years before they were ready.[70]

Another crisis between France and Germany developed in October. A German consul at Casablanca had attempted to assist six deserters from the French Foreign Legion to escape and the deserters were seized by the French authorities. Although there was no indication that Germany had any intention of going to war over the incident, both France and England were prepared to fight. Grey congratulated Paul Cambon on the strong stand France had taken and Cambon told him the spirit of the French army was very good and that the French "were quite prepared to defend themselves." Cambon also spoke of naval discussions concerning the form naval cooperation should take if war broke out.[71] Grey believed England should fight with France if Germany "fastened a war on France in connection with Morocco." He warned Reginald McKenna that the admiralty should be ready to make preparations to assist France.[72]

Major Victor Huguet, French military attaché, reported from London that Lord Esher considered eventual war with Germany a certainty, and thought it would be better to fight now with France than alone later. This would be, he said, an exceptional occasion for the British fleet to destroy the German fleet before it became a real menace to England. He told Huguet that if England took part in such a war she would do so with all her resources, and that the French and British fleets together with their combined financial resources "would provide the certainty of being able to continue the struggle unceasingly without mercy, until Germany, ruined and starving, acknowledged herself beaten and begged for peace."[73]

The subcommittee of the C. I. D. met in December to study the question of continental war. They concluded that the entente was of value only if it meant that the whole military and naval strength of both England and France would be brought to bear. The British army would fight on the French left wing, but aid to France could not be left to turn on the "mere point of Belgian neutrality." The report was adopted by the C. I. D., conferring "respectability on the strategy of intervention."[74]

October also saw the publication of an equivocal article in the *Fortnightly Review*. The author, who signed himself "Calchas," declared that "the greatest of all dangers to peace is the military weakness of Great Britain," which tempted Germany "to fling herself upon France." Paradoxically, he thought France was as strong as Germany, and that a Franco-German war would be at worst a drawn struggle. French artillery, he maintained, was better than that of any other country and France was stronger financially. France could put man for man in the field against Germany and "sustain equal armies for at least as long as the German financial resources...would be likely to last." Evidently he thought the balance of resources between France and Germany was unsatisfactory and British assistance was therefore needed to make it possible for France to dictate to Germany.[75]

The Bosnian crisis continued to excite the Powers in the early months of 1909. According to Delcassé the French army was in excellent shape. He thought it was very efficient, while the German army had deteriorated. France was also undertaking a large naval programme. She had twelve first-class warships afloat and six under construction, with twelve more projected, to bring the total to thirty.[76] The French ambassador at St. Petersburg alerted the Russians to the necessity of using the most recent loan from France to improve the mobilisation conditions of their army "in the eventuality of war with Germany."[77] Although Russia was not yet ready for war, the tsar believed a conflict with Germanism was inevitable in the future, and the president of the Duma declared that Russia would then be ready to fight for Serbia.[78] In France, *"Si vis pacem, para bellum* had become the favourite dictum of all politicians."[79]

The big event in Anglo-German relations was the naval scare which erupted in March of 1909. The press campaign engineered by Fisher produced a public panic of prodigious proportions. Frederic Harrison maintained in *The German Peril* that England's existence as a Great Power was threatened: Germany was challenging her command of the ocean, and British military and naval resources were "utterly inadequate."[80] In this desperate situation England could not count on keeping control of the sea, and needed an army of 400,000 or 500,000 men to defend against invasion.[81] At the same time, however, he believed the British fleet was stronger than any possible combination, and declared that "no power on earth will ever challenge our navy for years to come—and even then not without an ally."[82]

In April the *English Review* published an article by Hilaire Belloc in which he stated that England was now governed by panic. He suggested the possibility that Asquith might decide that the best course was to force a war with Germany as soon as possible. War was inevitable, and it might be better to have it at once.[83]

In a speech on the naval estimates Grey expressed the view that

England and Germany could exist in peace, but that two things would produce conflict. One of these would be an attempt by England to isolate Germany. There was, he maintained, "no reason to apprehend on our part that we shall pursue a policy of isolation of Germany." Could he have been oblivious to the fact that everyone in Europe believed that the main aim of British policy was to isolate Germany?[84]

At the end of the year Russia signed a military convention with Bulgaria providing for mutual assistance in case of war with Germany and Austria or with Turkey. Article V of the treaty stated that "the realization of the high ideals of the Slavic peoples upon the Balkan peninsula...is possible only after a favourable outcome of Russia's struggle with Germany and Austria-Hungary."[85]

Although 1910 was a quiet year with no crisis, both France and England continued to cherish the prospect of an early war with Germany. Lord Balfour, leader of the opposition, speaking at Hanley, England, in January, 1910, asserted that statesmen and diplomats of the lesser Powers were unanimous in the opinion that "a struggle sooner or later between this country and Germany is inevitable."[86] The French thought this was because England refused to look facts in the face and make adequate preparations to ensure victory.[87] The diplomats of at least one lesser Power, Belgium, believed, however, that it was England's determination to isolate Germany which would produce the war.[88]

In response to a proposal in the French Chamber to spend £56 million on naval construction in the next ten years, Grey told Bertie that he would prefer to have the French spend all they could afford on their army. His view was that "what really strengthens the moral obligations between us is that France should keep up an army and we a navy at the highest possible pitch of strength."[89]

Expectation of an early war was affirmed by many of those involved in its preparation. General Wilson was convinced "that a Franco-German struggle for the mastery must break out within a very few years, and that it might even break out within a very few months." General Ferdinand Foch, professor at the École de Guerre, warned Wilson that the year 1912 would be a dangerous one to live through, "for many reasons which he could not give."[90]

Russia was also intent on strengthening her army. The French were glad that Russia had decided to spend 350 million francs a year for ten years on her army, above ordinary expenditure.[91] A French publicist, Lémenon, voiced the view that the ties between France and Russia should be enhanced and that a Balkan confederation should be created. In particular, Serbia should be armed and built up, for "a strong Serbia would be a dagger in the flank of Austria."[92]

There was fear in France that Russia was redistributing her forces and would not make her main push against Germany.[93] The conference of the French and Russian Chiefs of Staff, which met in September, agreed, however, that the main Russian forces would act against Germany from the outbreak of war. The meeting confirmed that the mobilisation of the German army would oblige France and Russia to mobilise all their forces immediately and simultaneously without previous agreement, and the French were satisfied that the new Russian mobilisation plans responded to French requirements.[94] In November the French were assured that the Russian national defence programme was proceeding without interruption, especially the reinforcement of the artillery.[95]

The question of the redistribution of the Russian forces and the possibility that Russia might act only on the defensive arose again in December as a result of Russian foreign minister, Sergei Sazonov's, meeting with the Germans. The agreement that neither Power would enter into a combination of an aggressive character against the other alarmed both England and France, although both of them had long pretended that the Triple Entente was not aggressive.[96] Sazonov assured the French, however, that Russia would be faithful to the alliance, and General Brun, French chief of general staff, told Stephen Pichon, French foreign minister, he was sure the redistribution of the Russian armed forces had not lessened their offensive value.[97]

Meanwhile, the British government continued its preparations for the inevitable struggle with Germany. Grey took steps to strengthen the ties between Russia and England, a foreshadowing of the way in which England would follow in the wake of Russia's Balkan policy.[98] By this time over 150 schools and twenty universities each had their own Officer Training Corps. Young people were enrolled in organizations which dispensed patriotic propaganda, such as the Boy Scouts, the Boys Brigade, the Church Lads Brigade, the Lads Drill Association and the British Girls Patriotic League. The Navy League sent speakers to public schools, circulated pamphlets and persuaded headmasters to have patriotic Trafalgar Day celebrations.[99]

Events of the year 1911 played a prominent part in propelling Europe along the road to war. To this the French drive to complete the military conquest of Morocco made the most notable contribution. The French advance from both borders of the country culminated in May with the occupation of the capital Fez. A last attempt by Germany to wring from France some recognition of Germany's treaty rights produced a British reaction which threatened to unleash a war.

The French continued to concentrate on building up their armed forces on land and sea. Stephen Pichon appealed to the patriotism of the representatives in the Chamber to strengthen the military power of France.[100] A great French naval programme was projected, which involved the building, between 1910 and 1920, of sixteen battleships, six destroyer squadrons, twenty torpedo boat destroyers and fifty submarines. Three battleships of 23,000 tons were to be completed in three years.[101]

Théophile Delcassé, the minister of marine in the new Briand ministry, told Alexandre Isvolsky that his appointment was a sign that special care would be given to French military power. He guaranteed that the new cabinet would redouble its activity with regard to the army. He also promised to try to strengthen the ties between France and Russia. Monis, now premier, declared in the Chamber that the government would give special care to the army and navy, "with the aim of maintaining peace."[102]

The French military attaché at Berlin thought Germany's need to expand her commerce would lead her to go to war in the near future. He said the Germans had an exaggerated idea of their power, believing that their army was invincible, and that this led them to think they could get whatever they wanted by military threats. He believed that the German army had suffered from a long period of peace, and was therefore weak and deficient in some respects.[103]

In April J.M. Cruppi, the French minister for foreign affairs, probably anticipating trouble over France's Morocco policy, raised the question with Grey of Anglo-French military cooperation in case of war. He was concerned about a statement Grey had made in Parliament. Pacifist M.P. George Lansbury had asked whether there was any statement, implicit or explicit, obliging England to send troops to take part in the operations of the French army. Grey's deceptive reply was that British engagements were only those of the Anglo-French Agreement presented to Parliament.[104]

Cruppi proposed to make a statement in the Chamber about Anglo-French relations, and Grey objected to the words he intended to use. These would, he said, "have been construed as if an offensive and defensive alliance were pending," and there would have been a row in Parliament if Cruppi had implied that there was "a secret engagement unknown to Parliament all these years" committing England to a European war.[105] It had just been settled that in a war with Germany all six British divisions would embark on the 4th day, the cavalry on the 7th day and artillery on the 9th day of mobilisation.[106]

The President of the Russian Duma asserted that a Russo-German war was inevitable in one or two years. Russia, he said, could not always give in to German demands, and her military situation was now good enough that she could resist.[107] General Soukhomlinoff, the minister of war, told the French military attaché that the new mobilisation plan had shortened mobilisation time to a greater degree than expected, and that the Germans were very unhappy about it. He said: "Once mobilization is completed we shall act totally; no little bits!"[108]

When the *Panther* was sent to Agadir Sir Eyre Crowe thought the two opposing alliances were engaged in a test of strength, and the dominant question was whether England was prepared to fight along with France and Russia if necessary. The only hope of peace was to show a united front and overawe Germany.[109] The next day Jules Cambon suggested that military measures should be taken in case discussions with Germany broke down.[110]

On July 20, a pivotal conference took place at the Paris war ministry between General Dubail, chief of the general staff, and other members of the French general staff and General Sir Henry Wilson, director of military operations at the war office. This discussion defined the conditions of cooperation between France and England. It detailed the recruits of the British army, the arrangements for transportation and landing, plans for transport and concentration by railway and procedure for provisioning the British troops.[111]

On General Wilson's return to England from the conference he was sent for and asked when the expeditionary force could be ready.[112] Although Haldane asserted that England was then prepared to concentrate 160,000 men on the Belgian frontier in fifteen days,[113] Wilson thought the expeditionary force was in a bad way. He wrote in his diary, "The 4th and 6th Divisions will have no horses, no A.S.C. personnel, no mechanical transport or mechanical transport drivers and no medical units." He insisted, nevertheless, on sending the whole six divisions.[114]

Although there was no sign of any unusual military activity in Germany,[115] France was also preparing to fight. On July 31, Joseph Caillaux, the French premier, sent orders to the generals and admirals concerned in mobilisation to have everything ready.[116] Caillaux thought the men in the Quai d'Orsay had "bellicose perceptions." He himself was somewhat less enthusiastic, because the Russians had told him they would not be ready for war for at least two years.[117]

Caillaux expected to come to terms with Germany over Morocco, but foresaw an early war between Germany and the Triple Entente.[118] Many important people in France believed France was strong enough to risk war, since their chances of winning were good.[119] The public was "very confident of the efficiency of the French army."[120]

The seventh conference of the French and Russian general staffs met at the end of August, 1911. The French stated that they now had a greater effective army than the 1,300,000 foreseen by Article III of the military convention, that this army could concentrate as quickly as the German army, and that it could take the offensive against Germany on the 12th day of mobilisation "with the aid of the English army on its left wing." In reply to General Dubail's statement that France must receive instant and effective help from Russia in order that Germany should be attacked at the same time from east and west, General Jilinski, the Russian chief of general staff, reported that Russia could now take the offensive from the 15th day. When the reorganization of the Russian army was completed, it would be able to put in line much more than the 800,000 men envisaged in the convention. He thought, however, that Russia was not in a condition to undertake a war with Germany before at least two years "with certainty of success."[121]

The Russians gave France "formal assurance" of "diplomatic and military support,"[122] and an agreement was signed providing for an immediate offensive by both, to disrupt the German plan of knocking out France first.[123] At the end of August J.J. Joffre, French commander in chief, told the British military attaché that he and his staff were hard at work settling the details of their plan of campaign, which would be ready in a few days.[124]

Discussions about British cooperation with the French continued unabated, and an accord was reached concerning the cooperation of the two fleets. The two established a secret code and reached agreement on the role of France in the Mediterranean.[125] General Sir Henry Wilson, conversing with Grey and Churchill, advocated a policy of an offensive and defensive alliance of England, France, Belgium, Denmark and Russia. He insisted on the "enormous importance" of "an actively friendly Belgium."[126] He later estimated that a friendly Belgium would make a difference of twelve to sixteen divisions.[127]

In mid-September Grey was afraid the Germans might attack the British fleet without warning, but nevertheless told McKenna that no precautions beyond ordinary ones were needed.[128] Fisher, who had declared in June that "our navy at this moment could take on all the navies of the world," thought there would be no war because "we are too strong." He said he knew the Germans were "in a blue funk of the British navy."[129]

Fisher believed this was the time to fight, and that war should be forced on the Germans when it was so advantageous. A short time later he wrote: "If Pitt or Palmerston had been prime minister, they would have forced France to fight, as she now has the best artillery in the world, and a great military expert says her army is now really better than the Germans."[130]

Sir Arthur Nicolson, in agreement, told Grey that, if England and Russia supported France, Germany would come to an agreement, as "Our combination is a very strong one and Germany would not care to face it."[131] Lord Haldane thought the French and Russian forces were strong enough that England needed only a small army, and that the power of the entente was growing in relation to that of Germany.[132]

The French were, in fact, eager to fight, but the Germans were not interested. The British military attaché reported that the French army was ready for war, that the French thought their chances were better now than in

the future, and that they could win.[133] Grey did not like the indication "that
the French army are so ready that they might prefer war now," but he was
nevertheless glad they were ready.[134]

By November it was apparent that there was no prospect of war for the
moment, but the French did not abandon hope. Ferdinand Foch was sure
there would be war in the spring.[135] Paul Cambon, however, asserted that
France and Russia were of the opinion that war must be postponed until 1914
or 1915. Although France's material preparation for war was complete, the
organization of the upper command was not yet finished.[136]

At the same time the Russians were engaged in another attempt to open
the straits at Constantinople to Russian warships. They proposed a treaty by
which Turkey would agree not to oppose the passage of Russian warships
through the straits, in return for which Russia would guarantee to defend
Constantinople and adjacent territories for Turkey. As England maintained
the negative attitude she had assumed in 1908, nothing came of this
overture.[137] The Russians eventually concluded that the straits problem could
be resolved only as the result of a general war and, although both Austria and
Germany were ready to accept this proposed agreement with Turkey, the war
was to be waged against them.[138]

In the new year the French continued to expect an early war. Premier
Joseph Caillaux thought France had made a good deal on Morocco, but
feared Germany would give trouble and thought England should have a
stronger army. Clemenceau also deprecated British military weakness,
because he thought the Franco-German agreement on Morocco was full of
uncertainties which would enable Germany to raise difficulties when it suited
her. He professed a disinclination for war, but felt it would come.[139]

England also expected an early war. Raymond Poincaré informed the
French ambassadors at St. Petersburg and Berlin that Sir Francis Bertie had
told him the European situation made him apprehensive about the next
spring. He thought England and France should act in concert henceforth.[140]
Early in the year Asquith convened the "invasion committee" of the
Committee of Imperial Defence. Churchill tells us that the main question
discussed at the meeting of the invasion committee was a possible German
invasion of England, but that "many other aspects of a war with Germany
were patiently and searchingly examined."[141] General Wilson was working on
arrangements for transportation of the expeditionary force, especially with
relation to the ports of embarkation and disembarkation.[142]

Isvolsky reported from Paris in February that in spite of the end of the
Morocco crisis, military circles in France expected new international
complications in the spring, and that the war department was continuing to
prepare actively for military operations in the near future.[143] Joffre told the
Russian military attaché he was getting ready in case war broke out in the

spring, and that arrangements for the English landing had been made "down to the smallest detail," so that the English army could take part in the first big battle.[144]

The French conviction that war was imminent prompted the government to find out whether England would countenance a French invasion of Belgium. Paul Cambon wanted to know whether France must wait for the Germans to enter Belgium first.[145] Joffre wanted a French offensive through Belgium, but Poincaré feared this would cause difficulty with England.[146] He instructed Cambon to find out if responsibility for aggression could legitimately be imputed to France "if a concentration of German forces in the region of Aix-la-Chapelle" obliged France to penetrate Belgian territory.[147]

The British government insisted that Germany should be allowed to enter Belgium first, but British forces would then go into Belgium with or without Belgian permission. The British thought Belgium was unlikely to defend her neutrality, and were also aware that the Belgians believed England was more likely to violate that neutrality than Germany.[148]

In order to ensure that Belgium would join England and France, therefore, it was necessary to take steps to make sure that she would be friendly to the entente.[149] The French repeatedly urged that England should recognize the Belgian annexation of the Congo.[150] Sir Arthur Nicolson agreed that this was necessary, but thought the time was not yet ripe.[151]

Colonel Bridges, British military attaché in Brussels, suggested that England should secure Belgian good-will by recognizing the annexation of the Congo and by declaring her intention not to invade Belgium. Both steps were taken in 1913: on April 7, Grey reported that he had told the Belgian minister that he was "sure that this government would not be the first to violate the neutrality of Belgium;"[152] on June 27 England officially recognized the annexation of the Congo.

In deference to British wishes, Joffre decided on a plan of troop concentration "capable of lending itself to any possible plan of operations."[153] It was necessary to abandon the existing plan of concentration and devise the new plan XVII. This plan had variation A, to be put into effect if the Germans did not come through Belgium, and variation B, to be operational if, as was expected, the German offensive involved a passage through that country.[154] The whole of the work on the plan was concluded and inspected by June 1, 1914.[155]

The year 1912 also saw the broadening and consolidation of the Anglo-French entente. Naval plans were made which left the main responsibility for the Mediterranean to France, while England was to guard the French northern coasts. This made it impossible for the two countries to wage a naval war separately.[156] Viscount Esher wrote, quite correctly: "It means an alliance under cover of 'conversations'."[157] The recall to home waters of the British Mediterranean squadron involved the incorporation of eight King Edwards in the home fleet and the moving of four Duncans to Gibraltar, where they could act either in the Mediterranean or at home. This was described by Cambon as "part of the subordination of the whole naval policy to the eventuality of a war with Germany."[158]

As the British nevertheless insisted that they were not bound to fight alongside France, the French complained that then France was left with the need to protect the North Sea. Grey replied that it might be possible to devise a formula foreseeing common action without the cabinet being accused of contracting an alliance without the knowledge of Parliament.[159] France was assured that nothing would be done to impair Anglo-French relations, and that all six divisions of the expeditionary force would be sent to the continent.[160]

The Anglo-French entente was extended and further consolidated by the Grey-Cambon letters of 22/23 November, 1912. This initiative was presented as an assurance to those members of the cabinet who opposed Grey's policy that the recently revealed military conversations did not bind England to go to war with France. It stated, amongst other things, that the disposition of the two fleets was "not based on an engagement to cooperate in war," which was literally true, but it nonetheless irrevocably committed the British government to such cooperation.

The real significance of the Grey-Cambon letters lay in the statement that:

...if either Government had grave reason to expect an unprovoked attack by a third Power, or something that threatened the general peace, it should immediately discuss with the other whether both Governments should act together to prevent aggression and to preserve peace, and, if so, what measures they would be prepared to take in common.[161]

This statement changed the basis of the Anglo-French entente from England's limited agreement to support France in Morocco to a general agreement that the two Powers would act together in European affairs. It was, in fact if not in form, a recognition of the actual Anglo-French alliance. Haldane was confident enough that the war policy would be carried through that he told Prince Karl Lichnowsky, German ambassador in London, that, if the Balkan war spread to the Great Powers, England would fight with France and Russia to preserve the balance of power.[162]

Probably the most significant event of 1912 was the initiation of the Russian offensive in the Balkans. This began on February 29 with the Serbo-Bulgarian treaty of alliance negotiated under Russian auspices.[163] The Serbians were told by Nicholas II that the aspirations of Serbia against Austria would soon be fulfilled.[164] Nikola Hartwig, Russian minister at Belgrade and pan-Slav enthusiast with a burning desire to come to grips with Austria, was given the task of creating further alliances of the Balkan States.[165]

In June the French ambassador in St. Petersburg reported that it was clear that Russia thought that great events were near, and that the Russian government wanted to precipitate these events and prepare to profit by them. He also said, "Germany and Austria remain quiet."[166] When Poincaré and Isvolsky discussed the question of the need for a formal Anglo-French alliance, Poincaré said there was no need for any change. Recent events had shown that the understanding between France and England guaranteed that in case of serious complications they would follow a common policy. The signature of a formal document would add nothing to this guarantee.[167]

The Army Chiefs of Staff also held their annual conference in July. The French were improving their railway lines, which would allow a gain of one or two days in the concentration of their forces. General Joffre insisted that the Russian railroads to the eastern frontier should all be doubled and in some places quadrupled. France already had all double tracks to her frontier. Joffre and Jilinski agreed in declaring that "defensive war" did not mean they would conduct war defensively. On the contrary, it was absolutely necessary to take a vigorous offensive, as far as possible simultaneously.[168]

When Poincaré visited Russia in August, he insisted that doubling and quadrupling the railway lines and standardizing the gauge of the Warsaw lines to the German frontier was "very urgent." In particular, the doubling and quadrupling of the Smolensk and Briansk lines was very important. Sazonov showed him the Serbo-Bulgarian treaty, which Isvolsky had told him aimed at maintaining the *status quo*. Poincaré thought it was "a convention of war," because it was directed against both Turkey and Austria.[169] He warned Sazonov that France would fight in a Balkan war only if Germany was involved.[170]

Poincaré reassured Sazonov about the adhesion of England to the alliance. He said that, although there was no written treaty, the Chiefs of Staff of the army and navy were in constant contact and that there was verbal agreement that England would support France by land and sea in case of a German attack.[171]

Sazonov visited England, France and Germany in September, and was once again assured by Grey of support for Russia if war came. When he asked Grey if the British fleet could protect the Baltic coast, Grey replied that this would be dangerous, and that the fleet would confine its operations to the North Sea. He assured Sazonov, however, of the existence of "an Anglo-French agreement by which England bound herself, in case of war with Germany, to support France, not only by sea, but even by sending troops on the continent."[172] The British fleet would blockade the German North Sea coast and do all it could against Germany. He also made the usual pretence that no British government could go to war unless backed by public opinion, which would not support an aggressive war.[173] He was himself doing his best to confuse and deceive public opinion, and it may be assumed that neither Russia nor France took this very seriously. King George V told Sazonov that a war would have fatal consequences for Germany's fleet and for her commerce for "we shall sink every German ship we shall get hold of."[174]

Poincaré believed that, if Austria took action against Serbia, Russia could not be indifferent and there would be a general war. If Russia had to take military action against Austria or Turkey, France would give "energetic diplomatic support," but if the war involved German intervention France would not hesitate an instant in giving armed assistance.[175] Isvolsky reported that Poincaré knew that informed and responsible opinion viewed with a great deal of optimism the chances of France and Russia in case of a general war. The Balkan states would divert the Austrian forces and Italy would remain neutral.[176]

When the tsar decided on the mobilisation of certain districts against Austria Vladimir Kokovtsov, president of the council, feared that this would lead to war with Austria and Germany, and that Russia was not ready for war. He suggested lengthening the term of service by six months, thus increasing the standing army by one-quarter, and Sazonov agreed. Soukhomlinoff, the war minister, said it would be better to start the war as soon as possible, because both the tsar and he believed that "a war would bring us nothing but good." The Russian generals thought Russia was ready for war, and the tsar agreed that Russia was strong enough to put Germany in her place at any time.[177]

The Balkan situation forced Russia to increase greatly her military expenditures in the latter part of 1912.[178] Her increase over 1911 was £7 million, while Germany increased her expenditure by £2 million. The Russian expenditure exceeded that of Germany by £5.5 million.[179] The Duma consistently favoured an increase in military credits, and the press cried out for greater preparedness.[180]

At the same time the Dual Alliance was becoming more and more Balkanized. Isvolsky reported from Paris in 1912 that up to this time France had said that Balkan events would produce from France only diplomatic action. Now she recognized that Austrian territorial conquest would affect the balance of power and thus the interests of France.[181] Poincaré declared that in a question of interest to Russia it was up to her to take the initiative and France would support her. Isvolsky concluded that Poincaré meant that if Russia went to war France would do the same.[182]

France became greatly alarmed in December because Russia was not responding to Austrian military measures. The French feared that Austria was about to attack Russia, and that this would bring in Germany. They were much concerned that war was imminent and Russia appeared not to be preparing for it. Poincaré not only spoke of this to Isvolsky, but also addressed inquiries to Georges Louis, French ambassador in St. Petersburg, wanting to know if Russia was making preparations and what her intentions were.[183] Poincaré and his ministers were astonished when Georges Louis reported that the Russian general staff thought Austria's military measures were merely defensive, and that Russia would not go to war even if Austria attacked Serbia.

Isvolsky reported from Paris that the French government envisaged the possibility of war with composure, firmly determined to fulfil its alliance obligations. The French government, he said, had taken all the necessary measures. Mobilisation on the eastern front had been checked and the material was ready. Whereas a short time ago the French had blamed Russia for egging on Serbia, now Russia's indifference to the Austrian mobilisation was regarded with astonishment and anxiety.[184]

To quiet the distress in France over Russia's apparent disinclination to go to war at the moment, Sazonov informed the French that Russia had retained 350,000 reservists with the colours, allocated 80 million roubles for extraordinary military requirements and for the Baltic fleet, brought some divisions closer to the Austrian frontier and taken a series of further measures.[185] It appeared, however, that Russia was less eager for war than France, perhaps because she thought it wise to consolidate the gains of the Balkan war before going on to further adventures.[186]

Poincaré once again tried to get the British government to commit itself, but the answer, as usual, was that British action would depend on circumstances and be decided by public opinion. Isvolsky reported to Sazonov, however, that the military arrangements between France and England were more complete than those of the Franco-Russian military convention.[187]

In January the French still expected an early war,[188] and they naturally expected help from England, where "continental intervention had become the accepted dogma."[189] A further development of Anglo-French cooperation came with the completion of details for common action in the Far East, which involved secret signals, concentration, annual meetings of admirals and joint maneuvers.[190]

A dispatch from Sir Francis Bertie in France informed the British government of the outburst of chauvinism, as shown by the success of ultra-patriotic and anti-German shows. A note by G.H. Villiers warned that this jingo spirit was "a distinct danger to the peace of Europe." Grey, Nicolson and Crowe, however, all thought that the French government should "foster and take advantage of this spirit" to facilitate the passage of financial measures which would "ensure some equality of fighting efficiency between France and Germany."[191]

At the same time the Russian ambassador at Berlin wrote that all he saw and heard there convinced him that Germany wanted to avoid war at all costs, and that there was the same spirit in Vienna. The German government thought the result of a war would be doubtful in view of Russia's military preparedness and of French confidence in their army. Even if Germany was successful, her commerce would be destroyed if England took part.[192]

The appointment in February, 1913, of Delcassé as ambassador to St. Petersburg was a further indication of the French government's determination to hasten preparations for an early war. Isvolsky explained that this choice was made because, "in the eyes of leading French circles and of public opinion," Delcassé was regarded, "in the present exceedingly grave international situation, which may call for the application of the Franco-Russian Alliance," as a personification of that alliance. He added, on his own account, that Delcassé was entirely devoted to the idea of a close association between France and Russia, and might therefore play, "if the critical moment should come, a decisive part in overcoming any hesitation on the part of the government."[193]

Delcassé's specific task was to persuade the Russians of the necessity of increasing the number of strategic railway lines so the Russian army could be "more rapidly concentrated on the western frontier." He was also authorized to offer French financial assistance for this purpose.[194]

The return to three years army service in France was under active discussion in February, being presented as an answer to German army increases. In fact, there was no relation between the two developments, as was noted by Baron Guillaume, the Belgian minister in Paris.[195] Jules Cambon pointed out that France should always "make it appear" that her "immense military effort" was a result of German initiatives.[196] He also explained that the German army increase had nothing to do with the French efforts, but was the result of the re-awakening of patriotism in France, the weakening of Austria and the disturbance of the balance of power by the aggrandisement of the Balkan States.[197]

On February 25, Count Ai Benckendorff, Russian ambassador in London, reported from the London conference that his conversations with Paul Cambon had convinced him that, of all the Powers, France was the one which would envisage war without great regret. He said all the Powers were working for peace, but that France would accept war philosophically. He thought that, rightly or wrongly, France had complete confidence in her army.[198] This assessment of the French attitude was confirmed by the words and actions of the French government. Poincaré told Isvolsky that the events of the last eighteen months had aroused in French public opinion a patriotic feeling unknown in a long time. In view of this rising national sentiment neither he nor his ministers would allow a repetition of the Agadir incident or consent to any such compromise. This determination was reinforced by the fact that assurances given by the British government allowed France to count on the certainty of armed support in case of war with Germany.[199] Aristide Briand, the prime minister, read the Chamber a message from Poincaré which said, "No people can be really pacific unless they are always ready for war. We must turn toward our army and navy, and spare no effort or sacrifice to consolidate and strengthen them."[200]

Government, society and the press concentrated on the need for measures to counter the German army increase. The French newspapers demanded more money for arms and the passage of the three years law. The government decided to ask the Chamber for 500 million francs over five years, the first instalment to be spent mainly on artillery and training camps. Poincaré predicted that the three years law, about to be presented to the Chamber, would be passed by an enormous majority.[201]

British General Sir Henry Wilson talked with some of the leading military men of France who, he said, thought "it would be far better for France if a conflict were not too long postponed." They wanted to fight immediately over the Balkan difficulties so they would be sure of Russian assistance. Russia was so strong, both militarily and financially, that she was not dependent on France, and might take a line of her own. Both Nicolson and Grey erroneously thought the French government did not share the military view.[202]

Baron Guillaume, the Belgian minister in Paris, also remarked on the growth of chauvinism in France. Everyone he met told him an early war with Germany was certain and inevitable. People were demanding the immediate passage of any measure designed to increase France's military power.[203]

When Asquith stated in Parliament that England was under no obligation to send a military force to the continent, Paul Cambon complained that this might have an unfortunate effect in France.[204] The fact that the details of unloading and moving the British expeditionary force to the war zone were being completed at the same time should have shown the French that Asquith was merely acting under the necessity of deceiving Parliament concerning the government's policy. The arrangements for Franco-British cooperation were actually much more complete than those of France and Russia, which in turn were more elaborate than the vague arrangements between Austria and Germany.[205]

Jules Cambon reported to M. Jonnart, the French foreign minister, that a new German military law was to be introduced which he thought was likely to include a more severe application of military service. Forty-five thousand to fifty thousand men fit for service were enlisted each year into the Ersatz

Reserve, where they received no training. The German peace recruits, he said, fell short of the legal requirement of 1 percent of the population by 50,000 men: many of these would probably be called to the colours under the new law.[206]

The new German military budget involved an expenditure of 1,055 million marks, of which 999 million would be raised by a one-time levy on fortunes, to be collected over three years.[207] The French military attaché explained that there would be an increase in the annual number of recruits, which would amount to 58,500 recruits a year for the next two years. The immediate increase in the German effectives was 58,500 men, a second group to be added in October 1914.[208]

The three years law provided for an increase of the French army by 160,000 men in peace-time, with companies increased from between 130 and 150 men to 200 in the eastern regions. It was announced in May that the recruits of 1911, due to be discharged in October, would be kept in service, although the specific law authorizing this had not yet been passed by the Chamber.[209]

Pichon expected that the French Chamber would grant the 500 million francs required for army reorganization and increase of war *matériel* with enthusiasm.[210] The Belgian ambassador, Guillaume, thought the expenditures of the new law would be so exorbitant that there would be an outcry in the country, and that France would be faced with the necessity of renouncing the programme or going to war on short notice.[211]

The Russians decided that their response to the German army bill would be an increase of 260,000 men and a budgetary increase of the equivalent of 100 million roubles. The Warsaw district would get an increase of 75,000 men.[212] France and Russia therefore proposed to increase their already great numerical superiority over Germany by 360,000 soldiers.

The new situation was put in proper perspective by Colonel Repington, *The Times's* military correspondent, who wrote that the German army expansion was due to the changed situation in southeastern Europe, especially to the "enhanced power and prestige of Russia" as a result of the Balkan wars. He thought this change gave the German general staff "cause for serious anxiety" and that the new German armaments appeared perfectly justified.[213]

He praised the splendid way in which France had risen to the situation, being "ready to accept a very onerous extension of colour service in order to remain mistress of her destinies." Her infantry and artillery would be better trained than those of Germany and, "as France has been quicker with her riposte than Germany with her lunge, the new French peace establishments will be completed before those of Germany are begun."[214] In a later article he noted that France already had four million men in her reserves and that there would be more in future because service had been prolonged to twenty-eight years.[215]

With regard to Russia, Repington pointed out that since 1904 the Russian recruit contingent had averaged 440,000 men, and that with a period of service of three years, Russia never had fewer than 1,400,000 men under arms. During the last phase of the Balkan war one class had been kept with the colours, providing a total of more than 1,700,000. Russia's army expenditure in 1912 had been 815 million roubles, and her gold reserve was 1,846 million. Repington declared that Russia lacked neither men nor resources and that "the German army bill is condemned to sterility before it is passed, as far as Russia is concerned."[216]

In April the Russian Compulsory Service Act was amended so that all recruits born in 1892 would join the colours in 1913, not 1914.[217] Previously those born in the last quarter of the year were not called up until the next year.[218] In October the decision was taken to extend the legal term of service in the infantry from three to three and a half years, which would keep about 365,000 men on active service an extra six months. *The Times* report said it was not stated if the new regulation applied to the cavalry and artillery. If it did the army would be increased by 450,000.[219]

In a further article entitled "Europe's Armed Camp—the New Balance of Power," Repington expressed the view that the French sacrifices gave good hope that no attack by Germany could now succeed. He stated that it was no longer the case that the Russian army would be far behind in mobilisation. Railway construction and the reorganization of the army had reduced mobilisation time, and the Russian army now could take the field only a few days after the French army.[220]

French money was always available for strategic railways and to strengthen Russia's position in the Balkans. Delcassé's appointment to St. Petersburg coincided with the project of a loan to Serbia.[221] Isvolsky pointed out to Pichon that France was interested in increasing Serbia's strength, because in case of war Serbia would be on the side of France. Pichon promised to exert his influence to expedite a loan to Serbia.[222]

Russia's intention to make Serbia the spearhead of her attack against Austria was becoming more and more clear. In April, the Serbian minister at St. Petersburg reported that Sazonov had told him Serbia must work for the future, as she "would acquire a great deal of territory from Austria."[223] A week later Sazonov wrote to the Russian ambassador at Belgrade that Serbia had "passed only through the first stage of her historical career," and that her promised land lay in the territory of Austria-Hungary.[224]

Poincaré's letter recommending Delcassé to the tsar emphasized that the expeditious construction of the lines he had spoken of the previous August was now "particularly urgent." The great military effort France was making to maintain the balance of power called for corresponding efforts on the part of Russia.[225] France was, as usual, ready to provide the money.

Russia had, however, plenty of money to spend on her army. The Russian minister of finance had 400 million roubles for defence if it was needed, and the war ministry had over 200 million roubles of unused credits at its disposal.[226]

In June Pichon was authorized to tell Kokovtsov, the Russian minister of finance, that the French government would allow Russia to borrow 400 or 500 million francs a year to build railways throughout the Empire on two conditions. These were that the strategic railways planned with the French general staff would be begun at once, and that the peace strength of the Russian army would be considerably increased.[227] When an agreement was reached in November it was stipulated that 800 million francs would be spent on strategic railways in three years.[228]

Delcassé reported to Pichon on August 2, that the doubling of the Moscow to Warsaw line between Briansk and Gomel was nearly completed and that the quadrupling of the line Zabinka to Brest-Litovsk would soon be finished. The changing of the Polish line between Warsaw and Cracow to Russian gauge was about to begin. Works that were finished or were in progress would assure a gain of four days in the concentration of the army.[229] Russia would now be able to send thirteen army corps against Germany on the 13th day of mobilisation, which convinced Joffre, the French commander in chief, that satisfactory progress was being made for increasing the effectives on Russia's western frontier.[230]

Joffre pointed out that it was necessary for the French armies to have a marked superiority over the German forces in the west of Germany, which could be realized if Germany was obliged to send more forces to the east. He suggested that it would be advantageous for the Warsaw forces to be grouped so as to constitute a direct menace to Germany in peace-time. Russia's General Jilinski replied that the reorganization of the Russian army had in mind precisely the creation of an army corps in the Warsaw region. He also indicated that work had been completed on the doubling of the railway line between Orel and Warsaw and the quadrupling of the line between Zabinka and Brest-Litovsk. These were works which had been decided on at the 1912 conference.[231]

At the end of the year Russia and France continued their feverish preparations for war. Delcassé reported that the railway works requested by the general staffs in September, 1912, had almost entirely been completed. Significant increases had been made in the Russian peace effectives, with the forces on the western front receiving three successive reinforcements of 25,000 each. An increase of 90,000 was projected for 1914. Arrangements were completed at the end of December for Russia to borrow 500 million francs a year for five years to fulfill the railway programme.[232]

Sazonov addressed a significant report to the tsar on December 8, 1913, setting forth Russia's agenda for the near future. He spoke of the final dissolution of the Turkish Empire, which brought to the fore the question of the straits at Constantinople. Russia, he wrote, had spent hundreds of millions on preparation for the capture of Constantinople, but was still unable to accomplish it. He made detailed proposals for the further preparations which should be made to advance on Constantinople as soon as necessary. Finally, he concluded with plans for the European war without which Russia's aims could not be realized. He repeated his view that "the question of the Straits could hardly be advanced a step except through European complications," that is a European war. These "complications" would find Russia in alliance with France and possibly, although not certainly, with England. She could also count on Serbia and perhaps Roumania. He advocated a policy of conciliating Roumania to ensure her support, and hoped to reconcile Serbia and Bulgaria to the same end.[233] The Russians were now in agreement with France that a general war was needed if their aims were to be accomplished.[234]

Meanwhile, the desire of the Young Turks to reform the Turkish army brought about the appointment of the German general, Otto Liman von Sanders, to lead a military mission to accomplish the reforms.[235] The Russians strongly objected to the command of a Turkish army corps at Constantinople by a German general and were prepared to take strong measures to force his withdrawal from such a position. The matter was complicated by the fact that British Admiral Limpus was in command of the entire Turkish fleet, a greater position than that proposed for Liman von Sanders.

The members of a conference of Russian ministers and army and navy heads on December 31 all agreed that Russia could not allow a German general to be given any territorial command in Turkey. Sazonov outlined proposals for "measures of compulsion" which Russia should undertake to force Turkey to withdraw Liman von Sanders's appointment. The prime minister asserted that Germany was "looking for a way out of the situation created by Russia's demands," and that negotiations with Germany should be continued as long as there was a chance of success. He insisted that, before any decision was made on measures of compulsion, the extent of the support to be expected from England and France should be ascertained.[236]

Sazonov agreed that his scheme for compelling Turkey to withdraw Liman von Sanders's appointment required the collaboration of all the members of the Triple Entente. He was uncertain how far England would go, but stated that Russia could "count on effectual support to the uttermost limit" from France. Delcassé had assured him that France would go as far as Russia might wish. The French press criticized Russia for her intention to regulate the matter by friendly conversations with Germany. It was necessary to make sure of British support, however, as France and Russia were not in a position to deal Germany a mortal blow, even if they had military success in the possible war.[237]

Vladimir Kokovtsov asserted that the measures proposed would inevitably bring war with Germany, and asked if war with Germany was desirable and whether or not Russia could wage it. Sazonov agreed that a Russo-German war was undesirable, but said he did not consider himself competent to decide if Russia was now in a position to fight Germany. The minister of war and the chief of the general staff "declared categorically the complete readiness of Russia for a duel with Germany, not to speak of Austria." Such a duel was unlikely, however, as these two Powers would probably have to deal with the Triple Entente.[238]

After a discussion of the military and naval measures of compulsion which might be taken against Turkey, Kokovtsov insisted that a war at the moment would be a misfortune for Russia, and Sazonov wanted to know what should be done if the negotiations failed. The conference concluded that the negotiations with Germany should be continued until their lack of success became clear, whereupon measures of pressure should be applied in agreement with France and England. If the active participation of both those Powers could not be assured, it would not be possible to take measures which might lead to war with Germany.[239] It is thus evident that Russia was prepared to risk war with Germany if the cooperation of France and England was certain, although they expected that Germany would back down in that case. The Germans had never intended any provocation and were ready to compromise, so force was not needed.

Russia continued to pour money into preparation for war. In 1913, 816,500,000 roubles (nearly £85 million) was spent on national defence, 75 percent more than in 1904.[240] In the same ten years France and Russia spent 30 percent more on their navies than Germany and Austria.[241]

French financial support of the Russian position in the Balkans showed French concern to march with Russia in that area. When Roumania asked for a loan of 300 million francs, France required that Roumania abandon talks with the Triple Alliance.[242] Montenegro, already aligned with Russia and receiving military equipment from her, was granted a loan from France.[243] A loan to Serbia of 250 million francs was dispensed, with the condition that privileges should be given to French industry. Amongst these privileges was an order worth 3,500,000 francs to French arms manufacturer Creusot for shrapnel and an order for 400,000 rifles for 33,600,000 francs.[244]

There was little change in the policy of the British government in 1913.

It assumed that there would be war with Germany in the near future, and the arrangements for the British expeditionary force to fight with France were finalized. Six infantry and one cavalry division were to go into action on the 17th day of mobilisation. A memorandum was drawn up and signed which "resembled a de facto military convention."[245] The admiralty began to arm British merchant ships, thus turning them into warships.[246]

By the end of 1913 the German authorities were convinced, a few years too late, that war was unavoidable. Jules Cambon informed Pichon that the kaiser, who "had been considered a moderating influence on German policy had come to think war inevitable and necessary."[247] Pichon told Isvolsky that anti-French sentiment was growing in Germany, and even Wilhelm II, who had been noted for his strong pacific feeling for France, thought war was certain and that the sooner it came the better it would be for Germany.[248] Chancellor Bethmann-Hollweg was also "convinced that a great war was likely, if not inevitable," and that war was justified if Germany's "honour, safety and future" were threatened.[249] As the Franco-Russian plans and preparations threatened Germany's very existence, it was high time the Germans fully realized their danger.

The Liman von Sanders affair was resolved in January, but Russia was still concerned with the imminent demise of Turkey, and proceeded to make plans to deal with that desirable event. A conference of ministers and the heads of the army and navy which was held on February 8, 1914, discussed at length the issue of seizing the straits at Constantinople if the opportunity arose.

Sazonov opened the conference with a warning that events which might change the international situation of the straits might be very close. It was therefore necessary to prepare a programme to ensure that the straits question would be solved in accordance with Russia's wishes. Russia could not allow any other Power to control the straits and must prepare to seize possession of them immediately when the war began.[250]

Sazonov believed that the operations against the straits would be possible only in case of a general European war. The chief of the general staff and cavalry General Jilinski both agreed, and the latter pointed out that the possibility of sending troops against the Straits would depend on the general situation at the beginning of the war. If there was fighting on Russia's western front, all available troops would have to be sent there, because success on the western front would also mean success in the Straits question. Lieutenant-General Danilov supported this view, declaring that not a single army corps could be spared from the western front for other operations.[251]

After a long discussion of the means needed to seize the straits, the conference decided to take preparatory measures at once, because they might soon be required to execute them.[252] As all the participants who spoke agreed that this action could be taken only in conjunction with a general European war, it is evident that war was expected in the near future. This gives special significance to a passage in a memorandum by Nikolai Bazili, vice-director of the Russian secretariat of the foreign ministry, who was present at the conference. The memorandum reads in part, "The possibility of seizing the Straits depends on a favourable conjunction. To create it is the aim of the action of the Ministry of Foreign Affairs."[253]

The Russians expected that Serbia and Montenegro would fight with them when the war came, and they undertook to provide some of the needed armaments. Nikola Paschitsch, Serbian prime minister, had an audience with the tsar on February 2, 1914, at which he asked Russia to supply Serbia with 120,000 rifles, munitions and a few cannon. The tsar said the Serbs could not depend on Russia to manufacture arms for them but that she would do all she could, and asked what was needed. Paschitsch prepared a list for Sazonov. When the tsar asked how many soldiers Serbia could put in the field, he answered that she could field a half million well clothed and armed soldiers.[254]

Russia also assisted in the organization and equipment of the Montenegrin army, contributing two million roubles towards Montenegro's military expenditures and providing officers and non-commissioned officers (N.C.O.s) as instructors. The wartime army would number 50,000-60,000 men.[255]

At the same time the tsar began his campaign to arrange a closer relationship between Russia and England. In an interview with Paléologue, the new French ambassador, he deplored the fact that by England's fault the Triple Entente had not asserted its power better. Making it an alliance would allow its military, naval and financial power to give greater force to its representations. At the tsar's wish Paléologue offered to have the French minister for foreign affairs take up this matter with Grey. The tsar didn't think Wilhelm II wanted war, but it was necessary to be ready. He had, he said, recently increased his army by 75,000 men and would soon add 300,000 more.[256]

Preparations for the offensive against the straits involved strengthening the Russian naval forces in the Black Sea, and the minister of marine asked a secret session of the Duma for a credit of 270 million francs for this purpose.[257] Russia was also making a great effort to increase her naval power in the Baltic, the full effect of which would not be realized until the end of 1914.[258]

On June 13, 1914, the Russian minister of war inspired an article in the *Birshewija Vjedomosti* entitled "Russia is ready: France must be ready too." The article stated that Russia, having done everything to which the Dual Alliance obligated her, expected France to perform her obligations as well, in particular to maintain the three year term of military service. With regard to Russia's readiness for war, the article read as follows:

The reforms made in the Russian military departments during the training of Russia's armed forces exceed anything that has ever been done before in this line. The recruit contingent this year has...been raised from 450,000 to 580,000 men, and the period of service has been lengthened by six months. Thanks to these measures, there are in service every winter in Russia, four contingents of recruits under arms, making an army of 2,300,000 men.

The purpose of the peace-time increases was to effect rapid mobilisation, while a whole network of strategic railways aimed at "the most rapid concentration of the army in case of war."[259] *The Times* military correspondent wrote:

There are signs that Russia has done with defensive strategy. The increased number of guns in the Russian Army Corps, the growing efficiency of the Army, and the improvements made or planned in strategic railways are, again, matters which cannot be left out of account. These things are well calculated to make the Germans nervous.[260]

On June 18, ten days before the assassination of Archduke Franz Ferdinand of Austria-Hungary, Paléologue told René Viviani, the French premier, that "war would break out at any moment."[261] Before leaving for Russia on July 20, Poincaré called General Messimy, the war minister, to the Elysée and warned him that a conflict was imminent and that the three years law must not be touched.[262]

England was also well prepared for war. When the war came arrangements for the arrival and deployment of the British expeditionary force were complete.[263] On July 1, 1914, the navy issued "war orders no. 1 (war with Germany)."[264] From July 15 to 23, 1914, "the entire naval force in home waters was on a war footing." A return to peace-time organization had not gone far when on July 26 dispersal was cancelled.[265] Sir Julian Corbett wrote in the official history of the war that whether it was right or wrong to cling to the system of a small army and a large navy was debatable but that, given the scale of preparations decided on, "the machinery for setting our forces in action had reached an ordered completeness in detail that has no parallel in our history."[266]

The scale of entente preparations for war, in comparison with those of Germany and Austria, is shown by the defence expenditures of the Powers in the decade before the war. During these ten years the military expenditures of France and Russia exceeded those of Germany and Austria by £160 million, while the excess of their naval expenditures was £70 million. Thus these two Powers devoted £230 million more to defence in that decade than did Germany and Austria, an excess of 25 percent. The gap was greater in the last five years before the war than in the period 1905-09. Russia led the four

Powers in military expenditure, while Germany led all except England in naval expenditure. Austria trailed the others considerably in both categories.[267]

If England's spending on defence is taken into account, the entente superiority is overwhelming, because England led all the other Powers. According to A.G. Enock's figures, the excess on the side of the entente, including England, was £993 million. His calculations show England in the lead in every year but two: in 1909 the lead was taken by Germany and in 1913 by Russia.[268]

The Triple Entente led the way in war preparations in every respect during the last ten years before the war. France and Russia increased the numerical superiority of their armies during that decade, while the ability of the Russian army in particular to strike at Germany was greatly enhanced. The entente's preponderance in naval power was still greater, despite Germany's efforts to expand her navy. The outbreak of the war saw the Central Powers vastly inferior in both military and naval power to their prospective enemies.

Notes

1. Fritz Fischer, *War of Illusions*, p. 397.
2. V. R. Berghahn, *Germany and the Approach of War in 1914*, p. xii.
3. DDFI, VII, no. 289.
4. *Ibid.*, VIII, fn. p. 439.
5. *Ibid.*, nos. 434, 469, 482.
6. *Ibid.*, IX, no. 76.
7. DDF2, I, nos. 159, 281.
8. *Ibid.*, no. 329.
9. FO800/115.
10. *Ibid.*
11. The *Spectator*, August 9, 1902.
12. *Morning Post*, July 7, 1903, p. 6.
13. *Daily Telegraph*, July 10, 1903, p. 8.
14. *Westminster Gazette*, July 6, 1903, p. 1.
15. *Daily Telegraph*, March 25, 1904.
16. *The Standard*, April 11, 1904.
17. A. J. Marder, *The Anatomy of British Sea Power*, p. 479.
18. Peter Padfield, *The Great Naval Race*, p. 110.
19. Maurice V. Brett, (ed.), *The Journals and Letters of Reginald, Viscount Esher*, II, 62-3.
20. A. J. Marder, *Fear God and Dread Nought*, II, 20; Lord Fisher, *Memories and Records*, I, 35.
21. Padfield, pp. 121-2.
22. HCD, March 2, 1908, cols. 371, 374; A. G. Enock, *The Problem of Armaments*, pp.182-6.
23. Accounts and Papers, 1904, no. 129, LIII 83.
24. *Ibid.*, 1908, no. 281, LXV 371.
25. DDF2, III, no. 130.

26.*Ibid.*, V, no. 321.

27.*Ibid.*, no. 372.

28.S. R. Williamson, *The Politics of Grand Strategy: Britain and France Prepare for War*, pp. 45-6.

29.*Ibid.*, p. 56.

30.Lt. Col. C. à Court Repington, *The First World War, 1914-1918*, p. 14.

31.Marder, *Fear God*, II, 55.

32.*Ibid.*, p. 72.

33.O. J. Hale, *Germany and the Diplomatic Revolution*, p. 21.

34.Paul M. Kennedy, *The Rise of Anglo-German Antagonism*, p. 272.

35.E. D. Morel, *Ten Years of Secret Diplomacy*, p. 94.

36.Eugen Weber, *The Nationalist Revival in France, 1905-1914*, pp. 32-3.

37.Hale, p. 201.

38.Repington, p. 4.

39.*Ibid.*, pp. 6-9.

40.DDF2, X, no. 48.

41.Repington, p. 4.

42.*Ibid.*, p. 3.

43.Williamson, pp. 90-1.

44.F. Maurice, *Haldane, 1856-1915*, pp. 320-1.

45.J. E. Edmonds, *History of the Great War Based on Official Documents: Military Operations, France and Belgium, 1914*, pp. 4-5.

46.*Ibid.*, pp. 10-11.

47.FO800/49.

48.DDF2, VIII, no. 300.

49.BD, III, no. 244.

50.*Ibid.*, no. 299.

51.FO800/87.

52.Brett, II, 179-80.

53.*Ibid.*, p. 210.

54.Weber, pp. 39-42.

55.M. E. Durham, *Twenty Years of Balkan Tangle*, p. 134.

56.*Ibid.*, pp. 93, 157.

57.Marder, *Fear God*, II, 122-3.

58.DDF2, XI, nos. 17, 44, 47.

59.*Ibid.*, no. 95.

60.Marder, *Fear God*, II, p. 169.

61.*Ibid.*, p. 191.

62.Fisher, I, 35.

63.Brett, II, 294.

64.Caroline E. Playne, *The Pre-War Mind in Britain*, p. 145.

65.DDF2, XI, no. 417.

66.Weber, pp. 50, 86.

67.BD, VI, no. 79.

68.Williamson, p. 108.

69.Brett, II, 350.

70.M. Bogitshevich, *Causes of the War*, pp. 22, 111-2.
71.FO800/50.
72.FO800/73, 87.
73.DDF2, XI, no. 558.
74.Williamson, pp. 108-111.
75.*Fortnightly Review*, December 1, 1908.
76.FO800/51.
77.DDF2, XII, no. 69.
78.Bogitshevich, p. 112.
79.Weber, p. 72.
80.Frederic Harrison, *The German Peril,* pp. 113-4.
81.*Ibid.*, p. 120.
82.*Ibid.*, pp. 116, 130.
83.Playne, p. 133.
84.E. L. Woodward, *Great Britain and the German Navy*, pp. 232.
85.Bogitshevich, p. 90.
86.Francis Neilson, *How Diplomats Make War*, p. 126.
87.DDF2, XII, no. 392.
88.E. D. Morel, *Diplomacy Revealed*, pp. 43, 66, 67, 87, 157, 198.
89.FO800/52.
90.Major General Sir C. E. Callwell, *Field Marshal Sir Henry Wilson*, I, 88, 90-1.
91.FO800/52.
92.M. E. Durham, *The Sarajevo Crime*, p. 21.
93.DDF2, XII, no. 504.
94.*Ibid.*, no. 573.
95.*Ibid.*, XIII, no. 8.
96.*Ibid.*, nos. 63, 79.
97.*Ibid.*, nos. 81, 83.
98.B. de Siebert, *Entente Diplomacy and the World*, p. 525.
99.Kennedy, p. 375.
100.LN, I, 25.
101.*Ibid.*, p. 30.
102.*Ibid.*, nos. 26, 27.
103.DDF2, XIII, no. 204.
104.*Ibid.*, no. 208.
105.FO800/52.
106.Callwell, I, 92.
107.DDF2, XIII, no. 142.
108.*Ibid.*, no. 157.
109.BD, VII, nos. 392, 395.
110.DDF2, XIV, no. 79.
111.DDF3, II, no. 272.
112.Callwell, I, 97.
113.R. B. Haldane, *Before the War*, p. 168.
114.Callwell, I, 98.
115.BD, VII, no. 432.

116.FO800/52.
117.Joseph Caillaux, *Agadir: Ma Politique Extérieure*, pp. 143, 156.
118.FO800/52.
119.BD, VII, nos. 486, 488.
120.FO800/52.
121.LN, II, 420-3.
122.BD, VII, no. 496.
123.General J. J. C. Joffre, *Personal Memoirs of Joffre*, p. 23.
124.FO800/100.
125.DDF3, I, no. 336.
126.Callwell, I, 102.
127.*Ibid.*, p. 118.
128.FO800/87.
129.Marder, *Fear God*, II, 375, 380, 384.
130.*Ibid.*, fn. p. 384.
131.FO800/93.
132.Haldane, pp. 150, 180.
133.BD, VII, no. 644.
134.Williamson, p. 163.
135.Callwell, I, 104.
136.Bogitshevich, p. 109.
137.LN, II, 463-4.
138.*Ibid.*, pp. 469-70.
139.FO800/53.
140.DDF3, I, no. 603.
141.Playne, p. 250.
142.Callwell, I, 110.
143.LN, I, 194.
144.Weber, p. 123.
145.DDF3, II, no. 240.
146.Williamson, pp. 212-3.
147.DDF3, II, no. 269.
148.BD, VIII, nos. 315, 324.
149.Williamson, p. 214.
150.DDF3, II, nos. 82, 274, 369, 406.
151.*Ibid.*, no. 406.
152.BD, IX, no. 409.
153.Joffre, p. 69.
154.E. L. Spears, *Liaison*, 1914, pp. 35-9.
155.Joffre, p. 105.
156.Williamson, pp. 322-4.
157.Brett, III, 99.
158.DDF3, III, no. 145.
159.*Ibid.*, no. 448.
160.*Ibid.*, nos. 50, 71.
161.Grey of Falloden, *Twenty-five Years*, I, 93-5.

162.Padfield, p. 293.

163.DDF3, II, no. 297; Bogitshevich, pp. 100-107.

164.Bogitshevich, p. 30.

165.*Ibid.*, p. 27.

166.DDF3, III, no. 65.

167.LN, I, 269.

168.DDF3, III, no. 200.

169.*Ibid.*, no. 264.

170.Frederick L. Schuman, *War and Diplomacy in the French Republic*, p. 198.

171.LN, II, 339.

172.Foreign Affairs, Vol. I, no. 2, August 1919, p. 4.

173.FO800/94.

174.LN, II, 345.

175.LN, I, 324-6.

176.*Ibid.*, p. 326.

177.V. N. Kokovtsov, *Out of My Past*, pp. 345-9.

178.*Ibid.*, p. 339.

179.*Foreign Affairs*, Special Supplement, October 1919, p. 7.

180.Kokovtsov, p. 340.

181.LN, I, 342.

182.*Ibid.*, p. 346.

183.DDF3, V, nos. 22, 48, 103.

184.LN, I, pp. 368-70.

185.F. Stieve, *Isvolsky and the World War*, pp. 125-6.

186.*Ibid.*, pp. 126-7.

187.LN, I, 366-7.

188.Callwell, I, 122.

189.Williamson, p. 307.

190.DDF3, V, no. 303.

191.Weber, p. 114.

192.LN, II, 22-5.

193.Stieve, p. 137.

194.*Ibid.*, pp. 137-8; LN II, 49.

195.BDD, pp. 153-4.

196.DDF3, VI, no. 12.

197.*Ibid.*, V, no. 526.

198.LN, II, 303-6.

199.*Ibid.*, pp. 32-3.

200.Weber, p. 115.

201.*Ibid.*, pp. 33-6.

202.Nicolson, pp. 397-8.

203.Morel, *Diplomacy Revealed*, p. 247.

204.FO800/54.

205.Williamson, pp. 313, 317.

206.DDF3, V, no. 380.

207.DDF3, VI, no. 105.

208.*Ibid.*, no. 123.
209.LN, II, p. 87; Weber, p. 126.
210.BDD, pp. 157-8.
211.Morel, *Diplomacy Revealed*, p. 258.
212.DDF3, VI, no. 44.
213.*The Times*, March 10, 1913, p. 8a.
214.*Ibid.*
215.*Ibid.*, August 22, 1913, p. 3d.
216.*Ibid.*, March 10, 1913, p. 8a.
217.*Ibid.*, April 11, 1913, p. 5a.
218.*Ibid.*, April 11, 1913, p. 5c.
219.*Ibid.*, October 22, 1913, p. 8a.
220.*Ibid.*, pp. 3d, 3e.
221.LN, II, 49.
222.Stieve, p. 180.
223.Bogitschevich, pp. 99-100.
224.Stieve, p. 180.
225.*Ibid.*, pp. 52-4; DDF3, VI, no. 39.
226.Kokovtsov, pp. 364, 371.
227.DDF3, VII, no. 134; Stieve, pp. 169-70.
228.FO800/54.
229.DDF3, VII, no. 521.
230.*Ibid.*, VIII, no. 62.
231.*Ibid.*
232.DDF3, VIII, no. 698.
233.Stieve, pp. 188-90.
234.*Ibid.*, pp. 190-1.
235.S. B. Fay, *The Origins of the World War*, I, 501-503.
236.Stieve, pp. 219-24.
237.*Ibid.*, pp. 224-5.
238.*Ibid.*, p. 226.
239.*Ibid.*, pp. 228-9.
240.Kokovtsov, p. 462.
241.*The Naval Annual*, 1913, p. 96.
242.DDF3, VIII, no. 138.
243.*Ibid.*, no. 284.
244.*Ibid.*, no. 648.
245.Williamson, pp. 172-7.
246.Marder, *Fear God*, p. 407.
247.Weber, p. 132.
248.LN, II, 197-8.
249.Fischer, p. 270.
250.Stieve, pp. 230-1.
251.*Ibid.*, pp. 232-5.
252.*Ibid.*, p. 245.
253.Emile Laloy, *Les Documents Secrets Publié par les Bolcheviks*, p. 78.

254.Bogitschevich, pp. 130, 132.

255.*Ibid.*, pp. 95-6.

256.DDF3, IX, no. 322.

257.DDF3, X, no. 268.

258.*Ibid.*, no. 290.

259.*Kautsky Documents*, no. 2; DDF3, X, no. 369.

260.*The Times*, June 15, 1914.

261.Fischer, p. 431.

262.Weber, p. 142.

263.Williamson, p. 315.

264.*Ibid.*, p. 318.

265.Marder, *Fear God*, p. 52.

266.Julian Corbett, *History of the Great War Based on Official Documents: Naval Operations*, quoted in E. D. Morel, *Military Preparations for the Great War*, p. 3.

267.*Ibid.*, pp. 16-18. Enock's figures show a still greater disparity than those given by Morel.

268.A. G. Enock, *The Problem of Armaments*, pp. 182-6.

Ten

The War Aims of France and Russia

"The 'lost provinces' were a source of bitter humiliation and resentment to every Frenchman." The desire for *revanche* became "the keystone of French foreign policy." Paul Déroulède created the League of Patriots for agitation in Alsace-Lorraine and worked to arouse his countrymen to undertake a war of revenge. The French desire for pride and power to some extent found its expression in imperialism, but imperialism was regarded as a means to *revanche*, not a substitute for it.[1]

An isolated France could not afford to risk renewed war with Germany, and it was therefore imperative that France should acquire allies. Léon Gambetta reflected in 1881 that France should be very cautious until she had a strong army, and said, "The creation of that army is our present task. I occupy myself with it every day and it is the object of my principal preoccupation. When we possess a powerful army we will find allies."[2]

Gambetta's attempt to work towards an entente with Russia in 1881 was short-lived, but the idea was revived by Baron Mohrenheim, who became Russian ambassador in Paris in 1884. Mohrenheim sent memoranda regularly to the tsar concerning the advantages of a Franco-Russian understanding and was one of the most enthusiastic and faithful advocates of an alliance. The rise of General George Boulanger in 1886/7 increased French interest in an approach to Russia, but the tsar was frightened by France's wild talk of war with Germany. He was reassured of French reliability only when the League of Patriots was dissolved and Boulangism routed in 1889.[3]

When France replaced Germany as the source of loans to Russia hope for a closer relationship was raised in France. The outcome depended, however, on the Russian relationship with Germany. It was only when the Russian statesmen concluded that they could no longer count on German cooperation that they began to listen to the advances of France.[4]

For France the principal aim of the overtures to Russia was to forge a military alliance which could cope with Germany. As her military attaché at St. Petersburg wrote to Charles de Freycinet, then minister of war, in 1891, for Russia the main enemy was Austria. For France it was Germany, because she must recover the lost provinces.[5] When the Empress Victoria of Germany visited Paris she aroused the French nationalist press by expressing her desire for an end to *revanche*.[6] General Boisdeffre, deputy chief of the French general staff, told General Nicholas Obruchev that it went without saying that France wanted to take back Alsace-Lorraine.[7] Although a Franco-Russian entente was reached by 1892, it was not until the military convention was ratified by the tsar in January, 1894, that the French achieved their chief objective.

All the agreements between the two Powers were kept secret, and not even the Chamber of Deputies had any knowledge of the terms of the alliance. Public opinion was loud in its praise, although nothing was known of the commitments involved. The *revanchists* welcomed it as a means for the recovery of Alsace-Lorraine, and the conservatives, supported by the militarists and clerics, greeted it as a force for reaction in domestic politics.[8]

In 1895 the Russians wanted to know what France would do if Russia found it necessary to intervene militarily in the east. President Félix Faure replied that France would support Russia in a Balkan war only if it were justified by the possibility of recovering Alsace-Lorraine. "Faure repeated this warning during the visits to France by the tsar in 1896 and by Count Michael Mouravieff, the Russian foreign minister, a year later."[9]

When the tsar proposed a conference for the limitation of armaments, the French feared that this would involve the recognition of existing territorial arrangements. Paul Cambon, French ambassador in Constantinople, wrote that if the proposal had any practical consequences it would have the effect of forcing France to give up the idea of taking back Alsace-Lorraine by force of arms.[10] The *National Review* said that any French government which approved such proposals "would inevitably be swept out of office in a day."[11]

During the South African war France and Russia attempted to persuade Germany to act with them against British policy in the Transvaal. When Wilhelm II reacted by demanding that the three Powers should first guarantee their European territories, this was taken to mean that France would have to renounce any claim to Alsace-Lorraine. This not only made joint action with Germany impossible, but convinced Delcassé that France could make no agreement with Germany without reaffirming the Treaty of Frankfurt which had ended the France Prussian war. From this time on he minuted any dispatch which suggested an agreement with Germany with comments such as: "What? Approve the Treaty of Frankfurt all over again?" It was this conviction which led to his refusal to negotiate with Germany over Morocco and consequently to the first Morocco crisis.[12]

Delcassé's feeling was shared by President Loubet, who told Georges Bihourd, the French ambassador in Berlin, that he would rather have his right hand cut off than sign the Treaty of Frankfurt a second time.[13] The Marquis de Noailles wrote to Delcassé on June 20, 1902, that a *rapprochement* with Germany was impossible because France hadn't forgotten Alsace-Lorraine. He thought the Germans took too seriously the few French who spoke in favour of burying the hatchet.[14] Some Germans understood this, however, as Count Monts, the German ambassador to Italy, told Barrère, he knew Franco-German peace hinged on Alsace-Lorraine.[15]

Delcassé's resignation when his Morocco policy was repudiated brought little change in French policy because Rouvier opposed the assembling of a conference which would internationalize the Morocco question. The French newspapers represented Delcassé's fall as being entirely due to orders from Berlin, and before the end of June French opinion accepted the idea that war was preferable to submitting to German dictates. Barrère, ambassador in Rome, exclaimed, "Henceforth war is unavoidable." The possibility of war was taken for granted in the fall of 1905 and early in 1906. The French thus reacted strongly to what was considered a national humiliation. Henceforth any attempt by Germany to defend her rights would be treated as an insult to be resisted by war.

This nationalist revival, although a minority movement, dominated French policy for the next nine years. Moderates and anti-militarists won every election but were unable to influence foreign policy. Anti-militarism and anti-clericalism became official government policy. In 1905 the three years military service was reduced to two, and the separation of church and state was decreed.[16] Between 1906 and 1911, while France was constantly engaged in the military conquest of Morocco, "The French Chamber passed resolution after resolution by large majorities expressive of its determination to observe the Algeciras Act and disclaiming intervention in the internal affairs of Morocco."[17]

By the spring of 1906 the national feeling aroused by the Morocco crisis was overshadowed by a growing fear of social revolution. L'Echo de Paris published a series of articles on the coming revolution, with reference to the strikes of the miners and postmen. Some feared war as an alternative to social revolution, while the right considered war an antidote to social revolution. Paul Doumer believed France was in a desperate state, and said, "We must get out of it at any price by a violent crisis." He thought an early war was the only way to unite the French people "in the right feeling." The middle class, fearing for their lives and property, looked to the right to defend the existing social order.[18] These sentiments, naturally strong among the ruling class, strengthened the appeal of nationalism and chauvinism and enabled the nationalist minority to lead French policy in the desired direction.

La Revanche continued to preclude any move towards reconciliation with Germany. In July, 1907, Eugene Étienne, in Barthou's cabinet, met Wilhelm II at Kiel, and the kaiser expressed his desire for an understanding between France and Germany. Étienne replied that it would first be necessary to settle the territorial question, which ended the conversation.[19] The feeling of militarist circles was shown by speeches made at a farewell dinner held for Colonel Goepp of the 26th infantry regiment. He declared that, at the close of his career, "my poignant grief is…that the war of revenge which we are expecting every day has not taken place." General Bailloud, commanding at Nancy, said, "You remarked that we were within an ace of war in 1905. This war will take place. Let us hope that the 26th…will contribute to return to us the lost provinces."[20] In January, 1908, Stephen Pichon, faced with a proposal by Germany that France and Germany should sign a treaty guaranteeing their coasts on the North Sea, stated that France could not do this as it would mean the final ratification of the Treaty of Frankfurt.[21]

The nationalist revival gained force in 1908, partly through the growing influence of *action française*, an extreme nationalist and royalist group which provided a rallying point for the traditional nationalist forces.[22] In July premier Georges Clemenceau said he considered war with Germany inevitable.[23] Debates on foreign policy in the French Chamber showed that there could be no lasting conciliation between France and Germany without the restoration of Alsace-Lorraine. The settlement of the Bosnian crisis was considered a diplomatic defeat, and the conclusion was drawn in Paris that the entente "should pay attention to the systematic development of their armed forces."[24] *Si vis pacem para bellum* became "the favourite dictum of all politicians."[25] In 1910 the July 14 Bastille day celebrations showed a revival of enthusiasm for the army and the flag.[26]

Nationalist enthusiasm reached its peak in 1911, the year which saw the march to Fez and the Agadir crisis. In March the Belgian minister in Berlin noted Delcassé's return to the cabinet, which he thought was designed to play up to the growing anti-German feeling of public opinion. He noticed an intensification of the press campaign against Germany, and drew attention to a speech by the President of the Senate, in which he spoke more openly of *revanche* than had been done for years.[27] A Latin Quarter demonstration by 3,000 students evoked cries of "Vive l'Alsace! Vive la Lorraine! C'est l'Alsace qui nous faut."[28]

War was believed to be imminent, and French ministers thought Germany had "rallied France." Klotz, the finance minister, spoke of "the great and joyous confidence the nation in arms has in itself.[29] Colonel Arthur Boucher, in a book published in 1911, wrote that Agadir had shown that Germany was looking for an occasion to make war on France. The result was that "Patriotism, which a bad policy had enfeebled in her, has suddenly reawakened with the force of the great days of our history...the French people are now all ready to take up arms." His warning to Germany was that she should not attack, for France would win.[30]

Chauvinistic feeling reached its height with the signing of the Morocco agreement on November 4, 1911, which was represented as a defeat for France. The speaker who presented the treaty to the Senate said, "We negotiated under the cannon of Agadir...It is the counterpart of Fashoda." Albert de Mun wrote in L' Echo de Paris, that there had been a profound change in France in the most recent six months. The opportunity for revenge had been missed for lack of readiness, but "preparations for the inevitable should be ceaseless and untiring." Military circles expected a crisis in the spring of 1912.[31]

This revived national spirit was embodied in the person of Raymond Poincaré, who became premier of France on January 12, 1912. The fire-eating Lorrainer was determined to tighten the relations between France and Russia. One of his first acts was to reject a joint intervention by France and Germany in the Turco-Italian war, on the ground that it would give rise to the belief in a *rapprochement* between France and Germany and thus weaken the Triple Entente.[32]

Alexandre Isvolsky, Russian ambassador in Paris, evidently basing his opinion on the view prevalent in diplomatic circles, thought the Morocco agreement was a good one for France, who, he said, had won a material and moral success. He reported, however, that military circles expected new international complications in the spring, and that the French war department "continues to prepare actively for military operations in the near future."[33]

In March, 1912, Isvolsky wrote of the growth of national sentiment and a lively interest in the military forces. He reported that a subscription for the acquisition of airplanes for the army had raised a million and a half francs in two weeks. The aim was to maintain French superiority over Germany in military aviation. On Sunday, March 10, when a review of the troops of the Paris garrison had taken place on the Champs de Vincennes, a crowd of nearly a million people had turned out. They had sung patriotic songs and applauded the troops enthusiastically, to the accompaniment of shouts of "Vive l'Armée."[34] The *Daily Telegraph's* Paris correspondent wrote

I have never seen in Paris such a remarkable manifestation of military patriotism as that of last Sunday. The change in the national temper of the French people is one of the most notable events of contemporary Europe.[35]

In May, George Grahame wrote from Paris that the French press was full of talk about an Anglo-French alliance, based on the withdrawal of British ships from the Mediterranean. He thought the only idea of France was to recover Alsace-Lorraine.[36]

At the same time the agitation for a return to three years of military service, which had begun in 1911, was taken up by *Action française* in two long articles. The matter was soon raised in the Chamber and the struggle over this controversial proposal was under way.[37]

The first Balkan war produced an increase in anti-German demonstrations. Tattoos degenerated into demonstrations with loud shouts of *"à bas l'allemagne."*[38] General Lyautey praised the new spirit of the youth, particularly the fact "that it does not fear war." The right applauded a speech in the Senate which proclaimed that "In the present state of the world, the horrors of war must be veiled by its grandeurs, by its sacrifices, by its glories."[39]

In January, 1913, Raymond Poincaré was elected president of France, an event which some observers considered a signal for war. The minister of finance, Caillaux, thought it meant war after the general elections, and Armand Fallières, the departing president, agreed.[40] George Grahame wrote that he had listened to a high official in the ministry of foreign affairs holding forth on the danger of the existing situation. The official had expressed the belief that "one of the chief dangers of an explosion in Europe lies in the state of feeling in France, which has got back to the combustible sort of patriotism of the Boulanger days." He thought the French people were no longer afraid of war, but "would embark on one with the greatest enthusiasm." Poincaré, he said, was popular because he was a Lorrainer, as shown by the cries of *"Vive la Lorraine"* from the crowd around his house on the night of his election.[41]

Grahame also reported other signs of popular enthusiasm. Many things were occurring to revive bitter feelings about the lost provinces. Abbé Weltali was making a lecture tour to stir up trouble. One of the plays in vogue was *Alsace*, which excited French feelings against Germany, and Alsatian peasants were drinking to *"la revanche."*[42]

A short time after his election as president in January, 1913, Poincaré told Isvolsky that the events of the past eighteen months had aroused in the French public "a patriotic fervour unknown for a long time." In view of the rising national sentiment in France the French government would not consent to any such compromise as took place in connection with the Agadir incident.[43] In other words, the next time they would insist that Germany must submit completely to the dictate of the Entente.

Baron Guillaume, the Belgian minister in Paris, wrote that "public opinion in France is becoming daily more suspicious and Chauvinistic." He was continually meeting people who said an early war with Germany was inevitable. Minister for foreign affairs, Stéphen Pichon had just made a speech urging more preparation for war, and he believed Parliament would "grant with enthusiasm the 500 million francs demanded by the government" to complete French military organization.[44] Pichon noted that half the Paris theatres were producing patriotic or chauvinistic plays.[45] Guillaume thought the French government was encouraging this spirit of chauvinism in French public opinion.[46]

The Liman von Sanders affair brought further declarations of support for Russia. The French were very careful not to appear friendly with Germany. They avoided any agreement which public opinion might regard as sanctioning the existing territorial conditions, and thus as finally renouncing the lost provinces.[47]

Three interesting books by military men appeared in 1913 and early 1914. The most important of these was that by Colonel Arthur Boucher, entitled *L'Allemagne en Péril*. Boucher begins by saying that France has no quarrel with Germany except that when she took Alsace-Lorraine, Germany made of France an "irreconcilable enemy."[48] Germany no longer speaks of hegemony, but "proclaims that her only preoccupation is to defend her existence."[49] This results from the union of the four Balkan powers, which adds to Germany's three former enemies a fourth, which together can put a million men under arms. Germany is menaced on the north, the west and the east, and must now guard as well her southern flank. Germany can avoid being broken in this four-fold vise only by breaking the weakest and closest link, France. Thus "Germany's peril, great though it be, translates itself for France into a still greater peril."[50] He says that Germany, "to be in a position to resist the attacks which can menace her from all sides, is obliged to raise her military power to the supreme degree:" all this power is concentrated against France.[51]

Boucher does not believe, however, that Germany is strong enough to accomplish the task required of her. He thinks France alone can win against Germany. French morale is superior, now that "at last the reign of patriotism and justice has arrived."[52] The three years law has established equality of the French forces with those of Germany and changed the balance of power to the advantage of France.[53]

Russia has seen and applauded the awakening of patriotism in France, he says, and the three years law has shown her that France "is ready at all costs to be ready to resist Germany victoriously." Russia has strengthened her forces and taken measures to hasten the mobilization of her armies. France should insist that Russian forces are constantly ready to invade East Prussia. This will upset the German calculations and require them to keep more men in the east.[54] It can be seen that "on the perhaps early day when Slavism wishes to put an end to 'Germanism,' the friendship of Russia can serve us."[55] If Russia attacks Germany:

France becomes Mistress of the situation, and it will only be necessary for her to take up the sword at the opportune time to put Germany in a position where it will be impossible for her to defend the provinces she has taken from us.[56]

The most important fact which compromises Germany's future is the hostility of France, and France is Germany's enemy only because of Alsace-Lorraine. All Germany has to do is give up Alsace-Lorraine and she will have French friendship. A union of Germany, Russia and France could ensure permanent world peace.[57]

Major de Civrieux expresses similar ideas in *Le Germanisme Encerclé*. The Entente Cordiale, he writes, barred the great maritime routes to a Germany already pressed on the east by Russia and held in the west by France.[58] Now the victory of the Slavs over Turkey has struck a terrible blow to the Hapsburg Empire and to Germanism. "Encircled already on the north, the east and the west by the Triple Entente," Germanism is now barred on the south by "the victorious and aggrandized Slavs."[59] The dual monarchy is on the way to "early dissolution and decisive ruin." Austria had two choices: she could have become the protector and liberator of the Slavs and won their friendship, or she could have gone to war to prevent a Slav victory. She did neither and doomed herself. Russia has gained an army of 500,000 soldiers with which she can attack the Austrian flank.[60]

Passing to the question of Alsace-Lorraine, Civrieux says it can only be resolved in favour of France by force of arms. He maintains that French military thought has been dominated by the idea of defence, but that happily there are signs that this mentality is disappearing.[61] He quotes a Lieutenant-Colonel Montaigne as saying that victory requires the offensive, and that the three terms, "war, offensive, victory are linked together." Civrieux continues:

> *May all Frenchmen have these superb precepts in mind, in order that on that approaching day when the cannon will sound throughout Europe, they may be ready, with stout hearts and resolute spirits, to close the circle at the centre of which Germanism will struggle.*[62]

Germany does not face France alone, but all Europe. Pan-slavism rises up, in Russia and in the Balkans. An awakened and regenerated France is ready for every sacrifice.

> *On the day when the continent will rise...against the feudal empire which constitutes a constant menace to the peace of the world, England will close the ocean door through which this empire breathes and feeds itself; and, under the weight of its united enemies, it will perish, crushed, smothered.*[63]

Civrieux thinks it will be a beautiful war which delivers all the captives of Germanism and which "will establish at last on European soil the revenge of right against force. And in this beautiful war France will be at the head of the peoples—as in former times."[64]

Lieutenant-Colonel A. Grouard tells us in *France and Germany: the Possible War*, that for years French military power was weak, but that the harm will soon be repaired. He believes that "In no army has greater work been accomplished during the last thirty years than in the French army" and that "daily and incessant progress has been made in every branch of the military art." This has been most notable in recent years, "when the patriotic spirit seemed to be reborn in the country."[65] France can now effect mobilization and concentration of her forces as quickly as Germany, and be ready to begin hostilities at the same time.[66]

Early 1914 saw an intensification of the nationalist fervour. In May, Baron Guillaume wrote, "There is no doubt that the French nation has become more chauvinist and self-assured during the last few months." He knew well-informed men who two years before had been afraid of Germany who had changed their minds and were proclaiming the certainty of victory. He thought one of the most dangerous things was the French three years law, which was too heavy a burden to bear. A Parisian well-informed in international affairs had told him that in less than two years they would either have to abandon it or go to war.[67]

Although moderate and generally anti-militarist parties won every French election, the France of 1914 was dominated by a militant élite which thirsted for a war of revenge. The three years law was passed and maintained in the teeth of popular opposition, while the Russian alliance was strengthened and French support for Russia's Balkan policies increased.

French policy was designed to achieve objectives which everyone knew could be accomplished only by war. Negotiations which took place in St. Petersburg in early 1914 established the French war aim of restoring Alsace and Lorraine to France. There is no evidence that the French wartime aim of dismembering Germany and destroying her political and economic power was voiced before the war, although these intentions had materialized by October 1914.[68]

One of the crucial events which paved the road to the Great War was Russia's defeat by Japan. Russian expansionism was turned back on Europe and the blow to Russian power and prestige facilitated her agreement with England. The agreement ended the long Anglo-Russian feud over the safety of the approaches to India. This left the way open for the Russian politicians who favoured a European policy orientation. Amongst these was Alexandre Isvolsky, who became foreign minister in 1906.

From this time forward the principal aim of Russian policy was to gain control of the Bosporus and the Dardanelles and thus extend Russian power in the eastern Mediterranean. With this end in view, Isvolsky met the Austrian foreign minister, Count Ai von Aehrenthal, at Buchlau in September, 1908, where he agreed to the annexation of Bosnia and Herzegovina by Austria in return for Austria's support for the opening of the straits at Constantinople to Russian warships.

Unfortunately for Isvolsky's plans the determined opponent of Russian control of the straits was not Austria or Germany, but England. Aehrenthal immediately seized his share of the spoil, while Isvolsky was left with the task of persuading the British government to abandon its long-standing policy of resisting Russian access to the Mediterranean from the Black Sea.

In October, 1908, Isvolsky accompanied the tsar to England, where he asked for British agreement to the opening of the straits to Russian warships. Sir Edward Grey had foreseen that, if England was to remain on friendly terms with Russia, she "must abandon the policy of blocking her access to the sea," but he thought the moment was "inopportune."[69] He explained that he could not agree to a one-sided arrangement which would put Mediterranean shipping in danger from Russian warships, but must insist on "reciprocal rights." He had anticipated that the Anglo-Russian convention would eventually make the Russian desire possible, but Russian action in Persia had made a bad impression on English public opinion, which would make such a concession hard to defend.[70]

Isvolsky returned to the charge, intimating that a refusal to accommodate Russia in this matter would be fatal to good Anglo-Russian relations. Grey continued to maintain his position, however, and the question was dropped for the moment.[71]

The failure to obtain British agreement to the opening of the straits was a serious political defeat for Isvolsky, but he refused to admit that it was the result of his own miscalculation. His reaction was to deny that he had made any bargain with Aehrenthal and to stir up as much trouble as he could over the annexation of Bosnia-Herzegovina.

The Russians did not go to war over the two provinces at the time simply because they were not yet sufficiently prepared. The tsar stated to Nikola Paschitsch, the Serbian prime minister, that the question would be decided only by war. He felt that "a conflict with Germanism" was "unavoidable in the future and that preparations should be made for it."[72] The Russo-Bulgarian military convention of December, 1909, stated that "the realization of the high ideals of the Slavic peoples upon the Balkan peninsula...is possible only after a favourable outcome of Russia's Struggle with Germany and Austria-Hungary."[73]

The straits question was revived in 1911 during the Turco-Italian war. In October the Russians proposed a treaty in which Russia should support Turkey in maintaining her position in Constantinople and adjacent territories, in return for which Turkey would allow Russian warships to pass through the straits in time of peace or war.[74]

Isvolsky thought Russia's support for France during the Agadir crisis should induce France to take a favourable attitude "to the action Russia will sooner or later undertake concerning the Straits and the contiguous territory."[75] He assured Justin de Selves, the French foreign minister, that

Russia would adhere to the Franco-German agreement, but wanted France to support Russia regarding the straits. France had assured Russia in 1908 that she would support her action in the straits, and he now wanted France to recognize Russia's "liberty of action" there. Selves replied that France was ready to give Russia complete satisfaction, but refused to make any definite statement. Georges Louis was worried about the phrase "freedom of action," and wanted to know what Russia intended to do. Isvolsky told him Russia couldn't foresee what turn the straits question might take but that she could not allow control of the straits to be in other hands than her own.[76] Finally, in January, 1912, Selves replied that France confirmed in general the declarations she had made in 1908.[77] In June, 1912, Louis, now French ambassador at St. Petersburg, believed it was clear that Russia thought great events were near and that she wanted to precipitate these events.[78]

Meanwhile, Sir Arthur Nicolson had told Paul Cambon that the straits question must be negotiated with all the Powers signatory to the London convention. British opposition to Russian proposals regarding the straits remained unchanged until after the beginning of the Great War.[79] At the same time both Germany and Austria expressed their willingness to concede special rights to Russia regarding the passage of the straits.[80]

During negotiations aimed at limiting the first Balkan war Poincaré, wishing to prevent Austria from acquiring any territory in the Balkans, proposed that France, England and Russia should agree that no Great Power must be allowed to obtain land there. Sergei Sazonov, the Russian foreign minister, refused his assent to this proposal, because it could apply to Russia in the straits question. He suggested an agreement to oppose only territorial aggrandisement by Austria.[81]

By June, 1913, Russia had reaped great advantages from the Balkan wars. Her sphere of influence in the Balkans had been extended and the position of Austria was threatened, especially by the aggrandisement of Serbia. Russia still had not reached the straits, however, and it was evident that further action was necessary.[82]

Thus before the coming of the July crisis both France and Russia aimed at objectives which could be accomplished only by war, which they believed was imminent. The Russians were engaged in elaborating preparations for the seizure of the straits at Constantinople, which they knew could take place only in the context of a European war. The French had given them complete assurance that France would take part in such a war in support of Russia's Balkan projects and in the hope of regaining Alsace-Lorraine. The stage was set for an event which would provide the pretext for the outbreak of war.

Notes

1. Frederick L. Schuman, *War and Diplomacy in the French Republic*, pp. 130-1.

2.*Ibid.*, p. 132.

3.*Ibid.*, pp. 133-4.

4.*Ibid.*, pp. 136-7.

5.DDF1, VIII, no. 522.

6.Schuman, p. 139.

7.DDF1, VIII, no. 424.

8.Schuman, p. 150.

9.DDF3, II, no. 202; Christopher Andrew, *Théophile Delcassé and the Making of the Entente Cordiale*, pp. 134-5.

10.DDF1, XIV, no. 314.

11.Andrew, pp. 172-3.

12.*Ibid.*, pp. 172-4.

13.*Ibid.*, p. 269.

14.DDF2, II, no. 299.

15.*Ibid.*, V, no. 164.

16.Eugen Weber, *The National Revival In France, 1905-1914*, p. 23.

17.E. D. Morel, *Ten Years of Secret Diplomacy*, p. 102.

18.Weber, pp. 39-42.

19.FO800/50.

20.E. D. Morel, *Diplomacy Revealed*, p. 97, fn.

21.DDF2, XI, no. 263.

22.Weber, pp. 64-5.

23.*Ibid.*, p. 86.

24.*Ibid.*, p. 88.

25.*Ibid.*, p. 72.

26.*Ibid.*, p. 75.

27.Morel, *Diplomacy Revealed*, p. 171.

28.Weber, p. 95.

29.*Ibid.*, p. 98.

30.Colonel Arthur Boucher, *L'Offensive contre l'Allemagne*, pp. 67-8.

31.Weber, p. 99.

32.LN, I, 180.

33.*Ibid.*, p. 194.

34.*Ibid.*, pp. 212-13.

35.Weber, p. 102.

36.FO800/53.

37.Weber, pp. 110-11.

38.*Ibid.*, p. 105.

39.*Ibid.*, p. 106.

40.*Ibid.*, p. 112.

41.FO800/54.

42.*Ibid.*

43.LN, II, p. 32.

44.Belgian Diplomatic Documents, 1905-1914, no. 101.

45.*Ibid.*, no. 104.

46.*Ibid.*, no. 105.

47.LN, II, p. 175.
48.Colonel Arthur Boucher, *L'Allemagne en Péril*, p. 2.
49.*Ibid.*, p. 3.
50.*Ibid.*, pp. 7-8.
51.*Ibid.*, p. 181.
52.*Ibid.*, pp. 85, 184.
53.*Ibid.*, pp. 97, 188.
54.*Ibid.*, p. 161.
55.*Ibid.*, p. 167.
56.*Ibid.*, p. 190.
57.*Ibid.*, pp. 191, 193.
58.Commandant de Civrieux, *Le Germanisme Encerclé*, p. 23.
59.*Ibid.*, p. 40.
60.*Ibid.*, pp. 40, 57.
61.*Ibid.*, p. 72.
62.*Ibid.*, p. 76.
63.*Ibid.*, p. 105.
64.*Ibid.*, p. 110.
65.Lt. Col. A. Grouard, *France and Germany: The Possible War*, pp. viii-ix.
66.*Ibid.*, p. 70.
67.Morel, *Diplomacy Revealed*, p. 292.
68.Friedrick Stieve, *Isvolsky and the World War*, APP. IV, pp. 247-9.
69.Grey of Falloden, *Twenty-five Years*, I, 171-2.
70.*Ibid.*, pp. 173-5.
71.*Ibid.*, pp. 177-9.
72.M. Bogitshevich, *Causes of the War*, pp. 111-13.
73.*Ibid.*, p. 90.
74.LN, II, 463-4.
75.LN, I, 144-7.
76.Stieve, p. 42; LN, I, 166-8.
77.LN, I, 179.
78.DDF3, III, no. 65.
79.LN, I, 149-50.
80.Sir George Arthur (trans.), *The Memoirs of Raymond Poincaré*, I, 157-8.
81.LN, I, 343-5.
82.Stieve, p. 167.

Eleven

The Flowering of Anti-Germanism in England

The consummation of the Anglo-French entente ensured that in any confrontation between France and Germany, England would be ranged on the side of France. It also produced in France a belief that it was now possible to ignore Germany while proceeding with the conquest of Morocco, which made a Franco-German clash almost inevitable. The stage was set for continued Anglo-German conflict and eventual war.

Although the English people had already been convinced that Germany was England's foremost commercial and industrial rival, and that the traditional friendship with Germany was no longer possible, they were not yet persuaded in 1904 that Germany posed a serious threat to the existence of the British Empire and that an Anglo-German war was necessary. It remained for those who desired such a war to create an anti-German war psychosis which would prepare the public for the eventuality.

The main ideas of the militarist view of international affairs already dominated the public mind, in England as in other countries. Few questioned the belief that the way to have peace was to prepare for war, and the idea that the British navy should remain strong enough to control the sea was accepted even by such opponents of war as Liberal M. P. Arthur Ponsonby.[1]

The Social Darwinist idea that war was nature's way of eliminating unfit nations was promulgated by intellectuals and was widespread in military circles. According to William L. Langer in *The Diplomacy of Imperialism*, "the biological...conception of social and international relations was...more in vogue than on the continent." An early essay by Walter Bagehot declared, "The majority of groups which win and conquer are better than the majority of those which fail and perish, and thus the first world grew better and was improved."[2] The *Saturday Review* for February, 1896, carried an article, reputed to be by a professor Mitchell, which described the foreign policies of nations as "anticipation of, and provision for, struggles for existence between incipient species."[3] Professor Karl Pearson wrote in 1900,

> *History shows me one way, and one way only, in which a state of civilisation has been produced, namely, the struggle of race with race, and the survival of the physically and mentally fitter race...The path of progress is strewn with the wreck of nations; traces are everywhere to be seen of the hecatombs of inferior races, and the victims who found not the narrow way to the greater perfection. Yet these dead peoples are...the stepping stones on which mankind has risen to the higher intellectual and deeper emotional life of today.*[4]

J.A. Cramb, professor of modern history at Queen's College, London, expressed a similar militarist view in a series of lectures given during the Boer war. Cramb taught that, in the history of a state, war is "an attestation of the self-devotion of that state to the supreme end of its being, even of its power of concentration to the Highest Good."[5] War, he said, is a phase of "the perpetual omnipresent strife of all beings towards self-fulfilment."[6] It is "a manifestation of the world spirit" because "It is by conflict alone that life realises itself. That is the be-all and end-all of life as such, of Being as such. From the least developed forms of structure or organic nature to the highest form in which the world-force realises itself, the will and imagination of Man, this law is absolute."[7]

The press played a leading part in fanning the flames of antipathy to Germany, in cooperation with the foreign office, where some important figures had close connections with political writers. Eyre Crowe, for example, was a brother-in-law of Spencer Wilkinson, editor of the *Morning Post*, and his famous anti-German memorandum was a digest of Wilkinson's book, *The Great Awakening*. Sir Cecil Spring-Rice supplied journalists Chirol, Strachey, Leo Maxse and J. L. Garvin with material for articles on the German menace.[8] Sir Arthur Nicolson was friendly with Sir Donald Mackenzie Wallace of *The Times*, with whom he was in close contact at the Algeciras conference.[9]

In February, 1904, the *Navy League Journal* published a review of Erskine Childers's *Riddle of the Sands*, a novel about a German invasion of England. The reviewer believed the Germans had a plan for such an invasion and that some German railroads had been built specifically for the purpose of transporting the requisite troops. The idea of a German invasion was to become a standard scare tactic of the Germanophobe propagandists.

The Times' immediate reaction to the Anglo-French agreement was moderate in tone. The editor remarked that the day had gone by when Great Britain must follow in the wake of the Triple Alliance. *The Times* quoted the French publicist, Alcide Debray, as saying, "The quiescence of Germany is the result of certain changes to French advantage in international affairs." He thought the fact that England, Italy and Russia were on the side of France would moderate the zeal of the pan-German League.[10] Such comments foreshadowed the line taken in England, which credited the pan-Germans with significant influence on Germany policy. As Caroline Playne points out, the pan-Germans talked about action, but nothing was done to realize their dreams.[11]

The first fruits of the Anglo-French entente soon appeared. That summer of 1904 there was talk of the inevitability of an Anglo-German war, and the first reference to war plans against Germany appeared in the records.[12] In June Francis Bertie agreed with Mallet that British policy should be to isolate Germany, because she was "false and grasping and our real enemy commercially and politically."[13] When King Edward visited the kaiser at Kiel that same month, The Times expressed its disapproval of such a friendly gesture. Poisonous articles in The Times and the National Review aroused fears in Germany of an attack by the British fleet.[14]

When Count Metternich spoke to Lansdowne about the Open Door policy in Morocco, Lansdowne favoured him with the deceptive treatment which became standard practice when dealing with Germany. To the German ambassador's statement that he feared France would not accord fair treatment to Germany in Morocco, Lansdowne replied that according to their agreement both were "equally attached to the principle of commercial liberty both in Egypt and Morocco."[15] In fact, England and France were equally determined to turn Morocco into a French protectorate in which France and Spain would monopolize economic opportunities.

By the end of 1904 the clamour for war with Germany was loud and clear. In September, The Times published a long article about an imaginary secret treaty between Germany and Russia, which supposedly contained engagements exceeding those of Bismarck's Reinsurance treaty. Similar reports of German intrigues followed, with the Morning Post seconding the efforts of The Times.[16]

The Dogger Bank incident provides an instructive example of the lengths to which anti-German prejudice could be carried. It was rumoured, and believed, that the Germans had given warnings to the Russian fleet.[17] The German press sided with England in the affair.[18]

German economic power and the resulting commercial rivalry was a source of apprehension amongst British nationalists.[19] The tariff reform movement generated bitter attacks on Germany, and there was continuous criticism of the "dumping" of German goods in England.[20]

The year 1905 brought antagonism to Germany to a new peak of ferocity. A lull in January was followed on February 3 by a speech by Sir Arthur Lee, First Lord of the Admiralty, in which he declared that in case of war "the British navy will get its blow in first, before the other side has time even to read in the papers that war had been declared."[21]

The Germans naturally took this as a threat directed at them by a British cabinet minister. The conservative press in Germany took this view unanimously, and the furore assisted the Navy League's propaganda for a larger naval programme.[22] Admiral Thomsen of the German navy wondered why in England Germany was depicted as a robber waiting to seize other people's possessions. He said German officers did not believe in an unprovoked attack by England any more than British officers believed in a surprise German attack on the coast of England. Britain's Admiral Fitzgerald, in reply, defended Lee's statement, saying that Germany was not yet ready, but would attack England as soon as she could. He did not want war, but if it was inevitable it would be better to have it now than to wait until Germany was stronger. The anti-German section of the British press took the line that the Germans feared a British attack because they intended to attack England.[23]

A modern entente mythologist, Paul Kennedy, endorses this point of view, maintaining that the Germans were afraid the British would do to them what they were thinking of doing to their neighbours.[24] Since there is not the slightest evidence that anyone in a position of authority in Germany had any intention of doing anything to neighbouring countries except trade with them, and the influential people in England who advocated an attack on Germany had no German counterparts, it appears that it was the British who were eager to attack Germany.

The same writer tells us that one German author, a *Realpolitiker*, recognized that England would be quite right to present Germany with an ultimatum to reduce her naval armaments.[25] We are not told who this writer was, or exactly what he wrote, but it is hard to believe that anyone outside England would have made such a statement. It is obvious that the Germans had as much right to demand that the British should reduce their navy. This idea is another facet of the argument that Germany was an upstart with no right to independent nationhood.

The kaiser's visit to Tangier provoked a violent press campaign in England. Some observers thought *The Times* was trying to provoke war, and this idea was frequently echoed in France. Although Delcassé's policy was criticized in the Chamber and the French press, "the London journals loudly sang his praises." "French statesmen, unaccustomed to such Francophile enthusiasm in London, suspected that the English wished to embroil them with their neighbors across the Vosges."[26] The Nationalist leader declared in the French Chamber that France was exposing herself for England's benefit.[27] Clemenceau who was pushing for his resignation, accused the British press of excusing Delcassé's errors and increasing Franco-German difficulties.[28]

Early in April Fisher wrote to Lansdowne agreeing that Germany wanted a port on the coast of Morocco and asserting that this "would be vitally detrimental to us from a naval point of view."[29] Fisher later admitted that this statement was "rot," thus revealing that his real purpose was to strengthen Lansdowne's opposition to Germany.[30] Fisher, obviously eager for war, told Lansdowne it would be "a golden opportunity for fighting the Germans in alliance with the French." He hoped Lansdowne would be able to bring it about.[31] Statements by Fisher and General Wilson convinced the French that the British were keen to fight Germany, but Delcassé's colleagues repudiated his policy, much to Lansdowne's disappointment.

In June, 1905, Lansdowne told Metternich that France did not threaten the independence and integrity of Morocco and had "no designs upon the sovereignty of the Sultan or the rights of other Powers."[32] Lansdowne had endorsed the Franco-Spanish agreement of October 4, 1904, and he knew quite well the details of the French programme, as did the German government. One wonders why Lansdowne thought it was necessary to indulge in this kind of prevarication when he must have been aware that the Germans knew his statements were false.

The belligerency of the British press continued throughout 1905, with the papers voicing strong disapproval of France's acceptance of a conference on Morocco. The *Pall Mall Gazette* wondered why Berlin should dictate to the Powers, and thought that if England stood firm Germany would be forced to back down. It declared that "The defence of their own possessions against the Mailed Fist must be the bedrock principle of the friendship between England and France."[33] There was, of course, no German threat to any of their possessions, although there was a well-grounded German objection to the addition of Morocco to the French possessions without consideration for German rights and interests.

In October the Paris *Matin* published what purported to be an account of the June 6 meeting at which Delcassé had resigned. The article, which was generally supposed to be inspired by Delcassé himself, stated that he had urged the cabinet to reject the conference and had asserted that he was ensured of British support if war ensued. England had offered, it was said, to seize the Kiel Canal and land 100,000 men in Schleswig-Holstein. These revelations were widely believed in France and throughout Europe. The British press denied the truth of the story, but acknowledged that England would have assisted France if she had been attacked by Germany.[34] It is, in fact, quite clear that Delcassé was convinced that he had been assured of British support in resisting the German demand for a conference.

The report in the *Matin* that England had offered France armed support precipitated an anti-English crusade in the German press beginning in October, which produced a demand for further expansion of the German navy. The political parties were unanimous on the need to increase the fleet, because they were convinced that England had aimed at war and that Germany was in danger of a British attack. The French were not afraid of a German attack but of French involvement in an Anglo-German war.[35]

At the same time in 1905 a German syndicate wanted to acquire land on the Portuguese island of Madeira to build a sanatorium, which some British officials thought was intended for use eventually as a naval base. Portugal asked for British help in resisting the German request and the prospect of British opposition caused the Germans to relinquish the idea. According to historian G.W. Monger the British action shows that Lansdowne was ready "to go to extreme lengths against Germany," although he was not sure a German base on Madeira would be against British interests.[36]

Sir John Fisher's antipathy to Germany was a constant element arousing fear of Germany in the British public. An article in the *Fortnightly Review*, possibly instigated by Fisher, said in 1905 that the North Sea frontier of the British Empire had been threatened by the growth of the German navy. Fisher stated that England's only probable enemy was Germany and that because the whole German fleet was concentrated only two hours away, England must have a fleet twice as strong concentrated in the same way.[37] Fisher himself said that the British navy was four times as strong as the German navy, so it is evident that such statements were outrageous propaganda designed to stimulate public antagonism to Germany.

Fears concerning German trade competition with Britain were also fired during the year. An article in the *Fortnightly Review* spoke of Germany's capture of continental markets, and said that unless England met "force with force and violence with violence" these markets would be closed to British manufacturers.[38] The idea that Germany was using force and violence to conquer these markets existed only in the mind of the author. A similar misconception appears in the supposed German intention to conquer Belgium and Holland to expand German trade.[39] In fact, the Germans obtained a virtual monopoly of trade with these countries without military conquest.

A book by a British military writer, published in 1905, reiterated the Social Darwinist philosophy.

Major Stewart Murray wrote that the old rivalry of monarchical states had been replaced by the modern rivalry of races, a view which, we are told, was most widely voiced in Germany. They said the German people must be the chief naval, commercial, military and intellectual Power, and all who stood in their way must go under.[40] The Germans openly said that England stood in their way and must be overthrown, England would therefore be attacked as soon as Germany was ready at sea.[41] Who in Germany said these things Murray did not specify, nor did he estimate how many decades would pass before Germany could be ready at sea. Murray expected a German invasion of England and insisted that the present British army was "utterly inadequate." England should have an army on the continental scale, which required universal service to produce a million trained men.[42] He favoured a tariff on imports to raise money for this purpose.[43]

Lord Roberts's crusade for conscription got under full steam at this time. He resigned from his position in the army to become the leader of the National Service League.[44] The case for conscription was based on the assumption that England was threatened by a German invasion, and this belief therefore became an article of faith for those who advocated universal military service.

Caroline Playne wrote, "Probably there was no other propaganda pre-war organization which permeated the social life of England to the same extent as the National Service League." When it was founded it had the support of three members of Parliament, and by 1912 this number had increased to one hundred and eighty members. The League claimed the support of four English bishops, including the Archbishop of Westminster, head of the Roman Catholic church in England. One New Zealand canon waxed eloquent in his enthusiasm, climaxing his eulogy of military service with the statement "war is not murder, but sacrifice, which is the soul of Christianity."[45] One of the League's lecturers declared that "all boys should be separated from their mothers when infants and brought up in institutions where their upbringing would...lead to training in arms."[46]

A momentous change took place at the end of 1905, when the Liberals came to power and the Germanophobe Liberal imperialist Sir Edward Grey took over the foreign office. Grey's prejudice against and suspicion of Germany is evident on almost every page of his memoirs. He accepts without question the French propaganda view of the war of 1870, citing with agreement Bismarck's self-congratulatory account written twenty-five years later.[47] His account of a supposed German ultimatum concerning the conversion of the Egyptian Privileged Debt is so far removed from reality that it must be supposed that Grey had no information about the matter.[48] In discussing the Armenian massacres he asserts that the German government increased German influence in Turkey by winking at the massacres, while England's protests against the massacres received support from France and Russia.[49] This is the exact opposite of the truth, as was recognized by the British government at the time. Grey also states that England, "publicly through Joseph Chamberlain," offered Germany an alliance, which was refused.[50] Chamberlain, secretary of state for the colonies, at all times spoke only for himself, not for England, and no definite offer of an alliance was ever made. At the time, Grey says, the German army was the greatest in the world, but in fact the Russian army, the bugbear of the British foreign office, was much larger. And the French army was at least equal to that of Germany.[51]

Grey's description of Germany's attitude during the Boer war has almost no relation to the facts of the case. In his memoirs he says the feeling of sympathy with the Boers and dislike of England was even stronger in Germany than in other countries. He states that "it was suspected, if not entirely known," that Wilhelm II had encouraged Transvaal founder Paul Kruger in a policy unfriendly to England. He points to the fact that when Kruger came to Europe it was the German kaiser he asked to see. Grey is unimpressed by the fact that the kaiser refused to see him.[52] Later he declared that "nobody believes that France and Russia were more hostile than Germany was during the Boer War."[53]

The truth is that anyone who knew anything about the matter believed that France and Russia favoured the Boers. In November 1899 *The Times* reported that 400 French volunteers for the Boer cause were enrolled in France, 100 of them ex-officers or reserve officers. The next day the paper said that 1,500 volunteers had offered their services.[54] The German kaiser, however, had issued a proclamation forbidding German soldiers to go to South Africa. In November, 1900, Sir Edmund Monson reported that nine-tenths of French papers were "maliciously set against us."[55] In December, Émile Loubet, the French president, received Kruger in Paris.[56] Monson wrote to Lansdowne on January 10, 1902, "There is to be a great pro-Boer demonstration tonight at the Théâtre du Chatelet."[57] A short time later Chamberlain agreed that German policy had enabled England to localize the South African war.[58] When the Boer generals visited Paris "they had a private audience with President Loubet, and were received officially by Émile Combes, the prime minister, and by Delcassé." In Berlin, they were welcomed by the pan-Germans but were not received by the kaiser.[59] J. A. Spender later wrote in the *Westminster Gazette* that during the Boer war there was nothing in the German press like the Anglophobia of some French papers.[60]

It was this jaundiced attitude that Grey brought to the foreign office when the Algeciras conference was about to begin. He had already decided that Delcassé had been dismissed entirely as a result of German pressure, which had succeeded because German armaments were so much more ready for war than those of France.[61] That German armaments were in a better state of preparation than those of France was extremely doubtful. The reality was that the French leaders at that time were reluctant to undertake a war on behalf of Delcassé's policy of isolating and humiliating Germany. Grey obviously thought Delcassé's policy was correct, and was prepared to do all in his power to further it.

The question of tariff reform "was a major issue in the election of 1906, and it centered national attention, perhaps as never before, on the German trade danger."[62] Attacks on German dumping had been widespread in recent years, and the conservative press exploited this issue by denouncing cheap foreign goods from Germany and identifying protectionism with patriotism. The campaign inspired Gabriel Hanotaux to express the belief that Anglo-German commercial rivalry would lead to war.[63]

The relation of the tariff reform movement to Germany had its origins in a decision by Canada in 1897 to grant preference to British goods. This conflicted with the Anglo-German treaty of commerce of 1865, which stipulated that British and German goods would be given equality of treatment in British colonial markets. The Germans took the view that if Canada differentiated against them they were entitled to differentiate against Canada.[64] Germany and Canada then applied the general tariff to each other. In 1901 negotiations for a treaty of commerce took place between the two countries, but no agreement was reached, because it became clear that "Canada had no intention of treating Germany with even elementary equality."[65]

After England denounced the treaty of 1865, Germany passed a law giving most-favoured-nation treatment to the British Empire. This had been renewed each year until December 31, 1903. In April, 1903, the British ambassador in Berlin asked if it would be renewed again. Meanwhile, at the Colonial conference of 1902, all the self-governing colonies had promised to follow Canada in giving preference to British goods. The German government therefore replied that it could not tell in advance what the new Reichstag, soon to be elected, might do. This was characterized in England as a "deliberate blow" at the British Empire and an attempt to "terrorize the Colonies."[66]

Joseph Chamberlain, by 1903 virulently anti-German, attacked Germany for her policy with regard to the Canadian preference, which he called one of "dictation and interference." When Germany hinted that she might withdraw most-favoured-nation treatment from England as well as the colonies if the latter discriminated against Germany, The Times described this as a "direct menace" and "interference with the internal affairs of the Empire." An article in the Nineteenth Century charged Germany with trying to drive a wedge between England and her colonies to prevent the unification of the Empire.[67] England's press evidently thought that Germany's tariff policy, like the size of her navy, should have been determined by England.

By 1906 commercial rivalry had become a serious matter, of which the British were acutely aware, although less noisily than in the 1890s.[68] The threat by German trade was greatly exaggerated. The Times declared that England was in the "position of an industrially undeveloped country trading with another country on a far higher level of industrial efficiency." J. Ellis

Barker wrote in *Nineteenth Century*, "we have become hewers of wood and drawers of water for Germany."[69] The threat of German trade and shipping continued to excite the British press, which missed no opportunity to alarm the public about the issue. Periodic scares followed after 1906, usually coinciding with trade depressions, for which Germany was blamed.

On taking control of the foreign office Sir Edward Grey immediately espoused the French design of pushing forward to the conquest of Morocco. Although one of his first acts was to tell the Italian ambassador that England had no intention of using the Anglo-French entente to Germany's disadvantage,[70] he soon made it clear that he would oppose any attempt by Germany to take action of any kind outside her own borders.

At the same time Grey noted that England blocked German attempts to get a coaling station or port anywhere. He wondered if it was really necessary that all the efforts of British diplomacy should be used to prevent Germany from getting a port anywhere, but the policy continued without change.[71] Apparently he thought the lack of coaling stations and ports was no disadvantage to Germany.

Grey readily accepted as gospel any French propaganda, however ridiculous. He characterized the German attitude at the Algeciras conference as unreasonable because France was "ready to respect the sovereignty of the Sultan and the independence of Morocco."[72] A week later he spoke of the "economic guarantees" France had given England in Morocco as though these were also available to Germany. He wondered why Germany attached so much importance to political influence and so little to economic guarantees. He thought the French proposals were "exceedingly moderate and reasonable," and that England must support her.[73] It is pertinent to ask if Grey had read the Anglo-French and Franco-Spanish agreements, including the secret articles.

It is frequently said that Germany was isolated at the conference, but when France objected to the Austrian proposals for the organization of the Moroccan police it was France who was isolated. Both Grey and Nicolson thought France was in the wrong, but they insisted on standing alone with France against all the other participants in the conference. Grey told Paul Cambon France should accept the German view rather than break up the conference. Germany, he said, had given way on seven-eighths of the questions and had reserved this one point concerning the police to save a little prestige. The point at issue could not hurt French interests "for it would not bring in Germany, who apparently asks nothing for herself."[74] Grey nevertheless not only continued to support France, but was prepared to do so even if she invaded Morocco.[75] Obviously his policy was "France, right or wrong."

Sir Charles Hardinge had noted on a memorandum by Grey that if

Germany knew England would support France, "without any limitations as to whether action by France in Morocco is aggressive or not," she would not fight, as she would lose her entire merchant marine and almost her whole trade.[76] The French agreed that Germany would give way if England and France stood firm.[77] This turned out to be correct, since Germany had no intention of going to war over Morocco, and it was evident that France, with British support, was prepared to do so.[78]

O.J. Hale maintains that the Algeciras conference marked "a new chapter in the history of European relations." He says writers and statesmen recognized that the key to events was the growing Anglo-German hostility, which the European press saw as dividing Europe into two camps. Neutral observers agreed that this was the greatest danger to the peace of Europe.[79] Baron Greindl, Belgian minister in Berlin, commented: "The English Press has done all it could to prevent the Algeciras Conference being successful." It was, he said, "more irreconcilable than the French Press."[80]

When German mayors visited England in the summer of 1906, Grey not only felt it necessary to assure France that this had no political significance, but also made a statement in Parliament to the effect that "civilities and hospitality, which are promoted here by independent persons not connected with Government, do not imply any present or future change of policy."[81]

Sir Frank Lascelles reported from Berlin that Bülow hoped the reception of the mayors would lead to a friendly understanding between England and Germany. Crowe's minute on the report said that talk of an understanding was unreal. Understandings with France and Russia were based on differences to be adjusted, but with Germany there were no differences to be adjusted.[82] Quite clearly this made opposition to Germany imperative.

When German journalists visited England, Crowe thought it was necessary to take steps to counteract the impression caused by fraternization with them. Grey told the French ambassador that there was nothing of the nature of an entente between the two countries, and nothing of which an entente might be made. There was, he said, nothing to discuss with Germany except three minor matters, one of which was the German concession in Madeira, which was opposed by England. He remarked that if Germany kept quiet there was no reason for trouble.[83] Presumably this meant that Germany should take no action whatever outside her own frontiers. Evidently he felt there was no such prohibition on action by England, France or Russia. It is worthy of note that at this time, 1906, neither Grey nor Crowe considered the German navy a point of difference.

The Belgian ambassador in London commented on the use of press campaigns in England to isolate Germany. On May 23 he wrote,

For years Machiavellian steps which she has never taken, and ambitious plans such as she has never made, are systematically imputed to Germany. The repetition of these falsities has succeeded in establishing the idea that German policies are a menace to the tranquillity of Europe.

He thought the real danger came not from a Germany satisfied with what she had, but from the Powers which sought to change the map of Europe.[84]

Francis Bertie believed that the Franco-German friction was advantageous to England,[85] and he also worked to envenom Russia's relations with Germany. Alexandre Isvolsky told him that before coming to an arrangement with England he intended to find out what interests Germany considered she had in Persia: he did not want to adopt Delcassé's method and present Germany with a *fait accompli*. Bertie preferred Delcassé's method, which would probably produce conflict. He intimated that consideration for German interests would make an Anglo-Russian agreement very difficult.[86]

Although Grey stated that there was no idea of using an Anglo-Russian entente to create difficulties for Germany, England and Russia were already cooperating to shut Germany out of Persia. The British representative there noted that a German company had recently established a steamer service to the Persian Gulf. He thought an Anglo-Russian agreement should be arrived at soon to prevent any German infiltration into Persia.[87] England and Russia both at first refused to lend money to Persia, but when it appeared that a loan might be obtained from Germany, Grey thought England and Russia should advance the money.[88] Reports from Russia by Sir Arthur Nicolson showed that the two Powers were acting in concert to shut out German financial interests in Persia, unnecessarily as it happened.[89]

When Germany proposed to build a cable from Spain to the Canary Islands Grey thought it necessary to oppose this, as it might be developed to give Germany direct communication with South America and South Africa. The cable system between Europe and South America was almost entirely in English hands and it was undesirable for Germany to disturb this monopoly. There was, of course, no reasonable ground for opposition to the German project, which depended on rights already granted to England and France by Spain.[90]

Talk of a German invasion of England was in the air in 1906, but Fisher, in agreement with everyone except the conscription buffs, declared this to be impossible. He thought Germany was England's only possible enemy for years to come, but the British superiority was so great that it was hopeless for Germany to think of fighting her.[91]

The German proposal to lay a cable to the Canaries remained a live issue in 1907. Bertie's comments show that the British determination to prevent Germany from acquiring coaling stations anywhere was as strong as ever.[92] It must have been difficult for Lascelles, British ambassador in Berlin, to carry out Grey's instructions that his speeches should show that British policy was not inspired by animosity or hostility to Germany. The Germans were apprehensive that they might be attacked by England, but Admiral Fisher, who was spoiling for a fight with Germany, "could not understand how anyone in Germany could entertain such a preposterous idea."[93]

The Belgian chargé d'affaires in London remarked that all the efforts of English diplomacy aimed at bringing about the isolation of Germany.[94] Baron Greindl in Berlin, discussing in one of his dispatches at some length France's continuous violation of the Act of Algeciras, imputed this French conduct to the Entente Cordiale. Behind this friendly agreement he saw the hatred for Germany, "which, in London, is due to jealousy caused by the industrial, commercial and maritime development of the German Empire." He continued,

> The English Press pursues its campaign of slander with greater violence than ever. It sees the hand of Germany wherever anything disagreeable happens to England. When necessary it invents stories purely and simply, such as that of the alleged plan for closing the Baltic Sea.[95]

It was no wonder that, as Playne maintains, English belief in the inevitability of war with Germany had taken root.[96] An article in the *Fortnightly Review* raised the spectre of a German conquest of Holland and Belgium, which would be forced by the needs of her growing navy. This would be such a threat to England's independence that war was inevitable.[97]

When the kaiser visited England in September, 1907, Grey was greatly concerned for fear his visit would be thought to have some political significance. He insisted that it should be a purely private visit. Edward VII, however, agreed with Lascelles that it must be treated as a state visit, and Grey was obliged to give way.[98]

Lord Roberts's campaign on behalf of the National Service League, which propagated the fear of a German invasion, had by this time produced such public alarm that Herbert Asquith felt the need to appoint a committee—the so-called Invasion committee—to study the question. Although few of those in a position to know the situation took the matter seriously, this enquiry, "provoked by the action of Lord Roberts and Mr. Balfour,"[99] continued for six months. Asquith later described the idea of a German invasion as "a chimerical danger with which the authority of Lord Roberts alarmed the public imagination." The committee's report "demonstrated that such an enterprise was out of the range of practical warfare."[100]

The defence committee began its inquiry into the invasion scare on November 27, 1907.[101] The admiralty reported to it on the German port facilities and on the number of ships available for transporting troops, while a detailed study of the German railway system was also made. The committee set up to study these reports included five cabinet ministers as well as General J.D.P. French, a career military man, Admiral Fisher and others. It concluded that Germany could, without arousing attention, embark an army of 150,000 men, together with the required guns, horses and other equipment. This army could be ready to embark thirty-six hours after the orders were given, and could be at the English coast in another twenty-four hours.[102] General French (later Field-Marshall), incidentally, agreed with Fisher in thinking that the idea of a German invasion was absurd.[103]

Official suspicion of Germany grew with each passing year. In February, 1908, Grey remarked on the great number of German officers who spent their holidays on the English coast, obviously to make strategic notes. Presumably they were preparing for the coming invasion.[104] Grey thought that the German army could conquer England, but that there was no corresponding threat to Germany.[105] He knew very well that the possibility of the German fleet becoming superior lay far in the future, while combined armies far larger than her own already existed at Germany's frontiers.

Lord Esher swallowed a story by Fisher about a secret treaty between Germany and Sweden for the partition of Denmark. Sweden was to have the islands and Germany the mainland, which would give her control of the Belts and the Baltic. Esher thought England would have to spend a million pounds to counteract this by deepening the Sounds.[106] When Bülow expressed satisfaction with French explanations of their actions in Morocco, he was criticized by the German press. Crowe suggested that the German government wanted public opinion stirred up so it might later plead "the irresistible pressure of public opinion."[107]

The anti-German press echoed these official fantasies, publishing many articles on "the German danger." *The Times* and the *Standard* cultivated the German spy scare, with *The Times* suggesting that the secretary for war should be asked whether he knew of German spies operating in England. The *Observer* described the spying of German officers on the south-east coasts.[108] No doubt there were German spies acting clandestinely in England, but whether or not they were more numerous than English spies in Germany we have no way of knowing.

Some writers continued to develop the theme of the German invasion. Robert Blatchford in the *Clarion* declared that "the Germans are prepared to invade us at the first opportunity... The situation is one of deadly peril." H.M. Hyndman argued that Germany was making ready for an engagement in the North Sea, which would be followed by an invasion of England.[109]

Lord Roberts moved in the House of Lords that England should have an army strong enough to repel the most powerful nation, which was Germany. He stated that "vessels suitable for accommodating 100,000 men are at all times available in the northern part of Germany." The invasion would take the form of a surprise, coming when it was unexpected and the country was unprepared for it.[110] Lord Roberts's immense popularity gave his statements such special authority that they were certain to add to public alarm.

Alan Burgoyne's novel, *The War Inevitable*, published in 1908, scaled new heights of irrationality. In the midst of perfect peace the Germans launched a surprise attack which wiped out the British navy. They then accomplished the remarkable feat of landing 1,450,000 men in England, where their early success was turned into defeat by the heroic exploits of the untrained and vastly outnumbered defenders. The climax of absurdity was reached when the British remained courteous and friendly throughout and generously imposed an indemnity of only £100,000,000 on the defeated Germans.[111]

The anti-German fever reached new heights with the naval scare of March, 1909. The year began with an assertion by Reginald McKenna, First Lord of the Admiralty, that Germany was secretly breaking her naval law. Fisher joined him in insisting that there was certain knowledge that Germany was accelerating her building programme. Lloyd George correctly surmised that the alarm was deliberately engineered by Fisher, who he thought was disseminating false information to frighten people.[112]

One of the propagandists primed by Fisher was J.L. Garvin, editor of the *Observer*, who wrote,

> We stand in a crisis of national peril such as for two hundred years has never threatened us in peace or war. By an act of moral treachery, which would justify us in armed reprisals now, a foreign Power has doubled its naval programme in secret, and has gained a six month start in a conspiracy against our life...We must fight before 1910, while we have a full margin of power in our hands, or build eight Dreadnoughts now. There is no other way.[113]

Grey played his usual role as anti-German advocate in the cabinet. Metternich informed him of the actual number of Dreadnoughts Germany would have in 1912, but Grey told the cabinet that he did not believe him. He stated that if Germany was strong enough England would have to choose between diplomatic humiliation and war, apparently quite comfortable with the fact that the British navy's strength was already great enough to force Germany to make that choice.[114]

No one who knew the facts believed that the German navy threatened England, and it was freely stated that the British navy could easily wipe German shipping from the seas. The Germans believed England was determined to destroy German trade, by war if necessary,[115] and no one familiar with British statements on the subject could argue that their belief was unjustified.

The campaign for more battleships continued throughout 1909, growing more and more extreme as time went on. A crusade, led by a businessman named Mulliner, denouncing the government as "culpable and criminal" for not building faster was supported by *The Times*.[116] The *Daily Mail* carried a series of articles by Robert Blatchford, which were written, he said, because he believed Germany was "deliberately preparing to destroy the British Empire." He demanded twenty-six Dreadnoughts, a vote of £50 million for the navy and conscription for boys at the age of ten years. His articles were reprinted as a pamphlet and were widely read.[117]

Spencer Wilkinson, newly appointed professor of military history at Oxford, in a book published in 1909 clearly set forth the doctrine of militarism. The first business of government, he declared in *Britain at Bay*, is to be able to defend the state by war.[118] "The mark of the State," he says, "is sovereignty, or the identification of force and right." The use of force to maintain right is the foundation of all civilized human life.[119] Right and might are two aspects of the same thing.[120]

War with Germany was bound to come, because Germany was so overwhelmingly strong that she threatened to unify Europe under her control.[121] It was England's duty to preserve Europe from German dictatorship.[122] There was no visible cause for quarrel between England and Germany, but the German nation, "by the mere fact of its growth challenges England for the primacy."[123] The English were disturbed by the rise of Germany. They found themselves outstripped by a people whom they were used to looking on with the superiority with which "the prosperous and polished dweller in the city looks upon his country cousin from the farm."[124] When an Englishman saw Germany's successful efforts in science, education, trade and industry, he was puzzled and indignant. England found it hard to hold her own in industry, she had been passed in education and science, and even her navy had to make a great effort to keep its place.[125]

England's one chance lay in restoring the nation to its proper place in men's hearts and minds.[126] A strong navy was not enough, because a naval victory would not enable England to exert effective pressure on continental states. She needed the cooperation of a continental ally, and only an army able to take part in a continental war could make her the effective ally of a continental state.[127] England's naval supremacy preserved her from being constrained by Germany, but military weakness prevented her from pressuring Germany.[128] The essential thing was "to put the idea of the nation and the will to help England into every man's soul." This could be done "by making every citizen a soldier in a national army."[129]

Wilkinson thought an army based on the principle of universal service would cost no more than the existing army. The annual intake of recruits would number over 200,000, and by the sixth year there would be an army of nearly 1,000,000 men.[130] Curiously, he apparently believed England should adopt the German system, which he described at length and found admirable.

The election campaign of 1910 revived the issue of tariff reform which had been so contentious earlier in the decade. Joseph Chamberlain had led a campaign for the abandonment of England's traditional free trade policy and the imposition of tariffs to protect British business against German competition. The Conservatives attempted to arouse patriotism by exploiting the trade depression and the navy danger. Arthur Balfour, the Conservative leader, declared that he had known Germans who said that Germany would never allow England to adopt tariff reform. It made his blood boil that a German should have the audacity to say that the country should not be allowed to decide its own taxation system.[131]

The liberal press attacked Balfour for campaigning which exploited anti-German antagonism for party advantage, but right-wing organs applauded him. The *Morning Post* quoted a Briton doing business in Germany who knew a German manufacturer who expressed the opinion that Germany would never allow the British door to be shut in her face. The *Post* printed many articles from the German press showing that Germany would be alarmed at a victory for tariff reform. The *Pall Mall Gazette* published a cartoon showing Asquith, Churchill and Lloyd George teaching John Bull to curtsey to the kaiser. Albert Ballin told Wilhelm II that everybody was talking about tariff reform and a tariff union with the colonies, and that it was hardly possible to discuss things with friends "because the people here have turned mad and talk of nothing but the next war and the protective policy of the future." It was even suggested that tariff reform would ruin Germany economically and thus free England from German naval and imperial rivalry.[132]

German attempts to do business in Persia also disturbed Anglo-German relations. Sir Arthur Nicolson thought the Germans were trying to sow discord between England and Russia and weaken the Entente. Louis Mallett in the British foreign office noted a German objection to seven Frenchmen being appointed to the Persian ministry of finance, and suggested a firm British attitude might put a stop to German complaints. Hardinge argued that the British should wait until they were on stronger ground before remonstrating with Germany. If the Germans raised "captious objections" about Anglo-Russian policy, they could then remind her of her assurance that she had no political interests in Persia and refuse to allow any intervention. Germany, however, short-circuited the strategy; she waived her treaty right to most-favoured-nation treatment in Persia, and asked for discussions concerning concessions.[133] The Germans complained that England and Russia had talked of the Open Door in Persia, but were trying to shut

Germany out. Grey, in his usual style, denied any idea of excluding German commerce.[134]

On the question of naval rivalry, Grey insisted that public opinion in England considered the mutual arrest or decrease of naval expenditure as *the* test of whether an agreement with Germany was worth anything. There was, however, no British proposal for an agreement on mutual reduction. A political understanding was also impossible, because England must be able to help France if Germany took up "an aggressive attitude," as she had done in Morocco.[135] It is obvious that from Grey's point of view these discussions were a part of the pretense that England was concerned about the German navy.

In October the German government suggested that France and Russia should join in a naval agreement. Grey was at first enthusiastic about this idea, and thought Austria and Italy should be brought in as well. On second thought, however, he claimed that there was no hope for such an arrangement, because Germany would refuse to take part in it. He maintained the other five Powers would welcome an agreement of this kind, but for Germany it "would mean the renunciation of ambitions for the hegemony of Europe." No other Power, he said, had "designs of aggrandisement."[136]

One is stunned by Grey's irrational reaction to a proposal which had originated with Germany herself. When the aggressive activities of France in North Africa and Russia in Asia and the Near East are contrasted with the behaviour of Germany, the least actively aggressive of all the Great Powers, amazement turns to incredulity, and one is forced to wonder what unreal world haunted Grey's imagination.

The Agadir crisis was one of the most conspicuous landmarks on the road to war. As the French conquest of Morocco reached its climactic phase with the march to Fez, the German government decided to make a last attempt to wring from France some recognition of Germany's right to compensation for her exclusion from Morocco in violation of her treaty rights.

The Germans realized that there was every chance that France would simply try to prolong any discussion until the conquest was complete, unless she was given some reason to believe that German wishes should be taken seriously. They therefore decided, on the ground that German subjects were in danger, to send their gunboat, the *Panther*, to anchor off Agadir. They had exactly the same right to take such action as France, and the alleged danger to German subjects at Agadir was as real as the supposed danger to Europeans at Fez. The difference was that the scale of their action was infinitesimal in comparison with that of France.

The French government of the day understood the German signal and was disposed to effect a compromise which would end the long feud over

Morocco and restore some semblance of normal relations between France and Germany. The British foreign office, however, was by this time so caught up in the anti-German mania that it was determined to avert such a disaster. The British therefore intervened to ensure that France would resist the temptation to conciliate Germany and would continue to cooperate with England in thwarting her at every turn.

Belgian diplomats believed that British intervention would complicate the situation. Baron Guillaume thought the French might regret England's entrance into the discussion, and predicted that there would be much less likelihood that France could come to an understanding with Germany if England had any say in the matter.[137] He thought the key to the situation lay in London and that only there would there be any serious developments. Neither France nor Germany wanted war in his opinion, but he had less faith in England's desire for peace.[138]

A similar view was taken in France and Spain. *The Times's* correspondent reported from Madrid that "It is generally agreed that the main interest...centres in the attitude of England." The *Journal des Debats* said on July 5, "The turn which the conversations will take between Paris and Berlin must inevitably depend upon the attitude of England."[139] Joseph Caillaux, French minister of finance, believed some foreign office officials would be glad to see a war between France and Germany, in which England would take part.[140]

Grey naturally had some difficulty in convincing the radicals in his party and in the cabinet that his view of the situation was justified. The cabinet agreed that a new situation had been created, but not that it had been created by Germany. British foreign policy was carried on entirely by the liberal imperialist section of the cabinet. The opposition of the radicals, led by Lords Morley and Loreburn, prevented the cabinet from fully endorsing the foreign office policy.[141]

When Grey found that many of his supposed followers were not following him, he realized that dramatic action was necessary to bring the dissidents into line. Lloyd George had generally sided with the radicals, but his volatility made him susceptible to pressure from the Liberal imperialists. The result was that Grey and Asquith primed him to make a speech which insinuated that Germany was pushing England aside. The speech threatened Germany with war. The shock of Lloyd George joining the war party temporarily convinced Grey's opposition that his policy was warranted.[142] This enabled him to bring the country so close to war that all arrangements for opening the struggle were carried out.

The aftermath of Lloyd George's Mansion House speech on July 21 was a verbal reaction from Germany which caused Grey to fear a German attack on the fleet. The German fleet was on maneuvers at the moment, and

Grey described it as being mobilised, which, given his twisted view of German mentality, led him to expect the Germans might be about to attack the British fleet.[143] When he asked Goschen for evidence that Germany was preparing for war, however, no such evidence was forthcoming.

Sober second thought produced a left-wing reaction which resulted in the "Grey must go" campaign, but Grey was successful in misleading the opposition and maintaining his control of foreign policy. His November speech in Parliament was a masterpiece of deceptive sophistry, which aimed at increasing suspicion of Germany while feigning to lay the controversy to rest. He said that his policy had rested in part on a belief that Germany wanted territory in Morocco, although Germany had informed him by July 12 that this was not so.[144] In both France and Germany statesmen attempted, not too successfully, to quiet public opinion by making conciliatory speeches, but Grey would not even make the attempt.

In the end he managed to turn the radical opposition in the cabinet to his own advantage by engineering the acceptance of the Grey-Cambon letters. The small clique of liberal imperialists were thus able to continue the drive to war with Germany, which was by 1911 understood throughout Europe to be near at hand.

Meanwhile the conservative press had continued its campaign against Germany with increasing malevolence. Early in the year it emphasized the danger of German trade competition, and demonstrated the great alarm produced by Germany's economic progress.[145] After the dispatch of the *Panther* to Agadir, *The Times* led a campaign of vilification against Germany which mirrored the foreign office policy, and at times seemed to inspire it. Grey's conversation with the German ambassador on July 21 appears to have been based on a *Times* article of the day before. This article had spoken of "impossible demands" made by Germany and of the supposed landing of German forces at Agadir. The impossible demands were said to include the cession of the whole French Congo, although *The Times's* own map showed that the area from the Sangha River to the sea was less than half the French Congo. The furious press campaign in both France and England which followed Lloyd George's speech raged in England for three months, arousing great bitterness and resentment throughout Germany.[146]

The events of the year 1911 produced the situation which actually made a European war inevitable in the near future. Many Germans, including most significantly Wilhelm II, were convinced that England intended to force a war on Germany as soon as possible. The French, and through them the Russians, were certain of British support in a war against the German Empire. *Revanche*, dreamed of in France for forty years, stepped into the forefront of French politics, while the Russians were encouraged to open the offensive which was to destroy Austria-Hungary. The armaments race proceeded with increased intensity, as each Power hastened its preparations for the coming struggle.

At the same time inflammatory articles about the German menace continued to appear in England. *John Bull*, for example, wanted the German navy to be destroyed at once, because its destruction would be more difficult every year. England was the natural ruler of the sea, and Germany should be warned that her building more ships would not be allowed. If she paid no attention to the warning, every German ship should be sunk.[147] A writer in the *Navy League Annual* for 1911/12 described a German war plan for the invasion of England.[148]

J. Ellis Barker, in his book, *Modern Germany*, forecast the conquest of Holland by Germany, pointing out that a great part of German trade was carried out through the Low Country ports. German absorption of Holland would threaten the safety of England, and would not happen without a general European war.[149] Barker was also a proponent of tariff reform, which he thought would cripple Germany economically and force her to abandon hope of disputing British naval supremacy.[150]

Lord Roberts continued his campaign for conscription with increasing success. In a speech on October 22, 1912, he predicted a war with Germany as soon as the German forces were so superior as to be certain of victory. "Germany strikes when Germany's hour has struck," he said, and declared that this had been German policy from 1870 to the present time. Lord Roberts's great prestige and popularity influenced the public to take his words seriously, and the fear concerning England's security was increased.[151] By this time the National Service League had the support of 180 members of Parliament. Many leading Conservatives, including Curzon, Lansdowne, F. E. Smith, Arthur Lee and Bonar Law were in favour of conscription.[152]

The continuous propaganda about Germany's intention to invade England had by 1912 produced a sense of public panic which manifested itself in the most fantastic rumours and actions. People noted the number of barbers and waiters in London who were all "trained German soldiers;" suspicious-looking Germans were mapping the country and making drawings of buildings; estates near the south or east coasts were being bought by Germans; there were rumours of basements with concrete gun-platforms, usually near important railway lines. Inventories were made by the police of such items as carts, wheelbarrows and horses which people could provide when the Germans came.[153]

The *Daily Mail* started an airship scare by publishing accounts of sights in the heavens, and other papers followed suit. An article in the *Whitby Gazette* cited all the evidence of German airships over England and concluded that "Britain is at Germany's mercy now." In September, a book

entitled *England Invaded*, by Edward Ford and Gordon Home made its
appearance.[154]

Frederic Harrison, a professor of international law, saw Germany as a
country which posed the threat of war in 1913. The year 1912, he said, had
effected "a vast aggrandizement of the Slavonic race" in their struggle with
the Teutons. Germany was shut off from the Black and Aegean Seas, and
found herself "closed up in a ring fence." There was in Germany a large class
which lived only for war, and they controlled the whole civil and military
organization of Germany. "We all know," he wrote, "that for some years yet
peace is almost a condition of German development." Ninety percent of the
German people, he thought, wanted peace, and "the whole Government
machine works for peace—at present." Nevertheless, it was inevitable that the
Germans, "hemmed in a territory so inadequate to their needs and
pretensions" and dominated by a soldier caste, should "thirst to expand their
power and dominions at any sacrifice." Therefore, "England, Europe,
civilization is in imminent peril from German expansion."[155]

Professor Harrison's argument contained some curious internal
inconsistencies. Although Germany would not be ready for some years, she
threatened to unleash war in 1913; the whole civil and military organization
of Germany was controlled by a warrior caste, but the whole government
machine was working for peace; the Balkan war, "a startling blow to the
Teutonic peoples," had almost knocked the bottom out of the Triple
Alliance,[156] yet it was still as mighty a coalition as any in modern history.
Similar contradictions abound, and the essay provides a striking example of
the kind of dangerous nonsense which passed for reality in the England of
1913.

The *Navy League Annual* for 1913/14 attacked the 60 percent superiority
in completed capital ships proposed by Churchill, new First Lord of the
Admiralty, as inadequate, and called for a "two-keels-to-one" standard against
the next strongest naval Power. One writer complained that it was difficult to
get up steam for an increased programme now that Germany had slowed
down her rate of construction.[157] In fact Churchill had a hard fight to get the
increase of £3 million for 1914/15 through Parliament, because there was no
recognized danger or provocation.[158] The government had frequently said
that a reduction of Germany's rate of construction would moderate British
building as well, and no doubt some observers wondered why this did not
happen.

Further scares continued to cause public alarm in the last months before
the war. R.B. Haldane was asked in Parliament:

*Whether he had any information that there were 66,000 trained German
soldiers in England, or that there were in a cellar, within a quarter of a mile*

of Charing Cross 50,000 Mauser rifles and 7½ millions of Mauser cartridges, or 150 rounds per rifle.

He replied that the statement mentioned was "an exceptionally foolish one."[159]

Sir Edward Grey's account of the last days before the war reflects his weird interpretation of the European situation. Russia and France, he says, were preoccupied by fear of the German army.[160] France had given up the idea of *revanche*, and was, he told Prince Lichnowsky, the German ambassador in London, "peacefully disposed."[161] British relations with France and Russia, he said, "made it certain that they would not enter on an aggressive or dangerous policy."[162]

As Grey had been fully informed of the growing chauvinism in France it is impossible that he believed that France had given up the idea of *revanche* and was peacefully disposed. We have, of course, no way of knowing whether he was aware that articles from France and Russia, which were received and translated by the British general staff, showed that these Powers were bent on bringing about an early war with Germany.[163] He must have known, however, that they had no fear of Germany, as he had been assured that France was prepared to face her alone.

Commercial rivalry played a dominant role in the growing antipathy to Germany. According to R.J.S. Hoffman, the pre-war press was pervaded by "a nervous spirit of alarm and jealousy of German economic success." Discussion of the trade rivalry also appeared in parliamentary debates.[164]

The German threat was greatly exaggerated in the popular press. While Germany gained ground relative to England, British trade flourished in the world beyond Europe. By 1914 Germany had captured the continental markets, notably in Russia, where German trade was four times that of England.[165] Only in Greece and Turkey did England remain the dominant trader.[166] Elsewhere, however, British trade more than held its own. England was still ahead in every South American country, and in Colonial markets her trade was more than ten times that of Germany.[167] England continued to dominate the far Eastern market, although Germany made gains.[168] Throughout the pre-war period British business was as active and prosperous as that of Germany.

The growth of German shipping was another great concern, and attention was drawn to the close relation between merchant shipping and naval expansion.[169] The capture of trade by German shipping was emphasized, and the matter was greatly magnified by the press.[170] At the same time British shipping grew much more than that of Germany. At the end of 1912 *The Times* reported that British tonnage was four times as great as Germany's and half as big again as that of England's six nearest rivals combined.

On the eve of the war publicity over German trade and shipping was intensified. Several leading articles highlighted the fact that a British railway had ordered ten locomotives from a German firm. Another press alarm featured London gas companies ordering German coal.[171]

The greatest alarm, however, centred on the threat of German shipping. *The Times* ran a series of articles reporting the organization of societies for the promotion of German commerce. *The Times* viewed this as "the outcome of a fresh movement towards commercial and possibly even naval expansion." The Berlin correspondent of the *Daily Mail* wrote of a "German association for world commerce," whose mission was "to spread far and wide the gospel of German trade."[172]

When news was announced that German shipping lines intended to open a steamer service between Europe and New Zealand, *The Times* pointed out that British shipping would lose the annual trade of 100,000 tons of German cargo which had been sent to New Zealand in British ships. This design of German shipping companies to take over a larger share of German trade was decried by *The Times* as an "invasion of New Zealand" and an "aggressive policy."[173] A considerable quantity of German goods was still carried in British ships and *The Times* evidently considered the Germans' attempt to ship their own goods aggressive.

Hoffman regards commercial rivalry as "a powerful shaping factor in English national policy" and "a basic cause for the anti-German orientation of British world policy."[174] He concludes that "The British Government may stand acquitted of making war for the ends of trade, but that the anti-German orientation of the British mind and British world policy sprang chiefly from the great economic competition seems incontrovertibly proved."[175]

The outbreak of the war in August, 1914, inaugurated a campaign for the destruction of German trade, which became a great patriotic endeavour. The board of trade and the foreign and colonial offices immediately began working to substitute British for German orders and contracts throughout the world. On August 18, the *Daily Mail* published an article headed "Trade We Can Take from Germany." British manufacturers should seize the opportunity to replace German goods with British goods, in England and throughout the world. The *Pall Mall Gazette* captioned a leader "Get Back the Trade." "We are out for German trade," it said, "and we are determined to get it." *The Times* ran a series of articles under the title, "War on German Trade," drawing attention to markets open for attack all over the world, and to the opportunity for recapturing the chemical industry. It was also suggested that there were excellent openings for the engineering and electrical industries.[176]

This war on German trade was continued by the right-wing press and various anti-German associations throughout the war.[177] The Versailles Treaty of 1919, which wiped out Germany's merchant marine, her colonial empire and all her business connections outside her own frontiers, bears witness to the fact that the destruction of German commercial competition was England's foremost war aim.

Paul Kennedy, in his 1980 book, *The Rise of Anglo-German Antagonism*, agrees substantially with Hoffman. The most profound cause of war, he says, was economic.[178] Colonial quarrels, naval rivalry and disagreement about the balance of power reflected the relative shift in economic power between 1860 and 1914.[179] The rationale for the belief that the balance of power was in danger was Germany's rapid industrial and population growth.[180]

Kennedy maintains that in strategic and political terms the onus was on Germany. It is evident from his argument that he believes the Germans, an amoral and inferior people, had no right to develop industry and commerce or to increase in numbers. If Germany had remained an agricultural country and taken steps to limit her population, as she should have done, it would have been unnecessary for England to go to the trouble and expense of fighting her. Her failure to act properly in these respects shows a depth of depravity rarely seen in human affairs.

In his conclusion Kennedy demonstrates the usual conviction of entente apologists that words speak louder than actions. He tells us that England, France and Russia did not talk about "blood and iron" or "the mailed fist,"[181] but he fails to note that between 1870 and 1914 each of these Powers shed a great deal more blood and used a great deal more iron in war than did the German Empire. It might be added that while the British did not mention "shining armor," they declared their intention to fight alongside France on every possible occasion, and their preparations to do so were much more elaborate than anything done by Germany.

There is no evidence that any German statesman wanted a war with England for commercial supremacy. It would have been strange if they had, for it was understood everywhere, and not least in England, that Germany's ultimate triumph in the trade struggle was assured without a war. It is easy to quote fire-eating pan-Germans to the contrary, but they were always in opposition and had little influence on policy.

In England, on the other hand, the proponents of war with Germany dominated foreign policy. They directed the foreign office, controlled the cabinet, led the admiralty and influenced the press. They bear the responsibility for England's participation in the war and for her Pyrrhic victory.

Kennedy maintains that a change of personnel would have made no difference,[182] but it is at least possible that a genuinely liberal control of foreign policy might have produced some other solution than war to the problem of German trade competition. It is futile to speculate on what the result of a more rational course might have been, but what is certain is that it would have been almost impossible to devise a policy which would have been more disastrous for the British Empire than the one followed.

Kennedy tells us that if friendship with England was in Germany's best interests, then German statesmen failed their country. Anglophobia, he says, cost Germany dear.[183] This reasoning could be applied with equal force to British statesmen. Their Germanophobia was costly beyond measure for England, Europe and the world. It was one of the principal determining factors in the violent history of the twentieth century.

As we have seen, the German navy never came close to being a threat to British naval power. The real threat to British world supremacy was the spectacular growth of German industry and trade, which in a generation had made Germany a Great Power. The presumed necessity to block the German rise to power was the mainspring of Anglo-German antagonism. Perhaps too late British leaders now realize that, whatever may have been the case in the seventeenth and eighteenth centuries, in the twentieth century the way to cope with a trade rival is to out-trade her, not to defeat her in war. Two winning wars and eighty years later, England has fallen far behind, while defeated Germany ranks as one of the great commercial and industrial powers of the world. Her success rests on the same elements which operated in 1914—education, technology and efficiency.

At the turn of the century, the British government was faced with three choices: the first and best would have been to remain aloof from the continental alliance system in accordance with Lord Salisbury's wise advice; second best would have been to side with those Powers who wished to maintain the European *status quo* by joining the Triple Alliance; they chose the third and worst course by allying themselves with France and Russia, the Powers which were determined to change the map of Europe by force.

The fear of a continental coalition against the British Empire was the chimera which supposedly compelled a conjunction with one or other of the alliance systems. Given the permanent French antipathy to Germany this possibility was very remote: during the Boer war, when all Europe seethed with anger against England, the attempt to form such a coalition failed. There was no real compulsion for England to abandon her position as arbiter between the two balanced forces on the continent. Nevertheless, Salisbury's successors decided that isolation could not safely be maintained, which left the two remaining choices.

On the evidence it seems certain that Germany would have been happy to expand the Triple Alliance to include England, but the British rejected this in the belief that Austria-Hungary was a dying Power. They therefore attempted to make a one-sided bargain which would have protected the British Empire but would have left Germany alone in the centre of Europe at the mercy of France and Russia.

The remaining choice was to come to terms with France and Russia, their two principal rivals. The original intention may have been primarily to reach a bargain which would have relieved England of the continual danger of war with one or other of these Powers. When it became apparent, however, that agreement with France could be achieved only by joining an anti-German coalition, this was accepted by the British government.

Delcassé's programme of combining the conquest of Morocco with the flouting of Germany immediately involved them in conflict with Germany, which fed the fires of anti-German antipathy and soon led to a virtual alliance with France and then with Russia. They consequently became embroiled in the aggressive plans of these two Powers. The Anglo-French entente thus inaugurated a decade of almost continuous conflict, which culminated in the Great War.

Notes

1.HCD, Fifth ser., 41, col. 1407.
2.William L. Langer, *The Diplomacy of Imperialism*, pp. 86-7.
3.*Ibid.*, p. 87.
4.*Ibid.*, p. 88.
5.J. A. Cramb, *Origins and Destiny of Imperial Britain*, p. 118.
6.*Ibid.*, p. 127.
7.*Ibid.*, p. 152.
8.O. J. Hale, *Publicity and Diplomacy*, 287.
9.Harold Nicolson, *Lord Carnock*, p. 171.
10.*The Times*, April 14, 1904, p.3, April 18, p.5.
11.Caroline E. Playne, *The Pre-War Mind in Britain*, p. 204.
12.A. J. Marder, *The Anatomy of British Sea Power*, p. 479.
13.Peter Padfield, *The Great Naval Race*, p. 108.
14.Playne, pp. 117-8.
15.BD, III, no. 62.
16.O. J. Hale, *Germany and the Diplomatic Revolution*, pp. 56-8.
17.Playne, p. 117.
18.Hale, *Diplomatic Revolution*, p. 60.
19.Paul M. Kennedy, *The Rise of Anglo-German Antagonism*, pp. 308-9.
20.Ross J. S. Hoffman, *Great Britain and the German Trade Rivalry*, pp. 286-8.
21.Hale, *Diplomatic Revolution*, p. 72.
22.*Ibid.*, pp. 72-4.
23.*Ibid.*, pp. 73, 75.
24.Kennedy, p. 275.
25.*Ibid.*
26.Hale, *Diplomatic Revolution*, p. 106.
27.*Ibid.*, p. 110.
28.*Ibid.*, p. 115.
29.A. J. Marder, *Fear God and Dread Nought*, II, 55.
30.Padfield, p. 129.

31.Marder, *Fear God*, II, 55.
32.BD, III, nos. 117, 126.
33.Hale, *Diplomatic Revolution*, pp. 168-9.
34.*Ibid.*, pp. 196-7.
35.*Ibid.*, pp. 198-200.
36.George W. Monger, *The End of Isolation*, pp. 226-8.
37.Kennedy, p. 420.
38.Hoffman, p. 105.
39.*Ibid.*, pp. 295-7.
40.Stewart L. Murray, *The Peace of the Anglo-Saxons*, p. 95.
41.*Ibid.*, p. 113.
42.*Ibid.*, pp. 138-42.
43.*Ibid.*, pp. 236-7.
44.Playne, p. 150.
45.*Ibid.*, pp. 147-8.
46.*Ibid.*, pp. 151-2.
47.Grey of Falloden, *Twenty-five Years*, I, 88-9.
48.*Ibid.*, pp. 9-11.
49.*Ibid.*, pp. 126-7.
50.*Ibid.*, pp. 233-4.
51.*Ibid.*, pp. 41-2.
52.*Ibid.*, pp. 45-6.
53.FO800/50.
54.*The Times*, November 10, 1899, p. 5, November 11, p. 7.
55.FO800/125.
56.*The Graphic*, December 1, 1900, p. 902.
57.FO800/125.
58.Julian Amery, *The Life of Joseph Chamberlain*, IV, 193.
59.*Ibid.*, p. 197.
60.Hale, *Diplomatic Revolution*, p. 99.
61.Grey, I, 90-1.
62.Hoffman, p. 262.
63.*Ibid.*, p. 288.
64.*Westminster Gazette*, June 20, 1903, p. 1.
65.*Ibid.*, June 22, 1903, p. 1.
66.*Ibid.*, June 20 and 22.
67.Hoffman, pp. 286-7.
68.*Ibid.*, p. 261; Kennedy, p. 288.
69.Hoffman, p. 107.
70.BD, III, no. 206.
71.FO800/100.
72.BD, III, no. 281.
73.*Ibid.*, nos. 285, 296.
74.*Ibid.*, nos. 325, 338, 342, 344.
75 *Ibid.*
76.FO800/92.

77.BD, III, no. 342.
78.*Ibid.*, nos. 382, 384.
79.Hale, *Diplomatic Revolution*, pp. 210-11.
80.BDD, no. 17.
81.BD, III, no. 414; Grey, I, 112.
82.BD, III, no. 416
83.*Ibid.*, nos. 419, 420.
84.Playne, p. 404.
85.BD, III, no. 436.
86.BD, IV, nos. 230, 231.
87.*Ibid.*, no. 328.
88.*Ibid.*, nos. 336, 337.
89.*Ibid.*, nos. 344, 345, 456.
90.FO800/77.
91.Marder, *Fear God*, pp. 90-92.
92.FO800/50.
93.FO800/61.
94.BDD, no. 25.
95.*Ibid.*, no. 26.
96.Playne, p. 62.
97.Hoffman, pp. 288-9.
98.BD, VI, nos. 44, 48, 49.
99.Maurice V. Brett, *Journals and Letters of Reginald Viscount Esher*, II, 252.
100.H. H. Asquith, *The Genesis of the War*, quoted in Playne, p. 299.
101.Brett, II, 263.
102.DDF2, XI, no. 216.
103.Brett, II, 262.
104.FO800/61.
105.FO800/92.
106.Brett, II, 294.
107.BD, VI, no. 92.
108.Playne, pp. 118-9.
109.*Ibid.*, p. 145.
110.HLD, vol. CXCVI, 1908.
111.Alan H. Burgoyne, *The War Inevitable*.
112.Padfield, pp. 201-4.
113.*Ibid.*, p. 217.
114.FO800/61.
115.Padfield, p. 240.
116.Playne, pp. 130-1.
117.*Ibid.*, p. 145.
118.Spencer Wilkinson, *Britain at Bay*, p. 1.
119.*Ibid.*, p. 22.
120.*Ibid.*, p. 71.
121.*Ibid.*, p. 32.
122.*Ibid.*, pp. 93-4.

123.*Ibid.*, p. 95.
124.*Ibid.*, p. 50.
125.*Ibid.*, pp. 61-2.
126.*Ibid.*, p. 62.
127.*Ibid.*, p. 68.
128.*Ibid.*, p. 93.
129.*Ibid.*, p. 107.
130.*Ibid.*, pp. 152-4.
131.Hoffman, p. 289.
132.*Ibid.*, pp. 291-2.
133.FO800/93.
134.FO800/62.
135.*Ibid.*
136.Grey, I, 246.
137.BDD, no. 75.
138.*Ibid.*, no. 79.
139.E. D. Morel, *Ten Years of Secret Diplomacy*, p. 132.
140.Joseph Caillaux, *Agadir: Ma Politique Extérieure*, pp. 138-9.
141.W. S. Churchill, *The World Crisis*, I, 31.
142.*Ibid.*, p. 32.
143.FO800/87.
144.BD, VII, nos. 369, 373.
145.Hoffman, pp. 262, 303.
146.Morel, *Ten Years*, p. 146.
147.Playne, p. 139.
148.*Ibid.*, p. 141.
149.Hoffman, p. 299.
150.*Ibid.*, pp. 292-3.
151.Playne, pp. 133-4.
152.Kennedy, p. 385.
153.Playne, pp. 298-9.
154.*Ibid.*, pp. 102-3.
155.Frederic Harrison, *The German Peril*, pp. 155-166.
156.*Ibid.*, p. 186.
157.Playne, pp. 141-2.
158.Padfield, p. 366.
159.Playne, p. 406.
160.Grey, I, 267.
161.*Ibid.*, pp. 275, 294.
162.*Ibid.*, p. 292.
163.Playne, p. 367.
164.Hoffman, pp. 261, 264.
165.*Ibid.*, pp. 114-18.
166.*Ibid.*, p. 158.
167.*Ibid.*, pp. 196, 200-01.
168.*Ibid.*, p. 191.

169.*Ibid.*, p. 302.
170.*Ibid.*, p. 268.
171.*Ibid.*, p. 264.
172.*Ibid.*, p. 265.
173.*Ibid.*, pp. 266-7.
174.*Ibid.*, pp. 277, 279.
175.*Ibid.*, p. 304.
176.*Ibid.*, p. 327.
177.E. D. Morel, *Truth and the War*, 223-34.
178.Kennedy, p. 464.
179.*Ibid.*, p. 410.
180.*Ibid.*, p. 424.
181.*Ibid.*, pp. 467-8.
182.*Ibid.*, p. 434.
183.*Ibid.*, p. 468.

Twelve

■

The Entente Myth of German Foreign Policy

The second world war ended the rational discussion of the Great War of 1914-18 which was under way during the 1930s. Hitler's slaughter of six million Jews and millions of other civilians produced such strong anti-German feeling that a balanced judgement of pre-war German history became almost impossible. The result was reversion to the Versailles dictum of 1919 which held Germany solely responsible for the first world war.

The publication in 1961 of a book by the German historian Fritz Fischer, entitled *Germany's Aims in the First World War*, enshrined the accepted dogma that German policy was the sole cause of the Great War. The book made the unsubstantiated assumption that German aims during the war were implicit in Germany's pre-war policy. A preliminary section gave an account of the outbreak of the war based mainly on Karl Kautsky's *German Documents on the Outbreak of the War*, published in 1919. Fischer's second book, *War of Illusions*, was published in 1969. It blames Germany for all the conflicts which took place before the wars. Both books were flawed. The first defect was Fischer's belief that second-hand evidence is more reliable than first-hand evidence; the second was his almost complete ignorance of contemporary events in other countries. The common thread which runs through the works of Fischer and his followers is the eagerness for war which they say permeated German society.

Their account begins by maintaining that Chancellor of the German Empire Prince Otto von Bismarck's policy of iron and blood set Germany on the path of military aggression to bring about German unification. Fischer's view is that the main underlying cause of the Great War was the policy followed by imperial Germany. He shows no knowledge of the history of any country but Germany, and he never tells the reader which European country was unified or which empire was created without the use of iron or the shedding of blood.

The first instance of German "aggression" is the Franco-Prussian war. France had repeatedly stated that she would resist forcibly the unification of Germany and the French emperor Napoleon III had negotiated an alliance with Austria and Italy for this purpose. When they learned of Bismarck's plan to place a Hohenzollern prince on the Spanish throne they used this incident to force a war on Prussia.

The French began by demanding that the Prince's candidature should be withdrawn. Kaiser Wilhelm I of Prussia, the head of the Hohenzollern house, acceded to their request, presenting France with a diplomatic triumph. They were determined to bring on a war by forcing on Prussia a further humiliation, so they demanded that Kaiser Wilhelm should promise never to allow a Hohenzollern prince to aspire to the throne of Spain. The kaiser firmly refused to make such a promise and so informed Bismarck by a telegram from Ems where he was staying. He authorized Bismarck to make the contents of this telegram known to the public, and Bismarck paraphrased the contents in a press release. The French claimed they were forced to declare war because of the insult.

Bismarck stated in his memoirs written twenty-five years later that he had changed the meaning of the telegram to bring on the war. A comparison of the text of the telegram with the published press release shows that there is no difference in meaning between the two. In particular, the original telegram gives no suggestion whatever of negotiations to be continued at Berlin, as Bismarck asserts.[1] In fact, in the telegram Wilhelm I refused the demand of French ambassador Benedetti, saying that a promise of the kind requested was "neither right nor possible." He would not receive Benedetti again, and sent an aide-de-camp to tell him he had nothing further to say to him.[2]

Bismarck had blundered, and was himself responsible for the diplomatic defeat Prussia had received. He was rescued by the determination of France to provoke a war, but pretended that he had retrieved the position by his own cleverness. The information he published described exactly what had happened, as it was told in the telegram from Ems. If he had published the text of the original telegram from Ems, an unusual act, its effect could have been no different from that of his press release.

Fischer's followers emphasize the supposed error made by Germany in taking Alsace-Lorraine during the war that ensued. This cession was an almost inevitable result of German sentiment in favour of regaining the provinces lost to French aggression over the preceding two-and-a-half centuries: German military leaders believed that Alsace-Lorraine was required for protection against France. It is unlikely that France would have been reconciled to defeat even if she had not lost this territory. Although the French desire for *revanche* fastened on the loss of Alsace-Lorraine, there is no reason to believe France could not have found another rallying cry to precipitate the war it desired.

The indemnity of one billion dollars imposed on France in 1891, which has been described as a "tremendous sum,"[3] was a bagatelle compared with the indemnity imposed on Germany in 1919. Taking into account the increase of wealth and the change in the value of money, five billion dollars would have been an equivalent sum for the Germany of 1913, but not, of course, for the crippled and impoverished Germany of 1919. The French government was able to borrow the money to pay it off in a few years. German "reparations" of thirty-three billion dollars were designed to keep Germany paying forever.

Germanophobe historian Immanuel Geiss expatiates on the aggressiveness of German policy in supposedly threatening France in 1875 with "preventive war."[4] The incident began with the discussion in the German press of a large increase in the French army, already larger than the German army. The statement that Bismarck threatened France with war is pure fiction. In fact, the crisis, if it can be called a crisis, was engineered by the Duc de Decazes, the French foreign minister, to arouse Europe against Germany.[5]

Bismarck's Germany was generally recognized as a stabilizing influence working for peace. The British government frequently cooperated with Germany during the period of German dominance and joined France and Russia only after the Triple Alliance had been balanced by the Dual Alliance and Italy had been neutralized. This fact makes nonsense of the idea that England opposed Germany to maintain the balance of power. As everyone in Europe understood, the addition of England to the Franco-Russian alliance tilted the balance heavily against Germany and Austria. When the Triple Entente Powers spoke of preserving the balance of power what they were talking about was the maintenance of entente predominance.

There has been much controversy over Bismarck's alleged "conversion" to imperialism. One theory said that his acquisition of colonies was purely a matter of internal and international politics, and that he was never interested in commerce for its own sake. It is evident, however, that Bismarck was always interested in industry and trade, as is shown by his introduction of many measures to support these activities. These included subsidies for steamship lines, the establishment of bank branches overseas, consular support of trade, and special rates on railroads and canals for export goods.[6] He realized that an overseas policy was necessary to support trade, but his preference was to have businessmen take the initiative with support from the state when necessary. By the 1880s it appeared, however, that other Powers, particularly England, were intent on gobbling up the remaining unconquered parts of the world, and that Germany would be shut out. In these circumstances it was expedient to stake Germany's claim to at least some portion of the territories being acquired.

This "aggressive militaristic power" obtained all its overseas territories without the use of military or naval force. Geiss remarked on the "fraudulent" methods by which Germany obtained colonies.[7] In his eyes negotiation with native chiefs evidently was contemptible in comparison with the French and British method of military conquest. He mentions the revolts in some German colonies, ignoring the thirteen rebellions in British Africa in the 1890s alone.[8]

German colonial methods, Geiss tells us, were a combination of "paternalism, inexperience, arrogance, exploitation and racism," which led to revolts in all colonies except Togo.[9] All these terms, with the possible exception of inexperience, could be applied to every European empire as truthfully as to Germany, and resistance to European control was universal. The whole of Africa had been colonized by European Powers by 1914, and amongst all these colonies there was only one in which there had been no war either to acquire it or to keep it. That one colony was German Togoland.

German policy is supposed to have undergone a transformation in 1895, when a new line of conduct known as *Weltpolitik* was adopted and Germany embarked on a course of aggressive expansionism. This policy, Geiss tells us, "came into existence as a red herring of the ruling classes to distract the middle and working classes from social and political problems at home." He calls German imperialism "social imperialism."[10] He sees Germany's need for markets and sources of raw material as having no relation to its expansionist policy, although no doubt such economic motives were responsible for the far greater aggressive expansionism of France and England. According to Geiss, Germany's industrial development was also a result of the "aggressive" tendencies of German society, because it was "indispensable for power politics."[11]

The truth is that Germany's imperialism was a matter of words rather than of deeds. Her expansionism was largely an aspiration which rarely materialized in action. Fritz Fischer demonstrates this when he cites the many calls for an imperial policy by German writers, which continued until the outbreak of the war. In 1896 Rudolf Martin called for "an active colonial policy," and in 1900 Paul Voigt produced a collection of essays in which he advocated an increase in colonial possessions. Historian Hans Delbrück wanted a new partition of the world.[12] In 1912/13 many publicists were urging the German government to adopt an imperialist policy, which they obviously thought it did not have.[13] Paul Kennedy tells us that the demand for expansion was more organized and developed in Germany than in any other country.[14] He fails to note that there was no need for agitation for expansion in France or England, as both these countries were expanding as quickly as possible without public urging.

The groups which were demanding German expansion obviously did not have the ear of the German government. Fischer assumes throughout that the pan-Germans and their allies spoke for Germany, but in fact they formed the opposition to the government. Kennedy points out that in the Reichstag the right-wing parties opposed the government, and that the Pan-German League was part of the "national opposition" from its inception.[15] He notes the league's private influence in education, in business and in the right-wing parties, but does not see any significance in its constant opposition to the government.

There is an interesting passage in Winston Churchill's *World Crisis* in which he says that, concerned about the German navy and wanting a friendly agreement with Germany, he sent Sir Ernest Cassel to Berlin to discuss such an agreement with Kaiser Wilhelm. Cassel was armed with a memorandum which promised support for German colonial ambitions in return for a halt to the expansion of the German navy. Cassel reported on his return that the Germans were not interested in expansion: ten large companies in Berlin were importing labour into Germany, and over-population was not a problem.[16]

Germany's real policy, that which she actively followed, was aimed at increasing industrial efficiency by training her people and advancing scientific methods. She also worked to secure access to overseas markets. This was the policy forced on Germany by the rapid increase of her population. With no outlet in overseas territories suitable for white colonization, and no real prospect of obtaining any, Germany had to find work and food for her people, which could be done only by industrial and commercial development.[17]

For Germany, the central fact of foreign policy was that the expansion of foreign markets was a matter of life and death. The increase in the number of her people depending on foreign food was approaching a million a year. Her policy to expand markets was carried out so successfully that in the last twenty-five years before the war the rate of increase of Germany's trade was double that of England.

The institution of a "great navy" policy, V. R. Berghahn tells us, compensated for Germany's failure to increase the army. Germany "initiated" the naval arms race, although she was the last Power, with the exception of Austria, to decide on the expansion of her navy. No doubt in this case, as in so many others, the other Powers reacted in advance of German action.[18]

Berghahn admits that strong forces in German society demanded a naval armaments programme, and that these forces included the whole business world of bankers, industrialists and traders, as well as the educated bourgeoisie. He concludes, nevertheless, that Admiral Tirpitz's naval policy was "nothing less than an ambitious plan to stabilize the Prusso-German political system and to paralyze the pressure for change."[19] It was unwise to reveal such a purpose, which it may be supposed caused Tirpitz to pretend that his navy was related to foreign rather than internal policy.[20]

According to the ideas which prevailed universally at the time, a world policy and a naval policy were forced on Germany by her industrial and commercial development. Since in the eyes of the entente historians Germany had no right to undertake economic development, her natural reaction to such development was illegitimate, and must be explained by sinister forces operating in German society. This is a facet of the argument that Germany should have remained an agricultural country in order not to offend other Powers.

The tensions in German society actually lessened in the last twenty years before the war. The attempt to suppress the Social Democrats by law was abandoned and the party rapidly increased its representation in the Reichstag. The hope of moderate opponents of socialism was that the Social Democratic Party would become a party of reform. This hope was realized and the fear of socialism declined.[21] The success of the ruling classes in alleviating social strife is shown by the fact that emigration to the United States from Germany fell from over 500,000 in the decade 1891-1900 to under 350,000 in 1901-10, while total European emigration more than doubled, with increases from every country except Ireland and Germany.[22]

Berghahn also devotes several pages to the designs of using the German army against the German people, and particularly against the Social Democrats, but since he cites no instance in which it was ever so used, it must be assumed that this was unnecessary. It never occurs to him to wonder whether German society was less prone to violence, or the German leaders less eager to provoke a war, than he imagines.[23]

According to historian Paul Kennedy, Germany's restless, explosive and disconcerting activity caused in the other Powers a fear of German aims and irresponsible power. His examples of the German policies which produced this fear are the Kruger telegram, the fleet policy, the Bosnian ultimatum and the "*Panther's* Spring."[24] This is standard entente propaganda, designed to justify the encirclement and browbeating to which Germany was subjected by the policy of England and France. The Kruger telegram was certainly unwise, but it alarmed no one except the British press and public, while British conduct of the South African war aroused a storm of resentment throughout Europe. How Germany's tardy decision to follow the other Powers in expanding her navy constituted a restless, explosive and disconcerting activity must ever remain a mystery. In the case of the Bosnian crisis, the action which fits this description was taken by Alexandre Isvolsky, the Russian foreign minister, whose errors and prevarications created a crisis which was finally resolved by Germany. In the Agadir crisis the best example of restless and explosive activity was surely that of France, whose complete disregard of the Act of Algeciras and ten-year military campaign for the conquest of Morocco created the situation which led to the so-called *Panther's* Spring. The most prominent exercise of irresponsible power was the action of the British foreign office, whose eagerness to challenge Germany created a crisis where none existed.

Historian Michael R. Gordon maintains that British policy was "moderate and defensive," while in Germany domestic policy produced an aggressive foreign policy. This policy manifested itself in *Weltpolitik*, armaments programmes and quests for prestige.[25] As British historian E. D. Morel pointed out, "*Weltpolitik* has been the breath of our own nostrils since Elisabeth,"[26] and British defence expenditures during 1904-07, the period when the entente was consummated, were 42 percent greater than those of Germany.[27] The successful defence of the Empire against Boer aggression had just added 100,000 square miles to the British possessions, and other similar defensive actions were still in progress in various parts of the world in 1904.

Geiss claims that there were individuals in Germany who believed a war was necessary to unite German society or make Germany a world power.[28] Such statements are taken as the mainspring of German policy, despite the fact that no action by the German government indicates that they were ever taken seriously.

Fischer appears to believe that military leaders controlled German policy, and there was a constant desire for a preventive war. He tells us, for example, that in 1905 General Alfred von Schlieffen pushed the political leadership in the direction of war.[29] He does not note that the push was always unsuccessful.

From the time of the Morocco crisis onward Germany's determination to go to war is the central theme of this supposed German policy. Germany reacted aggressively to the policy of containment and pressed to increase her armaments.[30] But Berghahn says the German army "stagnated" from 1893 to 1912, and its growth did not keep pace with the increase in population, so it is obvious that this armaments policy did not include the army.[31] According to Berghahn, this stagnation was because the army leaders did not want to democratize the army by enlisting too many men of the middle and lower classes.

Fischer tells us that the kaiser's trip to Tangier arose from a desire to provoke a war with France after Russia's defeat at Mukden.[32] The reality, as usual, is quite different. The decision to oppose France's takeover of Morocco, and to send the kaiser to Tangier, took place well before the Russian defeat at Mukden. The German counterstroke was "pushed vigorously from January 1905."[33] Discussion of the kaiser's Tangier visit took place at the end of February, and it was designed specifically as a pacific demonstration which would not provoke France to war.[34]

If German society required a war and the German government was determined to fight one, it is incomprehensible that Germany did not force a war in 1905, when Russia was neutralized by the war with Japan and the Anglo-French entente was still in its infancy. Some writers have criticized German stupidity for not seizing such a golden opportunity. Major Civrieux, for example, remarks that Germany's historic moment came in 1905, when

France was isolated and England could have intervened only with her navy. A Bismarck, he says, would have launched the decisive war, but "happily for France a mystic was seated on the throne of the Hohenzollerns."[35] There is no evidence that Germany wanted a war, over Morocco or any other issue.

The emphasis on the German desire for war surfaces again concerning the crisis over the annexation of Bosnia. Her army leaders, Berghahn said, wanted war, partly because of domestic difficulties and partly because the army was well prepared. This was the army, it should be remembered, which according to Geiss had stagnated since 1893. One of the principal substantiators of this desire for war was the Russian ambassador in Berlin, who apparently was guiding German policy at the time. The reason the war did not take place was that "the political leadership as a whole" did not want one. At the same time the Chancellor had great difficulty in persuading the Reichstag to vote the money needed for defence expenditure. Thus while a few military men wanted war, the political leaders and the representatives of the German people opposed it. It is therefore not surprising that Germany, alone amongst the Great Powers, fought no war between 1870 and 1914; the only surprise is that anyone should cite these facts to indicate the warlike character of German society.[36]

Germany, it is said, provoked a second Morocco crisis in 1911.[37] Ignoring France's ten-year military campaign to subdue Morocco, which by this time involved nearly 100,000 French and Spanish soldiers, our mentors attribute a great crisis to Germany's sending a 1000-ton gunboat carrying 125 men, two 5" guns and six machine-guns to anchor off the Moroccan coast. Every German action regarding Morocco was a response to France's determination to ride roughshod over Germany's rights and interests there. The perverse perception which brands these actions as aggressive can be seen only as a supine surrender to the British propaganda of the time.

According to Geiss, Germany's readiness to go to war was so great that if war had come she would have been entirely responsible. The next year, however, Germany was "not yet prepared to go to war." Geiss admits that Alfred von Kiderlen-Wächter, the German foreign minister, did not think of going to war, and that even his limited belligerence was opposed by Bethmann-Hollweg and the kaiser.[38] What Kiderlen-Wächter said that was labelled belligerent by Geiss was that if France refused to make any concession Germany would insist on the maintenance of the Act of Algeciras.

The German determination to go to war is supposedly shown by accounts of a meeting held on December 8, 1912. The only first-hand account of this meeting is contained in Admiral Müller's diary, and it in no way supports the idea that a decision was made to go to war in one-and-a-half years. What it does show is that the German leaders believed that war was inevitable, and that preparations should be made for it. Tirpitz said the navy would prefer to have the war postponed, and Chief of the general staff, Helmuth von Moltke countered that the navy would not be ready in any case, which was obviously true. Müller concluded that "The result [of the meeting] amounted to almost nothing."[39] It was known before the war that the kaiser, who had always used his influence on the side of peace, was convinced by the Agadir crisis that war was inevitable. As this was also the belief held in all the capitals of the Triple Entente, its acceptance by the kaiser was a recognition of reality.

Fischer provides evidence that Wilhelm II was not aware of any decision to go to war at a certain time. He quotes a footnote in which the kaiser said "The struggle between the Slavs and the Teutons is unavoidable, it must come. When? We shall see." Moltke was also unaware of a decision: he advocated the adoption of universal conscription in October 1914, or at the latest October, 1915.[40]

These writers interpret evidence that Germans do not believe in the necessity of war in the opposite sense. For example, when Friedrich Meinecke denies that Germans hold the belief that Germany's future could be secured by a great war, this somehow shows how widespread was the conviction that war was necessary.[41] Press articles by even one newspaper are taken as German policy if they suggest a need for war. An assertion by the *Post* that war is the only means of achieving equality for Germany is a case in point.[42] The influence of the *Post* can be seen in the fact that when it allegedly called for a preventive war the whole German press opposed the idea.[43]

Fischer tells us that General Friedrich von Bernhardi advocated a preventive war to exploit the military superiority Germany still had.[44] Fischer does not say where this information comes from, but it does not appear in Bernhardi's *Germany and the Next War*, or in those parts of his book, *Unsere Zukunft*, which are quoted in J.B. Scott's survey of German-American relations.[45]

Bernhardi's actual view was that "France has succeeded in bringing her military strength to approximately the same level as Germany" and could increase it with levies from North Africa.[46] He believed that on the continent the Triple and Dual Alliances balanced each other, "provided that Italy belongs to the League. If Italy really withdraws from the Triple Alliance, very distinctly superior forces will be united against Germany and Austria."[47] He pointed out that French military writers were so confident that Italy would not fight with the Triple Alliance that they thought it was no longer necessary to maintain an army against Italy: they believed the entire forces of France were available against Germany.[48] He considered it doubtful that Italy would take part in a war in which England and France were allied against Germany, although he was evidently unaware that Italy was pledged not to fight against France. His opinion therefore was that "If we wish to attain an extension of our power...we must win it by the sword against vastly superior foes."[49] As regards naval forces, Bernhardi's view is shown by the statement that

"England and France together can collect in the North Sea a fleet of battleships alone three times as strong as that of Germany."[50]

Believing that Germany faced greatly superior forces, Bernhardi naturally did not advocate a preventive war. On the contrary, he warned the German government that the war was imminent and urged that preparation should be made for it before it was too late. He warned that "The period which destiny has allotted us for concentrating our forces and preparing ourselves for the deadly struggle may soon be passed."[51] "The first essential requirement," he wrote, "is to make the total fighting strength of the nation available for war."[52] He pointed out that only about half of the able-bodied men of Germany were actually called up for training, and that the country where universal military service truly existed was France. The first necessity, therefore, was to increase the number of trained men. This, however, would be a gradual process, and Germany could not hope "for a long time to equalize even approximately the superior forces of our opponents."[53]

Under these circumstances, efforts must be made to increase the "fighting capabilities and tactical efficiency" of the armed forces.[54] "The gradual enforcement of universal military service hand in hand with an increase of the regular army is the first practical requirement." But since equality in numbers was beyond reach, the greatest effort must be made to develop character, because "the army which contains the greatest number of self-reliant and independent personalities must have a distinct advantage."[55] He concluded that Germans "must use the respite we still enjoy for the most energetic warlike preparations," believing that, if the greatest effort were put forth, the superior fighting qualities of the German soldier would provide a chance for victory.[56]

Unfortunately for Germany, the German government did not take Bernhardi's advice, and Germany's preparations for war remained inadequate. When the time came too few men were available properly to carry out the Schlieffen plan, and the German army thus failed to envelop the French left wing. As French General Edmond Buat pointed out, if Germany had made as great an effort as France, they could have had an additional 600,000 soldiers to take part in the attack on France.[57]

It is true that Bernhardi believed that under certain circumstances preventive war was justified. It would have been difficult, if not impossible, to find a general in Europe who disagreed with him, and the same is true of most leading politicians. The idea that he urged Germany to start such a war under the conditions prevailing in 1911 or 1912, however, has no foundation in fact. This notion can be entertained only by those who have not taken the trouble to read his work.

Pursuing the theme of the readiness of Germany to go to war, Fischer presents Germany as ready to go to war if Austria is attacked while defending her Balkan interests, but admits that Germany's "real attitude" favoured peace.[58] He always assumes, of course, that generals speak for the German government, so when Count Alfred von Waldersee told Baron Franz Conrad von Hötzendorf that Germany hoped England would turn away from the entente, this proves to Fischer that the government was determined to go to war if England could be neutralized.[59] Bethmann-Hollweg, he says, was convinced by December, 1913, that a great war was likely, if not inevitable. Apparently he was unaware, too, that his government had "decided on" war on December 8, 1912.

Anti-German writers accept statements by publicists, particularly if they are pan-Germans, as established fact, although even a little study of such statements would show that it is the habit of propagandists to attribute their own views to the public at large. When Hans Plehn says that since the Morocco crisis it has become "almost universally accepted by the German nation that Germany can only be free to pursue her world political activity by fighting a great war," this shows nothing more than Plehn's desire to foist his idea on the German nation.[60] By the spring of 1914, according to Fischer, this feeling was even more widespread, so it must have been literally universal.[61] He wisely avoids citing evidence to support his statement.

In the discussion of economic preparations for war, we are shown the proper way to dispose of unwanted evidence. When Koerner, director of the commercial section of the foreign office, says that "this would be the moment for a war, but nobody is thinking of it," Fischer says it would have been more correct to say "Everybody is thinking of it."[62] As for economic preparations for war, Fischer's chapter on this subject shows that nothing was done.[63]

Many pan-German sources are reported as being keen for war, but there is no attempt to show that these had any effect on the actions or decisions of the German government. Max Warburg, a leading banker, was allegedly in favour of an "active foreign policy," but when the kaiser asked him on June 21, 1914, how he felt about a preventive war, he said that for Germany the economic trend could only improve. "Germany was becoming stronger with every year of peace."[64]

Fischer's attempt to show a widespread desire for war in any section of the German people, except possibly the pan-Germans, is a failure. He pretends that the pan-Germans speak for the German people and control the government, but the actual course of events shows clearly that the government paid little attention to them and that the policies they advocated were never followed.

Fischer mentions that in January, 1909, the Chiefs of Staff of Germany and Austria exchanged letters to coordinate the plans of the two armies in the event of war, and that this continued to 1914. He says there was "a strong body of opinion among the German leadership prepared to risk a war with Russia,"[65] although he supplies no evidence to support his assertion. The plans of the two armies were rudimentary in comparison with those of the entente Powers. The French and Russian staffs held annual conferences for many years, and France and England had elaborate plans, complete in every detail, for cooperation on the western front.

The Schlieffen plan is attacked as an example of Germany's "inflexible military plans," which were no more inflexible than anyone else's plans. In April, 1913, it is said, the Germans made war inevitable by scrapping a plan to attack Russia first, which pushed Germany on the road to offensive war in the west. The Germans should have counted on France being neutral or passive.[66] Kennedy tells us that Germany might have kept England neutral if she had returned to the strategy of defence in the west and an eastern offensive.[67] The "inflexible" Schlieffen plan "gratuitously" brought France into the war.[68]

The Germans made many mistakes, but they were not stupid enough to rely on French neutrality in a Russo-German war. Believing, quite correctly, that they would be forced to fight on two fronts against superior forces, they chose the plan which would give them a chance of knocking out France before the slower Russians could get under way. To get bogged down in the vast expanse of Russia while France attacked in the west would have been idiotic.

To believe that the Schlieffen plan brought France into the war these authors would have to be unaware of the existence of the Franco-Russian alliance. That seems incredible unless their preconceived belief in German guilt absolves them of the need to know what was happening in other countries. The assumption that only German policy is relevant is woven through the fabric of entente mythology.

Another facet of these authors' concentration on Germany is the assertion that Germany's lack of democratic institutions was one of the causes of Germany's supposed "predilection for war." Berghahn remarks that in Germany the question of war or peace was in the hands of a small "strategic clique."[69] According to Kennedy, the German constitutional position determined that the peace lovers in Germany had no influence on foreign policy. Majority control of the House of Commons was more decisive than control of the Reichstag.[70]

These facts supposedly contrast with the situation in England, which was ruled by the model democracy which Germany should have emulated. A cursory glance at the conduct of British foreign policy between 1906 and 1914 should dispel any such illusion. That policy was carried on by a half dozen Liberal imperialists, who concealed it not only from Parliament but from half the cabinet. The British Parliament was less well informed about foreign policy than the Reichstag, which at least knew what the German foreign policy was. On November 16, 1911, the editor of the *Daily News* wrote that "the control of the Reichstag over foreign affairs is very much greater than the control of our own House of Commons." On the eve of the war Grey felt it necessary to deceive Parliament about his negotiations for a naval agreement with Russia, because he knew that the bulk of his party would oppose closer relations with the tsarist autocracy.

With regard to a declaration of war, the British constitutional position was that the king declared war on the advice of his ministers. Parliament played no part until it was asked to supply money to carry on a war already declared. In the event even the cabinet made no decision either to send an ultimatum to Germany or to declare war on her: these decisions rested on the authority of the prime minister.[71]

The reality is that a small strategic clique controlled British foreign policy and took the British Empire into a disastrous war in support of Russia's offensive in the Balkans. While it is true that similar conditions prevailed to some extent everywhere, the deception of Parliament and the public in England with regard to foreign policy has no parallel elsewhere.

One of the remarkable features of the period 1870-1914 is that the satisfied, peace-loving Powers, England, France and Russia, all conducted military campaigns to expand their empires, while the army of warlike, aggressive Germany ventured outside German territory only once, to take part in the expedition against the Boxer rebellion. The British army, on the other hand, was constantly engaged in imperialist wars, usually in two or three at the same time. In the 1890s there were thirty-five wars, expeditions and campaigns, in addition to the suppression of several rebellions.[72] During that decade the British Empire acquired nearly two million square miles of African territory, while expansionist Germany added two Samoan islands with an area of 1,000 square miles to its empire. In 1904, the year of the Anglo-French entente, the British sent an expedition to extend the frontier of British India into Tibet, fought on the Afghan frontier, struggled to complete the conquest of Nigeria, and were engaged in suppressing a rebellion in Somaliland. Between 1871 and 1900 England and France added 4.5 million and 3.5 million square miles respectively to their empires,[73] while Germany acquired during the whole inter-war period one million square miles, all without moving a man or a ship.

Geiss tells us that after 1895 war became the "overriding preoccupation" of Germany.[74] If so, they never took advantage of any situation to make war, although attractive opportunities presented themselves. There was only one Great Power in the world which did not engage in a war of conquest during the reign of that erratic imperialist and expansionist Wilhelm II, and that Great Power was Germany.

Geiss engages his vivid imagination concerning the first Hague conference when, he says, Germany opposed the "disarmament and compulsory arbitration" suggested by the tsar, because she needed military power for *Weltpolitik*.[75] The tsar actually suggested non-augmentation of armaments and voluntary arbitration.[76] The idea that there was an attempt at the disarmament of Europe is fantasy. No government in the world took disarmament seriously, and none has yet done so, although some were prepared to humour the tsar at the time and numerous disarmament conferences have been held since.

The belief that German opposition prevented the adoption of compulsory arbitration is equally illusory. Since international law has not yet achieved either compulsory arbitration or the compulsory jurisdiction of the International Court, it is evident that this supposed German veto has had very long-term effects: the nations of the world are still not willing to risk the disapproval of Germany by disarming or instituting compulsory settlement of disputes.

According to Geiss the initiative is always taken by Germany, the other Powers react to Germany's aggressive moves.[77] The isolation of Germany according to this view was "self isolation."[78] Fischer tells us that the Triple Entente was created by fear and distrust of Germany.[79] German internal policy dictated that there should be no international agreements, and the policy of the free hand made it seem desirable to have political alliances with weak powers "but not with other Great Powers."[80]

There is not the slightest evidence that fear and distrust of Germany played any part whatever in the creation of the Triple Entente. On the French side the Anglo-French entente was mainly the creation of the French foreign office under Delcassé. His refusal to deal with Germany arose from his determination not to sign again the Treaty of Frankfurt to leave open the possibility of regaining Alsace-Lorraine. The road to his objective lay in the creation of an anti-German coalition. As far as French public opinion was concerned, fear and distrust of England was a dominant sentiment, remaining strong for some time after the signing of the Anglo-French agreement.

The idea that the British government acted through fear of Germany is ridiculous. The antagonism to Germany of the British public certainly played a part in the failure of England to move closer to Germany, but the British government was impelled by the fear of Russia and the need to come to terms with England's two foremost rivals.

In the last half of 1902 the important subject for British diplomacy was rivalry with Russia in Central Asia.[81] It was Russia's aggressive policy in that area that convinced Lord Lansdowne that concessions must be made to France in Morocco, against the advice of the war office and the navy. The service chiefs were evidently more afraid of France than of Germany, and wanted better arrangements for keeping France away from the strategic coast of Morocco.[82]

> The Cabinet's attention during 1903 was fixed upon Russia, and Germany was hardly ever mentioned in their correspondence; there was certainly no fear of Germany comparable to the fear of Russia which Balfour, Hamilton and Selborne so frequently expounded.[83]

The British were very happy when the Russian navy was almost annihilated by the Japanese at Tsushima on May 27, 1905, and at that time showed no concern about the balance of power on the continent or about a relative increase in the power of Germany.[84]

When Grey took over the foreign office in 1905 his rooted antipathy to Germany no doubt affected his determination to continue on the route mapped out by his predecessor. That he distrusted Germany is made abundantly clear in his memoirs, but there is no evidence that fear of Germany ever entered his head, nor is there any reason why it should have done so. His determination to support France at the Algeciras conference rested on his belief that it was imperative to maintain the Anglo-French entente. Otherwise England would be back where she had been between 1892 and 1895, "constantly on the brink of war with France or Russia or both, and dependent for our diplomatic position in the world on German good-will."[85]

As late as the July crisis in 1914 the enmity of Russia was considered more dangerous to the British Empire than that of Germany. On July 24, Sir Arthur Nicolson wrote, "Our attitude during the crisis will be regarded by Russia as a test and we must be careful not to alienate her."[86] A few days later he thought that, if Russia was disappointed in her hope for British support, "all hope of a friendly and permanent understanding with her would disappear."[87] Sir George Buchanan considered that, if England did not side with France and Russia, at the end of the war, whatever its outcome, "the Indian Empire would no longer be secure from attack by Russia."[88] It was generally believed when the war began that Germany posed no significant threat to England and that the entente could defeat her easily and quickly.[89]

The thesis that the initiative was always taken by Germany and that the other Powers simply reacted to German moves is supposedly illustrated by the long conflict over Morocco. England's agreement to support the conquest and partition of Morocco and the monopolization of its economy by France and Spain was thus a reaction to the kaiser's visit to Tangier, which in fact took place the following year. It is also clear to these reaction theorists, apparently, that France increased her financial, economic and military control of Morocco in reaction to Germany's attempts to preserve her own interests there. Similarly, they see the French military occupation of large areas of Morocco, culminating in the occupation of her capital by French troops, as a reaction to the dispatch of the *Panther* to Agadir.

Fischer's statement that Germany was ready to make political alliances with weak powers but not with Great Powers is followed immediately by his account of the attempt to form an alliance with Russia in 1904/05.[90] Geiss blames Germany for not accepting England's supposed offer of an alliance, an offer which was never made.[91] One writer, V.R. Berghahn, actually asserts that Germany turned down Lansdowne's "famous offer" of 1901 because "neither the Kaiser nor Bülow desired an alliance with Britain."[92] Lansdowne made no offer of an alliance to Germany either in 1901 or at any other time: this statement presumably refers to an idea for a common Anglo-German policy which Lansdowne discussed with Metternich in December, 1901.

This misleading statement about Lansdowne's famous offer confirms the impression given throughout the book that Berghahn knows nothing about British policy. It is evident that he considers it unnecessary to know anything about the policies of any Power except Germany. His application of the "analytical tools of social psychology and sociology" to German society[93] convinces him that Germany existed in a vacuum and her foreign policy was completely unrelated to the actions of other Powers. There is, of course, a relation between the domestic situation and foreign policy, in Germany as elsewhere, but a rational approach would make some allowance for the existence of other Powers.

Germany's alleged "self isolation" resulted from its "aggressive" policies. Fear of the German navy supposedly led England to a *rapprochement* with France and Russia, because British hegemony at sea was threatened.[94] In 1907 Admiral Fisher thought the British navy was four times as strong as the German navy, and since the French navy was by that time allied with that of England, the threat to British hegemony at sea which Fischer cites depends on a report from London by Wilhelm von Stumm, German naval attaché, who was taken in by British propaganda. There is no evidence that the German navy had anything whatever to do with the creation of the Triple Entente. In another flight of wrong-headed logic Fischer asserts that the Dreadnought was introduced because of British fear of the German navy.[95] Geiss accuses Germany of rejecting "mutual limitation" of naval building, which was never proposed by the British, who sought only German limitation.[96] Fischer ends by admitting that it was not the German navy which caused England to oppose Germany, although he argues as though he has forgotten this fact.[97]

According to Immanuel Geiss, Germany was not encircled, merely "contained." This containment supposedly began with the Anglo-Japanese alliance, whose aim was initially to contain Russia in the Far East.[98] It followed England's failure to enlist Germany for this purpose. Geiss claims the Triple Entente was formed to preserve the *status quo*.[99] He doesn't explain how the French conquest of Morocco or the division of Persia between Russia and England contributed to the maintenance of the *status quo*. Russia continued to pursue this objective by instigating the Balkan wars, which produced the greatest alteration of the *status quo* to take place during the whole period under discussion.

According to the wisdom of our time, the idea of encirclement was a figment of the German imagination. K.H. Jarausch mentions the "psychosis of encirclement," and Geiss calls it a spectacle conjured up by Germany. He quotes with approval Kantorowicz's phrase "the fairy-tale of encirclement."[100] Perhaps the French writer who originated the expression in· 1904 was imaginary, but Major Civrieux's book, *Germanisme Encerclé*, which actually exists, can hardly be imaginary. Colonel Arthur Boucher did not use the word encirclement, but he described vividly the "four-fold vise" which hemmed Germany in on all sides.[101] Many other writers have since used the term as a matter of course. Julian Amery, for example, announcing the death of the idea of an alliance with Germany, says that with its disappearance the "road was open now which was to lead to the founding of the Entente and the encirclement of Germany."[102]

Geiss confirms the reality of encirclement, which he calls "containment." He devotes a whole chapter to the containment of Germany, which he says was completed by the Anglo-Russian entente.[103] He does not explain the difference between containment and encirclement: perhaps containment was rectangular rather than circular. He later speaks of the "ring of containment" around Germany being "held and even strengthened,"[104] but apparently this ring was not a circle either. The distinction is, of course, that, since the other Powers had no policy of their own, the word "containment" signifies that encirclement was a reaction to German "aggression," not an independent policy. This stands Delcassé's policy of isolating Germany on its head, and paints a completely misleading picture of the creation of the Triple Entente.

The most significant policy of active aggression at this time was the French military conquest of Morocco. At the same time Russia was fighting a defensive war against Japan, probably to forestall Japanese occupation of St. Petersburg. Some historians act as if the Russo-Japanese war was prompted by German encouragement.[105] They can hardly believe that peace-loving Russia would undertake such a war unless urged to do so by aggressive Germany. The tsar would surely have been disturbed to learn that Russian policy was dictated by Germany. The British government took similar "defensive" action by agreeing to support the French conquest of Morocco and to back Delcassé in his determination to ride roughshod over Germany's treaty rights and legitimate economic interests in that country.

It is obvious that Germany proved unable to defend herself against the policy of the entente, but the idea that she herself was the creator of that policy runs directly counter to the voluminous evidence on the subject. It was the failure of Germany to adhere to her proper position as a supporter of the British Empire with no ambition to rise in the world which led England to her colonial deals with France and Russia. The idea that this action was caused by fear of Germany or by a threat to the balance of power is pure fiction.

Berghahn agrees with other writers on the subject that Tirpitz did not want war and had no notion of attacking England. Tirpitz's aim was to build a navy strong enough to prevent England from attacking Germany because she would be taking a risk in doing so. Berghahn realizes that Tirpitz never approached his aim, but he doesn't ask himself why the British government continued to act as though England was threatened by the German navy.

All the creators of this fictitious German policy pretend that a German agreement to limit naval building would have produced a settlement with England.[106] They are under the illusion that England agreed to limit her own building if Germany did so. The fact that some German leaders suffered from the same idea that they could conciliate England by naval concessions provides some excuse for this error.

Historian Fritz Fischer states that the idea of general disarmament was gaining ground in England and France. In both countries the legislatures were persuaded without difficulty to provide the funds the government wanted for defence. The United Kingdom led the world in armaments expenditures until 1913/14, when Russia took the lead. Per capita expenses were highest in the United Kingdom, with France in second place.[107]

The French electorate consistently gave a majority to parties which, theoretically at least, opposed an aggressive foreign policy, and this is also true in England and Germany. Unfortunately, neither the British Parliament nor the French Chamber had any more influence on foreign policy than the Reichstag. In England, Parliament was kept almost completely in the dark as far as foreign policy was concerned, and the French government paid no attention to resolutions in the Chamber with which ministers did not agree.

Immanuel Geiss states that in late 1912 the German Empire "had a more powerful position in Europe than ever before," as a result of its economic potential, its army and its rapidly growing fleet.[108] The truth is that it was recognized throughout Europe that the position of the Central Powers was greatly weakened by the Balkan war.[109] The idea that Germany was in a better position than ever can be taken seriously by no one who comprehends the situation.

Modern writers seem to accept without question the false statements made in England about Germany's pre-war power. If it was actually believed in England that Germany would have 200,000 more men than France,[110] this belief must have been instilled by French lies. Paul Kennedy tells us, falsely, that between 1910 and 1914 the German army budget rose from £40.8 million to £88.4 million. It is impossible to guess where this latter inflated figure originates: perhaps it includes the whole of the German capital levy, which was to be collected over three years. Kennedy notes that in 1910, Germany produced 13.8 million tons of steel to France's 3.2 million.[111] As France began the war in 1914 with more military equipment than Germany of every kind except heavy siege artillery, it is evident that France was devoting more steel to preparation for war than was Germany. The steel production of the three entente Powers was almost equal to that of Germany and Austria.

The fact is that, as Geiss says, the German army stagnated until 1912,[112] when the threat to Germany and Austria posed by Russia's Balkan offensive forced the German government to realize that expansion was imperative. The cost of maintaining the German military and naval forces was constantly criticized in the Reichstag,[113] and in 1912 that body refused to vote the money the chancellor and other officials thought was needed. The new army bill was not adopted until March, 1913, when it was too late to win a war.[114]

It was in their assessment of England's position in the European constellation that the Germans were most confused. They consistently underestimated the strength of the ties between England and France, and almost everyone except Wilhelm II thought these could be loosened by a naval agreement. Geiss claims to believe that Germany could have come to an agreement which would have neutralized England. The Haldane talks, he says, were "destroyed by German intransigence," although they succeeded to some extent in their real purpose, which was to quiet Grey's parliamentary opposition.[115]

According to Fischer, Germany was also to blame for growing Russo-German antagonism, although a tariff and trade war and a virulent press campaign were both initiated by the Russians.[116] German agitation against the "alleged threat" of the Russian military preparations was pretended and unjustified, he says, and the alarm concerning it was officially inspired. This false alarm was mounted by the German government to prepare the way for a preventive war.[117] Fischer nevertheless quotes Bethmann-Hollweg as saying that Russia was becoming a "greater nightmare" to Germany.[118] Apparently Bethmann-Hollweg was distressed by the assessment of German military men on Germany's relative strength in case of war. He thought it was necessary to "have a good deal of trust in God and count on the Russian revolution as ally in order to be able to sleep at all."[119]

General Buat, Major-General of the French armies at the time of the armistice, produced a book on the German army during the war, based on German documents. Buat declares that the general belief that at the outbreak of the war Germany was stronger than France and that she made better use of her reserves is false. He maintains that, on the contrary, "France alone at the beginning of the war, was at least equal, if not superior, to her formidable opponent in the number of large units," and that France made better use of her reserves than did Germany. He gives the strength of the active armies as 910,000 for France and 870,000 for Germany, and the reserves as 1,325,000 to 1,180,000.[120] In addition, he shows that Germany failed to train many of her young men: the number recognized as fit for service exceeded the number which budgetary provisions allowed to be incorporated into the army. In the year 1911 alone, of 1,200,000 young men presented to the medical boards, over 700,000 were turned down. Each year 135,000 well-qualified men were relieved of active service.

> *These men were tied down to a fictitious service of $12\frac{1}{2}$ years, legally represented by some period of training. In reality, for lack of money they were rarely called up. These are those who, to the number of 900,000 in 1914, constituted the ersatz-reserve.*

At the outbreak of the war the Germans had 2,000,000 mobilizable men, most of whom had received little or no training.[121]

The new German army bill projected a long-term plan, and the "sudden and massive expansion" of the German army[122] did not increase the army to the extent announced by Geiss until October 1914. The full effect on the reserves would be felt only in 1919.

Germany, who would never be able to match the Russian numbers, depended on quicker mobilization and better leadership. Russian military organization had been vastly improved in the last few years, however, and there had been steady progress in the supply of war material and the development of strategic railways.[123] In August, it was noted that railway construction and the reorganization of the army had greatly reduced mobilisation time, and that the Russian army could now take the field only a few days after the French army.[124] Russia had "unlimited reserves of trained men," but a shortage of officers limited the war strength to about 3,500,000 men.[125]

Fischer's statement that Germany launched a preventive war against the "unprepared entente" should convince any informed reader that he has not the faintest idea what was happening in Europe in the years before the war.[126] When the war broke out the standing armies of the entente outnumbered those of Germany and Austria by two to one, in trained reserves their advantage was eight to five, and their combined navies were three times as large as those of the Central Powers. The French army alone was slightly larger than the German army, and the French had more guns, more ammunition and more trained reserves. France and Russia spent 25 percent more on armaments than Germany and Austria in the five years before the war, while England led the world in defence expenditure until 1913/14, when Russia took the lead.[127] France and Russia thought they had a good chance of defeating Germany even without British help, and both believed they were well prepared. On July 20, 1914, the tsar told French ambassador to Russia, Maurice Paléologue, that unless Germany had "gone out of her mind altogether" she would "never attack Russia, France and England combined."[128]

Historian Hugh Trevor-Roper declares that Fischer's two books demonstrate that "Bethmann-Hollweg, like Hitler, aimed at German domination of Europe," and that the imperial government "sought consciously to achieve these aims by war."[129] The reader will search Fischer's books in vain for a single shred of evidence to support such a statement. Fischer's attempt to demonstrate a determination of Germany's leaders to go to war to achieve the aims developed in wartime is a complete failure. When a serious attempt is made to study the wartime aims of the entente Powers, these will certainly reveal the same kind of "continuity" with pre-war policy that Fischer sees in the case of Germany.

Bethmann-Hollweg, who as chancellor directed German policy in the last years before the war, apparently believed that Germany could acquire colonies and increase her trade without war.[130] He rejected the "militant imperialism of the Pan-Germans" and insisted on "peaceful *Weltpolitik*."[131] In June, 1914, he rejected the idea of a preventive war, and thought Germany should fight a war only if the "honour, security or the future of Germany" was at stake.[132] He opposed the idea that a war would strengthen conservatism, and thought as Grey did, that it would enhance social democracy and "topple many a throne."[133] He considered the maintenance of Austria a vital interest for Germany and was ready to fight if Austria's existence was threatened, as appeared to be the case in July, 1914.[134]

There is no evidence, either in Fritz Fischer's books or anywhere else, that the responsible directors of German policy in 1914 wanted a war for any purpose. German industry and trade were expanding, and could only be injured by war; there appeared to be a prospect of obtaining additional colonies without war; Germany had no aspirations for territorial expansion in Europe; and the Triple Entente disposed of what appeared to be overwhelming power, even if England remained neutral. Germany went to war because the existence of her one remaining ally was threatened by Russian intrigues, and if Austria was eliminated she would stand alone in the centre of Europe, completely at the mercy of the Triple Entente.

Notes

1. Otto von Bismarck, *The Man and the Statesman*, II, 99-100.
2. *Ibid.*, p. 96.
3. Immanuel Geiss, *German Foreign Policy, 1871-1914*, p. 28.
4. *Ibid.*
5. William L. Langer, *European Alliances and Alignments*, pp. 44-49.
6. James J. Sheehan, (ed.), *Imperial Germany*, p. 192.
7. Geiss, p. 48.
8. Byron Farwell, *Queen Victoria's Little Wars*, p. 370.
9. Geiss, pp. 49-50.
10. *Ibid.*, p. 78.

11.*Ibid.*, p. 77.

12.Fritz Fischer, *War of Illusions*, pp. 32-3.

13.*Ibid.*, p. 230-42.

14.Paul M. Kennedy, *The Samoan Tangle*, p. 264.

15.Kennedy, *The Rise of Anglo-German Antagonism, 1860-1914*, pp. 347-8, 371.

16.Winston S. Churchill, *The World Crisis*, I, 72.

17.K. H. Jarausch, *The Enigmatic Chancellor*, p. 144.

18.V. R. Berghahn, *Germany and the Approach of War in 1914*, p. 48.

19.*Ibid.*, pp. 28-9.

20.*Ibid.*, p. 34.

21.Fischer, pp. 19-20.

22.C. H. Lord and E. H. Lord, *Historical Atlas of the United States*, p. 207.

23.Berghahn, pp. 52-56.

24.Kennedy, *Antagonism*, p. 457.

25.Michael R. Gordon, "Domestic Conflict and the Origins of the First World War," *Journal of Modern History*, Vol. 46, 224-5.

26.E. D. Morel, *Truth and the War*, p. 244.

27.Arthur Guy Enock, *The Problem of Armaments*, pp. 182-6.

28.Geiss, pp. 78, 82.

29.Fischer, p. 55.

30.Geiss, p. 127.

31.Berghahn, pp. 6-9.

32.Fischer, p. 54.

33.Pierre Guillen, *L'Allemagne et le Maroc, 1870-1905*, p. 813.

34.*Ibid.*, p. 838.

35.Civrieux, *Germanisme Encerclé*, p. 104.

36.Berghahn, pp. 81-4.

37.Geiss, p. 132.

38.*Ibid.*, pp. 134, 140-1; Fischer, pp. 71 ff.

39.Geiss, pp.206-7.

40.Fischer, pp. 212, 399-400.

41.*Ibid.*, p. 196.

42.*Ibid.*, p. 244.

43.*Ibid.*, pp. 271-2; Jarausch, p. 140.

44.Fischer, pp. 243, 267.

45.J. B. Scott, *A Survey of International Relations Between the United States and Germany, 1914-1917*, pp. xcii-cxii.

46.Friedrich von Bernhardi, *Germany and the Next War*, pp. 90, 137.

47.*Ibid.*, p. 102.

48.*Ibid.*, p. 138.

49.*Ibid.*, p. 152.

50.*Ibid.*, p. 145.

51.*Ibid.*, p. 168.

52.*Ibid.*, p. 169.

53.*Ibid.*, p. 170.

54.*Ibid.*, p. 173.

55.*Ibid.*, p. 180.

56.*Ibid.*, 286-7.

57.General Edmond Buat, *L'Armée Allemande pendant la guerre de 1914-1918*, p. 10.

58.Fischer, pp. 156-9.

59.*Ibid.*, p. 173.

60.*Ibid.*, p. 196.

61.*Ibid.*, p. 319.

62.*Ibid.*, p. 440.

63.*Ibid.*, p. 441.

64.*Ibid.*, p. 457.

65.*Ibid.*, p. 60.

66.Geiss, p. 148; Fischer, pp. 178, 139.

67.Kennedy, *Antagonism*, p. 429.

68.*Ibid.*, p. 445.

69.Berghahn, p. 168.

70.Kennedy, *Antagonism*, pp. 380-1.

71.Churchill, p. 178.

72.Farwell, p. 370.

73.Paul M. Kennedy, *The Rise and Fall of the Great Powers*, pp. 220, 224.

74.Geiss, p. 26.

75.Geiss, pp. 90-91.

76.J. B. Scott, (ed.), *The Hague Conventions and Declarations of 1899 and 1907*, pp. xvii and xviii.

77.Geiss, p. 106.

78.Fischer, p. 50; Gordon, p. 225.

79.Geiss, p. 21.

80.Fischer, pp. 50-1.

81.G. W. Monger, *The End of Isolation*, p. 87.

82.*Ibid.*, pp. 130-2.

83.*Ibid.*, p. 134.

84.*Ibid.*, pp. 201, 205-6.

85.Sir Edward Grey, *Twenty-five Years*, I, 100.

86.BD, XI, no. 101, fn.

87.*Ibid.*, no. 239.

88.*Ibid.*, no. 490.

89.Earl Loreburn, *How the War Came*, p. 135.

90.Fischer, pp. 50-1.

91.Geiss, pp. 62, 82, 87.

92.V. R. Berghahn, *Germany and the Approach of War in 1914*, p. 45.

93.*Ibid.*, p. 65.

94.Fischer, p. 58.

95.Geiss, p. 107; Fischer, p. 123; A. J. Marder, *Fear God and Dread Nought*, II, 26.

96.Geiss, p. 109.

97.Fischer, p. 123.

98.Geiss, p. 96.

99.*Ibid.*, p. 124.

100.Jarausch, p. 98; Geiss, pp. 101, 122.

101.Colonel Arthur Boucher, *L'Allemagne en Péril*, p. 7.

102.Julian Amery, *The Life of Joseph Chamberlain*, IV, 170.

103.Geiss, p. 105.

104.*Ibid.*, p. 121.

105.*Ibid.*, p. 97.

106.Geiss, p. 130; Jarausch, p. 130; Berghahn, p. 109.

107.F. R. Mertens, *Militarism and Wages*.

108.Geiss, p. 139.

109.*Ibid.*, p. 146.

110.Kennedy, *Antagonism*, p. 426.

111.*Ibid.*, p. 424.

112.Geiss, p. 79.

113.BDD, no. 69.

114.Geiss, p. 79.

115.*Ibid.*, p. 137.

116.Fischer, pp. 366-8, 374.

117.*Ibid.*, pp. 371, 373, 375, 376-7, 388.

118.*Ibid.*, p. 224.

119.Jarausch, p. 96.

120.Buat, pp. 1, 7, 9, 14.

121.*Ibid.*, pp. 4,6.

122.Geiss, p. 147.

123.*The Times*, March 10, 1913, p. 8a.

124.*Ibid.*, August 22, 1913, p. 3d.

125.*Ibid.*, September 10, 1913, p. 6f.

126.Fischer, p. 397.

127.E. D. Morel, *Military Preparations for the Great War*, pp. 15-26.

128.Maurice Paléologue, *An Ambassador's Memoirs*, p. 13.

129.John Rohl (ed.), *1914: Delusion or Design*, pp. 11-12.

130.Jarausch, p. 111.

131.*Ibid.*, p. 116.

132.*Ibid.*, pp. 146-7.

133.*Ibid.*, p. 152.

134.*Ibid.*, p. 153.

Thirteen

The Road To Sarajevo

The assassination of Archduke Franz Ferdinand, heir apparent of the emperor of Austria-Hungary, on June 28, 1914, marked the culmination of a long period of conflict provoked by the continuing decline of the Ottoman Empire. The Treaty of Paris, which ended the Crimean War, "admitted Turkey to the Public Law of Europe, recognized it as a European state, and guaranteed its position."[1] The European Powers agreed to respect the independence and territorial integrity of the Ottoman Empire, an obligation which was substantiated by a guarantee "in common."[2]

The treaty also provided that the principality of Serbia should "preserve its Independent and National Administration, as well as full liberty of Worship, of Legislation, of Commerce, and of Navigation."[3] Although Serbia was considered a "subject and tributary nation," she enjoyed a considerable degree of autonomy under her own prince.[4]

At the same time a convention was signed according to which the Turkish sultan declared that he would maintain the ancient principle that no foreign ship of war should be admitted into the straits of the Dardanelles and the Bosporus so long as his empire was at peace.[5] By a treaty signed in 1871 the sultan was given the right to open the straits in peace-time to warships of friendly and allied Powers if he thought this was necessary to secure the execution of the stipulations of the Treaty of Paris.[6]

An uprising against Turkish misrule in Bosnia and Herzegovina broke out in 1875. The defeat of the insurgents prompted Russia to make war on Turkey, and in order to protect her flank against Austrian intervention Russia agreed to Austrian annexation of Bosnia and Herzegovina. The most significant provision of the Treaty of San Stefano, which ended the successful Russian war, was the creation of a great Bulgarian state, which England and

Austria believed would be a Russian satellite. These Powers therefore insisted on a European congress to revise the treaty.[7]

The Congress of Berlin and the treaty which emerged from it set the stage for the subsequent events of many years. Article XXV of the treaty provided that the provinces of Bosnia and Herzegovina should be occupied and administered by Austria-Hungary.[8] The independence of Montenegro was established and stipulations were made guaranteeing religious equality and freedom of worship.[9]

The population of Bosnia and Herzegovina was divided in its attitude to the imposition of Austrian control. "The Catholics greeted them as saviors, the Serbs were hostile, and the Moslems were in a state of ferment."[10] It took 200,000 Austrian soldiers almost a year to suppress Muslim and Serb uprisings.

British writer M.E. Durham maintains that by 1908 Austria had turned a ramshackle Turkish province into a flourishing state, with fine schools, model farms and irrigation works, and with impartial laws for Muslim, Catholic and Orthodox people.[11] Vladimir Dedijer says the Austrians built roads and railroads, opened coal and iron mines and established iron and chemical industries, but that these advances in industry were counteracted by the retention of serfdom, with Muslims as landlords over Christian serfs. The fine schools left 88 percent of the population still illiterate in 1914.[12] He gives no figures on literacy prior to the tutelage of the Austrians in Serbia or other Slavic states.

After 1878 Serbia was considered to be in the Austrian sphere of influence, and Prince Milan Obrenovitch worked to increase Austrian domination. On June 16, 1881, a secret treaty was signed between Serbia and Austria giving Austria control of foreign affairs and renouncing any Serbian claim to Bosnia and Herzegovina. It also stated that Serbia would not tolerate any political or religious intrigues against Austria-Hungary.[13]

Milan Obrenovitch's policy of subservience to Austria was extremely unpopular with the Serbs, and Serbian politicians immediately began planning for the expansion of Serb territory. On June 8, 1881, the Serbian Radical Party adopted the Great Serbian programme, aimed at uniting all Serbs by military force. The programme emphasized the necessity of creating an efficient, well-armed national army, ready for action when the proper time came. Meanwhile a propaganda campaign would be organized to awaken consciousness of national unity in lands under the control of other Powers. The achievement of these aims required the break up of the Austro-Hungarian and Ottoman Empires, and therefore could be accomplished only with the assistance of other Great Powers.[14]

The Serbs were left in no doubt as to which Great Power would assist them. Peter Shuvalov, one of the Russian delegates at the Berlin conference, told them that "the occupation of Bosnia and Herzegovina by Austria would last at the longest fifteen years and thereafter Russia would settle her accounts with Austria without fail."[15] The Russians supported the Radical party and supplied money for intrigues against King Milan and propaganda against Austria.[16] The Serbian army was expanded and developed in the 1890s and from that time forward it played a major role in the country.

Subservience to Austria continued, at least outwardly, until 1903, when 180 army officers led by Dragutin Dimitrievitch, later known as Colonel Apis, plotted and carried out the assassinations of King Alexander Obrenovich, of Serbia, and his queen. This brought Austrian influence to an end, increased Serbian prestige among the Austrian Slavs, and intensified the national struggle of the south Slavs in Austria and Turkey.[17]

Serbia replaced Bulgaria as the Russian *agent provocateur* in the Balkans, because the Bulgarians had shown themselves unwilling to act as a cat's-paw for the Russian Empire. France signalled her support for Russia's Balkan projects in 1906 by undertaking to supply Serbia with arms, and the Serbian army was reorganized and supplied with modern weapons with the assistance of French loans. The British government, which had hitherto refused to recognize the regicides, now gave them recognition and support.[18] It was evident that Serbia had joined the combination engaged in the "containment" of Germany.

The Serbs relished their role as the spearhead of the offensive against Austria-Hungary, and saw themselves as heir to all the Slav lands under Austrian control. When Prince Nikola of Montenegro appeared as a possible rival for leadership, a plot to assassinate him was hatched in Belgrade and the plotters were supplied with bombs from the royal Serbian arsenal at Kraguyevatz. The plot failed when a student in Belgrade informed the Montenegrin government.[19]

Events of the year 1908 intensified the struggle for control of the Balkans. The Young Turk revolution was followed by an attempt to reclaim Turkish sovereignty over Bosnia and Herzegovina, and some action by Austria was needed to prevent this.[20] After preliminary negotiations in June, Baron Ai von Aehrenthal of Austria secured Alexandre Isvolsky's consent to the annexation of Bosnia and Herzegovina at Buchlau on September 16.[21] In early October Austria annexed the two provinces without giving Isvolsky time to prepare Russian public opinion or to sound England and France concerning the opening of the straits to Russian warships, which Aehrenthal had agreed to support.[22]

The Serbians reacted to the annexation by condemning the violation of the Treaty of Berlin and preparing for war. At the same time they demanded compensation for their supposed territorial loss. Their plea for Russian support fell at first on deaf ears, however, because Isvolsky did not want the Serbs to make trouble until he had secured his half of the Buchlau bargain.[23]

When he found that he could get no support in Paris or London for the opening of the straits, he tried to foil Aehrenthal by proposing a conference of the Powers. His anger at being forestalled by Aehrenthal led him to broadcast false representations of their dealings with each other and to pretend that no bargain had been made. As the European Powers had been quite ready to acquiesce in an Austrian annexation of Bosnia and Herzegovina in 1878, and Russia had on at least two previous occasions expressed her own consent, Isvolsky's ire resulted from his annoyance at his own stupidity. With the cooperation of England and France he nevertheless succeeded in turning a relatively unimportant incident into a European crisis.

The British government had shown little interest in Austria's intentions towards Bosnia and Herzegovina before the annexation, and in fact Sir Charles Hardinge had agreed that "any developments arising in Bosnia and the Herzegovina from the constitutional changes in Turkey should be considered as purely internal matters affecting Austria-Hungary and not involving any question of international policy."[24] British suspicion that Austria was supporting a declaration of independence by Bulgaria, however, aroused the hostility of the foreign office and led to British acceptance of a French suggestion that England and France should make a serious protest and refuse to accept the annexation.[25] Grey therefore denounced the annexation on the ground that it was a violation of the Treaty of Berlin.[26]

Isvolsky now pushed his proposal for a conference to discuss the matter and supported Serbia's demand for compensation, but with German support Austria succeeded in resisting the idea of a conference. The dastardly Germans even suggested that Aehrenthal should make use of the documentation of the Buchlau meeting to show that Isvolsky had agreed to the annexation.[27]

Austria settled with Turkey by making a money payment to console her for the loss of nominal sovereignty over the two provinces. The continued agitation in Serbia, encouraged by Isvolsky, however, threatened to produce an Austro-Serbian war. The crisis was finally defused by a German proposal, made on March 14, 1909, that Austria should request the Powers to give their formal sanction to the annexation of Bosnia and Herzegovina provided that Russia promised beforehand to give her sanction when asked to do so. This was designed to secure for Austria recognition of the annexation by the Powers. It would meet the demand that the consent of the Powers was required for any change in the Treaty of Berlin. At the same time it relieved Isvolsky of the difficulty of formally withdrawing his demand for a conference.[28]

Isvolsky recognized the conciliatory spirit of this German proposal, but hesitated to accept it, because he still hoped that his conference idea might be agreed upon. Meanwhile the outbreak of war between Austria and Serbia seemed imminent, and Chancellor Bernhard von Bülow feared that an immediate answer to his proposal was needed to preserve peace. He therefore instructed his ambassador in St. Petersburg to tell Isvolsky that he must have an immediate answer, yes or no, or Germany would "draw back and let things take their course." Isvolsky realized that he was required to accept the "regulation of the annexation question by an exchange of notes" or Serbia would probably be invaded. Isvolsky replied in the affirmative the next day.[29]

In the end the Russians had to give way because they were still too weak to go to war in support of Serbia. In Immanuel Geiss's opinion they would have been quite justified in going to war to salve Isvolsky's wounded pride if they had been strong enough to do so.[30] But Russia was not yet ready, and the Serbs were forced to accept recognition of the annexation and to renounce south Slav agitation against the Hapsburg monarchy, a renunciation which they fulfilled neither in the letter nor in the spirit. Serbia also agreed to restore her army to its state of the spring of 1908.[31]

Since from the entente point of view it was necessary to ascribe any European crisis to German aggression, the German intervention to solve the crisis was represented as a threat to go to war with Russia. Bülow's proposal to publish the documents to counteract the entente legend of a German threat of force was rejected by Isvolsky, who was unwilling to reveal the deception he had practised.[32]

The legend is resurrected in its modern form by Geiss, who tells us that the Russian retreat was the result of "massive intervention" by Germany, when Bülow risked a European war by threatening to "let developments take their course."[33] As the only threat of war arose from Isvolsky's encouragement of Serbia's designs on the Austro-Hungarian Empire, and this policy was based on his falsification of the events preceding the annexation of Bosnia and Herzegovina, it is easy to see which power was risking a European war.

The Russians told the Serbs quite plainly that although at the moment they were too weak to go to war this deficiency would soon be remedied and aid for Serbia's aims would be forthcoming. Kosutitch, the Serbian minister in St. Petersburg, reported that Isvolsky, the tsar and leading members of the Duma assured him that the inevitable war was coming and that it would bring about the downfall of Austria and fulfil the Serb dreams of a greater Serbia.[34]

The Serbs responded to this encouragement by escalating their subversive activities in Austria-Hungary, in violation of their agreement to curtail them. "Secret and illegal contacts were established with Serbs in both provinces. They received weapons and were trained for sabotage and guerrilla warfare."[35]

These activities were directed from Serbia by two new secret societies which were closely linked with each other and with the Serbian government and army. *Narodna Odbrana* or National Defence was established in October, 1908, on the initiative of the minister of foreign affairs. Among its founders were several ministers and other notables, including Nikola Paschitsch, prime minister and leader of the Radical party. The organization also included Serbian military officers and important civil servants.

Narodna Odbrana supposedly was concerned with cultural matters and nationalist propaganda, but it enrolled volunteers and trained them in throwing bombs, blowing up railways and bridges and other operations useful for a guerrilla war against Austria. It also established a network of agents on Austrian territory who were trained for sabotage and guerrilla warfare.[36] After the agreement by Serbia to cease her anti-Austrian propaganda, a pretence was made of changing *Narodna Odbrana* into a purely cultural organization, but it continued to maintain its activities on Austrian territory and its relations with the other revolutionary society, Union or Death, known as the Black Hand.[37]

The Black Hand was formed in 1911 by a group of patriots who were dissatisfied with the decision of *Narodna Odbrana* to play down its subversive activities and mark time until Russia's military preparations were completed. Most of the leaders were military men, but it included some notable civilians and many officials.[38]

Narodna Odbrana and the Black Hand were closely related and had many members in common. For example, Major Milan Vastitch was a member of the central administration of the Black Hand and also secretary of *Narodna Odbrana*. The two organizations used the same network of agents in Austrian territory and the same "tunnel" through which these agents were introduced. Gavrilo Princip, the man who shot Franz Ferdinand and his wife, was a member of both organizations, as were some of those who helped him and his companions on the way to Sarajevo.[39]

The goal of the Black Hand was the union of all Serbs, and the method was the organization of revolutionary activity in all the lands inhabited by Serbs. It was pledged to fight those who opposed its aims in these lands "with all means" and to support peoples struggling for national liberation "in every way."[40] One of the important ways of supporting such peoples was by assassination. Many leading figures in the Black Hand had been involved in the murder of King Alexander and his queen, and this tradition was continued in the fight to disrupt the Austro-Hungarian Empire.

Secret societies had been formed in Serbia and in Bosnia-Herzegovina from the turn of the century. The rules and goals of these secret societies were not written, minutes of meetings were not recorded and correspondence was in code, all measures to preserve secrecy.[41] The annexation of Bosnia and Herzegovina caused a surge of activity. Many young Bosnians went to Serbia

for training in guerrilla activities by the *Narodna Odbrana*. Vladimir
Gatchinovitch was one of about thirty who got stipends from the Serbian
government to attend Vienna University. During summer vacations he visited
Bosnia-Herzegovina, where he organized secret societies and established
links between them for gathering military information for Serbia. He joined
both Union or Death and *Narodna Odbrana*.[42] During the Balkan wars
members of these secret societies flocked to Serbia to join the Serbian army.[43]

It is evident that much of the unrest in Bosnia-Herzegovina was a result
of the subversive activities directed from Serbia. The Serbs were concerned,
not with the alleged sufferings of their brothers in Bosnia-Herzegovina, but
that Serbian propaganda might be less effective if the lot of those in
Bosnia-Herzegovina were ameliorated. Their antagonism to Franz Ferdinand
arose from the fact that he was an advocate of "trialism," a policy of giving the
Slavs equality with the Germans and Magyars in the Empire.

The Serbian bourgeoisie was on the side of the Austrian government,
and all the leading Serbian parties in Bosnia-Herzegovina accepted their
annexation without protest. There was a gulf between the generations of
Bosnian Serbs, and the revolt of the young was partly a rebellion against their
parents.[44] Nedeljiko Cabrinovitch, who threw the first bomb at Archduke
Franz Ferdinand, was in conflict with his father and quarrelled with him on
the morning of June 28 because his father wanted to put up the Hapsburg
imperial flag.[45] After the assassination some cousins of Princip and
Cabrinovitch changed their names to express their disgust, and when the war
broke out a large number of leading Serbs presented a petition asking that
they be sent to the front at once in order to prove "by their own deeds that
they had nothing to do with the assassination."[46]

Between 1912 and 1914 the "Young Bosnians," in collaboration with the
secret societies in Serbia and elsewhere, were involved in a dozen plots. The
most important of these was an attempt to kill the governor of Croatia on
June 8, 1912. Weapons, bombs and instructions were supplied by the same
Major Voja Tankositch who was to figure so prominently in the assassination
of the Archduke Franz Ferdinand and his wife. The attempt on the governor
of Croatia failed, but such schemes provided dress rehearsals for the successful
conspiracy against the heir to the Austrian throne.[47]

The idea that the Serbian government was unaware of these activities
and therefore had no responsibility for them was a convenient fiction. It
enabled the Serbian government to pretend innocence in the assassination of
the archduke and allowed the entente governments to justify their support of
Serbia by accepting this pretence. The British government probably believed
these Serbian protestations, but the Russian government certainly knew better
and it is likely that the French government was equally well informed.

In fact Nikola Paschitsch was kept informed about the undertakings of the Black Hand by individuals with membership in both organizations. Even without these links, however, it is not credible that the Serbian government did not know what these supposedly secret societies were doing. According to English writer M.E. Durham, Serbia was a country riddled with spies, where everyone was dogged by the police and where it was impossible even to buy a carpet without their knowledge.[48]

In fact the evidence given at the Salonika trial in 1917 clearly shows the close connection between the Serbian government and the Black Hand. At least one cabinet minister was kept informed of its activities and others almost certainly knew of them as well. Colonel Apis stated at his trial "that the Government was kept informed of the doings of the Organisation, that the Minister for Foreign Affairs knew and approved of it." No attempt was made, either by the court or by government officials, to deny the truth of his statement.[49]

The Russians encouraged and supported these subversive activities directed from Serbia. The great Serbian propaganda directed against Austria was fostered by Russia and was presided over by Paschitsch, who had been under Russian influence throughout his career.[50]

A secret supplement to the Serbo-Bulgarian treaty revealed the hand of Russia in its preparation. If the two countries agreed on a military operation, Russia was to be informed and the undertaking would be carried out if Russia had no objection; if no agreement was reached the matter would be examined by Russia and her decision would be binding on both parties. The treaty was accompanied by a military convention: the treaty, the secret supplement and the military convention were to be submitted to the Russian government for approval.[51] The third article of the military convention provided that if Austria should under any pretext advance her troops into the Sandjak of Novi-Bazar, Bulgaria would join Serbia in war with Austria.[52] The Serbian minister, Milowanich, expressed the view that the downfall of Austria-Hungary would very much simplify the territorial problems of the Balkan states, since Serbia would acquire Bosnia and Herzegovina.[53] This treaty was followed by a treaty between Bulgaria and Greece by which they agreed to help the people of Macedonia to obtain their rights and to support them if it involved war with Turkey.[54]

Montenegro went to war with Turkey in October, 1912, and was shortly joined by Serbia, Bulgaria and Greece. The war was begun without Russian consent and although Russia had prepared the war she did not approve of its timing and pretended she had nothing to do with it.[55] The Balkan allies astonished Europe by the rapidity with which they overwhelmed Turkey and practically relieved her of her European possessions except Constantinople. The Serbs were elated by successes, which doubled their territory, and they looked forward to future triumphs at the expense of Austria.

Russia's support of Serbia's claims to Albanian territory and a port on the Adriatic did not receive encouragement from England and France and Serbia was forced to abandon these demands.[56] The French and Russian ministers at Bucharest advised the Serbians that they should be satisfied with their gains, because Serbia would be at least twice as large as before. Serbia should strengthen herself and "await, with as great a degree of preparedness as possible, the important events which must make their appearance among the Great Powers." On December 27, 1912, Sazonov told the Serbian minister at St. Petersburg that in view of Serbia's great successes he "had confidence in our strength and believed we would be able to deliver a shock to Austria." Serbia should therefore be satisfied with what she would receive "and consider it merely as a temporary halting place on the road to further gains, as the future belonged to us." In February Sazonov declared that "Serbia was the only state in the Balkans in which Russia had confidence, and that Russia would do everything for Serbia."[57]

The Balkan wars set the stage for the confrontation between Austria and Russia which brought about World War I. The creation of the Balkan League signalled the launching by Russia of an offensive whose ultimate aim was the destruction of the Austro-Hungarian Empire. The primary interest of the Russian Empire was to gain control of the straits at Constantinople. Russia believed that Austria was the main obstacle to this ambition, and that the road to the straits lay through Vienna.

The wars themselves wrecked what was left of the "Concert of Europe" and brought the division of the continent into stark relief. The conference of all the Powers in London demonstrated the solidarity of the Triple Entente and resulted in a resounding diplomatic defeat for Austria.[58] The ambassadors agreed with the Austrian aim of creating an independent Albania. Nevertheless Austria was forced to give way to Russian demands that town after town which Austria contended should belong to Albania should be surrendered to Serbia and Montenegro. In return for these concessions, the town of Scutari was not to go to Montenegro, but when Montenegro refused to accept this decision and captured Scutari the Concert was helpless, and Austria was left to solve the problem herself by threatening Montenegro with war. This crisis demonstrated that Sir Edward Grey valued entente solidarity more highly than the Concert or the peace of Europe.[59]

The second Balkan war in 1913 resulted in another increase in Serbia's power and a diplomatic defeat for Austria, with Paschitsch boasting of preparing for the next round against her.[60] Isvolsky wrote that the treaty of Bucharest, which ended the war, had struck a blow to Austria and strengthened Serbia both morally and physically. Austria was isolated, and her position was threatened by the advance of Serbia, whose expansionist dreams could be fulfilled only at Austria's expense.[61]

From this time forward the Austrians realized that it was useless to look to the Concert of Europe to protect their interests. This view was strengthened by a Serbian invasion of Albania aimed at a further expansion of Serbian territory or even the elimination of Albania. The Powers talked but took no action, and again Austria was forced to act independently. When Austria sent an ultimatum demanding the evacuation of Albania within eight days, the Serbians gave way. "Although the Serbs had undoubtedly been in the wrong, and although Austria-Hungary was acting to enforce a decision of the Concert, [Austro-Hungarian foreign minister] Berchtold's 'precipitate action' was the object of indignant comment in the Triple Entente camp."[62]

These experiences with the Concert of Europe were of crucial importance in the crisis of 1914. The Austrians realized that the Concert was dominated by the Triple Entente, which would inevitably side with Russia where her interests were in conflict with those of Austria. After the assassination of Archduke Franz Ferdinand, therefore, they resisted the calling of a conference of the Powers, which could only inflict on them another diplomatic defeat and further weaken their Empire.

Austria's resentment at her failure to halt the relentless advance of Russian power produced another significant development. Diplomats of that time and historians since agree unanimously that during the whole period of the Balkan wars Germany worked consistently for peace and used her influence to restrain any Austrian inclination to follow an adventurous policy. By the fall of 1913, however, Germany was alarmed lest she might lose Austria-Hungary's support, and in order to regain Austrian confidence she supported the Austrian ultimatum which forced Serbia out of Albania.[63] Germany was also worried about the growing weakness of Austria, but saw no alternative to trying to maintain her as a factor in the European balance. Late 1913 thus saw Germany "unreservedly identifying herself with Austria-Hungary against Serbia and the South Slav movement."[64]

At least one principal actor in the drama which was about to unfold had undergone a conversion which would affect his reaction to the Sarajevo crime. Late in October, 1913, Wilhelm II told Count Berchtold that Serbia should be brought to heel, by force if necessary, and promised German support if war ensued.[65] In July, 1914, therefore, neither Austria nor Germany was willing to suffer meekly another disastrous defeat which would seriously weaken their position.

Notes

1.Sir Augustus Oakes and R. B. Mowat, *The Great European Treaties of the Nineteenth Century*, p. 158.

2.*Ibid.*, p. 177.

3.*Ibid.*, p. 182.

4.*Ibid.*, p. 174.

5.*Ibid.*, p. 184.

6.*Ibid.*, p. 330.

7.Sidney B. Fay, *The Origins of the World War*, I, 86.

8.*Ibid.*, p. 345.

9.*Ibid.*, p. 345-6.

10.Vladimir Dedijer, *The Road to Sarajevo*, p. 64.

11.M. E. Durham, *The Sarajevo Crime*, p. 40.

12.Dedijer, pp. 78-81.

13.*Ibid.*, p. 82-3.

14.Durham, p. 20.

15.Dedijer, p. 83.

16.M. Bogitschevich, *Causes of the War*, pp. 7, 10.

17.Dedijer, pp. 83-5.

18.Durham, p. 28.

19.M. E. Durham, *Twenty Years of Balkan Tangle*, pp. 183-4.

20.Immanuel Geiss, *German Foreign Policy, 1871-1914*, pp. 33, 114; F. R. Bridge, *Great Britain and Austria-Hungary, 1906-1914*, pp. 100-101.

21.Bridge, p. 107.

22.*Ibid.*, p. 115.

23.Fay I, 378-80.

24.BD, V, 827-30, App. IV.

25.Bridge, pp. 111-113.

26.BD, V, nos. 296, 350.

27.Geiss, p. 114.

28.Fay, I, 388-9.

29.*Ibid.*, pp. 389-91.

30.Geiss, p. 114.

31.Fay, I, 393.

32.*Ibid.*, p. 391 fn.

33.Geiss, p. 116.

34.Fay, I, pp. 384-5.

35.Geiss, p. 117.

36.Fay, II, 80-1; Dedijer, p. 378; Geiss, p. 117.

37.Fay, II, 84-5.

38.Fay, II, 89-91; Durham, Sarajevo, pp. 52-3.

39.Dedijer, p. 378.

40.Fay, II, 87.

41.Dedijer, pp. 177-80.

42.*Ibid.*, p. 180.

43.*Ibid.*, p. 192.

44.*Ibid.*, pp. 207-8.

45.*Ibid.*, pp. 198-9, 315.

46.*Ibid.*, p. 328.

47.*Ibid.*, pp. 261-5.

48.Durham, *Tangle*, p. 185, *Sarajevo*, p. 12.

49.Durham, *Sarajevo*, pp. 56, 64.

50.Bogitshevich, pp. 18-19.

51.*Ibid.*, pp. 102, 104.

52.*Ibid.*, p. 106.

53.Max Montgelas, *The Case for the Central Powers*, p. 53.

54.*Ibid.*, pp. 54-5.

55.Bogitshevich, pp. 37-9.

56.Bridge, p. 199.

57.Bogitshevich, pp. 98-9.

58.Bridge, pp. 200, 202.

59.*Ibid.*, p. 202.

60.*Ibid.*, p. 203.

61.LN, II, 134-5.

62.Bridge, p. 204.

63.Geiss, p. 153.

64.*Ibid.*, pp. 155-6.

65.G. P. Gooch, *Before the War*, II, 424.

Fourteen

The Outbreak Of The War

The selection of the Archduke Franz Ferdinand as a murder victim was no accident. As an advocate of reforms which would improve the position of the south Slavs in the Austrian Empire he was a threat to Serbia's expansionist plans. The fact that these changes were already well under way made his early elimination no less desirable. A Russian report of January 7, 1914, listed promised reforms aimed at conciliating the Croats. These included the calling of a Croat assembly, abolition of the state of siege, freedom of press and assembly, returning cities to their Slav names and efforts to solve the language problems of the railway. Most of these reforms had already been carried out.[1]

Vladimir Dedijer tells us that the assassination of the Archduke Franz Ferdinand and his wife was neither an underlying nor an immediate cause of the war. It merely gave the Viennese war party a pretext for attacking Serbia which it had sought ever since 1908-09.[2] This is true only if we consider the assassination an independent occurrence, ignoring the role of Serbia and assuming that because the murder took place in Bosnia it was purely a Bosnian affair.

The assassination of the heir to the Austrian throne on June 28, 1914, was not, however, an isolated incident but the culmination of a long campaign aimed at the destruction of the Austro-Hungarian Empire, of which Russia was the instigator and Serbia the enthusiastic tool. This campaign was punctuated by assassination plots against Austrian officials, hatched in Serbia by government-supported terrorist organizations and encouraged by the Russian Empire. Seen in its proper perspective, the murder was the real and sufficient cause for Austria to attempt to put an end to the Serbian threat to her existence.

In June, 1914, the Austrian government was in the process of developing a policy initiative which it hoped would repair some of the damage caused by the Balkan wars. A memoir by Count Leopold von Berchtold, the Austrian foreign minister, penned on the eve of the murder, outlined the ideas which inspired the proposed policy. The memoir began by surveying the results of the Balkan wars, which it accurately asserted were unfavourable to Austria and the Triple Alliance. Berchtold believed that France and Russia were not satisfied with the results, however favourable to them, and were endeavouring to patch up the differences between the Balkan states to create a new Balkan league. Now that Turkey had been expelled from Europe, such a league would be directed against Austria-Hungary. He saw that the main problem facing the Franco-Russian combination lay in the difficulty of effecting a reconciliation between Serbia and Bulgaria, while their greatest success had been the detachment of Roumania from its allegiance to the Triple Alliance.

Before taking any action, Berchtold wished to establish an understanding with Germany, to ensure that the two Powers would work together to frustrate the joint action of France and Russia and to safeguard their vital interests. He proposed that they should form an alliance with Bulgaria, in accordance with that country's expressed desire, and that they should attempt to bring about an alliance between Turkey and Bulgaria. This would thwart the formation of a solid Balkan bloc under Russian auspices against the Triple Alliance.[3]

The Austrian government at once assumed that Serbia was responsible for the outrage at Sarajevo, and that supine acceptance of this blow would pose a deadly threat to the existence of the Austro-Hungarian Empire. The fact that the Austrians could not prove the Serbian government's complicity in 1914 does not indicate that they were not aware of it. The Austrians can hardly have believed that so many important officials were involved in the plot without the Serbian government's knowledge. It can be assumed that the Austrians knew quite well that the civilian authorities were privy to the conspiracy.

The Serbian government was in fact deeply involved in the plot to murder the archduke. The Austrian government could not prove this in 1914 for the simple reason that the Serbians were successful in covering their tracks. The weak link in the Serbian armour was Milan Ciganovitch, a railway official at Belgrade, who was an important figure in the assassination plot. Ciganovitch was a member of the Black Hand, but was also in the pay of Paschitsch for whom he spied on the organization. He was under the orders of Major Voja Tankositch, who in turn took orders from Colonel Dragutin Dimitrievitch, known as Apis, chief of the military intelligence section of the Serbian general staff and leader of the Black Hand. Ciganovitch supplied the assassins with revolvers, bombs, ammunition and money. He and Tankositch also arranged for them to cross into Bosnia "by means of one of the 'tunnels' consisting of the trusted agents of *Narodna Odbrana,* who smuggled printed matter, arms and conspirators into the Monarchy."[4]

The Serbian government spirited Ciganovitch out of Belgrade three days after the murder and sent him to Albania, not to return to Belgrade until a month after the war began. The military commandant of an important railway station arranged his escape, and instructed the railway service to remove his name from its personnel books. The Austrians were told that he was unknown in Belgrade, where he was in fact a well-known figure. The Serbs informed them that a warrant had been issued for his arrest, but that he could not be found.[5] Ciganovitch was an Austrian subject and if extradited to Austria, might have attempted to mitigate his situation by assisting the Austrian authorities.

Ljuba Jovanovitch, minister of education in the Serbian cabinet in 1914, tells us in *The Murder of Sarajevo* that late in May or early in June Stojan Protitch, the justice minister, informed the cabinet that a group of young men was on the way to Sarajevo to murder the archduke. The cabinet decided that the border guards should be instructed to prevent them from crossing into Austrian territory.[6]

Ljuba Jovanovitch played a large role in the organization of the Black Hand, and had a close relationship with Apis. Apis was the principal organizer of the plot to kill the archduke, and he signed a declaration, not only that he had planned the outrage, but that the court, the Russian minister and the Russian military attaché knew about it.[7] Another civilian member of the Black Hand was Bogdan Radenojevitch, who in 1910 became an official in the Serbian ministry of foreign affairs. The first president of the Black Hand was Colonel Ilija Radenojevitch, chief of the Serbian gendarmerie.[8]

Among the papers seized by the Austrians in 1914 in the aftermath of the assassination was an order from the Serbian war minister to the border guards to prevent the plotters from crossing the frontier. The names of the young men were given, and it is evident that the Serbian government was informed even of the identity of the assassins.[9]

When so many members of the Serbian cabinet and so many government officials knew of the plot to kill the archduke it could hardly have been concealed from Nikola Hartwig, Russian minister at Belgrade, who was one of the most influential men in Belgrade. Apis confirms that Hartwig was informed, and that he also told Colonel Artimov, the Russian military attaché, who he says consulted St. Petersburg and was told Russia would back Serbia whatever happened. While it is certain that Artimov knew of the conspiracy, there is no proof that he told the Russian government, although he may have informed some of his military superiors.[10] In any case, however, it cannot be doubted that the Russian authorities knew quite well that the Serbian government supported the organizations which carried on subversive activities in Austria and that this was approved in St. Petersburg.

The fact that the Serbian government knew of the plot and even the names of the assassins and that no serious attempt was made to inform the Austrian government shows clearly that the Serbians had little interest in preventing the murder. The Serbian minister in Vienna, Jovan Jovanovitch, received a telegram from Belgrade which instructed him to warn the Austrians, but the information was given in general terms which did not justify alleging that a plot existed. When Jovanovitch spoke to the Austrian finance minister, Doctor Bilinsky, he therefore merely warned him that it would be dangerous for the archduke to lead the troops at Sarajevo. The maneuvers on the holiday of Vidov Dan, so close to the Serbian border, would be a provocation, he said, and "among the Serb youths there may be one who will put a live cartridge into his rifle or revolver in place of a blank one."[11]

The conspirators were not only supplied with weapons and instructed in their use at Belgrade, but were assisted to cross the border by officials under orders of Colonel Apis. They were sent to official contacts wherever they went, and many people who were in official positions knew what they were doing and helped them.[12] Jakov Milovitch, the Bosnian peasant who took Gavrilo Princip and Trifco Grabez over the Drina river to Bosnia was used as a link by the Serbian military intelligence department and was also an agent of *Narodna Odbrana*. It was through him that the Serbian cabinet learned of the plot to kill Franz Ferdinand, but it seems likely that Paschitsch knew beforehand and did nothing until other members of the cabinet were informed. Some of the men who helped the youths after they crossed into Bosnia were members of both *Narodna Odbrana* and the Black Hand.[13] It is therefore hardly surprising that the Austrian authorities failed to distinguish between the two organizations.

Dedijer emphasizes the fact that the Austrian government was unable to prove the complicity of the Serbian government in the assassination. Ljuba Jovanovitch describes how the Serbs tried to get through the task of giving satisfaction to Austria as cheaply as possible, and says that "From all this it might have been expected that Vienna would be unsuccessful in establishing any connection between official Serbia and the event on the Miljacka [River]."[14] This was, of course, the case, but the Austrians were quite correct in their belief, based on the facts which the investigation did reveal, that there was a connection. It was to be expected that the Serbian government would be able to prevent them from finding the evidence to prove this conclusively if they undertook the proper obstructive action, which they did.

On July 1, the Austro-Hungarian chargé d'affaires at Belgrade asked the secretary general of the Serbian ministry of foreign affairs about the Serbian government's plans for an inquiry into the connection of the assassins with

Serbia and Belgrade. The reply was that nothing had been done and that the matter did not concern the Serbian government. This was the same day on which the Serbians acted to remove Ciganovitch from Belgrade, so it is evident that every effort was being made to prevent Austria from linking them with the crime.[15]

It was also on July 1 that Paschitsch undertook a campaign of lies designed to deceive Europe into believing that Serbia had no connection with the crime at Sarajevo. In a circular directed to all Serbian legations abroad he declared that "it was of the greatest interest to Serbia to prevent the perpetration of this outrage," but that she had been unable to do so because both the assassins were Austrian subjects. He asserted that Serbia had been "careful to suppress anarchic elements" and that she would now "redouble her vigilance." If such elements existed within her borders she would take "the severest measures against them."[16]

On July 19 another circular stated that "By their attitude and the measures they have taken the Serbian government have irrefutably proved that they are working to restrain excitable elements." Their diplomats were requested to impress on foreign governments Serbia's desire to "suppress every attempt directed against the peace and public safety of the neighbouring monarchy." The circular also asserted Serbia's willingness to bring to trial in her own courts "any accomplices in the outrage who are in Serbia—should such, of course, exist."[17] The contrast between these statements and the actual activities of the Serbian government is obvious.

When the second circular was received at Berlin, Gottlieb von Jagow, German foreign minister, merely replied that he would inform Vienna about the Serbian démarche. He then called the attention of the Serbian chargé d'affaires to the fact that Serbia had done nothing to improve its relations with the monarchy, and said he could understand if Austria now decided to take more energetic measures.[18]

It has been maintained that Serbia did not want war, because owing to internal problems she was not ready for it. Ljuba Jovanovitch, however, says that he did not doubt for a moment "that Austria-Hungary would make this the occasion for declaring war on Serbia."[19] His view was no doubt shared by other members of the cabinet so it is curious that if they did not want war they did nothing to prevent the crime. As a matter of fact Paschitsch had told the tsar on February 2, 1914, when the latter had asked him how many soldiers Serbia could put in the field, that he believed they could put "half a million well clothed and armed soldiers into the field." The tsar said, "That is sufficient, it is no trifle, one can go a great ways with that."[20] At the end of the interview the tsar said, "For Serbia we shall do all."[21] It was obvious that Serbia never would be able to fight Austria alone, but since she was assured of Russian support this was irrelevant.

After the assassination of the archduke, Austrian foreign minister Berchtold's memoir was forwarded to Germany with a covering letter from the Emperor Franz Joseph to the kaiser. In this letter he declared that the crime was "the direct consequence of the agitation carried on by Russian and Serbian Panslavists, whose sole aim is to weaken the Triple Alliance and shatter my Empire." He believed that the "bloody deed" was "the result of a well-organized plot, the threads of which lead to Belgrade." He looked to the formation of a new Balkan league "under the patronage of the Triple Alliance," which would "stop the progress of the panslavist flood." This would be possible only "by pushing aside Servia and preventing it from becoming a factor of power in the Balkans, as it is at present the cornerstone of panslavist politics."[22] Berchtold added to his memoir the statement that it was now "necessary for the monarchy to seize the threads which its enemies are weaving over its head with a strong hand and tear them once for all."[23]

The Austrians strongly believed that the very existence of their empire was threatened, and that to accept the murder of the heir to the throne without some decisive action would be a blow from which it would never recover. The Germans accepted this view, realizing that the issue was a life and death matter for Germany as well, because the demise of Austria would leave her alone in the centre of Europe to face armies three times the size of her own. Later historians have endorsed this view of the situation, without agreeing that it justified action to prevent the collapse of Austria.[24]

There can be no doubt either of the Russian determination to destroy Austria or of the part assigned to Serbia in this plan. It appears that in the eyes of the entente the Russian aim was quite legitimate, because the polyglot Austro-Hungarian Empire was an anachronism which had forfeited its right to existence and therefore should have allowed its enemies to dismantle it without a struggle. The entente historians are unanimous in their condemnation of Austria-Hungary's determination to make war on Serbia in defence of her existence, and of Germany's decision to assist her. They are, however, equally unanimous in their approval of Russia's going to war in defence of her use of Serbia as an instrument for Austria's destruction.

The Austrian government believed that the assassination, which they incorrectly supposed would be condemned even by Russia, provided them with an opportunity to force Serbia to abandon its campaign to destroy the monarchy. They were, of course, well aware that behind Serbia stood the Russian Empire. By engineering the Balkan wars Russia had struck the first blow in her campaign to crush Austria-Hungary. If Russia was now ready to unleash a European war in support of Serbia's campaign to shatter the monarchy, the crucial moment had arrived when Austria must decide whether to go down fighting or to surrender without a battle.

Berchtold, the Austrian foreign minister, recognized the possibility that

Russia might decide to make any attempt to chastise Serbia a cause for war, but the Austrians believed that the tsar and his government would be so horrified by the crime that they would refuse to support Serbia. Historian Luigi Albertini, who appears to take an idealized view of the tsar's character, believes that if he had been aware of Serbia's involvement in the murder of the archduke he would not have supported her.[25] The tsar's statements showing his personal knowledge of and support for Serbia's anti-Austrian activities do not lend much encouragement to this opinion. Furthermore, it is hard to credit the tsar with so little knowledge of his own government's activities. Russia's decision to back Serbia was almost certainly made in the full knowledge of the Serbian government's responsibility for the crime. Berchtold's decision was made in the conviction that, even if Russia decided to make an attempt to chastise Serbia a cause for war, the monarchy had no alternative but to fight for its life. "That the war was lost and the Hapsburg Empire disappeared never altered his conviction that no other course was open in 1914."[26]

It would be hard to argue that Berchtold was wrong in his belief that the Austro-Hungarian monarchy was forced to take some action to remove the Serbian threat or perish. To submit tamely to the murder of the heir to the throne by a conspiracy hatched in Serbia by Serbian officials with the knowledge of the Serbian government would have shown their lack of confidence in their ability to defend themselves against Serbia's intrigues. This would have encouraged the Serbians to believe that there were no extremes to which they could not go in their campaign to destroy Austria-Hungary. The result would undoubtedly have been an intensification of their subversive activities in Austria. To Berchtold and his colleagues it was clear that "the security of the Empire depended upon the suppression of these subversive activities" organized in Belgrade.[27]

Stephen Tisza, the premier of Hungary, was informed on July 1 that Berchtold intended "to make the horrible deed of Sarajevo the occasion for reckoning with Servia." Tisza thought this would be a "fatal mistake" and refused to share the responsibility for it. He made it clear that he thought the diplomatic situation made the moment unfavourable for the unleashing of a war, and that this should wait until diplomacy could "change the proportions of military power in our favour."[28] Berchtold was therefore faced with the necessity of persuading Tisza to change his mind if his plan for the reduction of Serbia was to go forward.

The next day Berchtold declared to German ambassador Heinrich von Tschirschky that Serbia's intrigues could be stopped only by a regardless action against Serbia. The ambassador agreed and advised that only "firm and energetic" action would produce the desired result. He said Berchtold must know that in Balkan politics Germany would always stand on Austria's side.

When Berchtold remarked that this had not always been the case, Tschirschky said this was because the Austrian government always expounded ideas but never formed a definite plan of action. He advised that Austria must be clear about how far she intended to go and about what was to be done with Serbia. He thought a favourable diplomatic situation must be created and that Italy should be consulted before war was decided on. Berchtold replied that it was up to Austria to decide how far to go and what was to be done with Serbia, and rejected the idea that Italy should be consulted.[29]

On July 4, Berchtold attempted to change Tisza's stand by implying that Germany was urging immediate action against Serbia. The lever he used was a supposed message from the German government, which Tschirschky was said to have delivered through someone named Ganz, who was the Vienna correspondent of the *Frankfurter Zeitung*. Count Johann Forgach at the Austrian foreign office, was told that "the sooner Austria attacked the better" and that Germany would stand by her "through thick and thin" whatever action she decided to take.[30] Presumably the journalist Ganz did in fact visit the foreign office, but Forgach's urge to help Berchtold convert Tisza may have coloured the message. The idea that an experienced diplomat in one of the most important posts in the German foreign service should have delivered such a momentous message via a press agent is rather unlikely. The Austrian letter setting forth the monarchy's proposals had not yet been delivered in Berlin, and the German government had had no chance to make any decision concerning its attitude toward the action Austria might take. The report of Count Lazlo Szögyény-Marisch, Austrian ambassador in Berlin, that same day said Alfred Zimmermann considered energetic action on the part of the monarchy "perfectly justified," but that "he would advise great discretion and would not like to see that humiliating conditions were proposed to Servia."[31] The ambassador's account of the definite German decision was not sent until July 6, and there is no evidence that Tschirschky received any such instructions on or before July 4 as reported by Forgach. Tschirschky's dispatches to Berlin also fail to reveal any sign of such an initiative on his part.

The German government recognized that the assassination of the Archduke Franz Ferdinand was a serious threat to the existence of Austria-Hungary if left unpunished, but its "initial reaction" was "hesitant, groping, and generally peaceful."[32] "It took some days before a clear political decision crystallized."[33]

The eventual German decision to support the Austrian plan to eliminate Serbia as a political factor in the Balkans was at least partly determined by the reaction of Wilhelm II. Outraged by the murder of his friend, the kaiser did not use his influence in the cause of peace, as he had so often done, but pressed for immediate action. His comments on Tschirschky's dispatch reporting that he had advised against too hasty steps by Austria set the tone of Germany's response. He wrote that "The Serbs must be disposed of, and that right soon." He thought Austria was in danger and that Germany's vital interests demanded her preservation.[34]

The Germans believed, correctly, that the collapse of Austria and complete Russian control of the Balkans would make the position of the Teutonic race in central Europe untenable.[35] Bethmann-Hollweg thought that the crime would disgust the Russian leaders with Serbia, and both he and Zimmermann thought Russia would not intervene. If Russia did insist on supporting the Serbian assassins by war, the conflict was inevitable and would be better entered immediately than later.[36]

The German government therefore decided to give its full support to whatever action Austria should determine to take against Serbia. The German reply to Franz Joseph's letter, delivered by Tschirschky, pledged the kaiser to "faithfully stand by Austria-Hungary, as required by the obligations of his alliance and of his ancient friendship," while rejecting any intention of interfering in the quarrel between Austria-Hungary and Serbia. Germany thus pledged herself to support whatever action Austria should decide to take.[37] The kaiser told Bethmann-Hollweg that Germany must refrain from making direct suggestions "because we must use all means to prevent the Austro-Serbian conflict from widening into an international conflict."[38] The German government was naturally aware that Russia might decide on war, but they believed that the Russians would hesitate to support regicide. Also they appear to have been of the opinion that Russia had not yet completed her war preparations. In any case, they clearly thought they had no alternative but to maintain Austria. The idea, as suggested by Kennedy, that at this point Germany could abandon Austria and come to terms with Russia is baseless. No one familiar with Russian policy during the previous five years could seriously entertain it.

There was nothing new in this. Germany had always been ready to fight to save Austria from destruction. The crucial conclusion, that Austria's existence was threatened, imposed on Germany the necessity of sustaining her. Similarly, England had frequently shown her readiness to fight to save France from destruction, or even from recognizing German rights in Morocco. The difference was that the preservation of Austria was a matter of life and death for Germany, while the defeat of France would have been an inconvenience for England.

Before leaving on his annual northern cruise, which was carried out as planned in order not to arouse comment, the kaiser saw representatives of the army and navy. He informed them of his talk with Count Szögyény, but gave no orders for military or naval preparations. Lieutenant General Bertrab on the army staff and Admiral Eduard von Capelle, acting secretary of the navy, are both agreed that the kaiser stated that he did not believe there would be any warlike complications and that no orders for military preparations were necessary.[39] General Erich von Falkenhayn, Prussian minister of war, although he was told that Austria intended to invade Serbia if necessary, received the impression that the kaiser's conversation with the Austrian ambassador had been concerned mainly with such political steps as making a treaty with Bulgaria. He thought that Austria did not intend to take any decisive action. He was not ordered to make any military preparations and neither he nor General Helmuth von Moltke, chief of the German general staff, whom he informed by letter, thought there would be military complications.[40]

On July 7, the Austrian council of ministers held a meeting for the purpose of deciding on measures to be taken for dealing with the evils which resulted from the events at Sarajevo. Count Karl von Stürgkh stated that the first order of business should be to decide whether the moment had come to put an end to Serbian intrigues by a demonstration of power. All those present except Tisza agreed that a purely diplomatic success would be useless even if Serbia were humiliated, and that the demands to be addressed to her should make a refusal almost certain so the problem could be solved by military action. Tisza agreed that the demands to Serbia should be hard, "but not such as to make our intention of raising unacceptable terms clear to everybody." If Serbia accepted the demands, Austria would have a diplomatic success which would increase her prestige; if Serbia refused he would vote for war. He insisted, however, that he would never consent to the annexation of any part of Serbia. Tisza also maintained that it was not for Germany to decide whether there should be war or not, indicating that he accepted the accuracy of Berchtold's arguments but was not convinced by them.[41]

The next day Berchtold made another attempt to change Tisza's position by exaggerating the terms in which Tschirschky had delivered the message from Berlin. His letter to Tisza expressed the German point of view even more strongly than Szögyény had done in his reports of his conversations with Wilhelm II and Bethmann-Hollweg.[42]

Tisza's report to the emperor emphasized his objections to Berchtold's plan of provoking a war on Serbia under the present unfavourable conditions. He agreed that energetic action should be taken against Serbia, but thought she "must be given the possibility to avoid a war by suffering a heavy diplomatic defeat." The demands to be made on Serbia should be far-reaching, and a Serbian refusal would force Austria to go to war in self-defence. He advised that to conciliate Italy and England and to make it possible for Russia to remain inactive Austria should declare that she had no intention of annihilating Serbia or annexing any of her territory. He thought, however, that in case of a successful war Serbia should be reduced in size by giving some of her territory to Bulgaria, Greece and Albania. This report shows, first, that Tisza's view of the situation was not so different from that of his colleagues as has often been supposed, and, second, that Berchtold's reports of German support had little influence on his attitude. On the contrary, he cited the fact that Germany was no longer opposed to an active policy in his argument for postponing war until the two Powers could improve their position in the Balkans and thus have a better chance of winning when war came.[43]

Count Franz Conrad von Hötzendorf advised that the diplomatic moves against Serbia "must avoid everything that would delay action by protracted negotiations, so that our antagonists would gain time for military preparations." This agreed with the advice coming from Berlin, where it was believed that immediate advantage should be taken of the revulsion aroused by the murder of the archduke and his consort. Berchtold used the argument of the military difficulties that would be caused by delay to convince Tisza to accept a time limit of forty-eight hours for Serbia's reply to the ultimatum.[44]

A conference held on July 14 agreed on the demands to be addressed to Serbia, but the text was not definitely settled until the council of ministers met on July 19.[45] Meanwhile, Berchtold informed Berlin that he wanted to delay the action at Belgrade until Poincaré had left Russia, because to begin it during the diplomatic festivities at St. Petersburg "might naturally be regarded in the light of an intended affront." He also thought it would be unwise to take a "threatening step" while the peace-loving tsar and the cautious Sazonov were under the influence of the warlike Isvolsky and Poincaré. He deplored the delay, because he was having difficulty controlling the press, which he feared might "get up too much steam, so that other powers might think of mediation."[46] Gottlieb von Jagow agreed that Austria's action should wait until Poincaré had left St. Petersburg, but regretted the delay because he feared "that the sympathetic approval of this step and the interest in it will be debilitated by this delay" in both Austria and Germany.[47]

When the council of ministers had approved the note it decided to present it at Belgrade on July 23 at 5 p.m., requiring the answer to be received on July 25 at the same time. This would make it possible to publish the mobilisation order that same night. Count Berchtold believed Poincaré would have left St. Petersburg before the news became known there, so the duties of etiquette would have been preserved. The time had actually been fixed on July 17, according to the counselor of the German embassy at Vienna. Tisza was successful in persuading the ministers to pass a resolution that, if there was a war, as soon as it began the monarchy would declare to the foreign powers that no annexation was intended.[48]

Meanwhile, two important telegrams had been sent to Vienna from Berlin, neither of which had any influence on Austrian policy. Jagow wrote on

July 11 that, while Germany did not want to take part in formulating the demands on Serbia, he believed Vienna "should collect sufficient material to show that there exists a Greater Serbia agitation in Serbia which threatens the Monarchy" in order to convince European opinion of the justice of Austria's cause. He advised that this material should be published before the ultimatum was sent to Serbia. Berchtold agreed with this idea, but the Austrian dossier arrived too late to have any effect.[49] It is improbable, however, that earlier action would have changed the outcome, except possibly in England, for Russia and France were unlikely to be influenced by any such evidence.

A long telegram dated July 15 urged the Austrians to come to some agreement with Italy. Jagow thought it was "of the greatest importance that Vienna should come to some understanding with the Cabinet at Rome regarding its aims to be sought in Serbia in case of war." He stated that Italy had the right to claim compensation for any change in the Balkans to the advantage of Austria, and suggested the cession of the Trentino in compensation.[50] Tschirschky did not reply to this dispatch until July 20, when he reported that Berchtold insisted that Italy had no right to compensation and refused to discuss the matter with her.[51] Similar advice was given by the counselor of the embassy at Vienna on July 18, but again Berchtold refused to initiate any discussions with Italy.[52]

On July 17, Jagow, the German foreign minister, asked for information about Austria's intentions concerning the future of Serbia, because this question would influence the attitudes of Italy and England. He denied any attempt to influence Austria's ideas on the subject, but wanted "to be informed to a certain extent about where the road is likely to lead us."[53]

The main features of the Austrian note to Serbia soon became public knowledge throughout Europe. Sir Maurice de Bunsen, British ambassador in Vienna, reported on July 16 that Austria was preparing an indictment against the Serbian government for "alleged complicity" in the plot to kill the archduke, and that Serbia would be "required to adopt certain definite measures in restraint of nationalist and anarchist propaganda." If Serbia failed to comply, force would be used. The next day he wrote that the note would demand that Serbia "should take effective measures to prevent the manufacture and export of bombs, and to put down the insidious and murderous propaganda against the Dual Monarchy."[54]

The French government was informed on July 20 that severe demands would be made on Serbia. A consular report stated that Serbia would be required to dissolve propagandist societies, to suppress nationalism, and to control anti-Austrian tendencies in the schools. A short interval would be given for reply, and if Belgrade refused, which the "imperious tone" of the Austrian note made almost certain, military operations would begin.[55]

The German government was better informed. On July 18, the Bavarian chargé d'affaires at Berlin reported that Zimmermann had given him important particulars of the Austrian note. These were, first, that the king of Serbia was to issue a proclamation stating his disapproval of the Greater Serbia movement, second, that Austrian officials should participate in an inquiry to discover those implicated in the murder, and third, that a time limit of forty-eight hours would be given for reply. Zimmermann also expressed the view that if Austria contented herself with chastising Serbia and refrained from taking Serbian territory the conflict might be localized. Austria was to be advised against mobilising her whole army, especially in Galicia, because this would trigger Russian mobilisation, followed by that of Germany and France, which would "conjure up a European war."[56]

The next day Jagow instructed Tschirschky to request that Berchtold communicate the text of the proposed note to Belgrade as soon as it was formulated, so Berlin could prepare its *démarches* toward the other Powers in time. Berchtold promised that Tschirschky would be given the note in time to have it delivered to Berlin by the evening of July 21, but he did not keep this promise.[57]

Disturbing reports of Vienna's intentions also reached Sazonov in St. Petersburg, and in a conversation with Sir George Buchanan, the British ambassador, on July 18 he said he intended to ask the French government to give a word of warning at Vienna. In answer to a question from Buchanan he replied that "anything in the shape of an Austrian ultimatum at Belgrade could not leave Russia indifferent, and she might be forced to take some precautionary military measures."[58] The Russians had already made known their determination to allow no action to be taken against Serbia. On July 16 Baron M.F. Schilling, in the Russian foreign office, had told the Italian ambassador in St. Petersburg that he was in a position to declare that "Russia was firmly determined not to permit any weakening or humiliation of Serbia."[59]

One of the difficulties involved in unravelling the threads of the rapidly approaching crisis is that all the continental Powers adopted a policy of deliberate deception, attempting to gain an advantage by concealing their real aims behind a veil of dissimulation. In the case of France and Russia their purpose was to ensure themselves of British support by pretending moderation and love of peace. Germany's principal aim was to procure England's neutrality She shared with Austria the desire to postpone any Russian military preparations to enable Austria to attack Serbia before Russia could intervene. Even Sir Edward Grey was not entirely immune from this tendency. In conversation with Lichnowsky he inferred that he was urging moderation on Russia, while there is no evidence that he took any such action.

An outstanding feature of the pro-entente history of the crisis is a touching belief in the honesty and sincerity of everyone except the Germans. The greatest beneficiaries of this blinkered view are the Russians, whose prevarications were so obvious that only a strong determination to look the other way could enable anyone to believe them.

The Austrian government adopted a two-faced policy on July 18. When Sazonov saw the Austrian ambassador that day to warn him that Russia would not "permit any attempts against the independence of Serbia," Count Szápáry assured him that Austria had no intention of "rendering relations with Serbia more acute." He spoke so peaceably that Sazonov was convinced that Austria had no warlike designs.[60] As we shall see, Sazonov was understating Russian aims, which were to resist even any request for "explanations" from Serbia.

On July 20, Grey suggested that Austria and Russia should discuss things if they became difficult. Poincaré thought conversations between Austria and Russia would be "very dangerous" and wanted "moderating counsels" by France and England at Vienna. Sazonov agreed that the three entente Powers should counsel moderation at Vienna, but thought this should not be "collective action," presumably so Austria would not understand that she was being threatened by the Triple Entente. Officials at the British foreign office believed it would be unwise to make representations at Vienna, but Grey did warn Count A. von Mensdorff-Pouilly, the Austrian ambassador in London, that Austria's demands should be reasonable.[61] Poincaré's reaction shows his usual concern for the solidarity of the Triple Entente and avoidance of any separate talks with members of the Triple Alliance. The incident indicates that the Entente Powers had already decided, before the dispatch of the Austrian note, that Austria should be told that they would not allow her to take any steps which might reveal Serbia's connection with the crime.

On July 21, at a reception for the diplomatic corps in St. Petersburg, President Poincaré told Count Szápáry that in the present condition of Europe every government must act with caution, because the Serbian affair could develop dangerously. Serbia had warm friends among the Russian people. He concluded by saying that "Russia has an ally, France. What complications are to be feared here." After delivering this threat to Austria he offered a few words of condolence to the Serbian minister who was also present at the reception.[62]

Buchanan informed Grey that Sazonov and Paléologue had told him that the result of Poincaré's visit to St. Petersburg had been to establish perfect agreement between France and Russia concerning the maintenance of general peace, and to affirm the obligations imposed on the two countries by their alliance. It had also been decided "to take action at Vienna with a view to the prevention of a demand for explanations," or any summons which involved intervention in Serbia's internal affairs or which that country might consider an attack on her sovereignty and independence. The determination not to allow even a demand for explanations from Serbia indicates that Russia intended to insist that Austria must recognize that Serbia had nothing whatever to do with the archduke's murder.[63] Sazonov had instructed his ambassador at Vienna to give "friendly counsels of moderation" in concert with his French and British colleagues.[64] The British foreign office thought any such step at Vienna would be unwise and did not propose to take part in it.

The German government informed the British ambassador in Berlin that their attitude was that Austrian action to clear up relations with Serbia was justified, that the question at issue was one between Austria and Serbia alone and that there should be no outside interference. Jagow advised the Serbians to give way to Austria's requests for measures to put Austro-Serbian relations on a proper footing.

Sir Eyre Crowe's minute to this report is instructive. The German government, he wrote, was not being straightforward. If they really wanted to keep Austria in check, they should say so at Vienna. The Germans had given no indication that they wanted to keep Austria in check, but had on the contrary supported action by Austria. They were certainly not showing a lack of straightforwardness. Crowe also opposed any attempt by the British government to suggest moderation at Belgrade or St. Petersburg, because this would create a breach between England and Russia. It is clear that he had already decided that Austria had no right to take any action concerning Serbia's involvement in the assassination, and that any attempt by her to do so should be opposed by the Triple Entente. It is significant that he assumed as early as July 22 that a confrontation between the two Alliance systems was in prospect and that England should maintain solidarity with Russia.[65]

On July 22, Grey told Count Benckendorff he thought the Russian government should communicate directly with Austria. Sazonov might ask the Austrian government what demands they felt it necessary to make of Serbia, and it might then be possible to arrange that these should be kept within reasonable limits. The Russian ambassador thought such an approach by Russia would be difficult. Grey also said that, if Austria could prove that the plot to assassinate the Archduke had been organized on Serb territory, Grey could urge in Belgrade that Serbia should give Austria "the utmost assurances they could for the prevention of such plots against Austria being carried on in Servia in the future."[66]

The next day, July 23, Grey was informed by the Austrian ambassador of the general tenor of the demands to be made on Serbia. He hoped that if there were difficulties Austria and Russia would discuss them directly with each other. Grey deplored the fact that there was to be a time limit, as this might "inflame public opinion in Russia" and make a settlement more difficult. He had spoken to Benckendorff about the influence of public opinion in Russia, indicating to him that he took this matter seriously.[67] Public opinion had almost no influence on the conduct of diplomats anywhere, and the view that it played an important role in Russia is ridiculous.

Berchtold did not give the Germans a copy of the Austrian note until the evening of July 22, but there is no evidence to show the purpose of this delay. If the intention was to prevent Germany from suggesting changes, his previous experience with German lack of support for Austrian initiatives may have led him to fear that the Germans would consider the ultimatum too harsh. However that may be, Jagow at once assured Szögyény that the German government agreed entirely with the note.[68] He could hardly have done anything else, because Germany had not only given Austria a completely free hand but had already informed her representatives abroad that she fully supported Austria's procedure and demands.[69]

The Austrian *démarche*, presented at Belgrade at 6 p.m. on July 23, required an answer within forty-eight hours. After quoting the Serbian government's declaration of March 31, 1909, by which Serbia had promised to change its policy and to live on terms of friendly and neighbourly relations with Austria-Hungary, the note cited the ways in which Serbia had failed to keep this promise. In particular, it mentioned the Serbian government's toleration of societies whose activities had resulted in acts of terrorism and a series of murders and attempted murders.

In order to put an end to these actions, the Austrian government demanded that Serbia should publish in its official press organ the following declaration:

> *The Royal Servian government condemns the propaganda directed against Austria-Hungary…whose ultimate aim is to disjoin parts of the territory belonging to the Austrian-Hungarian monarchy and regrets sincerely the horrible consequences of these criminal ambitions. The Royal Servian government regrets that Servian officers and officials have taken part in the propaganda above-mentioned and thereby imperilled the friendly and neighbourly relations, which the Royal government had solemnly promised to cultivate in its declaration of 31st March 1909.*

The Royal government, which condemns and rejects every thought and every attempt to interfere in behalf of the inhabitants of any part of Austria-Hungary, considers it a duty to warn officers, officials and indeed all the inhabitants of the kingdom, that it will in future use great severity against such persons, as will be found guilty of similar doings, which the government will make every effort to suppress.

This declaration was also to be communicated to the army by order of the king and published in the official army organ.

Then followed the ten points to which the Serbian government was required to pledge itself. These were:

1. to suppress publications "likely to inspire hatred and contempt against the monarchy;"

2. to dissolve the *Narodna Odbrana* and all other societies which promote propaganda against Austria-Hungary;

3. to remove from the schools, teachers and books which foster this propaganda;

4. to dismiss all officers and officials who have taken part in such propaganda;

5. to consent that Austrian officials should assist in suppressing the subversive movement directed against the territorial integrity of the monarchy;

6. to institute a judicial inquiry against those who took part in the plot to murder Franz Ferdinand, with Austrian officials taking part in the inquiry;

7. to arrest Tankositch and Ciganovitch, both compromised by the results of the Austrian inquiry;

8. to take effectual measures to prevent the smuggling of weapons and explosives across the frontier with the connivance of Serbian authorities, and to punish the frontier officials who had assisted the Sarajevo criminals;

9. to explain the remarks of Serbian officials who had spoken of Austria in hostile terms after the murder;

10. to inform the Austrian government without delay that all these measures have been taken.

The Serbian government was informed that the Sarajevo court set up to investigate the murder of Franz Ferdinand had shown that the plot had been devised in Belgrade by the assassins and by Milan Ciganovitch, with the help of Major Tankositch, that the bombs and pistols had been procured and given to the assassins Gavrilo Princip and Nedeljiko Cabrinovitch by Ciganovitch and Tankositch and that Ciganovitch had taught them how to use the weapons. The implication of Serbian officials in the transport of the criminals and their weapons was also described.[70]

On hearing the news of the Austrian ultimatum Sazonov exclaimed "*C'est la guerre européenne,*" and proceeded to set Russia on the road to war.[71] The Russian council of ministers met at 3 p.m. on July 24 and passed the following resolutions:

to have the Great Powers try to persuade Austria to extend the time-limit;

to advise Serbia to offer no resistance in case of an Austrian invasion, but to appeal to the Great Powers;

to mobilise the four military districts of Kiev, Odessa, Moscow and Kazan and the Baltic and Black Sea fleets;

to have the war minister speed up the stockpiling of war materials;

to reduce the Russian money deposited in Germany and Austria.

The council specified that military measures were to be directed against Austria-Hungary alone. After the meeting Sazonov, according to his account, advised the Serbian minister that there should be extreme moderation in respect of the Serbian reply to the Austrian note.[72] That Sazonov advised Serbia to a course of moderation in her reply to the Austrian note is the first of a long series of prevarications on the part of the Russian foreign minister.

Sazonov met Maurice Paléologue, the French ambassador, and Sir George Buchanan on July 24. He told Buchanan that France and Russia had decided to take action at Vienna to prevent any demand for explanations or any summons to Serbia which she might consider an attack on her sovereignty and independence. He considered that some of Austria's demands were absolutely unacceptable. He asserted that France and Russia were in complete agreement and that France would support Russia, and expressed the hope that England would proclaim her solidarity with them. Sazonov also disclosed his view that Russia would have to mobilise. Buchanan thought there was little chance that England would declare solidarity with France and Russia, but promised to acquaint Grey with their views. He informed Grey that it seemed from Paléologue's language that "France and Russia were determined to make a strong stand even if we failed to join them." Crowe's minute to this dispatch indicates his view that the Triple Alliance and the Triple Entente were engaged and that England should support France and Russia regardless of the merits of the Austrian case. He suggested the mobilisation of the fleet to indicate that England would fight and thus to induce Germany to back down.[73]

In fact it was Russia, not Serbia, which rejected the Austrian ultimatum. Serbia would have accepted all the Austrian conditions if Russia had not insisted that some were unacceptable and promised intervention if Serbia rejected them. Up until noon on July 25, Serbia was prepared to accept the whole ultimatum, asking only for an explanation of point six. After receiving the Russian promise of support for rejection of some points, the Serbian government drew up a cleverly worded but evasive reply calculated to influence British opinion, and at the same time ordered mobilisation of the army.[74]

Having thus made certain that an Austrian attack on Serbia would be forthcoming, the Russian government at once initiated preparations for a general war. While Austria was still awaiting the Serbian reply the Russian council of ministers decided to "enforce throughout the entire Empire the order for the period preparatory to war laid down in both schedules" and to empower the war minister to take such other measures as he thought necessary in the circumstances.[75]

This procedure for the period preparatory to war had been authorized by the tsar on March 2, 1913. Its purpose was to enable Russia to undertake the early stages of mobilisation without actually declaring it and thus lull an enemy into believing no military measures were being undertaken. It would make it possible for Russia to close the gap between her mobilisation time and that of Germany. This was completely successful in 1914. Russia was able to "surprise the world by the rapidity with which she poured her troops into East Prussia and Galicia."[76] Russian advance troops crossed into East Prussia on August 3, the same day on which the Germans entered Belgium.[77]

The measures to be taken under authority of the Russian regulation encompassed the first stages of mobilisation, including the calling up of reservists and the territorial reserve.[78] The territorial reserve would secure the frontiers, the lines of communication and the telegraph system; horses and wagons were to be bought for the baggage trains and the baggage transported to its destination. The council of ministers had authorized the war minister to take still further measures if he thought it necessary. General Dobrorolsky, in charge of mobilisation, who thought "the war was already a settled matter," indicates that the actions taken went beyond the instructions, especially on the German frontier. The order to institute the regulations went out on July 26 at 3:26 a.m.[79] The German government received numerous reports of activities on the German frontier, but did not declare *Kriegsgefahrzustand*, the corresponding measure, until July 31.[80]

Meanwhile, Sir Edward Grey launched his first plan for defusing the critical situation. The Austrian note to Serbia was "the most formidable document I had ever seen addressed by one state to another that was independent," Grey said later.[81] He told the German ambassador that as long as the ultimatum did not lead to trouble between Austria and Russia he had no concern with it, but that he feared the Russian reaction would be unfavourable. The only chance of effective intervention he could see was that England, Germany, Italy and France should work together for moderation at Vienna and St. Petersburg.[82]

It appears that for the moment Grey was ready to accept the German view that Austria should be treated as a Great Power with a justifiable grievance against Serbia. He agreed that the Austro-Serbian conflict could be localized and that the other Powers had no role to play unless a quarrel between Austria and Russia ensued. He abandoned this position when it became evident that France and Russia were determined to support Serbia in her role as an instrument for the destruction of Austria-Hungary. Curiously Grey, unlike his counterparts in France and Russia, probably believed Serbia's protestations of innocence.

Grey broached the idea of the other Powers working for moderation at Vienna and St. Petersburg to Paul Cambon. The French ambassador said that once Austria moved against Serbia it would be too late for mediation, and that the important thing was to gain time by mediation between Austria and Serbia. Cambon thought Germany should propose this to the other Powers.[83] Cambon's report to Paris did not mention Grey's original proposal to defuse the situation, but said that he and Grey had agreed that Germany should be asked to "take the initiative in approaching Vienna with the object of offering the mediation, between Austria and Servia, of the four Powers which are not directly interested."[84] The French government was thus never informed of Grey's idea that a moderating influence should be exercised at St. Petersburg.

Count Benckendorff, when told of Grey's proposal for mediation at Vienna and St. Petersburg, was apprehensive lest this "would give Germany the impression that France and England were detached from Russia." Grey replied that France and England would be no more detached from Russia than Germany would be from Austria. He reiterated his belief that the dispute between Austria and Serbia was no concern of his, and said he would intervene only between Austria and Russia. Grey assumed that Russia would mobilise, and said he was asking Germany not to mobilise if Russia did so, but to join in intervention between Austria and Russia. Because this would throw away her advantage of rapid mobilisation, he feared Germany would refuse his proposal.[85]

British historians maintain that Sazonov's statement in response to Grey's proposal, that if Serbia appealed to the Powers Russia would stand aside and leave the matter in the hands of the four Powers, shows that he accepted Grey's proposal for mediation at St. Petersburg. It is, however, obvious that if Russia were to "stand aside" what he was accepting was mediation between Austria and Serbia. This is proved by Sazonov's response to a telegram from Isvolsky in Paris which reported a suggestion on July 26 by Bienvenu-Martin, French minister of justice, that the four Powers should take steps at St. Petersburg and Vienna. Sazonov's reaction was to state that "If there is a question of exercising a moderating influence in Petersburg we reject it in advance, as we have adopted a standpoint from the outset which we can in no way alter." Isvolsky replied that France "did not for a moment admit the possibility of exercising a moderating influence in Petersburg."[86]

Jagow's acceptance of Grey's suggestion that the four Powers should work for moderation at Vienna and St. Petersburg was sent to London at 3:16 p.m. on July 25, before the receipt of Lichnowsky's second telegram urging a favourable reply.[87] Luigi Albertini maintains that the German acceptance of Grey's proposal was "bogus" because Germany could not seriously mean to let Russia make preparations against Austria. Germany did allow Russia to mobilise against Austria without taking similar action herself. There was no reason why Germany should not agree to Grey's proposal, since it supported the German plan for localization.[88]

The plain fact, unpalatable though it may be to pro-entente historians, is that Germany accepted this neutral proposal and that it was turned down by France and Russia. Grey's plan provided a possibility that the Powers could work out a compromise between Austria's intention of eliminating Serbia as a power factor in the Balkans and Russia's determination to maintain Serbia as "a dagger pointed at the heart of Austria." Unfortunately Grey's overriding need to maintain entente solidarity enabled France and Russia to divert him to the necessity of undertaking mediation between Austria and Serbia, leaving Russia to "stand aside," with its lethal outcome.

The idea that the proposal that the four Powers should work for moderation at Vienna and St. Petersburg was a gross error on Grey's part and that he should have given Germany a "severe warning" to abandon Austria rests on an incorrect premise. It assumes that Austria had no case against Serbia and that Russia was justified in her determination to go to war rather than allow Austria to defend herself against Serbian plots and intrigues on her own territory. This is, in fact, Luigi Albertini's opinion. He says the question is whether politically and morally Austria had a better right to defend her existence or Serbia to liberate her brethren.[89] Ignoring the internecine conflicts endemic to the Balkan area, he equates the Serb aim of ruling over the multinational, multi-religious Balkan Slavs with the Italian desire to be free from Austrian rule.

The opinion that Russian policy was completely justified did not receive unanimous support from entente diplomats. Francis Bertie did not think that if Russia picked "a quarrel with Austria over the Austro-Serb difficulty public opinion in France would be in favour of backing up Russia in so bad a cause." A few days later he wrote to Grey suggesting that France "should be encouraged to put pressure on Russia not to assume the absurd and obsolete attitude of Russia being Protector of all the Slav states whatever their conduct, as this would lead to war."[90] Paul Cambon said on July 24, that if Russia supported Serbia she would be initiating aggression against Austria, that Germany would have to support Austria, and that this would mean general war.[91] Sir Horace Rumbold, counsellor at the Berlin embassy, told the Russian ambassador that "Russia was so great and so important that she could afford not to consider the question of prestige in dealing with Slav opinion."[92]

In fact it was not Russian prestige that was at stake, but whether or not the Russian offensive against Austria could proceed without hindrance. Any Austrian attack on Serbia must be resisted, "or the whole Pan-Slavist programme of expansion in the southeast would be frustrated."[93] The worst that could have happened to Russia would have been the loss of some of the advantages she had gained by instigating the Balkan wars. In other words, while Austria was prepared to fight for her existence, Russia insisted on fighting to maintain Serbia as a threat to that existence.

Late on the evening of July 25, Grey received an alarming telegram from Russia which told of the imminence of Russian mobilisation and of the determination of Russia to go to war if Germany did not restrain Austria. Sir George Buchanan expressed the "earnest hope that Russia would not precipitate war by mobilizing" until Grey had time to use his influence for peace. He said that if Russia mobilised Germany would not give her time to complete mobilisation "but would probably declare war at once." Sazonov said that Russia could not allow Austria to crush Serbia and that "secure of the support of France, she will face all the risks of war." He appealed for England to stand solidly with France and Russia to force Germany to give way and thus avoid war. Buchanan could not give any promise of British support to Russia and advised prudence, but to Grey he urged that England should not fail to support Russia, whose friendship with England was at stake.[94]

The telegram from Russia also mentioned a suggestion by Sazonov that Serbia should appeal to the Powers, in which case Russia would be ready to stand aside and leave the question in the hands of England, France, Italy and Germany. This produced a recommendation from Sir Arthur Nicolson that Grey should propose a conference of these four Powers in London. It is obvious from the context that this conference would deal with the Austro-Serbian conflict and thus avoid any pressure on Russia. While it would have the appearance of neutrality its result could be only an attempt to force Austria to retreat. Such a proposal was certain to be turned down by Germany, because Italy would side with England and France and Germany would be put in the wrong.[95]

Grey's conference proposal provided only for the suspension of military operations, while it allowed the Russians to mobilise. This ensured that while the entente was administering a diplomatic defeat to Austria, the military situation of the Central Powers would become more precarious. If they should then decide that the decisions of the conference were intolerable, as was to be expected, the possibility of carrying on a successful war, already very doubtful, would be even more remote.[96]

The question of Russian military preparations was addressed by Bethmann-Hollweg on July 26. He wrote to Lichnowsky that he had information that Russia was about to call up several classes of reservists, and that this pointed to mobilisation against Germany, to which she would have to respond. Bethmann-Hollweg has been accused by Albertini of falsely stating that Russia had called up reserves and of threatening that Germany would also do so. He actually stated that he had been informed that this action was imminent in Russia, and if this proved true Germany would be forced to take counter action.[97] As the calling up of Russian reservists had been authorized before dawn that morning, Bethmann-Hollweg's information was correct, and Germany would have been quite justified in taking similar action, although she did not do so.

The falsehood on this subject was actually committed by the Russians. Count Pourtalès, German ambassador in St. Petersburg, forwarded that night a report from the German military attaché at St. Petersburg, who had been told by the minister of war that "not a horse was being conscripted, not a reservist called to the colours." The attaché was not deceived, and thought that "complete mobilization may not yet have been ordered, but preparatory measures are very far-reaching."[98]

Bethmann-Hollweg, as was to be expected, rejected the idea of a conference on the ground that Germany "would not be able to summon Austria before a European court of justice in her case with Serbia." Bertie, who evidently sympathized with the Austrian viewpoint, thought Austria would consider she was "being treated as a minor Balkan State." Bethmann-Hollweg recalled Grey's distinction between the Austro-Serbian and an Austro-Russian conflict, and said that Germany's "mediation activities must be confined to a possible Austro-Russian clash." He then suggested the feasibility of a direct understanding between Vienna and St. Petersburg. This had been Grey's favourite idea since July 20, and he continued to believe that this "would be the best possible solution." If there was a chance of its taking place, he would "suspend every other suggestion."[99]

France did not reply immediately to Grey's conference proposal, but accepted it on the afternoon of July 27, with the proviso that Germany first speak with the Austrians with some success.[100] French premier René Viviani saw at once that Grey's proposal meant mediation between Austria and Serbia, and thought it would allow Germany to withdraw with dignity from her untenable position that the Austro-Serbian conflict could be localised.[101] Sazonov was ready to accept a conference if his direct conversations with Austria led to no result.[102]

It has generally been maintained that Germany committed a grave error in rejecting the conference. This means she should have accepted a procedure which was certain to inflict on Austria a much greater humiliation than she had suffered as a result of the previous conference in London in 1912. Bethmann-Hollweg was well aware that Austria would refuse the idea of such a conference, as in fact happened when the British ambassador presented it to Berchtold. Bethmann-Hollweg remarked that if Austria accepted mediation "Serbia would feel itself encouraged to go on doing what it has done in the past," and war would merely be postponed.[103] Ultimately, the argument that the conference should have been accepted means that Germany should have agreed to the destruction of Austria and the complete domination of the Triple Entente. This judgement depends on foreknowledge of the result of the war, which was not certain, despite the seemingly overwhelming superiority of the entente Powers. The argument cuts two ways: it is evident that even the complete destruction of Serbia, which Germany and Austria agreed not to bring about, would have inflicted much less injury on the entente Powers than they suffered from the war.

It is doubtful that anything could have been done after July 26 to avert a European war. The actions of the Russian government on July 25 and 26 indicated that war was already a decided thing. Albertini says that the first critical date was July 5, when Germany gave Austria the "blank cheque," and the second was July 26, when Russian military measures were taken. He thinks the Russian period preparatory to war was more significant than her partial mobilisation against Austria.[104]

Although Sazonov may have thought until July 28 that war might still be avoided, the Russian military leaders had no such idea. According to General Dobrorolsky, chief of the mobilisation section of the Russian staff, the militarists and the general staff believed on July 25 that the war "was already a settled matter." The flood of telegrams between governments merely provided "the stage setting of a historical drama."[105]

Paléologue believed on July 25 that the steps taken by Russia indicated that war was imminent. He thought efforts to avert it were useless, but that the entente would try to do so, "or at least to make it clear on whom the terrible responsibility rests."[106] The same day the Russian ambassador, Benckendorff, vainly tried to persuade Grey to make it absolutely clear to Germany that England would not be neutral if war came, but reported that Grey "barricades himself behind the hope of negotiations." He thought Sazonov's moderate attitude and language was very necessary to ensure English cooperation.[107] The Russian ambassador obviously agreed with Paléologue that war was imminent, that negotiations were useless, and that the important thing was to make sure England would fight with France and Russia.

Only Sir Edward Grey amongst the major participants still soldiered on, hoping to find a magic formula which would bridge the unbridgeable gap between Austria and Russia without sacrificing entente solidarity. Bethmann-Hollweg, it is true, continued to press for localization, but he should have known by then that Russia would not allow it. Sazonov also continued to make proposals ostensibly aimed at averting war, but since he appears to have decided by July 28 that war was certain, these can be intended only as window-dressing to parade his desire for peace. Austria had no intention of giving up her attempt to stop the Serbian threat, Germany would not abandon her ally, and France and Russia were resolved to fight unless

Austria backed down. Only a buoyant optimist or a reckless gambler would have wagered a wooden nickel on the chances of peace.

It is customary, however, to assume that the war still could have been prevented at some later date, which gives entente writers the fullest scope to expatiate on the way in which Germany frustrated the heroic efforts of the entente Powers to preserve peace. Some even claim piously that war was not certain even after the Russian general mobilisation, if only Germany had refrained from mobilising as well. This enables them to accomplish the amazing feat of branding the last continental Power to mobilise as the author of the act which precipitated the catastrophe.

The task of demonstrating that Germany was entirely responsible for Austria's uncompromising attitude requires some inventiveness, and employs several stratagems. Almost all the documents showing that Germany pushed Austria to extremes come from Austrian sources. Luigi Albertini's ingenious explanation of this is that Bethmann-Hollweg avoided documentary evidence of his inflammatory messages to Vienna by giving them verbally to Szögyény.[108] When two diplomats talk together their reports of the conversations often differ considerably. It is obvious that Berchtold and Forgach, at least, exaggerated German enthusiasm for action in order to convert their colleagues, and Szögyény may well have done the same.

Another device is to read into German statements or documents more than they said. When Jagow asked for information about Austria's plans for Serbia, some writers interpret it as evidence that Germany wanted a partition of Serbia, for which there is no justification whatever in the document.[109] Geiss quotes two documents which supposedly show German displeasure that Vienna "was not showing the requisite spirit of resolution" but neither shows such a thing.[110] When Szögyény is quoted as reporting that everyone in authority in Berlin urges Austria "to undertake an action against Serbia which may eventually end in war," this is represented as urging immediate *military* action.[111]

A third trick of historical interpreters consists of ignoring evidence of Austrian determination to press forward, which often precedes the supposed evidence of German responsibility for Austria's intransigence. Germans are always assumed to be devious and dishonest, while everyone else is honest and straightforward. These tactics are the mark of researchers whose conclusions are known in advance. Only the fact that such accounts frequently contradict themselves allows some light to shine through the fog.

It was not until July 27 that an account of the Serbian reply to the Austrian note was known in the entente capitals. On the previous day the French foreign office had received a dispatch from the French minister at Belgrade which stated that he had been told by a Serbian chargé d'affaires that Serbia had accepted all the points unconditionally, merely asking for more information concerning the participation of Austrian government officials in the judicial enquiry. The French probably took this dispatch, which substantially misrepresented the actual Serbian reply, as an accurate summary of Serbia's note to Austria.[112] The Serbs sent a similar message to London, giving an even briefer version of the Serbian reply and stating that Austria should accept it as giving full satisfaction if she did not want war.[113] These machinations were simply part of Serbia's campaign of misrepresentation, aimed at deceiving England and France, carried out through the month of July. No doubt it influenced these Powers to accept the idea that the reply gave in to all the Austrian demands and should be considered satisfactory.

The actual Serbian reply to Austria began with the assertion that neither the Serbian government nor any of its organs had made any attempt to change the condition of either Bosnia or Herzegovina. The government could not be made responsible for newspaper articles or the "peaceful work" of societies. It was therefore "painfully surprised, when the assertion was made, that Servian subjects were supposed to have taken part in the preparations for the crime of Sarajevo." Serbia expressed its willingness to take legal proceedings against any Serbian subject "of whom proofs are given that he has participated in the crime of Sarajevo," and to publish in the official gazette a statement condemning all propaganda against Austria-Hungary and all efforts to detach parts of Austrian territory.

The implication that the Serbian societies were engaged in peaceful work was as hypocritical as the "painful surprise" that Austria should suppose that Serbian subjects had taken part in preparing the Sarajevo crime. Part of the declaration requested by Austria was omitted, and there was no acknowledgement that those parts which were included would be communicated to the army by the king or published in the official army organ.

Passing to the specific points of the Austrian note, the Serbian reply accepted the first point, but made no indication concerning when the action would be taken to control the press. Serbia agreed to dissolve *Narodna Odbrana* and other societies, but not to prevent them from appearing under other names or in other forms. Doubt was expressed that such societies had actually committed any criminal actions, although the Serbian authorities were well aware of their activities. Point three was accepted unconditionally. To point four, which asked for the dismissal of officers and officials who had taken part in anti-Austrian propaganda, the reply promised only to dismiss those proved guilty in a Serbian court of actions against the monarchy's integrity. The reply to point five is vague and evasive. With regard to point six, which was refused on the ground that it "would be a violation of the constitution and of the law of penal procedure," the Austrian demand itself is hard to interpret. The expectation that a Serbian court would convict any Serbian of anything on evidence supplied by Austria was, to say the least, bizarre. Austria insisted in the critique of the Serbian reply that it did not intend that Austrian officials should take part in judicial proceedings but only in the police researches, and that the language used made this clear. The answer to point seven was completely false: it asserted that the Serbian authorities had been unable to find Ciganovitch and requested the Austrians to tell them the grounds on which he and Tankositch were suspected so that an inquiry could be instituted. The three remaining points were conceded, although the reply expressed ignorance that remarks hostile to Austria had actually been made.[114]

The Austrian government, with five years of experience of the way in which Serbia kept promises, felt justified in rejecting this reply as inadequate. From the Serbian point of view, however, the reply was a great success, because not only was it declared satisfactory by the entente Powers but even accepted by Bethmann-Hollweg and the kaiser as sufficient, provided Austria could obtain guarantees for its fulfilment. This approval must have been the result of a superficial study of the document.

The most interesting comment came from Sazonov, who told the French that the Serbian reply exceeded all his expectations "by its moderation and its readiness to give Austria the fullest satisfaction."[115] He did not mention that the Serbian note would have been much more moderate if he himself had not insisted on some points being rejected. Perhaps the Serbian agreement to disband the *Narodna Odbrana* exceeded his expectations, since he had declared this point unacceptable.

Sazonov had already told Sir George Buchanan that he had done his best to induce Serbia to accept all of Austria's demands, and he now repeated to the British government his statement that the Serbian reply had exceeded his expectations.[116] Grey accepted these lies at face value, and told Lichnowsky, the German ambassador in London, he "assumed that the Servian reply could not have gone as far as it did unless Russia had exercised conciliatory influence at Belgrade."[117] It is evident that Grey's grasp of the reality of Russian policy in the Balkans was very weak, and that he was an easy mark for the deceptions of his allies.

In the conversation with Lichnowsky Grey stated that Serbia had agreed to all the Austrian demands except one point, and, according to Lichnowsky, Grey requested Germany to use her "influence at Vienna either to get them to accept the reply from Belgrade as satisfactory or as the basis for conferences." It appears that Grey still based his view of the Serbian reply on the incomplete information supplied by the Serbian chargé d'affaires. Austria's slowness in providing a correct copy and her delay in producing her dossier on Serbia's actions were disastrous errors. Grey's account of his talk with Lichnowsky says that he told Lichnowsky that the "Servian reply should at least be treated as a basis for discussion and pause." He said the "German government should urge this at Vienna."[118]

Late on the night of July 27, Bethmann-Hollweg forwarded Lichnowsky's telegram outlining his meeting with Grey to Tschirschky for consideration of the Vienna cabinet. He requested Berchtold's opinion on it and on Sazonov's desire to negotiate directly with Vienna.[119] The Austrian government replied late on the 29th that since it was now at war with Serbia, the Serbian reply had been superseded by other events.[120] A few hours after his dispatch had been sent to Vienna, Bethmann-Hollweg replied to London, definitely refusing to ask Austria to accept the Serbian reply as satisfactory, but agreeing to act on the second part of Grey's request, i.e., to accept it as a basis for conferences.[121]

It does not seem as though Grey was renewing his proposal for a conference, although Lichnowsky may have understood it that way. Even this is not certain, however, because Lichnowsky's telegram speaks of "conferences," which implies discussions rather than a formal conference. From Grey's account it appears that what he wanted was pressure on Vienna either to accept the Serbian reply as satisfactory or to delay action and discuss it.

Although Tschirschky received Bethmann-Hollweg's message early on the morning of July 28, it appears that he did not speak to Berchtold until after the declaration of war at 11 a.m.[122] In any case, however, it is unlikely that Austria could have been persuaded to consider the Serbian reply as satisfactory, or even as a basis for discussion.

There has been much controversy over this incident, based on a telegram which Count Szögyény directed to Vienna on the evening of July 27, which is supposed to show double-dealing on Bethmann-Hollweg's part. This view is based on failure to read carefully the relevant documents.

Szögyény's telegram to Berchtold states that "If Germany candidly told Sir E. Grey that it refused to communicate England's wishes to Austria-Hungary, which [England] thinks will be more regarded, if they pass through Germany's hands," then "the wire still working between Germany and England" might be broken. The next paragraph states that "The German government will, whenever England has such a request to make, declare with decision that it cannot support such proposals...and only passes them on to please England." If anything, the text supports Germany's attempt to keep open the lines of communication with England. In fact, Bethmann-Hollweg told Grey bluntly that it was impossible for him to advise Vienna to accept the Serbian reply as satisfactory. That he should have spoken so forthrightly if his purpose was to deceive Grey by pretending to accede to his wishes is unlikely.

The next paragraph of the Szögyény telegram speaks of a British wish that Austria's note to Serbia should be modified. German foreign minister Jagow is supposed to have replied that he would send Grey's proposals to Berchtold but that he could not support them. This nullifies the alleged German deception, because Jagow has told England exactly what he intends to do. Finally, Bethmann-Hollweg's telegram to Tschirschky mentions no note from Grey and clearly says that, when it arrives, the English proposal is to be submitted to the Vienna cabinet. The telegram requests Berchtold's opinion on the British suggestion and on Sazonov's desire to negotiate directly with Vienna.[123]

No rational conclusions can be drawn from Szögyény's telegram and the momentous deductions concerning Bethmann-Hollweg's two-faced policy which depend on it are the products of groundless speculation. Szögyény's document does not fit together with the other documents, as Fischer says.

It is alleged that Bethmann-Hollweg waited to send his proposal to Vienna until he was sure that the declaration of war would have taken place but in fact it arrived at 5:30 a.m. on July 28. Bethmann-Hollweg did not know definitely that the declaration of war was to take place on July 28, because Tschirschky's telegram of the 27th informing Berlin that it was imminent said that the declaration would be sent "tomorrow, or the day after tomorrow at the latest," that is, on the 28th or the 29th.[124]

Some historians also put emphasis on the supposed fact that war was declared because Germany insisted on it. This is based on Szögyény's telegram of July 25, which stated that in Germany the "general belief" is that if Serbia's reply is unsatisfactory a "declaration of war and war operations will follow immediately." Szögyény urged Austria to proceed with "war preparations" without delay, which advice agrees with Szögyény's own view.[125] To show that Austria declared war because of this telegram, Luigi Albertini misquotes Tschirschky's report to Berlin. He quotes Franz Conrad von Hötzendorf, German chief of staff, as saying that "a formal declaration of war would doubtless be necessary," while Tschirschky reports that what he said was "a formal declaration of war would probably prove superfluous," because he expected hostile action by Serbia within a few days.[126] Albertini suggests that Austrian foreign minister Berchtold pretended to agree with the German view that the Austrians should not delay declaring war because he was intimidated by Tschirschky. In fact, Berchtold decided after Tschirschky left to postpone the declaration of war, but to discuss it again if diplomatic reasons made it necessary. The next morning he persuaded Conrad von Hötzendorf to agree to the declaration of war if Berchtold thought the diplomatic situation required it.[127] It appears that Berchtold favoured the war declaration but that Conrad von Hötzendorf did not want war declared until he was ready to fight it.

The German belief that if the Serbian reply was unsatisfactory war would follow immediately was shared by the Russians, who expected military operations immediately after the time-limit expired. The Russians already knew that the reply would be unsatisfactory, since they had insisted on this themselves.[128]

Berchtold stated that military operations must be delayed until the end of deployment so the blow could be dealt with full strength. Albertini interprets this to mean that Berchtold did not think the declaration of war would necessarily be followed by war. The natural meaning of his statement, if one is not hampered by the necessity of emphasizing German responsibility for all Austria's actions, is that war was not certain until it was declared, and that therefore no large-scale military measures had yet been taken.[129]

German foreign minister Gottlieb von Jagow's reaction to the information that the offensive could not begin until August 12 was regret that "military action" should be delayed so long.[130] This reaction is cited as further proof that Germany desired to rush things forward, but there is no reason to suppose it had any influence on the declaration of war. Germany had insisted from the beginning that Austria's action should be taken quickly. This was partly to take advantage of the revulsion which it was expected would be felt everywhere by the crime of Sarajevo.[131] It was also hoped that the action could be taken before Russia had time to prepare for military intervention.[132]

Fritz Fischer and his cohort have completely misinterpreted the German insistence on speedy action. The purpose was not to hurry up the outbreak of a European war, but to prevent it. Bethmann-Hollweg and Jagow both believed that, if the shock wave produced by the assassination was given time to recede, opposition to strong measures by Austria would be more likely. They also thought prompt steps would temper reaction by the other Powers and would deprive the entente of time to coordinate its normal opposition to any move made by the Central Powers. It was hoped that this would enable Austria to achieve her purpose of putting a stop to Serbia's intrigues before the Entente could take counteraction.

This German plan was frustrated by the insistence of the Hungarian premier, Count Tisza, that Austria must take diplomatic steps before attacking Serbia to justify a declaration of war if Serbia refused to comply. There was a long delay while the Austrian note was being drawn up and approved, and then a further postponement to avoid delivery of the note while Poincaré was in St. Petersburg. Nearly a month went by before the Austrian ultimatum was sent to Belgrade.

As time passed the German authorities grew more and more nervous, because it became apparent that the long delay was making more probable the miscarriage of their strategy. They kept hoping against hope that it could still be executed without unleashing a general war, and by the time all hope was gone it was too late to avert the catastrophe. It is not, of course, certain that even the rapid stroke projected by Bethmann-Hollweg would have prevented Russia from intervening, but to assume that his intention from the first was to produce a European war is unjustified.

As early as July 7, Tisza had assumed that a refusal would bring a declaration of war. He clearly believed that a decision to mobilise would also mean that war would be declared.[133] The Austrian cabinet agreed that war was necessary, but Tisza insisted on diplomatic action first.

Conrad von Hötzendorf had emphasized on July 10 that "our diplomatic steps must avoid everything that would delay action by protracted negotiations, so that our antagonists would gain time for military preparations." If Austria's mind was made up for war, there should be an ultimatum with a short term, "which, if it be answered in the negative, must immediately be followed by the order for mobilisation."[134] On July 19, it was decided to publish the order for mobilisation on the night of July 25. Conrad von Hötzendorf was in favour of "a speedy beginning of the impending action."[135] He wanted mobilisation proclaimed on July 25 in view of the Serbian mobilisation actions.[136] Tisza warned on July 24 against the slightest hesitation in mobilising if the Serbian answer should be unsatisfactory.[137] It is therefore certain that Austria intended to take immediate military action if Serbia replied in the negative. It is thus hardly surprising that Germany expected and supported immediate military action and assumed that it would be preceded by a declaration of war.

The Serbians also expected an immediate attack on Belgrade as soon as the Austrian minister left and accordingly the government was removed from Belgrade. The Serbian army was mobilised on the afternoon of July 25, before the delivery of the reply to Austria, indicating that the government realized its reply would produce war and depended on the promised Russian support to avert disaster.[138]

July 28 was a day of considerable activity. The kaiser read the Serbian reply and said that "on the whole the wishes of the Danube Monarchy [Austria] have been acceded to" and that the few reservations could be cleared up by negotiation. However, because the Serbs were "masters of evasion," he suggested that Austria should take Belgrade hostage, "as a guaranty for the enforcement and carrying out of the promises," and should occupy it until Austria's demands had been complied with.[139] Bethmann-Hollweg sent a long telegram to Tschirschky in Vienna that evening, which said that, since Sazonov had conceded that Serbia would have to receive her "deserved lesson,"[140] he might even agree to an invasion of Serbia, particularly if Austria repeated her declaration of territorial disinterestedness and stated that she intended only a temporary occupation of parts of Serbia to ensure fulfilment of her demands. When these had been complied with, evacuation would follow. Bethmann-Hollweg ended with the following instructions:

> You will have to avoid very carefully giving rise to the impression that we wish to hold Austria back. The case is solely one of finding a way to realize Austria's desired aim, that of cutting the vital control of Greater-Serbia propaganda, without at the same time bringing on a world war, and, if the latter cannot be avoided in the end, of improving the conditions under which we should have to wage it, in so far as is possible.[141]

It is commonly asserted that this telegram presents the kaiser's "pledge plan" for the occupation of part of Serbia as a guarantee in a "distorted" form, but this requires some imaginative interpretation. Bethmann-Hollweg's telegram omits the kaiser's statement that there is now no cause for war, but since the kaiser suggests the occupation of Belgrade and other parts of Serbia, it is obvious that he expects military action, which would be hard to distinguish from war. It is unlikely that Wilhelm II intended Austria to invade Serbia without a declaration of war. He also wants the Austrian army to have "the external *satisfaction d'honneur* of an ostensible success in the eyes of the world," which again suggests military action. The kaiser also wants a "guaranty for the enforcement and carrying out of the promises." Bethmann-Hollweg says the temporary occupation is to "force the Serbian government to the complete fulfilment of [Austria's] demands, and for the creation of guarantees of future good behaviour." The difference seems to lie in the word "complete," but the promises to Austria could not be carried out unless they were carried out completely. The kaiser's statement that the few differences could be settled by negotiation cannot mean that Austria is not to be satisfied, and it is not included in his suggestions for the proposed dispatch. Whether this was submitted to him before it was sent, as he requested, is not clear. The last paragraph is too much concerned with catering to Austria's sensibilities, but it does not materially distort the kaiser's plan, which was clearly designed to enable Austria to stop the Serbian intrigue without bringing on a world war.

If the sole purpose of this telegram to Tschirschky was to provide false evidence that Germany was trying to avoid war, and Bethmann-Hollweg was aware that Szögyény had told Vienna to pay no attention to proposals coming from Berlin, his last paragraph was both dangerous and unnecessary. It is also difficult to understand why two further telegrams were sent, one inquiring whether Bethmann-Hollweg's message had arrived and the other urging immediate action on its instructions.[142]

Late on the night of July 29, Tschirschky reported back to Bethmann-Hollweg that he had carried out the instructions and that Berchtold was ready to repeat his declaration of territorial disinterestedness, but with regard to Belgrade he could not reply at once. The report concluded,

"In spite of my representations as to the urgency of the matter, I have up to this evening received no further communication."[143]

Meanwhile a message had arrived in Berlin from Lichnowsky in London, which reported a suggestion by Grey that Germany should take part in mediation *à quatre*, already accepted in principle. Apparently Grey still believed he was talking about mediation between Austria and Russia, which his allies had refused. Grey also made a proposal similar to the kaiser's pledge plan, which envisaged occupation of Belgrade and other places by Austria, who would then announce her conditions. Grey said to the Italian ambassador that there was "no longer any question of a humiliating retreat by Austria, as the Serbs would in any case be punished and compelled, with the consent of Russia, to subordinate themselves to Austria's wishes."[144] How Grey arrived at the unrealistic idea that Russia would consent to Serbia's subordination to Austria is incomprehensible. It appears that he was as yet unaware of the Russian position, which was that no action against Serbia could be tolerated. The kaiser's plan also would have had no chance of acceptance by Russia even if Austria had agreed to it.

This message from Lichnowsky contained the unwelcome news that any hope of England's neutrality must be given up. In the early morning of July 30 Bethmann-Hollweg forwarded Lichnowsky's telegram to Tschirschky, instructing him to "urgently and impressively" suggest acceptance of mediation as proposed by Grey. Five minutes later he sent another message protesting Austria's alleged refusal to exchange opinions with Russia.[145] In both these messages he strongly insisted on Austrian acceptance of mediation.

Fritz Fischer insists that these two telegrams represent a change of attitude consequent on the news on the evening of July 29 that England's participation in the war was certain. His statement that they find no parallel among the documents of the night of July 29/30 ignores Bethmann-Hollweg's two telegrams concerning the pledge plan, which went out on July 29 at 10:18 and 10:30 p.m. Fischer's view is partly derived from his unjustified interpretation of Bethmann-Hollweg's version of the kaiser's pledge plan for the temporary occupation of parts of Serbia, but probably even more from his faith in Szögyény's telegram of July 27 which, according to his interpretation of it, told Vienna to pay no attention to mediation plans forwarded from Berlin. It seems certain that Bethmann-Hollweg was unaware that Vienna had been sent such a message and that he took the pledge plan seriously. Tschirschky's reply shows that he too took it seriously and that it was refused by Austria. It is true that Bethmann-Hollweg's language became somewhat stronger after Lichnowsky's July 29 telegram was received, because in the pledge plan message he had told Tschirschky to discuss the idea "thoroughly and impressively," while later he wanted him to speak "urgently and impressively."[146] Obviously the danger of war was becoming more acute.

Fischer's bias is shown by the fact that he considers everything Bethmann-Hollweg says in the worst possible light, but accepts any statement by an entente statesman as gospel. No mention is made, for example, of a telegram from London which reports Grey as giving Lichnowsky the false information that "the French are using all their influence at Petersburg toward a peaceable outcome" and that France has made no "actual war preparations."[147] This indicates the kind of falsehood with which France was deceiving Grey, who believed this misinformation. It is evident that the argument which assumes that Bethmann-Hollweg followed a double-faced policy throughout the crisis rests entirely upon Szögyény's telegram of July 27.

Sir Edward Grey still believed on July 29 that direct conversations between Austria and Russia were the best method, and evidently also believed that his proposed mediation between Austria and Russia was still a live issue. It appears that he never realized that France and Russia would accept mediation only between Austria and Serbia. Bethmann-Hollweg, too, was ready to give up on mediation as a solution, but only on July 30, when it was too late. Concentration on Germany's failure to put sufficient pressure on Austria to force her to back down before the superior power of the entente enables the heroes of entente mythology to draw attention from the plain fact that Germany was the only Power even to suggest that an ally should modify its policy during the whole course of the crisis. According to entente myth-makers, Russia must be considered entirely in the right, and any attempt to thwart her aim of destroying the Austro-Hungarian monarchy constitutes aggression.

Both Austria and Russia refused throughout to budge from their original positions. Austria insisted that Serbia must accept her demands completely, and refused to discuss the modification of her note with anyone. Russia took the stand from the outset that any Austrian attempt even to ask for explanations from Serbia would mean war.

On July 14, Austrian foreign minister Berchtold reported that in conversation with Premier Tisza he had argued that even after mobilisation a peaceful arrangement might be possible "if Serbia gives way in good time."[148] He never changed his view that complete Serbian submission was necessary. His instructions to Baron Wladimir von Giesl in Belgrade regarding the presentation of the ultimatum to Serbia stated that Austria "could not on any account consent to a prolongation of the term" and that she could not "enter into negotiations with Servia" with regard to her demands. Only "unconditional acceptance within the stated time" would be satisfactory. Giesl was told to avoid discussion of the contents or interpretation of the note.[149] On July 25, Berchtold categorically refused to accept any change in the forty-eight-hour time-limit, and declared that only "the unconditional acceptance of our demands could bring about a peaceful solution."[150]

When the Russians said they wanted the time extension so the Powers could examine the dossier, Berchtold replied that the dossier was for information only, and that there was no intention of asking the Powers for their objections.[151] When he received Grey's proposal for a conference, he rejected any idea of mediation based on the Serbian reply, and said that Austria required an "integral acceptance" of her demands.[152] He accepted talks with Russia, which were strongly advocated by both England and Germany, only with the stipulation that the Austro-Serbian question should not be discussed. He was ready to talk only about Russia's interests concerning Serbia. This meant he would discuss the maintenance of Serbian territorial integrity and sovereignty, but not the contents of the Austrian note to Serbia.[153]

The fact that Berchtold paid little attention to suggestions from Germany is apparent, but it is pretended that this is explained by Szögyény's telegram of July 27, which supposedly dictated her actions. Berchtold resented Grey's opinion that Austria was being urged forward by Germany, and made it clear that Austria was being pushed by nobody, but was "counselled by the vital interests of our monarchy."[154]

Even Russia's last offer to continue negotiations did not alter Berchtold's stand. On July 30, he telegraphed to Count Szápáry, his ambassador to Russia, that he wanted to continue the exchange of views with Russia. He stated that he was willing to explain his note to Serbia, but not to yield on any of the points it contained.[155] Szápáry reported that he had decided to resume the conversations, partly because he did not want to disavow the kaiser's statement that Austria was willing to continue them, and partly because he thought it better that Austria should appear to be the one attacked, and therefore to give "an ultimate proof of good will and thus put Russia in the wrong as much as possible."[156] When Szápáry saw Sazonov the next day he told him Berchtold was ready to discuss the interpretation of the note, but not to modify it.[157] This was exactly the attitude Berchtold had taken from the start.

Russian policy was settled on July 24 and was fixed in stone from that time on. It was Sergei Sazonov who decided that the Austrian note was unacceptable and reacted by declaring that it meant a European war. The Russian government immediately began to make military preparations, and the decision to institute the period preparatory to war was made the next day, before the Serbian reply had been given to Austria. By July 26 it was generally understood, although perhaps not by Sazonov, that a definite decision for war had been made.[158]

It is true that Sazonov made several proposals for a settlement, but every one required concessions by Austria, not by Russia. Three such proposals made on July 25, 26 and 27, are mentioned by Sir Arthur Nicolson, who remarked that "one really does not know where one is with M. Sazonov."[159] Sazonov's proposals were, first, that if Serbia appealed to the Powers Russia would "stand aside" and leave the matter in the hands of the other four Powers; second, that England and Italy should collaborate with Austria to settle the matter; third, that Russia would converse with Vienna. The first suggestion required mediation between Austria and Serbia and required concessions by Austria. The second accompanied the statement that some of Austria's demands were impossible and repetition of his request that England should intimidate Germany by proclaiming solidarity with France and Russia. The third meant a discussion concerning re-drafting the Austrian note to Serbia but required no change in the Russian position.[160] All these proposals appear to be part of Sazonov's plan to ensure Russia of England's support by a "moderate" policy rather than attempts to avert war.

All the Powers at one time or another expressed the view that Russia might be satisfied with a promise to respect the territorial integrity of Serbia. Sazonov definitely rejected this as inadequate.[161] Sazonov's final offer, made too late to have any significance, was that Russia would stop her military preparations if Austria declared her "readiness to eliminate from her ultimatum those points which violate the sovereign rights of Serbia."[162] The points which were supposed to violate the sovereign rights of Serbia were numbers five and six, which demanded that Austrian officials should take part in inquiries instituted against those who had been involved in the assassination plot. Austria had informed Russia on July 25 that in demanding collaboration of Austrian officials they "were thinking of establishing in Belgrade a secret *"bureau de sureté,"* similar to the Russian establishments in Paris and Berlin, which would cooperate with the Servian police and administrative authority."[163] The Russians naturally did not want any Austrian collaboration, because then there would be a genuine investigation. This might have revealed the full extent of Serbian responsibility for the crime, and might have uncovered the complicity of the Russian representatives in Belgrade. Their concern was not to preserve Serbian sovereignty, which was not threatened, but to conceal the truth about the archduke's murder and thus justify their determination to unleash a European war.

It was asserted in both England and France that Russia had done everything possible to ensure peace. Bienvenue-Martin and Grey maintained that Serbia's reply to the Austrian note of July 23, which they thought was almost completely satisfactory, was attributable to Russian advice.[164] No doubt Grey, at least, was not aware that it was Sazonov who had decided that some points were unacceptable and had so advised Serbia. Sazonov's acceptance of any measure France and England might propose to maintain peace was based on the knowledge that neither would propose any modification of Russian policy.

A telegram from the kaiser induced the tsar to reverse his decision for general mobilisation at 11 p.m. on July 28. It made no difference to the Russian mobilisation, because the Russian war minister secretly had given instructions that the general mobilisation should proceed.[165]

Sazonov's last offer was made July 30 after he had decided that war was inevitable and the tsar's consent to general mobilisation had been obtained: it is clear that its purpose was merely to delay German mobilisation while Russia completed her preparations for war.[166] His proposal reached Germany after Russia's general mobilisation had been authorized by the tsar for the second time.[167] That it was not serious is made plain by a series of telegrams between Paris and St. Petersburg, which showed that Russia was hastening her military measures while attempting to conceal them.[168]

Russian mobilisation was again, finally, decreed the next afternoon, and at 6 p.m. on July 30 the wires throughout the Russian Empire hummed with orders for general mobilisation. So died the last faint hope that Europe might be spared the catastrophe which brought an end to its domination of the world.

So much that is false has been written about mobilisation that the subject must be examined at length. Entente historians almost unanimously assert that German mobilisation meant war but that the mobilisation of other countries did not. In 1914 no one believed this except Sir Edward Grey, whose ignorance of military matters was almost complete. The assertion cannot be taken seriously, but it seems to be a necessary part of the indictment against Germany.

It was generally believed in 1914 that the first Power to declare general mobilisation would be blamed for the outbreak of war. It was considered such a momentous step that the culpability which flowed from it should be left to others. Jules Cambon wanted the French government to take appropriate action "to place the responsibility where it belongs." On July 30 he thought Germany intended to make France publish her mobilisation orders first. He urged France to foil this plan by declaring mobilisation only after Germany had done so, "so that British public opinion...cannot attribute to us any decision that led to war."[169]

The Russians pretended that their general mobilisation was an answer to that of Austria, which in fact took place later. According to historian Immanuel Geiss, the delay in German mobilisation was designed to put the responsibility for this act on Russia.

In the negotiations for the Franco-Russian alliance General Obruchev insisted that the French and Russian armies must be mobilised immediately and simultaneously as soon as either Power received news of mobilisation by the forces of the Triple Alliance. Mobilisation by France and Russia would be "followed immediately by active deeds, acts of war, in a word be inseparable from an aggression."[170] After the approval of the military convention, French General le Mouton de Boisdeffre, in conversation with the tsar, said that "mobilization is the declaration of war," to which the tsar replied, "That is exactly the way I understand it."[171] Russian General Dobrorolsky, in charge of mobilisation, took the same view.[172]

The most important military requirement of the Franco-Russian alliance was that on mobilisation the Russians should immediately launch an attack on Germany in order to force her to fight simultaneously in the east and the west to prevent her from shuttling her forces from one border to the other.[173] The greatest care of France throughout the succeeding years was to speed up Russian mobilisation to ensure the achievement of this objective.

On July 27, 1914, the English ambassador at St. Petersburg, Sir George Buchanan, told Sergei Sazonov, the Russian minister of foreign affairs, that if war were to be averted Russia must "do nothing to precipitate a conflict," and that he hoped mobilisation would be delayed as long as possible.[174] On July 30 Buchanan wrote that, if Austria rejected Sazonov's proposal of that day, Russia would proceed with general mobilisation and war would be inevitable. He did not know, of course, that Sazonov intended to proceed with the renewed general mobilisation at once. Also on July 30 Lieutenant-Colonel Repington, the military correspondent of *The Times,* wrote that "in a very short time after Russian mobilization is announced it will be a miracle if all Europe is not aflame."[175] *The New Cambridge Modern History* says, "The Russian general mobilization was the decisive calamity...There was no question in 1914 but that general mobilization by a great power must be followed by hostilities."[176]

There is no reason to believe that the Russian leaders, including the tsar, were not aware of the significance of mobilisation. On July 29, the tsar's telegram to the kaiser said, "I foresee that very soon I shall be overwhelmed by the pressure brought upon me, and be forced to take extreme measures which will lead to war."[177] Baron Schilling's description of the tsar's long hesitation in renewing the order for general mobilisation shows that both he and his advisors understood that they were making the final decision for war.[178]

Schilling says the tsar "still cherished the hope of preventing the general mobilization from becoming an irrevocable *casus belli,*" and that he therefore sent word to the kaiser that as long as negotiations continued his troops would not "make any provocative actions."[179] All the actions of the Russian government were authorized by the tsar, who must have understood that Russian policy aimed at deliberately deceiving a prospective enemy by concealing military preparations, thereby delaying enemy counteraction. Whether he believed it was possible to stop his armies on the frontier, or if this was simply a further device to gain time we cannot know. What is certain, however, is that he would have been unable to keep this promise, because the chief of the general staff had smashed his own telephone to prevent the tsar from contacting him.[180] The German leaders would have had to be very naive to take his promise seriously. To quote General Boisdeffre in 1894, they would have been placing themselves "in the situation of an individual who, with a pistol in his pocket, should let his neighbour put a weapon to his forehead without drawing his own."[181]

Sergei Sazonov stated on several occasions that mobilisation did not mean war, but there is no doubt that this assurance was part of the plan to lull the Germans into a sense of false security, and to pretend that Russia did not want war. At the same time that he stated that peace could be maintained in spite of Russian mobilisation, he took steps for it to proceed secretly "to avoid rendering more acute our relations with Germany."[182] The French advised Sazonov that Russia should declare her willingness to slow down her military measures, while continuing to strengthen them.[183]

On July 31, Sazonov told Buchanan there was "no chance of averting a general war unless Germany and France would agree, as Russia was ready to do, to keep their troops mobilized on their own side of the frontier pending final attempt to arrive at settlement." If we believe this, it means that Sazonov thought Germany's mobilisation did not mean war either, and that all the armies could remain mobilised without fighting.[184] In the light of all that had gone before, however, it is not credible that Sazonov was doing anything more than throwing dust in Grey's eyes, as he had been doing for the previous week.

The pretense that only German mobilisation meant war is an idea imposed on the entente apologists by the unfortunate fact that Germany succeeded in saddling all the other continental Powers with the onus of declaring mobilisation before her. They also insist that Germany's delay in mobilising was a trick designed to ensure this result.

The second decision for Russian general mobilisation was made on the afternoon of July 30, and the orders were sent out at 6 P.M. that evening. Luigi Albertini, straining to find a reason to blame Germany for any action which led to war, pretends that the Russian general mobilisation was the result of German threats.[185] Germany, threatened by Russia's extensive military measures on her eastern frontier, which had been proceeding since July 26, decided on July 29 to instruct Count Pourtalès, the German ambassador in St. Petersburg, to call Sazonov's attention "to the fact that further continuation of Russian mobilization measures would force us to mobilize, and in that case a European war could scarcely by prevented." Pourtalès delivered this message, which he described as a friendly communication, after the tsar had made the initial decision for mobilisation and before he changed his mind.[186] After the tsar had rescinded the order on July 28, the efforts of his advisers were almost continuously devoted to persuading him to renew it. Their success had nothing to do with a threat from Germany.

Austria decided on general mobilisation on the morning of July 31 and ordered it shortly after noon. This action was in response to the Russian partial mobilisation against Austria, since Vienna had not yet been informed about Russia's general mobilisation.[187]

Mobilisation of the French army was decreed at 3:40 p.m. on August 1: the telegram announcing it was sent out at 3:55 p.m.[188] As the time was 4:55 in Germany, French mobilisation came exactly five minutes before that of Germany.[189] Thus both France and Russia, whose alliance obligations required them to mobilise immediately when Germany did so, took this step before Germany.

While German mobilisation was forced by that of Russia, France was simply getting as quick a start as possible for the projected offensive against Germany. That France fully realized the significance of mobilisation is shown by a telegram from the new French premier, René Viviani, to Paul Cambon in London on August 1. The telegram stated that Russian mobilisation had followed that of Austria, and that German mobilisation was actually under way, although not yet proclaimed. French mobilisation was, he said, forced by the premature steps by Germany.[190] These statements were false. Russian general mobilisation had preceded that of Austria, and German preparations for war had lagged behind those of France and Russia.

There remain the controversial relations of England with Germany in the last few days before the British entered the war. Theobald von Bethmann-Hollweg has been severely criticized for the proposal to Sir Edward Goschen for British neutrality which he made on July 29. He offered a pledge to take no French territory in Europe, to respect the neutrality of Holland, and to maintain the integrity of Belgium if she did not side against Germany. In return for this England was to remain neutral and to look towards a general understanding with Germany.[191] It was not disgraceful for Bethmann-Hollweg to have made such a proposition, although it would certainly have been disgraceful for England to agree to it, in view of her obligations to France. Bethmann-Hollweg's mistake was his failure to understand that England was bound to assist France in a Franco-German war and that the British government was determined to fulfil its engagements. He did not realize that the relation between England and France was virtually an alliance. Bethmann-Hollweg is quoted as saying in 1912 that a new naval increase would make the Anglo-French bond "completely unbreakable." Apparently he did not perceive that it was already unbreakable.[192]

Bethmann-Hollweg was not altogether to blame for this misunderstanding. Grey's need to conciliate the left wing of the Liberal party had forced him to make some friendly gestures to Germany, and this no doubt deceived some Germans as well. He was also misled by Grey's policy during the crisis. Grey's acceptance of localization and his repeated statements that he had no interest in the Austro-Serbian dispute and wanted only Austro-Russian mediation seemed to indicate a friendly attitude towards Germany. Grey's statement that a general war would involve four nations, omitting England, was also misleading. Bethmann-Hollweg could not know that Grey's policy was not a sign of British disinclination to fight Germany if war came, but of his fear that too strong a stand on his part would alienate opinion in the cabinet and in Parliament.

Although Bethmann-Hollweg's proposal for British neutrality in the war has been castigated as a colossal blunder, it had little influence on the course of events. His telegram did draw Grey's attention to the question of Belgium and alert him to the possibility of using the question of Belgian neutrality to influence some members of the cabinet. It is probable, however, that he would have thought of this expedient anyway, since care had been taken after Agadir to ensure that France would allow Germany to enter Belgium first. As it turned out the Belgian question made little difference to the cabinet's final decision.

An incident which took place on August 1 illustrates the extent to which Fritz Fischer goes to show Germany's responsibility for France's entry into the war. Just before noon that day Lichnowsky sent a telegram to Berlin in which he said that Grey had "asked me if I thought I could assure him that in case France would remain neutral in a Russo-German war we would not attack the French."[193] Sir William Tyrrell, Grey's private secretary, had suggested that in this case England would guarantee France's neutrality."[194] The German government was delighted at the prospect of keeping France neutral. Bethmann-Hollweg immediately replied that German troops would not cross the French border until 7 p.m. on August 3, pending agreement on French neutrality.[195] Less than seven hours after Lichnowsky's first telegram was received, he informed Berlin that there was no prospect that such an English proposal would be made.[196] A telegram from King George V informed the kaiser that there had been a misunderstanding.[197]

The only light thrown on this incident by the British documents comes from telegrams exchanged between Grey and Sir Francis Bertie in Paris. Grey informed Bertie that he had suggested that after mobilisation the French and German armies might remain on their borders without crossing the frontier. He did not know, he said, if this would be consistent with France's obligations under her alliance, but if so England could agree to remain neutral as long as the German army did not cross the frontier. Bertie naturally replied that he could not imagine that this would be consistent with France's obligations to Russia.[198] Why Grey should have made such a suggestion is a mystery. Cambon had told him on July 29 that France "was bound to help Russia if Russia was attacked."[199]

Fischer maintains that there was a genuine offer that England would guarantee French neutrality if Germany would refrain from attacking France. He tells us that Germany's rigid military plans prevented her from taking advantage of the offer, and that an opportunity to keep France neutral was lost.[200]

No such English proposal was ever made, and the German response was based on informal conversations about a remote possibility. There is, therefore, no substance to Fischer's story that Moltke's opposition forced Germany to carry on with the invasion of France.

In fact, German military plans were no more rigid than those of any other Power. General Moltke's distress when it appeared his plans might be overthrown was similar to that of the Russian generals when they were ordered to carry out partial mobilisation. Fortunately for their peace of mind, neither general staff had to alter its plans.

Germany's plan to throw the bulk of her army against France and attempt to hold Russia in the east was forced on her because she was faced with a war on two fronts against armies outnumbering her own by at least 800,000 men. Unfortunately for Germany, this strategy was based on the historical slowness of Russian mobilisation, which provided the possibility of defeating France before the Russians could penetrate far into east Germany. By 1914 the Russian delay in mobilisation behind that of Germany had been reduced to four days, and Russia's early adoption of the measures preparatory to war had enabled her to make up this time. Russia was therefore able to send her armies into Prussia at the same time that Germany could move against France. Nevertheless, the German plan of campaign still offered her the only possible chance of success. To get bogged down in the vast spaces of Russia while being attacked in the rear by France would have been an irrational strategy. An argument that this would have been a superior plan rests on the assumption that French neutrality was a real possibility.

Drawn aside by the red herring of Germany's rigid plan of campaign, some historians ignore the real significance of this incident, which was that Germany was eager to avoid war with France if that were possible. It was impossible, not because of the rigidity of Germany's military plans, but because France had not the slightest intention of shirking the obligations imposed on her by the Franco-Russian Alliance. She had already made this clear to Russia, England and Germany, and was within half an hour of ordering the mobilisation of her army when Lichnowsky's first telegram about Grey's odd "proposal" arrived in Berlin from Vienna. The question of whether Germany could have stopped the invasion of France if Grey's supposed offer had been genuine is thus entirely irrelevant.

The final significant event in Anglo-German relations concerns the neutrality of Belgium. On July 31, Grey told French ambassador Paul Cambon that the preservation of Belgian neutrality would be an important factor in determining the British attitude. He then addressed to France and Germany requests for the assurance that Belgium's neutrality would be respected. Grey's false statement in his memoirs that this was done without any previous arrangement with France is intended to persuade his readers that France and Germany were being treated equally.[201] In fact, arrangements had already been made which provided that France would allow the Germans to enter Belgium first. Plan 17B was put into effect on August 2, 1914.

The British foreign office had been afraid for some time that Belgium might allow a German passage without fighting, as she could have done quite correctly. To prevent this Grey sent Belgium a note informing her that England expected she would "to the utmost of her power maintain neutrality."[202] Belgium was thus faced with the necessity of judging which side was likely to win, and as it appeared at the time that there was little doubt of Entente success, it was imperative for the Belgians to oppose Germany.

When the British cabinet first discussed the Belgian question on July 29, it was decided that "if the matter arises it will be rather one of policy than of legal obligation." The cabinet considered it doubtful that a single state was bound to maintain Belgian neutrality if the others did not do so.[203]

Sir Edward Grey informed Prince Lichnowsky, the German ambassador, on August 1 that the neutrality of Belgium would play an important role in England's decision to take part in the war, but when Lichnowsky asked him if England would remain neutral if Germany respected Belgian neutrality he replied that he could not promise that.[204] Germany was thus advised on August 1 that a change of plan on Germany's part with regard to Belgium would not keep England neutral.

The decision that England should take part in the war was made at the cabinet meeting which began at 11 a.m. on Sunday, August 2. At that meeting the cabinet authorized Grey to tell Paul Cambon that the British fleet "would not allow the German fleet to make the channel a base of hostile operations."[205] Grey assured Cambon that if the German fleet came "into the channel or through the North Sea to undertake hostile operations against the French coasts or shipping" the British fleet would oppose it with all its power.[206] Viscount John Morley and John Burns resigned from the cabinet in protest against the decision to enter the European war.

Grey states that the German promise not to attack the French coast eliminated the naval question as a factor in the British government's decision.[207] His promise to Cambon, however, included the phrase "or shipping," which means that he had promised to protect the French merchant marine from German attack. There was no mention of any obligation by France not to attack German shipping: the French could have wiped German commerce from the seas and the British navy would have prevented Germany from protecting it or retaliating. The Germans agreed not to attack the French coast, but made no mention of French shipping until Bethmann-Hollweg declared on August 4 that Germany would, "in case of reciprocity," agree not to attack French "commercial navigation."[208] This decision of August 2 therefore bound England to go to war with Germany at sea, and the probability that this would not involve war on land as well was extremely remote. The French assumed that British cooperation was now assured.[209]

It is possible that the German invasion of Belgium helped Prime Minister Herbert Asquith to take his cabinet into the war with the loss of only two members, but it was not a determining factor in the decision to take part in the war. Part of the explanation for the cabinet's agreement to the statement that England would protect the French coasts and shipping can be found in a letter from Conservative leader of the opposition Bonar Law which reached Asquith before the morning meeting. It assured him of the united support of the opposition "in all measures required by England's intervention in the war."[210] This not only ensured a House of Commons majority for a war policy, but showed that there would be no difficulty in forming a coalition if this should prove necessary. The position of the opponents of the war policy was greatly weakened, and the question of whether the country would go to war gave way to the problem of what their attitude would be when war was declared.

From this time on, Asquith's main concern was to preserve the unity of his cabinet. After the Sunday evening cabinet meeting, Sir John Simon and Lord Beauchamp decided to resign, which meant the possible loss of four members. Asquith was determined to make the war a Liberal struggle, and thus prevent the rise of an anti-war party. He therefore wished to retain as many ministers as possible, to preserve the appearance of substantial unanimity and save the unity of the party.

When the cabinet assented to the principal points of Grey's speech to Parliament on August 3, it looked as though there would be four resignations. Asquith's talk at the cabinet meeting showed that the only decision left for the dissenters was whether they were ready to remain in a war cabinet.[211] During the course of the day Simon and Beauchamp decided to stay in the cabinet. No doubt the threat to Belgium had some influence on their decision, but at least in the case of Simon, Asquith's appeal to maintain the unity of the party was an important consideration.[212] Simon's conversion was far from thorough, and he remained a reluctant warrior for some time.[213]

It is evident that the British cabinet's decision to enter the European war was made before the presentation of the German ultimatum to Belgium. The question of Belgian neutrality helped Asquith to maintain his cabinet almost intact and to ensure that the war would be fought by a Liberal government and not by a coalition.

There is no evidence to support the belief that either Germany or Austria wanted a European war. After the murder of Archduke Franz Ferdinand, however, the Austrians were convinced that the time had come to put a stop to the subversive activities which were being carried on in the monarchy by Serbian secret societies. On the one hand, they believed that Serbia would take supine acceptance of the crime as evidence that Austria was helpless to protect herself against their intrigues, and on the other they thought that abhorrence of the deed would deter Russia from active support of its authors. It therefore seemed that strong action was necessary and that conditions were favourable for its success.

Germany, which for some time had been discouraging Austria from taking venturesome steps, now believed that action was necessary to prevent her collapse. To maintain Austria as a Great Power was considered a matter of vital interest to Germany, and it had always been held that a serious threat to her existence would compel Germany to support her.

The Balkan wars, instigated by Russia, had altered the balance of power drastically to the detriment of the Central Powers and greatly increased the territory and influence of Serbia. That country had been given hope to expect that Russia would support still further expansion at the expense of Austria-Hungary, and Russian agents had encouraged Serbia to work for Austria's disintegration.

Germany and Austria recognized that Serbia was the spearhead of the Russian offensive against the monarchy, and that Russia might be prepared to go to war to prevent her weapon from being blunted. They hoped that Russia would hesitate to launch a war in the cause of assassination, but believed that if she did so her determination to carry her offensive against Austria to the point of embarking on a European war would be apparent. In that case, to allow a further weakening of Austria while Russia continued to strengthen her armed forces would be suicidal. Self-preservation required that the Russian challenge should be accepted under circumstances which would never be as favourable again.

In the event, the Russians immediately determined to fight to prevent any action by Austria which might reveal the truth about Serbia's connection with the crime of Sarajevo. Although their military preparations would be still further advanced in a few years, they were already confident that the Dual Alliance could defeat Austria and Germany, and they were certain that Italy would not intervene on the side of her nominal allies. Russia's war aim, determined before the crime of Sarajevo, was the dismemberment of Austria-Hungary.

The primary goal of French policy had been for many years the recovery of Alsace-Lorraine. This too could be achieved only by war. For this purpose France had allied herself with Russia, neutralized Italy and formed the Entente with England. To strengthen her ties with Russia and weaken the Central Powers she had involved herself more and more in Russia's expansionist policies. She was fully aware of the role Serbia was expected to play in the weakening of Austria, and no doubt had as little faith in Serbia's innocence as Russia had.

In contrast to these definite aims of France and Russia, which both recognized could be achieved only by war, Germany and Austria aimed at defending the right of the Austro-Hungarian monarchy to exist. Austria specifically denied any aim of acquiring territory from Serbia, and repeatedly stated that she wished only to secure herself against the subversive activities of Serbian organizations on her soil. As for Germany, neither Fritz Fischer nor any of his disciples has produced a shred of evidence to indicate that Germany went to war to achieve any of the aims which appeared as German policy during the war. When someone undertakes a genuine study of allied aims during the war these will naturally show the same kind of continuity with pre-war policy that Fischer claims for German war-time aims. For example, the decision of the British colonial office on August 7, 1914, that England should attempt to acquire all of Germany's African colonies has obvious continuity with British pre-war policy. No one has claimed that England went to war to acquire Germany's colonies, but this conclusion would be at least as plausible as the blanket assumption concerning German war aims.

In summary, the Triple Entente fought to dismember the Austro-Hungarian monarchy and reconquer Alsace-Lorraine, while the Central Powers fought to defend their existing territory. France and Russia played their traditional role as the expansionist Powers of Europe, Germany and Austria remained the conservative Powers who wished to maintain the *status quo*. Germany's wartime aims no more prove that Germany began the war to achieve those aims than the Treaty of Versailles proves that the allies began the war to impose its terms on Germany.

Notes

1.LN, II, 373-6.

2.Vladimir Dedijer, *The Road to Sarajevo*, p. 446.

3.ARB, I, 9-13.

4.Luigi Albertini, *The Origins of the War of 1914*, II, 55-8.

5.*Ibid.*, p. 97; M. E. Durham, *The Sarajevo Crime*, p. 87.

6.Ljuba Jovanovitch, *The Murder of Sarajevo*, p. 3.

7.Albertini, II, 69, 75-80.

8.Durham, p. 52.

9.Albertini, II, 97.

10.*Ibid.*, pp. 82, 86.

11.*Ibid.*, pp. 102-5; Durham, p. 153.

12.Dedijer, pp. 290-7.

13.*Ibid.*, pp. 278, 288.

14.Jovanovitch, p. 8.

15.KD, no. 12.

16.Collected Diplomatic Documents Relating to the Outbreak of the European War, Serbian Blue Book, no. 8.

17.SBB, no. 30.

18.KD, no. 91.

19.Jovanovitch, p. 4.

20.M. Bogitshevich, *Causes of the War*, p. 132.

21.*Ibid.*, p. 134.

22.ARB, I, 1-3.

23.*Ibid.*, p. 13.

24.Immanuel Geiss, *German Foreign Policy, 1871-1914*, p. 172; K.H. Jarausch, *The Enigmatic Chancellor*, pp. 153, 155-6.

25.Albertini, II, 65-6.

26.G. P. Gooch, *Before the War*, II, 446-7.

27.F. L. Schuman, *War and Diplomacy in the French Republic*, p. 206.

28.ARB, I, no. 2.

29.*Ibid.*, no. 3.

30.S. B. Fay, *Origins of the World War*. II, p. 227.

31.ARB, I, no. 5.

32.Jarausch, p. 153.

33.Geiss, p. 164.

34.Jarausch, pp. 155-6.

35.Geiss, p. 172.

36.Jarausch, pp. 153-4, 156.

37.KD, no. 15.

38.Albertini, II, 140.

39.Fay, II, 211, fn.

40.*Ibid.*, pp. 212-13.

41.ARB, I, no. 8.

42.*Ibid.*, nos. 6, 7, 10; KD, nos. 15, 18, 19.

43.ARB, I, no. 12.

44.*Ibid.*, nos. 13, 14, 19.

45.*Ibid.*, nos. 19, 26.

46.*Ibid.*, no. 21.

47.*Ibid.*, no. 23.

48.*Ibid.*, no. 26; KD, no. 65.

49.KD, nos. 31, 40.

50.KD, no. 46.

51.KD, no. 94.

52.KD, no. 63.

53.KD, no. 61.

54.BD, XI, nos. 50, 56.

55.*French Yellow Book*, no. 14.

56.KD, Supp. IV, no. 2.

57.KD, nos. 83, 88.

58.BD, XI, no. 60.

59.M. F. Schilling, *How the War Began in 1914*, p. 25.

60.Immanuel Geiss, July 1914, p. 131.

61.BD, XI, no. 67.

62.F. Stieve, *Isvolsky and the World War*, p. 212; KD, no. 134; ARB, I, 45.

63.BD, XI, no. 101.

64.*Ibid.*, no. 84.

65.*Ibid.*, nos. 73, 77.

66.*Ibid.*, no. 79.

67.*Ibid.*, no. 86.

68.ARB, II, no. 6.

69.KD, no. 100.

70.ARB, I, no. 27.

71.Schilling, pp. 28-9.

72.Ibid; pp. 30-31; Geiss, July 1914, pp. 186-7, no. 59.

73.BD, XI, no. 101.

74.Albertini, pp. 352-60.

75.Geiss, July 1914, pp. 207-8, no. 76.

76.Fay, II, 308, 314, 321.

77.E. D. Morel, *Truth and the War*, p. 136.

78.Fay, II, 317-18.

79.*Ibid.*, pp. 317-21.

80.L. C. F. Turner, "The Russian Mobilization in 1914," *Journal of Contemporary History*, Vol. 3, no. 1, January, 1968, pp. 76, 87.

81.BD, XI, no. 91.

82.*Ibid.*, no. 99.

83.*Ibid.*, no. 98.

84.FYB, no. 32.

85.BD, XI, no. 132.

86.Gisbert von Romberg, *The Falsifications of the Russian Orange Book*, pp. 26, 28, 36.

87.BD, XI, no. 122; KD, nos. 179, 192.

88.Albertini, II, 343-4.
89.*Ibid.*, p. 372.
90.FO800/55.
91.DDF3, XI, no. 12.
92.BD, XI, no. 160.
93.Schuman, p. 206.
94.BD, XI, no. 125.
95.*Ibid.*
96.*Ibid.*, nos. 139, 140.
97.Albertini, pp. 343-4; KD no. 199.
98.KD, no. 242.
99.BD, XI, nos. 192, 218, 263; KD no. 248.
100.BD, XI, no. 183; DDF3, XI, no. 123.
101.DDF3, XI, no. 190.
102.Romberg, pp. 27-8.
103.ARB, II, no. 90.
104.Albertini, pp. 305, 309.
105.S. Dobrorolski, *The Mobilization of the Russian Army*, p. 103, quoted in Fay, II, 319-20.
106.Albertini, II, 308.
107.LN, II, 329-30; BD, XI, no. 132.
108.Albertini, II, 449-50.
109.KD, no. 61.
110.Albertini, II, 261-3.
111.ARB, I, no. 15.
112.DDF3, XI, no. 63.
113.BD, XI, no. 114.
114.ARB, II, no. 47.
115.Romberg, pp. 28-9.
116.BD, XI, nos. 153, 208.
117.*Ibid.*, no. 176; KD, no. 258.
118.KD, no. 258; BDXI, no. 176.
119.KD, no. 277.
120.*Ibid.*, no. 400; ARB, III, no. 25.
121.KD, no. 279.
122.KD, nos. 311, 313.
123.ARB, II, no. 68; KD, no. 277.
124.KD, no. 257.
125.ARB, II, no. 32.
126.Albertini, II, 454; KD, no. 213.
127.Albertini, pp. 455-6.
128.ARB, II, no. 93; KD, no. 339.
129.ARB, II, no. 69.
130.*Ibid.*, no. 67.
131.ARB, I, no. 15.
132.*Ibid.*, no. 14.
133.*Ibid.*, no. 7.

134.*Ibid.*, no. 14.

135.*Ibid.*, no. 26.

136.ARB, II, no. 21.

137.*Ibid.*, no. 22.

138.BD, XI, no. 221.

139.KD, no. 293.

140.*Ibid.*, no. 282.

141.*Ibid.*, no. 323.

142.*Ibid.*, no. 377, fn.3, p. 332.

143.*Ibid.*, no. 388.

144.*Ibid.*, no. 368.

145.*Ibid.*, nos. 395, 396.

146.*Ibid.*, nos. 323, 395.

147.*Ibid.*, no. 435.

148.ARB, I, 19.

149.*Ibid.*, no. 28.

150.ARB, II, nos, 27, 28, 29, 30.

151.*Ibid.*, no. 39.

152.*Ibid.*, no. 93.

153.*Ibid.*, no. 95; III, no. 19.

154.ARB, III, no. 13.

155.*Ibid.*, no. 45.

156.*Ibid.*, no. 75.

157.*Ibid.*, no. 97.

158.Schilling, pp. 28-9; Geiss, July 1914, no. 76.

159.BD, XI, nos. 125, 170, 179 fn., 239.

160.Romberg, pp. 24-5.

161.Schilling, pp. 50-51, 66.

162.Romberg, p. 47.

163.ARB, II, no. 38.

164.FYB, no. 85; KD, no. 258.

165.*Foreign Affairs* Special Supplement, October, 1919, p. 13.

166.Schilling, pp. 49-50.

167.KD, no. 421.

168.Romberg, pp. 40, 48-9.

169.DDF3, XI, no. 203; Geiss, July 1914, p. 313.

170.DDF1, IX, no. 409.

171.*L'Alliance Franco-Russe*, p. 95 ff, quoted in Fay, II, 480.

172.*Ibid.*, p. 481.

173.DDF1, IX, no. 444.

174.BD, , no. 179.

175.*The Times*, July 30, 1914, p. 7f.

176.*New Cambridge Modern History*, XII, 354.

177.KD, no. 332.

178.Schilling, pp. 65-6.

179.*Ibid.*, pp. 66, 72.

180.*Ibid.*, pp. 64, 66.

181.Fay, II, 480.

182.KD, nos. 343, 365, 445; Schilling, pp. 69, 102.

183.Romberg, p. 49.

184.BD, XI, no. 459.

185.Albertini, II, p. 556.

186.KD, nos. 342, 378.

187.ARB, III, nos. 49, 50.

188.Romberg, p. 58; DDF3, XI, no. 507.

189.KD, no. 554, fn.

190.DDF3, XI, no. 523.

191.KD, no. 373.

192.Jarausch, pp. 113, 135.

193.KD, no.562

194.*Ibid.*, no. 578.

195.*Ibid.*, nos. 57, 578.

196.KD, no. 603.

197.BD, XI, no. 612.

198.BD, XI, no. 419.

199.BD, XI, no. 367.

200.Fritz Fischer, *Germany's Aims in the First World War*, pp. 86-87.

201.Sir Edward Grey, *Twenty-Five Years*, I, 319.

202.BD, VIII, no. 315.

203.CAB 41/35/22.

204.KD, no. 596.

205.H. H. Asquith, *Memories and Reflections*, II, 12.

206.BD, XI, no. 487.

207.Grey, II, 3.

208.KD, nos. 714, 829; BD, XI, no. 531.

209.R. Poincaré, *The Memoirs of Raymond Poincaré*, pp. 227-8; FYB, no. 143.

210.A. Chamberlain, *Down the Years*, p. 99.

211.John Morley, *Memorandum on Resignation*, p. 25.

212.Christopher Addison, *Four and a Half Years*, I, 34.

213.G. A. R. Riddell, *War Diary*, p. 14.

Fifteen

Conclusion

Historians of the future, if indeed the human race has a future, will no doubt look back on the twentieth century as a period when militarism achieved a dominance in human affairs never before equalled in history. When the Romans coined the phrase, "*Si vis pacem, para bellum,*" they could not have dreamed that it would one day be accepted throughout the world as a pearl of political wisdom.

It would have been impossible to impose this conviction on the general public without the cooperation of militarist historians, who propagate the theory that war is caused by evil nations who refuse to get along with the good nations, of which their own nation is obviously a shining example. This requires the falsification and distortion of history, in order to show how all the conflicts preceding a war, and the outbreak of the war itself, were caused by the actions of the nation chosen as the scapegoat. That nation is the loser of the most recent war, as the now-dominant winners can impose their view on the world, sometimes even with the cooperation of sycophant historians from the losing nation.

The Great War provides by far the best example of the falsification of history for propaganda purposes. The history of the last ten years before the war is a classic example of the kind of manipulation used to produce the beliefs which support militarism. It gives strong support to the view that war is unrelated to any failure in political organization, but exists only because evil nations oppose good nations.

The currently popular history of Europe between 1870 and 1914 is pure mythology. The picture of Germany as an aggressive, expansionist disturber of the peace is completely unrelated to the actual events of the period. Until after the turn of the twentieth century it was almost universally recognized that the German Empire was a conservative, stabilizing force whose policy upheld the *status quo*. It was equally apparent that the restless, aggressive Powers on the continent were France and Russia, whose policies frequently led them into near collision with the British Empire.

The predominance of Bismarck's Germany was brought to an end in 1894 by the Franco-Russian alliance, which balanced the Triple Alliance and produced a temporary equilibrium. The aim of French policy, however, was to destroy this equilibrium and construct a combination which could overpower Germany and restore Alsace-Lorraine to France. The first step in this plan was the detachment of Italy from the Triple Alliance; the second was the making of the Anglo-French entente.

When England decided that compromise with France and Russia was preferable to continued conflict, it became necessary to find a method of conciliating France. The French requirement was that England should join an anti-German coalition, and because the British foreign office judged that friction with Germany was less dangerous than the continual clashes with France and Russia, this condition was accepted.

The Anglo-French entente was the crucial event which determined the history of the twentieth century. England's decision to ally herself with France involved her in France's aggressive designs and inevitably brought her into conflict with Germany. The immediate result was the beginning of a period of continental strife, initiated by French foreign minister Théophile Delcassé. He had the conviction that with British support he could challenge Germany by ignoring her interests in Morocco and proceeding with the conquest of that country.

The propaganda view of history is particularly important for England, because the disastrous results of the policy followed make it imperative for her advocates to insist that there was no alternative. They do this by perpetuating the idea that German policy left England no choice other than to support France and Russia against a German attempt to destroy the British Empire and dominate the world.

Germans of the Fritz Fischer school are impelled by the need to find a scapegoat for the disasters which overtook Germany, and the imperial government is readily available. As they no doubt realize that Germany had no way to escape being crushed by the Triple Entente once it came into being, they must make Germany responsible for its creation and for her own isolation. They dismiss the defection of Italy by the fiction that Italy remained loyal to the Triple Alliance but did not fight in 1914 because her allies were fighting an offensive war. This requires a complete disregard of Franco-Italian relations after 1902.

These historians then imagine that the Anglo-French entente was instigated by German policy. The British decision to ally herself with France had nothing whatever to do with the German navy or with the balance of power. The Franco-Russian alliance had already balanced the Triple Alliance, even before the detachment of Italy, as everyone in Europe understood.

For France the attraction of the entente lay in her desire to create a coalition which could overawe Germany and force the restoration of Alsace-Lorraine. Delcassé made no secret of the fact that he believed in the certainty of a German defeat in a war in which France had British support. It can, of course, be argued that it was Bismarck's annexation of Alsace-Lorraine which fuelled the French desire for revenge, but few people familiar with French history would assume that even without this annexation France would have been reconciled to her defeat.

The perpetrators of the perverse mythology which condemns Germany for trying to protect her treaty rights against French encroachment cannot take such a view seriously. It was Germany's methods which were objectionable, they say. It would be hard to devise a less warlike gesture than the kaiser's visit to Tangier, so perhaps it is Germany's pacific attitude which is objectionable, as is her peaceful method of acquiring colonies. The reality is that in their eyes Germany, as an inferior upstart Power, had no business attempting to protect herself against the violation of her rights by the established legitimate Powers.

Having embarked on a policy which brought England into conflict with Germany, the British government was faced with the necessity of rationalizing this policy. The method chosen was to raise the spectre of a German threat to British naval supremacy. Although the German navy was never close to being a threat to England's naval power, most historians have accepted this as a real reason for Anglo-German enmity. Here again British propaganda has triumphed over fact and reason.

The real threat, if one existed, was the threat to England's commercial supremacy, but the exploitation of this as an expressed threat would have been less respectable and less effective than a campaign involving the German navy. The spectacular growth of German industry and trade had made Germany a world power in a single generation: it was the desire to block this German rise to power that provided the mainspring of Anglo-German antagonism.

It becomes quite clear as we follow the imaginary history written by entente myth writers that Germany was a usurper who had no right to be treated as an equal amongst the European Powers. She had no right to follow all the other Powers in building a modern navy, no right to acquire bases or coaling stations, no right to have an army to defend herself against the larger armies of her neighbours, and no right to compete for the trade of the world. In fact, Germany had no right to exist as a Great Power, but should have been satisfied to remain disunited, a permanent parade ground for French armies.

At the same time, Germany is described as the *deus ex machina* which determined the whole course of events after 1900. She not only encircled herself by creating the Triple Entente but supposedly initiated all the events which threatened the peace of Europe in the succeeding years. No reader of this mythical history could guess that France was the country which undertook the military conquest of Morocco in 1900 and carried it forward continuously until its completion in 1912, or that every German move was a reaction to this French campaign.

Reliable evidence, according to Fischer and his disciples, comes exclusively from German sources, because the Germans are not only omnipotent but omniscient. When some German says that Russia is not ready for war and France wants peace, these opinions become gospel truth. An examination of French or Russian policy is unnecessary. If some Germans believe in the strength and efficiency of their army, no further proof of that army's superiority over the French and Russian armies combined is needed. The belief of the French and Russian staffs that they have a good chance of defeating Germany and Austria without British help is irrelevant.

In a sense this picture of pre-war history is very flattering to Germany, since Germany is the only Power with a policy and the other Powers simply react to German actions, like planets revolving around a sun. At first sight it seems difficult to understand how such a view is sustainable, but it soon becomes apparent that the origin of these effusions lies in the fact that the authors know very little about what was happening in any other country. They begin by assuming German responsibility for everything that took place, which relieves them of the task of relating German actions to those of other countries, and requires only some knowledge of German society, politics and foreign policy. Their conclusions are inherent in their premise that Germany was the only Power that counted.

The superior power and knowledge of the Germans is called into question, however, by their almost incredible stupidity in understanding their own interests. The German leaders, supposedly determined to dominate the world by military force, lacked the elementary common sense to perceive that the situation in 1905 presented them with a glorious opportunity which was unlikely ever to occur again. Instead of seizing this opportunity, they waited until their enemies had amassed such overwhelming power as to render their attempt at domination almost hopeless.

German interventions in Morocco were almost equally stupid: according to these mentors, they never knew what they wanted, but simply made trouble in the hope of annoying the other Powers, or perhaps disrupting their alliances. We are also told that they usually attained none of their objectives, although they say the Germans did not know what they wanted.

Immanuel Geiss tells us that Germany developed a modern industry in order to use it as an instrument of power. As this policy of industrialization was illegitimate in his eyes, Germany had no right to compete with other Powers for world markets, raw materials, or areas of investment, no right to create a large merchant marine. It had no right to build a navy, a right freely conceded to England, France, Russia, the United States and Japan. In other words, Germans were an inferior people, who should have recognized their inferiority and been content to allow others to enter the modern world without them.

Another characteristic of entente history is the belief that words speak louder than actions. This is seen in the discussion of both imperialist expansion and war. When some Germans, usually without much influence on the German government, agitated for an imperialist policy and bewailed the fact that Germany did not have one, they represent Germany's rampant imperialism. When British or French politicians stated that their empires were large enough and they did not want more territory, this demonstrates that they were "satisfied Powers." The fact that they were continually engaged in expanding their empires by military force, while Germany took no such action is ignored. The circumstance that in both cases the words were directly opposed to the conduct of the governments concerned is irrelevant.

Entente myth-makers apply the same twisted logic to the discussion of war. When a few individual Germans say that Germany needs a war, this indicates that Germany has an irresistible urge to start one. The fact that Germany fought no war between 1871 and 1914 while British and French armies fought almost constantly is immaterial. A statement by German leaders that they will fight to preserve the existence of Austria-Hungary demonstrates the warlike tendencies of Germany, while repeated declarations by British statesmen that they will fight to prevent the defeat of France shows the strictly defensive attitude of England.

The question of war preparations is usually disposed of by extensive falsification. Entente historians commonly assert, for example, that the French army was much smaller than the German army, although every military writer of the time maintained that the two armies were evenly matched, and that France could meet Germany on equal terms. Germany's armed forces and number of trained men are inflated, while those of France and Russia are reduced. The same tactic is applied to the discussion of armaments expenditures, if these are mentioned at all.

Emphasis on Germany's preparations for war while ignoring those of other Powers once again highlights the historians' determination to pay no attention to events in any country but Germany. The reality that the expenditure of the entente Powers on war preparations greatly exceeded that of Germany and Austria is presumably beside the point. If one depended on these historians' accounts of the matter it would be impossible to guess that France alone had more military equipment than Germany in every category except heavy siege artillery. Accounts of the supposed Anglo-German naval race are designed to obscure the reality that England began racing long before Germany and raced so far in advance that Germany never came close to threatening British naval supremacy.

The Agadir crisis was a great step along the road which led to war. British foreign secretary Grey's eagerness to support France in defying an international treaty and flouting Germany convinced the kaiser that England was determined to force a quarrel on him at the earliest opportunity. It was soon known throughout Europe that he could no longer be as firmly counted on to use his influence on the side of peace as he had done in the past. The arms race was given a new impetus, and an early outbreak of the European war was everywhere expected.

Russia in the fall of 1911 launched an offensive designed to organize the Balkans under Russian control and achieve her avowed objective of destroying the Austro-Hungarian monarchy. The most significant achievement of the Balkan alliance created under Russian auspices was a great expansion of Serbia, the state selected by Russia as the spearhead of her attack on Austria.

The Balkan wars substantially weakened Austria and altered the balance of power in favour of the entente, forcing Germany to increase her army to make up the loss. Despite this gain by the entente Powers, Germany nevertheless used her influence on the side of peace throughout the crisis caused by the Balkan wars, which was no doubt a major factor in postponing the war.

The climax of the Serbian programme of subversion, espionage and assassination came on June 28, 1914, with the murder of Archduke Franz Ferdinand and his consort. Although the intention to commit the crime was known in advance to the Serbian government and to the Russian military and diplomatic representatives in Belgrade, no serious attempt to warn the Austrian government was made.

It was believed in Austria and Germany, and must have been well understood throughout Europe, that passive acceptance of this outrage would encourage the Serbians and their Russian sponsors to intensify their campaign for the destruction of the monarchy. The Austrians therefore decided that the existence of their Empire required that an effort should be made to bring the long-continued Serbian provocations to an end.

The German government concurred in the opinion that Serbia's activities posed a deadly threat to Austria, and decided to support her in a serious attempt to stop them. The kaiser and his chancellor therefore agreed to give Austria a free hand in taking whatever action she thought necessary.

The German decision to back Austria represented no new policy. It was understood that the maintenance of Austria was vital to the security of

Germany, and that if Austria's existence was threatened Germany would go to war if necessary to prevent her downfall. The acceptance of the idea that Austria was so menaced made a German determination to support her almost automatic.

The Austrian government, correctly convinced that Serbia was deeply involved in the plot to murder the archduke, decided to present Serbia with an ultimatum which, if accepted, would impose on her a severe humiliation and a great loss of prestige, thus weakening her position as the leader of the attack on the integrity of Austria-Hungary. If Serbia refused her consent, which was considered highly probable, military action would be taken to force her acceptance.

The Russian government decided from the outset that it would countenance no investigation of Serbia's complicity in the crime of Sarajevo. Having ensured that Serbia would reject the Austrian note and that Austria would attack Serbia, the Russian leaders proceeded to authorize the inception of "the period preparatory to war," an action taken before the Serbian reply to Austria was known. Their purpose was to allow Russia to begin mobilisation without actually declaring it, to enable her to compensate for her slow mobilisation and to lull her prospective enemies into a sense of false security.

The situation when Serbia gave an unsatisfactory reply to the Austrian note was that Austria was determined to force its complete acceptance by making war on Serbia. Russia, on her part, was equally resolved that an attack on Serbia would be the signal for a European war. Neither power retreated from this position in any degree at any time during the crisis which followed.

The Balkan wars, following on Russia's creation of the Balkan league, had shifted the balance of power in the Balkans heavily in favour of the Russian Empire. It was Austria's attempt to prevent a further, and possibly fatal, tilting of the balance which posed a supposedly deadly threat to Russia and thus made it necessary to launch a European war to defend her gains.

A proper judgement on each Power's share of responsibility for the outbreak of the war must weigh the extent to which these attitudes were justified. The implied answer of entente historians is that Austria had no right to go to war with Serbia to maintain her existence, but that Russia was entitled to start a European war to sustain Serbia's ability to threaten that existence and to bolster her own prestige in the Balkans.

The only possible basis for such a judgement is that the polyglot Austro-Hungarian monarchy was an anachronism which had no right to exist, and that Russia was therefore quite correct in using Serbia as an instrument for its destruction. Evidently no such strictures applied to the multinational Russian Empire, or to the continued extension of French and British rule over subject peoples by military force. Apparently the beneficent deity who had given the entente powers the divine right to rule over alien nationalities had neglected to bestow this gift on Austria. It was an omission which was to cost Europe oceans of blood and mountains of treasure.

The same reasoning applies to Germany. As an illegitimate upstart Power she had no right to defend either her existence or her interests, but should have been content to exist on the sufferance of the established Powers and to cut her cloth to suit their interests. Germans should have been satisfied with their pre-eminence in science, philosophy and education, and should have left industry and commerce to those whose earlier rise to power had bestowed on them the god-given right to dominate the world.

If the German leaders had had the good sense to accept quietly the destruction of Austria, the aims of the Triple Entente could have been accomplished much more easily. Germany might then have realized the futility of struggling to maintain herself against odds of more than three to one, and the entente could have strangled her without the trouble and expense of fighting a great war. It was Europe's tragedy that this misbegotten upstart refused to surrender without a fight, thus imposing on the entente Powers the necessity of defeating her in war.

It is unnecessary to dwell at length again on the negotiations between July 26 and August 1, but a few comments are in order. It is frequently stated that Germany refused all proposals for a peaceful settlement of the growing conflict and that France and Russia gave full cooperation. The fact is that Sir Edward Grey, British foreign secretary, made only one neutral suggestion for intervention by the four Powers, a proposal that they should work for mediation at St. Petersburg and Vienna. This was accepted by Germany, ignored by France and refused by Russia. Later proposals either involved putting pressure on Austria to give way or ensured that she would be outvoted and defeated.

Germany has also been criticized for failing to influence Austria in the direction of compromise soon enough to have any effect. Germany did attempt to influence Austria: Germany was the only Power which made any attempt at any time to suggest that an ally should make concessions in the interest of peace.

During the period under discussion all the Powers based their policy on military and naval strength; all believed and acted on the ancient Roman dictum that preparation for war was the best insurance for peace; all used war and the threat of war as instruments of policy. Between 1870 and 1914 Germany was, in practice, the least warlike of all the European Powers, and in preparations for war, both naval and military, she trailed the Powers of the Triple Entente. France, the only Power which carried out a policy of universal military service, was much more highly militarized than Germany, where little more than half the annual contingent of young men received military training, and which began the war with millions of untrained men of military age.

All the Powers were prepared to go to war for what they believed to be their interests. In this case, however, the interest of the Central Powers was to maintain Austria as a factor in the European balance, while the interest of Russia, supported by France, was to eliminate her, and the specific interest of France was to regain Alsace-Lorraine. In other words, Germany and Austria fought to maintain the *status quo*, while France and Russia fought to change it.

There is no reason to believe that either the conflicts leading to the war or the outbreak of the war itself were caused exclusively by one Power. If it were necessary to single out a Power or a number of Powers whose policies were responsible, it would be easier to make a case against other Powers than against Germany, on the basis of actions and events. In the pre-war period, France was the Power which organized an anti-German coalition and proceeded to act as though Germany was of no account in the family of nations. It was Russia who precipitated the Balkan wars and upset the balance of power in the east. As for the outbreak of the war, a better case could be made against Russia than against Germany.

Attempts to assess responsibility for the coming of the war have, however, no relevance to its basic causes. Until the international community creates a superior authority to which nations can appeal to maintain their interests or to protect their rights, war will remain the instrument of last resort, to which nations will inevitably appeal when they think it necessary. They will continue to build up the armaments which militarist mythology tells them will prevent war, and they will use them when they believe it is expedient to do so.

The same conditions exist today which prevailed in 1914. An organization such as the United Nations, where diplomatic representatives of sovereign states meet to further the interests of their states, has nothing to do with preventing international war. The United Nations, like the League of Nations, was created by the Great Powers who had won the most recent war, in the hope that it would enable them to maintain the dominant position they had gained without fighting another great war.

The result of two wars has been that Germany has risen from the devastation of the last war to play as important a part on the world stage as Wilhelm II could have envisioned for her. An economic union of western Europe in which Germany is the dominant Power is a magnified manifestation of the visionary *Mitteleuropa* of 1913. The end result of the great victories of the Triple Entente has been the elevation of Germany to greater influence and prosperity than that enjoyed by England, France or Russia. The enthusiasts of militarism might well reflect on the goal they have achieved by the sacrifice of fifty million victims to the god of war.

Bibliography

Abbreviations

ARB *Austrian Red Book*.

BD *British Documents on the Origins of the War, 1898-1914*.

CAB Cabinet paper.

Cd Command paper.

DDF *Documents Diplomatiques Français, 1871-1914*.

FO Foreign Office.

FYB *French Yellow Book* (in *Collected Diplomatic Documents Relating to the Outbreak of the European War*).

HCD House of Commons. Debates.

HLD House of Lords. Debates

KD Karl Kautsky (ed.), *Outbreak of the World War, German Documents collected by Karl Kautsky*.

LN *Un Livre Noir*.

SBB *Serbian Blue Book* (in *Collected Diplomatic Documents Relating to the Outbreak of the European War*).

Works Cited

I. Primary Sources:

Austrian Red Book (3 vols.), London: HMSO, 1920.

Belgian Diplomatic Documents. Berlin: E.S. Mittler and Sons, 1915.

Collected Diplomatic Documents Relating to the Outbreak of the European War. London: HMSO, 1915.

France. Ministère des Affaires Etrangères. *Documents Diplomatique Français*. Paris: Imprimierie Nationale, 1938.

Dugdale, E. T. S. *German Diplomatic Documents* (4 vols). New York: Barnes and Noble, 1969.

Gooch, G. P. and H. Temperley, eds. *British Documents on the Origins of the War, 1898-1914*. London: HMSO, 1926-30.

Great Britain. Accounts and papers.

Great Britain. Foreign Office. Papers.

Great Britain. Cabinet. Papers.

Great Britain. Parliament. House of Lords. Debates.

Great Britain. Parliament. House of Commons. Debates.

Great Britain. Public Records Office, Foreign Office Papers:

Angra Pequena, Cromer, Grey, Lansdowne, Morocco, Turkey.

Kautsky, Karl. *Outbreak of the World War: German Documents Collected by Karl Kautsky*. New York: Oxford University Press, 1924.

Marchand, René (ed.) *Un Livre Noir: Diplomatie d'avant guerre après les documents des Archives Russe, Novembre 1910 - Juillet 1914* (2 vols.). Paris: Librairie du Travail, 1922-23.

Romberg, Gisbert von. *The Falsifications of the Russian Orange Book*. London: George Allen and Unwin, 1923.

Schilling, M. F. *How the War Began in 1914*. London: George Allen and Unwin Ltd., 1925.

II. Secondary Sources

Addison, Christopher. *Four and a Half Years*. London: Hutchinson, 1934.

Albertini, Luigi. *The Origins of the War of 1914*. Westport, Conn.: Greenwood Press, 1980.

Amery, Julian. *The Life of Joseph Chamberlain*. Vol. 4. London: Macmillan, 1951.

Anderson, E. N. *The First Moroccan Crisis, 1904-1906*. Chicago: University of Chicago Press, 1929.

Andrew, Christopher. *Théophilé Delcassé and the Making of the Entente Cordiale*. London: Macmillan and Co. Ltd., 1968.

Ashmead-Bartlett, E. *The Passing of the Shereefian Empire*. London: William Black and Sons, 1910.

Asquith, H. H. *Memories and Reflections*. Boston: Little Brown, 1928.

Aydelotte, William O. *Bismarck and British Colonial Policy*. New York: Russell and Russell, 1970.

Barlow, I. C. *The Agadir Crisis*. N.p.:Archon Books, 1971.

Bell, H. C. F. *Lord Palmerston*. Vol II. Hamden Connecticut: Archon Books, 1966.

Berghahn, V. R. *Germany and the Approach of War in 1914*. London: Macmillan, 1973.

Bernhardi, Friedrich von. *Germany and the Next War*. New York: Chas. A. Eron, 1914.

Bismarck, Otto von. *The Man and the Statesman*. London: Smith, Elder, 1898.

Bogitshevich, M. *Causes of the War*. London: George Allen and Unwin, 1920.

Boucher, Arthur. *L'Allemagne en Péril*. Paris: Berger-Levrault, 1914.

Boucher, Arthur. *L'Offensive contre L'Allemagne*. Paris: Berger-Levrault, 1911.

Brett, Maurice V. *The Journals and Letters of Reginald Viscount Esher*. London: Ivor Nicholson and Watson, 1934.

Bridge, F. R. *Great Britain and Austria-Hungary, 1906-1914*. London: Weidenfeld and Nicolson, 1972.

Broh, Dagobert. "Hardinge, the Tirpitz Plan and Anglo-German Relations, 1906-1910." Unpublished M. A. Thesis, Concordia University, 1985.

Buat, Edmond. *L'Armée Allemande pendant la guerre de 1914-1918*. Paris: Librairie Chapelot, 1920.

Buchanan, George. *My Mission to Russia*. London: Cassell, 1923.

Bülow, Bernhard von. *Memoirs*. London: Putnam, 1932.

Caillaux, Joseph. *Agadir: Ma Politique Extérieure*. Paris: Albin Michel, 1919.

Callwell, C.E. *Field Marshal Sir Henry Wilson, His Life and Diaries*. London: Cassell, 1927.

Chalmers, W.S. *The Life and Letters of David, Earl Beatty*. London: Hodder and Stoughton, 1951.

Chamberlain, Austen. *Down the Years*. London: Cassell, 1935.

Churchill, Winston S. *The World Crisis, 1911-1918*. London: Odhams Press, 1938.

Civrieux, (Commandant) de. *Le Germanisme Encerclé*. Paris: Henri Charles-Lavauzelle, 1913.

Contamine, Henry. *La Revanche, 1871-1914*. Paris: Berger-Levrault, 1957.

Cramb, J. A. *Origins and Destiny of Imperial Britain*. New York: E.P. Dutton, 1915.

Dedijer, Vladimir. *The Road to Sarajevo*. New York: Simon and Schuster, 1966.

Dunn, Ross E. *Resistance in the Desert*. Madison: University of Wisconsin Press, 1977.

Durham, M. E. *The Sarajevo Crime*. London: George Allen and Unwin, 1925.

Durham, M. E. *Twenty Years of Balkan Tangle*. London: George Allen and Unwin, 1920.

Edmonds, J. E. *History of the Great War Based on Official Documents: Military Operations, France and Belgium, 1914*. London: Macmillan, 1922.

Enock, A. G. *The Problem of Armaments*. London: Macmillan, 1923.

Farwell, Byron. *Queen Victoria's Little Wars*. London: Allen Lane, 1973.

Fay, Sidney B. *The Origins of the World War*. New York: Macmillan, 1930.

Fischer, Fritz. *Germany's Aims in the First World War*. New York: W. W. Norton, 1967.

Fischer, Fritz. *War of Illusions*. London: Chatto and Windus, 1975.

Fisher, Lord John. *Memories and Records*. New York: George H. Doran Company, 1920.

Garvin, J. L. *The Life of Joseph Chamberlain*. Vols. 1-3. London: Macmillan, 1934.

Geiss, Immanuel. *German Foreign Policy, 1871-1914*. London: Routledge and Kegan Paul, 1976.

Geiss, Immanuel. *July 1914. The Outbreak of the First World War: Selected Documents*. London: B.T. Batsford, 1967.

Gifford, P. and W. R. Louis. *Britain and Germany in Africa*. New Haven: Yale University Press, 1967.

Gooch, G. P. *Before the War*. Vol. 2: *The Coming of the Storm*. London: Longmans, Green and Co., 1938.

Gordon, Michael R. "Domestic Conflict and the Origins of the First World War," *Journal of Modern History*, Vol. 46, pp. 224-5.

Goudswaard, J.M. *Some Aspects of the End of Britain's "Splendid Isolation."* Rotterdam: W. L. & J. Brusse, 1952.

Grey, Edward. *Twenty-five Years*. Toronto: The Ryerson Press, 1925.

Grouard, A. *France and Germany: The Possible War*. Paris: Librairie Chapelot, 1913.

Guillen, Pièrre. *L'Allemagne et le Maroc, 1870-1905*. Paris: Rabat, 1967.

Haldane, Richard Burdon. *Before the War*. London: Cassel, 1920.

Hale, O. J. *Germany and the Diplomatic Revolution*. Philadelphia: University of Pennsylvania Press, 1931.

Hale, O. J. *Publicity and Diplomacy*. New York: D. Appleton Century, 1940.

Harrison, Frederic. *The German Peril*. London: T. Fisher Unwin, 1915.

Herwig, Holger H. *"Luxury" Fleet*. London: George Allen and Unwin, 1980.

Hirst, F. W. *The Six Panics and Other Essays*. London: Methuen, 1913.

Hoffman, Helmuth. "The English Periodical Press and the End of British Isolation, 1894-1904." Unpublished M. A. Thesis, Concordia University.

Hoffman, R. J. S. *Great Britain and the German Trade Rivalry*. New York: Russell and Russell, 1964.

Hurd, Archibald and Henry Castle. *German Sea Power*. London: J. Murray, 1913.

Jane, Fred T. *Jane's Fighting Ships, 1905-06*. Arco Publishing Company, 1970.

Jane, Fred T. *Jane's Fighting Ships, 1914*. Arco Publishing Company, 1969.

Jarausch, K. H. *The Enigmatic Chancellor*. New Haven: Yale University Press, 1973.

Joffre, J. J. C. *Personal Memoirs of Joffre*. New York: Harper & Brothers, 1932.

Jovanovitch, Ljuba. *The Murder of Sarajevo*. London: British Institute of International Affairs, 1925.

Kennedy, Paul M. "German War Policy and the Alliance Negotiations with England, 1897-1900," *Journal of Modern History*, 1973, pp. 606-07, 610.

Kennedy, Paul M. *The Rise and Fall of the Great Powers*. New York: Random House, 1987.

Kennedy, Paul M. *The Rise of Anglo-German Antagonism, 1860-1914*. London: George Allen and Unwin, 1980.

Kennedy, Paul M. *The Samoan Tangle*. New York: Barnes and Noble, 1974.

Koch, H. W. "Anglo-German Alliance Negotiations: Missed Opportunity or Myth?" *History*, Vol. 54 (1969), pp. 388-390.

Kokovtsov, Vladimir. *Out of My Past*. Palo Alto: Stanford University Press, 1935.

Laloy, Emile. *Les Documents Secrets Publié par les Bolcheviks*. Paris: Editions Brossard, 1919.

Langer, William L. *The Diplomacy of Imperialism*. New York: Alfred A. Knopf, 1965.

Langer, William L. *European Alliances and Alignments*, 1871-1890. New York: Random House, 1950.

Langer, William L. *The Franco-Russian Alliance, 1890-1914*. New York: Octagon Books, 1977.

Lloyd George, David. *War Memoirs*. London: Odhams Press, 1933-34.

Lord, C.H. and Lord, E.H. *Historical Atlas of the United States*. New York: Henry Holt and Company, 1953.

Loreburn, Earl. *How the War Came*. London: Methuen, 1919.

McKenna, Stephen. *Reginald McKenna, 1863-1943*. London: Eyre and Spottiswoode, 1948.

Marder, A. J. *The Anatomy of British Sea Power*. Hamden, Conn: Archon Books, 1964.

Marder, A. J. *Fear God and Dread Nought*. Oxford: Alden Press, 1956.

Marder, A. J. *From the Dreadnought to Scapa Flow*. Vol. 1: *The Road to War*. London: Oxford University Press, 1961.

Maurice, F. *Forty Days in 1914*. London: Constable and Company, 1920.

Maurice, F. *Haldane, 1856-1915*. London: Faber and Faber, 1937.

Medlicott, W. N. *The Congress of Berlin and After*. London: Methuen, 1938.

Mertens, F. R. *Militarism and Wages*. N.p.: Labour Party Pamphlet, n.d.

Monger, George W. *The End of Isolation*. London: Thomas Nelson and Sons, 1963.

Montgelas, Max. *The Case for the Central Powers*. London: George Allen and Unwin, 1925.

Morel, E. D. *Diplomacy Revealed*. London: The National Labour Press, 1921.

Morel, E. D. *Military Preparations for the Great War.* London: The Labour Publishing Company, 1922.

Morel, E. D. *Ten Years of Secret Diplomacy.* London: National Labour Press, 1915.

Morel, E. D. *Truth and the War.* London: The National Labour Press, 1916.

Morley, John. *The Life of William Ewart Gladstone.* London: Macmillan, 1903.

Morley, John. *Memorandum on Resignation.* London: Macmillan, 1928.

Murray, Stewart L. *The Peace of the Anglo-Saxons.* London: Watts & Co., 1905.

Neilson, Francis. *How Diplomats Make War.* New York: B. W. Hubsch, 1915.

Newton, Lord. *Lord Lansdowne.* London: Macmillan, 1929.

Newton, Lord. *Lord Lyons.* London: Edward Arnold, 1913.

Nicolson, Harold. *Lord Carnock.* London: Constable, 1930.

Oakes, Augustus and R. B. Mowat. *The Great European Treaties of the Nineteenth Century.* Oxford: Clarendon Press, 1918.

Oncken, H. *Napolean III and the Rhine.* New York: Russell and Russell, 1967.

Padfield, Peter. *The Great Naval Race.* London: Hart-Davis, MacGibbon, 1974.

Paléologue, Maurice. *An Ambassador's Memoirs.* New York: George H. Doran Company, 1925.

Playne, Caroline E. *The Pre-War Mind in Britain.* London: George Allen and Unwin. 1928.

Poincaré, Raymond. *The Memoirs of Raymond Poincaré,* translated by George Arthur. London: William Heinemann, 1926.

Poincaré, Raymond. *The Origins of the War.* London: Cassell, 1922.

Porch, Douglas. *The Conquest of Morocco.* New York: Alfred A. Knopf, 1983.

Repington, Charles a'Court. *The First World War, 1914-1918.* London: Constable, 1920.

Riddell, Lord. *More Pages from My Diary, 1908-1914.* London: Country Life, 1934.

Riddell, Lord. *War Diary.* London: Nicholson & Watson, 1933.

Ridpath, J. C. *et al. The Story of South Africa.* Guelph: World Publishing Co., 1902.

Rohl, John (ed.). *1914: Delusion or Design.* New York: St. Martin's Press.

Russell, Bertrand. *Justice in War Time.* London: The Open Court Publishing Co., 1917.

Sandiford, K.A.P. *Great Britain and the Schleswig-Holstein Question, 1848-1864.* Toronto: University of Toronto Press, 1975.

Schilling, M. F. *How the War Began in 1914.* London: George Allen and Unwin, 1925.

Schuman, Frederick L. *War and Diplomacy in the French Republic.* New York: Howard Fertig, 1969.

Scott, J. B. *The Hague Conventions and Declarations of 1899 and 1907.* New York: Oxford University Press, 1915.

Scott, J. B. *A Survey of International Relations Between the United States and Germany, 1914-1917.* New York: Oxford University Press, 1917.

Sheehan, James J. (ed.) *Imperial Germany.* New York: New Viewpoints, 1976.

Siebert, B. de. *Entente Diplomacy and the World.* New York: The Knickerbocker Press, 1921.

Snyder, Louis L. *Historic Documents of World War I.* New York: Anvil Books, 1958.

Sontag, Raymond. *Germany and England.* New York: D. Appleton-Century, 1958.

Spears, E.L. *Liaison, 1914.* New York: Doubleday Doran, 1931.

Spender, J.A. *Life, Journalism and Politics*. London: Cassell, 1927.

Steinberg, Jonathan. *Yesterday's Deterrent*. Macdonald, 1965.

Steiner, Zara S. *Britain and the Origins of the First World War*. Macmillan, 1977.

Stieve, Frederick. *Isvolsky and the World War*. Freeport, N.Y.: Books for Libraries Press, 1971.

Taylor, A. J. P. *Germany's First Bid for Colonies, 1884-1885*. London: Macmillan, 1938.

Temperley, H. and L. M. Penson. *Foundations of British Foreign Policy, 1792-1902*. London: Frank Cass, 1966.

Turner, L. C. F. "Russian Mobilization in 1914", *Journal of Contemporary History*, Vol. 3, (1968), pp. 76, 87.

Weber, Eugen. *The National Revival in France, 1905-1914*. Berkeley: University of California Press, 1968.

Wilkinson, Spencer. *Britain at Bay*. London: Constable, 1909.

Williamson, S. R. *The Politics of Grand Strategy: Britain and France Prepare for War*. Cambridge: Harvard University Press, 1969.

Woodward, E. L. *Great Britain and the German Navy*. Hamden, Conn: Archon Books, 1964.

III. Periodicals Consulted

Daily News and Leader (London).

Contemporary History.

Daily Telegraph (London).

L'Echo de Paris.

Edinburgh Review.

Foreign Affairs.

Fortnightly Review (London).

The Graphic (London)

History.

L'Humanité (Paris).

Journal of Modern History.

Manchester Guardian (London).

Le Matin (Paris).

The Naval Annual (Portsmouth).

Navy League Annual.

Navy League Journal.

The Observer (London).

Pall Mall Gazette (London).

The Spectator (London).

The Standard (London).

Sunday Times (London).

The Times (London).

Vanity Fair (London).

Westminster Gazette (London).

Index

---■---

Also published by

NATIONALISM AND CULTURE

Rudolf Rocker, *translated by Ray E. Chase*

Nationalism and Culture is a detailed and scholarly study of the development of nationalism and the changes in human cultures from the dawn of history to the present day and an analysis of the relations of these to one another. It tells the story of the growth of the State and the other institutions of authority and their influence on life and manners, on architecture and art, on literature and thought.

It traces the evolution of religious and political systems; it analyzes the Nation as alleged community of race, of culture, of language, of interest. It presents in its 592 pages a series of cross-sections of European society at successive historical periods and relates them to one another; it offers copious illustrations of the literature of every period and country. It is at every point illuminated by the interpretative comment of the author, scholarly, brilliant, poetic, human; it is the ripened fruit of thirty years of intensive and devoted study by a man in every way fitted for the task.

.. an important contribution to political philosophy and a brilliant criticism of state-worship.
  Bertrand Russell

Worthy to be placed on the same shelf that holds Candide, The Rights of Man and Mutual Aid.
  Lewis Mumford

Extraordinarily original and illuminating. Presented in it in a novel and convincing fashion.
  Albert Einstein

Rocker is tolerant, modest, and aware of the essential values in culture.
  Herbert Read

592 pages, bibliography, index
Paperback ISBN: 1-55164-094-5 $28.99
Hardcover ISBN: 1-55164-095-3 $57.99
L.C. No. 97-74153
1998

BLACK ROSE BOOKS

has also published the following books of related interest

Anarchist Collectives, *by Sam Dolgoff, editor*
Anarchist Organisation, *by Juan Gómez Casas*
Bitter Thirties in Québec, *by Evelyn Dumas*
Civilization and its Discontented, *by John F. Laffey*
Cuban Revolution, *by Sam Dolgoff*
Global Trap, *by Hans-Peter Martin, Harald Schumann*
Great French Revolution, *by Peter Kropotkin*
History of Canadian Business, *by R.T. Naylor*
Killing Hope: US Military and CIA Interventions Since WW II, *by William Blum*
Looking East Leftwards, *by David Mandel*
Military in Greek Politics, *by Thanos Veremis*
Politics of Obedience, *by Etienne de la Boétie*
Rethinking Camelot, *by Noam Chomsky*
Russian Literature, *by Peter Kropotkin*
Unknown Revolution, *by Voline*
When Freedom Was Lost, *by Lorne Brown*
Women Pirates, *by Ulrike Klausmann, Marion Meinzerin, Gabriel Kuhn*
Zapata of Mexico, *by Peter Newell*

send for a free catalogue of all our titles
BLACK ROSE BOOKS
C.P. 1258, Succ. Place du Parc
Montréal, Québec
H3W 2R3 Canada

or visit our web site at: http://www.web.net/blackrosebooks

To order books in North America: (phone) 1-800-565-9523
(fax) 1-800-221-9985
In Europe: (phone) 44-0181-986-4854 (fax) 44-0181-533-5821

Printed by the workers of
VEILLEUX IMPRESSION À DEMANDE INC.
Boucherville, Quebec
for Black Rose Books Ltd.